NEW DEAL LAW AND ORDER

NEW
DEAL
LAW
AND
ORDER

HOW THE WAR ON CRIME
BUILT THE MODERN LIBERAL STATE

ANTHONY GREGORY

Harvard University Press   Cambridge, Massachusetts I London, England   2024

Publication of this book has been supported through the generous
provisions of the Maurice and Lula Bradley Smith Memorial Fund.

Library of Congress Cataloging-in-Publication Data

Names: Gregory, Anthony, 1981– author.
Title: New Deal law and order : how the war on crime built
the modern liberal state / Anthony Gregory.
Other titles: How the war on crime built the modern liberal state
Description: Cambridge, Massachusetts ; London, England : Harvard
University Press, 2024. | Includes bibliographical references and index.
Identifiers: LCCN 2023041735 | ISBN 9780674290303 (cloth)
Subjects: LCSH: New Deal, 1933–1939. | Law enforcement—
United States—History—20th century. |
Liberalism—United States—History—20th century. | Criminal justice,
Administration of—United States—History—20th century. |
United States—Social conditions—1933–1945. | United States—
Politics and government—1933–1945.
Classification: LCC E806 .G834 2024 | DDC 973.917—dc23/eng/20231031
LC record available at https://lccn.loc.gov/2023041735

For Nicole and Alfred, who keep my heart full every day

CONTENTS

NEW DEAL LAW AND ORDER

INTRODUCTION

President Franklin D. Roosevelt spoke proudly of his record on crime as he campaigned in 1936. Four days before voters emphatically re-elected him, the incumbent reminded a Brooklyn audience of his first term's accomplishments, from the National Recovery Administration to the Tennessee Valley Authority. Roosevelt then credited his "successful war on crime" for making the country's "homes and places of business safer against the gangster, the kidnapper and the racketeer." In response to those who might decry his New Deal and crime policies as "meddling and interference," the president celebrated these "new stones in a foundation" for "a structure of economic security for all our people—a safer, happier, more American America." The struggle against crime, Roosevelt suggested, was a significant part of his plan to secure the nation.[1]

The phrase "war on crime" was not new. Politicians and journalists used the same language to describe national efforts under Roosevelt's predecessor, President Herbert Hoover, who faced a sensationalized rise in racketeering and kidnappings. But just as his 1936 campaign speech suggested, Roosevelt made the war on crime his own. He dramatically escalated it into a sweeping, multipronged offensive against lawlessness.[2]

As journalist Herbert Corey explained that same year, Roosevelt delivered action where his predecessors and critics offered empty talk. According to Corey's book *Farewell, Mr. Gangster: America's War on Crime,* President Hoover spent half a million dollars on a major crime commission whose "report got nowhere at all." Roosevelt and his attorney general, Homer Cummings, in contrast, produced results. Although America was "still the most lawless nation," the new national leadership was inspiring governors to convene state "conferences on crime."[3]

Corey described matters accurately. The New Dealers indeed overhauled America's approach to crime. They immediately amplified President Hoover's reactive war, targeting the infamous outlaws of the early 1930s like John Dillinger and "Pretty Boy" Floyd. Then the New Dealers brought longer-term changes to law enforcement and relations between the federal government and the states. After Prohibition ended, even as crime fell, the federal criminal code swelled. The Roosevelt administration flexed its interstate-commerce muscles against bank robbers and targeted new classes of contraband, from automatic firearms to marijuana. Creative constitutionalism and progressive social welfare ideas accommodated this muscular strategy. Modern regulation and criminology converged in pursuit of what would become known as white-collar crime. Alcatraz became a civilian penitentiary, prison construction accelerated, and incarceration, parole, and probation rates broke national records. In 1939 the inmate population reached a per capita peak that would not be reached again until the late 1970s. J. Edgar Hoover's Bureau of Investigation was modernized and renamed the Federal Bureau of Investigation (FBI) as it achieved new powers and prestige and stamped its imprimatur on police departments nationwide. Roosevelt recognized the importance of these criminal justice developments, even alongside his many other groundbreaking policies.

In those same years when the New Deal gave rise to the modern American state, law and order became good national politics. For all of living memory, many factions distrusted law enforcement, particularly at the federal level. The New Dealers prevailed where previous attempts had failed to build enduring law-and-order relations across society and the different scales of government. To achieve this, Roosevelt and Cummings in effect created a war-on-crime coalition to transcend the institutional and ideological divisions that had precluded a nationally cohesive effort. Academia, the legal community, and law enforcement found their place. Essential Democratic constituencies—organized labor, white southerners, and Black Americans—had traditionally regarded national law enforcement as a source of hostility or neglect. The New Deal war on crime brought these groups deeper into Roosevelt's ambit, reconciling and fusing individualism and progressivism, which in past eras had been in tension.

This political triumph altered liberalism and federalism. American liberalism, a political program seeking to balance freedom and social needs in pursuit of democratic stability, has periodically adjusted to accommodate each momentous development in government. Federalism, the balancing of both deferential and adversarial relations between national and state authority, has also undergone major changes in accordance with the great ruptures in US history. The changes in federalism and liberalism are often understood together. Consequential constitutional innovations have coincided with commensurate refinements in liberalism, both of which have often turned on the tension between the freedom that politics and law have promised to secure and the limitations on power they have presumed to respect.[4] The histories of federalism and liberalism have together tracked the rise of what we might call the modern liberal state. More specifically, over time liberalism and federalism have each made demands on law enforcement while constraining its activities. It makes sense that the 1930s metamorphosis in crime policy, no less than economic policy, chaperoned the country's constitutional and ideological evolution.

The war on crime was vital to the New Deal's transformation of America: It advanced a new and lasting settlement across jurisdictions, among institutions and factions, and between freedom and authority. In short, the New Deal war on crime built American law and order. But it did so not only in the narrow sense of modernizing law-enforcement and criminal-justice infrastructure. It also built law and order in the broader sense of bringing institutional and ideological stability to the American state. Roosevelt and Cummings's crime policies delivered legitimacy to national enforcement authority—accommodating economic reforms and laying the foundations of modern government. These crime policy accomplishments were more than a "radical moment," to borrow Ira Katznelson's phrase, but an enduring departure for American governance.[5] By the late 1930s the transformed federalism and liberalism could accommodate a distinctively durable and politically acceptable type of security infrastructure. The modern liberal state that would define the twentieth century, with its unity of welfare liberalism, carceral repression, and national security regimentation, arose largely from the crucible of Roosevelt's anti-crime campaign.[6]

Contemporaries of the New Deal war on crime acknowledged its importance, and so have commenters and scholars ever since.[7] But as historians have written the story of those years, crime policy has mainly been relegated to the periphery. Other aspects of the New Deal have dominated our historical imagination, and thus popular narratives and scholarly treatments tend not to spotlight law and order. Our general understanding of the New Deal has widened thanks to exciting work since the 1980s, but accounts of interwar liberalism rarely feature its dialectic with crime. Rarely do the early 1930s shootouts, New Deal criminology, and the 1940s security and surveillance story all come together.

The few focused studies of the New Deal war on crime do suggest something quite significant. In 1995 Mary M. Stolberg observed that anti-crime efforts revealed complexities in the development of federalism from the Progressive Era through the Roosevelt years.[8] In 1998 Claire Bond Potter's *War on Crime* unveiled the cultural importance of FBI operations in the early New Deal.[9] Some historians have stressed the tensions between the Bureau of Investigation's expansion and the New Deal.[10] Others have stressed the affinities.[11] Political scientist Matthew G. T. Denney has recently argued that the New Deal war on crime had a ratchet effect in state building, driven by a political consensus that excluded Black Americans.[12] Historian Emily M. Brooks has explored what northern urban policing in the 1930s and 1940s reveals about the limitations of "law-and-order liberalism" in addressing an "unequal society."[13]

One nagging question is whether the war on crime was simply one of many programs sustained by the Roosevelt administration's general state-building energy, or whether it was more central to defining the New Deal state. Focused on the 1930s war on kidnapping, Kathleen J. Frydl has highlighted the "coterminous advance of the social welfare state with the security state" in a project that "legitimized and extended the case for federal power in general."[14] Scholars have shown the larger importance of 1930s law to liberalism, and Michael Willrich has suggested that crime policy in the 1930s should be viewed as a major constitutional moment.[15] And although crime and punishment narratives usually feature Progressive Era reform and the postwar origins of mass incarceration more than the eight pivotal years between the end of Prohibition and World War II, the "New Deal war on crime" has been called out by name in recent work, from Lisa McGirr's examination of Prohibition to James Sparrow's history of the "warfare state" in the Second World War.[16] Meanwhile, scholars have integrated the trajectories of postwar liberalism and the modern carceral state. Jonathan Simon, Naomi Murakawa, Elizabeth Hinton, and others have underlined the breach between the egalitarian aspirations and punitive reality.[17]

The importance of New Deal law and order should be intuitive, given that the political and constitutional arc of the twentieth-century state was fused by three stories: the anti-crime struggle, the transformation of liberalism, and the reformation of state power around national security.[18] The formative New Deal decade would, unsurprisingly, have a lot to say about how these three stories interlace. Margot Canaday, writing about the midcentury criminal construction of homosexuality in peacetime and during war, has lamented that "historians . . . have responded to the vastness and complexity of the state (until fairly recently) by not writing about the state at all."[19] Twenty years earlier, Claire Potter asked "historians of the New Deal to consider the crucial importance of enforcement to other statist agendas of the period."[20] Despite many great histories of the state, New Deal law and order deserves more attention.

My response to Potter and Canaday, and to the vast relevant literature, is that the New Deal war on crime delivered political legitimacy to the modern state through the transformation of liberal ideas, liberal governance, and constitutional structure. By "political legitimacy," I refer to a social status government achieves by obtaining sufficient state capacity and public support. Legitimacy is the site of political mediation where subjective valuations provide for objective institutional stability. Social theory has emphasized this connection between the subjective and objective ever since Weber's formulation of the modern state.[21] Sociologists continue to locate legitimacy in the relationship between institutions and the relevant populations.[22]

In building law and order, the New Deal war on crime adopted an extensive approach to what was understood as the problem: lawlessness. The construction of political and legal legitimacy in opposition to lawlessness offered a special opportunity for state building in America, where constitutional and ideological traditions had constrained the power of government and especially the federal government. Protecting people from crime is often seen as a canonical government activity, but in the United States crime was traditionally treated as a local, even private matter. But even though *crime* was seen as a local and personal danger, *lawlessness* was seen as a social and national problem—warranting collective and federal action. American lawlessness had proven too much for previous generations of leadership, whose ideological and constitutional commitments undercut attempts at building law and order. But it also offered a new opportunity to remake liberalism and the constitutional order.

In any political system the narrower and broader law-and-order challenges are linked, but their connection was conspicuous in the United States in 1933. Law enforcement challenges awaiting Roosevelt revealed deeper problems with the government's structure and supporting ideology. These interlocking problems had frustrated national leaders since Reconstruction. By 1933 the New Dealers had inherited a legitimacy problem, generations in the making and punctuated by interwar emergencies. In addition to the Depression, an early-1930s crime surge and Prohibition scandals cast serious doubt on law enforcement's instruments and authority.

As Frydl has observed, a state's coercive management of relatively small threats is especially revealing: "The logic of survival might legitimize the response to a predator, but a more careful consideration of norms and limits governs the response to the pest."[23] What made the 1930s special was that these pests achieved a critical mass that invited new modes of peacetime focus and political action. Without wide support for federal enforcement authority, Roosevelt would suffer the distrust and skepticism that constrained the 1920s Republicans. He hoped to legalize liquor without undercutting public trust, all while managing intense and conflicting political pressures.

Two concepts—law and order, and lawlessness—enjoyed a capacious meaning in the 1930s, and the New Dealers were especially well situated to address both concepts in their expansive forms. For them lawlessness included political corruption and racketeering, corporate malfeasance, and fraud. It could include anti-Black lynching and anti-labor vigilantism. It came to include foreign despotism and war. The perception of rampant lawlessness offered not just a threat but an opportunity for a new kind of governance. As for law and order, the words meant institutional competence, civil rights, and democratic equality, a system promising accountability for all. The term "law and order" at its most expansive included liberatory meanings. Lawlessness, often tolerated by law officials, was a chief mechanism of reactionary politics from Reconstruction through the 1920s. Law and order was a rallying cry to expose the hypocrisy of reactionary lawlessness and a hopeful appeal for genuine change. Black activists, labor radicals, and egalitarians called, without irony, for law and order—and continued to do so for the celebrated decades of the New Deal order.

The Roosevelt administration's solution to lawlessness was to reform the war on crime—to redirect and escalate it across many dimensions, and to integrate it as a permanent feature of government. To do so the New Dealers nurtured an informal war-on-crime coalition that transcended partisan, regional, and ideological lines. It included Republicans and Democrats, Prohibitionists and anti-Prohibitionists, conservative crime hawks and progressive idealists, practitioners and academics, national and local enforcers, industrialists and labor activists, white supremacists and civil rights activists. These coalitional efforts turned a narrow and immediate challenge of law and order into a larger political undertaking at the heart of American state power, with far-reaching consequences for liberalism and federalism.

To appreciate the New Dealers' relationship to the war-on-crime coalition, and the stakes it carries for the thorny concept of liberalism, some terminological clarification is in order. I use the term "New Dealers" rather conventionally, referring to those who shared Roosevelt's goals of restructuring political economy. This included his top officials, especially those directly influencing economic policy, as well as local and state politicians, journalists, and activists who championed New Deal reforms.[24] The reforms that united New Dealers varied in design and implementation but shared a discernable family resemblance. Not all New Dealers were liberals, as the term came to mean. Jim Crow Democrats and other socially conservative interests offered their numbers to a state-building movement ultimately directed toward Roosevelt's vision of liberalism. And even though the New Dealers and the war-on-crime coalition overlapped, they were not identical groups. Cummings was a consummate New Dealer, liberal, and crime warrior, as was his advisor Justin Miller, but many key New Dealers had little involvement in crime. On the other hand, Roosevelt's advisor Raymond Moley began as an archetypal New Dealer; when he later became a famous anti–New Dealer, his loyalty to the war on crime remained steady. FBI chief J. Edgar Hoover, Narcotics Bureau chief Harry Anslinger, and many American Bar Association personalities backed the war on crime but were indifferent or hostile to New Deal economics.

The coalitional flexibility of both the New Deal and the war on crime helps account for the dynamic complexity in how Roosevelt's state building changed liberalism. Such an account is possible despite disagreements over how to define liberalism. Reflections on modern American liberalism often grapple with its different connotations—as an ideology, as an approach to governance, as a description of political mobilization. But these different aspects of liberalism did not exist in isolation. Liberal ideas guided the experience of governing and mobilizing politically, which in turn forced liberal ideas themselves to change. These shifting ideas and ideals motivated self-identified liberals and how they saw themselves in the political tradition they inhabited and hoped to carry forward.[25] Even if liberalism eludes a fixed definition, some generalizations are possible. Across historical settings, liberalism has evinced an affinity toward human flourishing, equality of rights, commercial society, civilizational harmony across classes and trades, and state power directed and constrained by democratic voice and predictable legal principles. These values distinguish all forms of liberalism from anarchy, autocracy, theocracy, the ancien régime, and the utopian total state. But the tensions among liberal values have meant that, in practice, they could never all be realized perfectly. Under pressure, liberals have rebalanced and reprioritized their fidelity to these values, and these attempts to recalibrate liberal ideas, beliefs, and policies have fueled much of the history of liberalism in transformation.

How New Deal liberalism and the larger history of liberalism are related is itself no small question.[26] Whether one stresses the continuities or differences between New Deal liberalism and other varieties, the development of law and order offers stark, if neglected, inflection points where the liberal tradition reimagined itself. Before the New Deal, both liberalism and law and order looked much different. The nineteenth-century liberalism of free labor, contractual relations, private property rights, and constitutional subsidiarity lost its dominance in the Progressive Era, whose reformers embraced domestic and international intervention. Their progressivism eschewed radical or aristocratic class interests in favor of a middle-class urban sensibility, and faced constitutional limits to power, particularly federal authority. I will return to the contestable relationship between progressivism and liberalism. For now, suffice it to note that progressivism dominated politics between the eras of nineteenth- and twentieth-century liberalism, and its relevant personalities, agendas, and institutional history formed an important bridge between the two liberal eras.[27] Progressive state building climaxed and collapsed during World War I, the Red Scare, and Prohibition. As a testament to the volatile 1920s, so-called classical liberalism thrived in a perhaps more unwaveringly contractual form than ever in the federal judiciary. The 1920s Republicans restored an older liberalism as compared to Woodrow Wilson's experimentation, while accommodating immigration control, protectionism, and uneven alcohol enforcement. The chaos of Prohibition exacerbated the political and constitutional contradictions.

It is hardly controversial to say that Roosevelt aimed to remake liberalism.[28] He came to power with big plans for government but wary of utopian crusades and the illiberal movements reshaping Europe and Asia. He hoped to temper the individualist legacies of his own Democratic Party while restraining the impractical impulses of earlier progressivism. To be sure, New Deal liberals clung to the banner of progressivism and sometimes used the term "progressive" interchangeably with "liberal."[29] At any rate, for Roosevelt, progressivism served as both inspiration and cautionary tale. His redefinition of liberalism synthesized past traditions, the wisdom of experience, and the aspiration to rebalance constitutional values.[30] New Deal liberalism thus branded itself as a middle position between anachronistic laissez-faire and unbridled collectivism. Its welfare state recognized the contractual and civil-libertarian expectations of a capitalist culture jealous of its heritage of freedom: social welfare framed as social insurance, federal spending disbursed through the states, the positive "freedom from fear" articulated as the negative freedom to be left alone. Law and order assisted in coupling these positive and negative freedoms, as a robust criminological state promised a return to the government's mythical primary function of securing the domestic peace. Modern liberalism would deliver this primordial political aim where earlier liberalism failed.

As evidence of Roosevelt's national significance, the New Deal refashioned a liberalism with both partisan and nonpartisan legacies. Sometimes the partisan version is called left-liberalism, as it came to define the Democratic Party, which emphasized social welfare and economic equality and accommodated veteran reformers along with swaths of the labor left who straddled anticapitalist radicalism and statist compromise. For decades this left-liberalism infused the Democratic Party with an economic program that maintained the loyalty of factions not otherwise very left-wing or liberal at all—namely, the Jim Crow southern Democrats who, aside from economic planning priorities, stuck out as some of the most culturally and socially conservative of their time. But the liberalism established by the New Deal also harbored another paradox, as it constrained and arguably defined the politics of the oppositional Republicans during and after Roosevelt's presidency. Liberalism can indeed refer not only to the partisan actions of the midcentury Democratic Party, but more broadly to a shared constellation of values and practices in governance that also captivated much of the contemporaneous Republican Party. Even elements of the postwar conservative movement, and most clearly the presidencies of Dwight Eisenhower and Richard Nixon, would often advance policy corollaries to the New Deal framework.[31] Liberal Republicans as well as non-liberal Democrats thus bolstered broad waves of political development in which New Deal liberalism triumphed as the central force.

The war on crime helped give New Deal liberalism this robustness. Not only did law and order strengthen the New Deal coalition, securing the loyalty of Democrats with views on racial and social issues outside the party's rising liberal camp. The popularity of crime policies also bridged New Deal liberals with liberal-adjacent, moderate, and conservative factions across the aisle. Indeed, anti–New Deal conservatives who joined the war-on-crime coalition, however unwittingly, helped build one of the pillars of the New Deal liberal state. From the 1930s through the late twentieth century, conservatives would define their creed against the New Deal and its legacies. While they largely remained a recalcitrant movement within the broader tradition of liberalism, a right-liberal faction whose clearest differentia would be contingent on whatever best characterized left-liberalism at the moment, conservatism long harkened back to its 1930s opposition to social spending, corporate regulation, and labor protections. But on crime, these conservatives were mostly allies—and in that ecumenical sense of building law and order they were junior partners in remaking liberalism. This overlooked 1930s consensus on law and order foreshadowed the conservatives' accessory relationship to the breadth of liberal state making later in the century. And so, the notorious bipartisan war-on-crime consensus predated the conventionally accentuated postwar period—or the later neoliberal period—and was consequential in the foundational years of modern liberalism and its conservative foil.

All that said, in this book I emphasize the overlap between the New Dealers and the war-on-crime coalition, for three major reasons. First, many officials in political economy had major roles in crime control— Roosevelt himself, Cummings and later attorneys general (two of whom became Supreme Court justices), Treasury Secretary Henry Morgenthau, key congressional allies, Works Progress Administration workers, as well as local liberal politicians. Second, because crime fighting and state building fueled each other, those invested in one project often became invested in the other. Third, as the war on crime developed alongside Roosevelt's agenda for liberalism, criminological forces earlier discernible as "progressive" gained traction in unifying idealistic social welfare and pragmatic social control. Activists from the American Civil Liberties Union (ACLU), lawyers at the National Association for the Advancement of Colored People (NAACP), criminal procedure reformers, and idealist criminologists found real hope and voice in the rising liberal state—not only in their concrete accomplishments but as they pursued unrealized aspirations. New Deal law and order, no less than its economics, accommodated and even empowered progressive, radical, and left-egalitarian factions.

Especially vexing in this coalitional story are the twists of racial politics. The New Deal unfolded at a turning point for racialized policing, when lawless racial terror was being socialized into both overtly segregationist and purportedly colorblind systems of state discipline—modern policing, prisons, and the death penalty. This took place as even racist law enforcers saw the benefit of taming lynching and brutality and bringing social control under respectable auspices. This undertaking commenced amid enforcement centralization. These changes presented New Dealers an anomalous challenge and opportunity, as their reactionary, liberal, progressive, and even radical constituencies could find agreement on the short-term importance of modernizing criminal systems. From Roosevelt's vantage, this modernization required a balancing of ultimately incompatible views about the end purpose of law and order. While it broke ground in enforcing the slavery statute, the Roosevelt administration was infamously slow to act nationally on lynching. But in the 1930s the federal goal of carceral state construction was not always or even usually racial. The continued policing of so-called street criminality was a given, complete with the racial and class disparities. At the same time, federal officials subsidized federal and state incarceration, having in mind new targets seen as necessary to make law and order more equitable. The New Deal war on crime affirmed the importance of punishing corporate crooks and middle-class white bandits alongside the perpetuation of the traditionally regressive aspects of the carceral state. The national New Deal thus unfolded atop and alongside the continuities and ruptures in racial policing inside and beyond the South. The conscious mediation between conflicting racial visions and the conceit of purportedly race-neutral national policymaking reinforced structural disparities of an older racist regime even as they aspired to a future freed of white supremacist lawlessness. Many scholars, appropriately, have critically engaged the racial dimensions of postwar mass incarceration uneasily juxtaposed with midcentury tales of civil-rights triumphs, but the conflicting aspirations for law and order in the 1930s mark the earlier origins of these postwar ironies.[32]

Central to the modernization of liberalism and criminal justice was the transfiguration of the constitutional order. Under the Constitution, crime fighting never became a fully national occupation; mundane lawbreaking has always been treated as a paradigmatically local matter. But the social condition of *lawlessness* has been nationally legible since at least the 1794 Whiskey Rebellion. Nevertheless, in what Trevor George Gardner has called the "traditional" model of police federalism, outright federal control over "routine subfederal police activity" was resisted until well after World War II.[33] Local officials' support has always been key to legitimating a national role against lawlessness, and to outlive an exigent crisis any sustained national role would require a new understanding among officials.

In regard to the larger history of state building, the importance of law and order has received attention among scholars of jurisdiction and federalism. Jonathan Obert has identified the late nineteenth-century's simultaneous rise of private and public legal coercion as a peculiarly American story, fueled by republican community enforcement of rights but complicated by the "jurisdictional decoupling" where state capacity, claims of authority, and responsibilities became mismatched during the Market Revolution and the Civil War.[34] This concept of "jurisdictional decoupling" could be extended to the paradoxes of federalism persisting in later decades, as national and local legal obligations contradicted governing capacity or practical politics. Scholarship has moreover shown how the twentieth-century modernization of law and order largely coincided with jurisdictional innovation. Daniel C. Richman has noted that while violent crime is the classical example of local jurisdiction, local officials have at times called upon federal assistance.[35] Focusing on the FBI, Richman and Sarah Seo have also shown how the national–local relations have at times circumvented development at the intermediary state level.[36]

When Roosevelt took office, public clamoring for anti-crime action alongside disillusionment with Prohibition provided a unique peacetime opportunity to experiment with federalism. Yet the New Dealers' ambitions had to contend with venerated constitutional tradition. Cummings in particular saw himself as carrying a heavy burden of constitutional history, which threatened to weigh down the activist state, even as he knew the limits on power could not be abandoned altogether.

As with political ideology, the New Dealers staked out a middle position. They championed an approach between federal inaction and total nationalization, which they leveraged toward steady federal expansion. This posturing as moderates between extremes had analogues in their redefinition of liberalism, of which one traditional feature was the constitutional separation of powers. The American national government would never become a unitary state with plenary crime-fighting powers—a reminder of its grand paradox. Nothing is more fundamental to authority than law and order, and yet these supposedly basic functions were among those most out of the federal government's reach. Through the Civil War, Indian wars, Reconstruction, Prohibition, and other major mobilizations at home and abroad, the US government expanded its life-and-death powers to all corners of the world but was (and remains) jurisdictionally constrained in local courtrooms and pedestrian law-breaking. An implication is that the federal government can balloon toward empire without ever obtaining its supposedly minimal night-watchman role. And so long as the Roosevelt administration forswore the goal of usurping the last local law-and-order powers, the New Deal could call itself constitutionally limited. The New Dealers could meanwhile lavishly encourage states and localities to assert their own power against lawlessness. And that is what they did.[37]

Roosevelt and Cummings, with enthusiastic state and local participation, exploited the room they had to expand government power at all levels. By the end of the 1930s, law and order led to some of the New Deal's greatest watersheds in federalism. These included new frontiers of interstate cooperation and the federal prohibition of marijuana, achieved without the kind of constitutional amendment that authorized the national alcohol ban. But the formula did not mainly rely on national usurpation. Cummings negotiated a new settlement, which I call war-on-crime federalism, that finally overcame the zero-sum jurisdictional contest of previous eras when officials expended great energy competing over control. Under the New Deal, federal, state, and local enforcement authorities cooperated innovatively to expand their scope in concert. Federal officials encouraged state reforms in drug policy, criminal procedure, incarceration, and rehabilitation, and consulted localities for their criminological expertise. Innovations in federal–state relations allowed constituents with sharply opposed racial and social goals to cooperate—most conspicuously Black activists agitating to make white-supremacist terror legally legible, and white southerners seeking modern systems of racial discipline.

The changes in federalism and liberal politics stimulated each other through the 1930s, providing the institutional and ideological conditions for a new kind of security state. Blurring the lines between domestic policy and national defense, the New Deal constructed a stable war on crime from the beleaguered remnants of World War I—particularly J. Edgar Hoover's policing apparatuses, surveillance and detention systems for wartime enemies, and Treasury powers that harmonized regulation and criminal justice—and refashioned this machinery into a permanent security state. The jurisdictional jealousies that previously plagued state and local governments, federal authorities, and Treasury and Justice officials, yielded to a new cooperative arrangement in which all had expansive roles to play, even as they observed a new deference toward one another. By the late 1930s those who had spent the 1920s repressing dissidents, and some of the dissidents themselves, could join in the hopes that the instruments of domestic control would in the end serve the public good.

An ever-expanding power to suppress crime through a remodeled federalism was thus baked into the defining contours of modern liberal governance. Roosevelt and Cummings successfully synthesized humanitarian reformism and old-fashioned state violence. Although the ties between welfare and warfare have received attention, it was the war on crime that consummated their domestic partnership in their most precarious years. The experimentalism of war-on-crime liberalism, uniting conservative and reformist elements, already yielded a remarkably stable program in the twilight of the 1930s—a political program I call security-state liberalism. With this fusion the New Dealers shepherded enforcement machinery through World War II. Their collaboration made the wartime security state, including its great injustices, much smoother and more stable than it had been in World War I. In the 1940s this stabilized infrastructure of repression could withstand the pressures of World War II and the Cold War and became a permanent fixture of the American landscape. By transforming federalism and liberalism—by turning the mess of lawlessness into a refined security apparatus with social stability—the New Deal war on crime built American law and order and the modern liberal state.[38]

THIS BOOK IS ORGANIZED into five parts and twelve chapters to clarify the larger political arc and examine its thematic components. Part I narrates the long predicament for law enforcement, political authority, and liberalism from Reconstruction through the Progressive Era, with the structural and ideological enforcement contradictions hitting a fevered pitch in the interwar period. Part II shows how in its first two years the Roosevelt administration navigated the political predicament, revolutionized the criminal code, and grappled toward new coalitional means of legitimating national authority. Part III explores war-on-crime federalism, with chapters on a neglected consensus in constitutional and legal thought, the jurisdictional watersheds of drug control, and how racial reformers within changing legal structures sought to define the New Deal's law-and-order promises. Part IV shows how the nation's relations across society and the states produced penological and criminological innovations that married progressive reform to the repressive state, yielding a vision at once aspirational and pragmatic. Part V describes how the preceding developments gave rise to a security state, steeped in a new class consciousness and political consensus, blurring the lines between war and peace, and remaining stable through World War II—thus avoiding the collapse of the infrastructure of repression that came after World War I.

America entered the post–World War II era with most of the paradoxical components of its later twentieth-century war on crime already in place. To those seeking the origins of these paradoxes, I argue that there was no immaculate conception of the modern liberal state, for one of its founding purposes was to convert the chaos of repression and lawlessness into an ecumenical and stable system of law and order. To fully understand the difficulties this system would face in the late twentieth and early twenty-first centuries, it is fruitful to begin with how Roosevelt's generation addressed the mounting challenges it inherited.

PART I

THE LIMITS OF LIBERAL MOBILIZATION,

1865–1932

Lawlessness reigned when Roosevelt became president in 1933. Homicide and property crimes were on the rise. Prohibition staggered along, haunted by corruption and black markets. Economic dislocations fueled violent strikes and strikebreaking, and Black Americans suffered surging racial terror. Roosevelt had a limited toolbox for managing these crises. The symbiotic relations between government and vigilantes were in disrepute. Statutes shackled Pinkerton agents and the Secret Service. Prohibition enforcers were poorly equipped. J. Edgar Hoover's controversial Bureau of Investigation had few officers or legal powers of arrest or investigation, and its agents were outgunned by gangsters with automatic weapons. Hoover himself was hesitant to fight violent crime directly.[1] The Treasury Department and Justice Department had trouble cooperating with each other. State governments pursued crime without credible national leadership or coordination. Practitioners and criminologists enjoyed few institutional ties.

Roosevelt's economic and crime agendas required a reliable expansion of federal enforcement power. Yet in living memory the national state had not achieved legitimacy. Historians have pondered the legitimacy crisis that peaked with Prohibition. They recognize that Roosevelt's promise to rein in corruption and lawlessness by legalizing alcohol helped him win the presidency.[2] Looking farther back, the predicament of social order animates the literature on Progressivism, corruption drives stories of the Gilded Age, and the struggle over jurisdiction frames scholarship on Reconstruction.[3] It is worth considering the full weight of the intergenerational quest for order that Roosevelt inherited in 1933.

Anxieties about crime had become a moral panic, but the threat was not imaginary. From 1865 through the mid-1930s Americans witnessed disorder and violence beyond what future generations experienced. Industrial warfare, political violence and assassinations, lynchings, labor unrest, homicides, property crimes, Indian wars—this chaotic violence largely subsided by the end of the decade. Whether coincidental or a policy success, the taming of lawlessness is an unappreciated triumph of New Deal America and the first national war on crime.

But wars, and the shadow cast by their mobilization, typically mutate domestic politics. Roosevelt's contemporaries were familiar with two wars that had radically altered national power, political economy, and public ideology—the US Civil War and World War I. Both crises drove ideological and constitutional change, but each inaugurated contradictions that peacetime liberalism could not reconcile with stable rule. The Civil War helped finalize continental consolidation, but frontier conquest, battles between capital and labor, and the failure of Gilded Age liberalism to manage racial divisions yielded to seemingly ubiquitous lawlessness. Progressives attempted to defeat lawlessness under a new politics attentive to security and social welfare, but were unable to unite Americans across class, party, race, region, and institutions by the eve of World War I. In Chapter 1, I consider this multigenerational frustration.

In Chapter 2, I explore the perpetual mobilizations, beginning with World War I, that raised the stakes of social unity but could not achieve it. Domestic repression and Prohibition inflated enforcement power, but it was not sustained. The contradictions reached a breaking point as reactionary repression, alcohol control, and conservative economics converged in the Herbert Hoover administration and its mistrusted war on crime, providing both the sense of urgency and opportunity that welcomed the New Dealers when they inherited power.

CHAPTER 1

"THE MOST LAWLESS NATION"

The Civil War marked the culmination of mounting antebellum violence. Through the 1850s, anti-abolitionist mobs, protracted guerilla combat in Kansas Territory, and John Brown's uprising anticipated the unparalleled destruction of America's deadliest war. But after the war, law enforcement, especially at the federal level, faced continual resistance for fifty years. Those seeking national unity and order saw each obstacle as the specter of lawlessness. Beginning with the bloody contests in the 1860s over jurisdiction, the "lawlessness" trope inhabited frontier narratives and drifted eastward to haunt the national story. Prompted by the 1864 massacre of Cheyenne Indians at Sand Creek, Colorado, the federal Indian Peace Commission downplayed the perpetrators' operational ties to military authority and depicted the atrocity as the "aggressions of lawless white men."[1] This motif of lawlessness reappeared to mark Indigenous Americans, whose fights for sovereignty thwarted federal assimilation. Through Reconstruction and the Gilded Age, the national press described as lawless everyone who obstructed the rational, continental production of order. *New York Times* readers learned of Georgia's "lawless Negroes" in 1869 and Harlem's "lawless Italians" two decades later.[2]

They read horror stories of "lawless strikers," "lawless gamblers," "lawless coal miners," and "lawless Chinese."[3] In 1874 the New York paper condemned "lawless Kentucky" and in 1889 the *Los Angeles Times* warned of "lawless Texas."[4] Governments themselves suffered the affliction, from the "lawless law" of Southeast Asian despotisms to New York's own "lawless" state senate.[5]

Some phantoms of "lawlessness" were very real and others were largely imaginary, and their suppression carried conflicting social and moral implications. But they shared a function in defining oppositional aspirations for political and legal order. Concern about lawlessness did not cleanly track violent crime rates, but the qualitative contrast between enforcement legitimacy and lawlessness nevertheless shaped national politics.[6] Fear of lawlessness undermined democratic stability and frustrated the more ambitious plans of national leaders. Indeed, as an opposition to lawlessness served the ideological construction of lawful order, law itself became defined in terms of its opposite—lawless resistance. Resistance appeared in the vigilant defense of Indian sovereignty, the terroristic overthrow of Union authority, and violent labor strikes. Having subdued recalcitrant Southerners and Northerners through the Civil War, the United States faced continuing intransigence during its military domination of the South and conquest of the western Plains.

Achieving law and order was the principal institutional and ideological domestic challenge from the 1860s to the eve of World War I. These difficulties revealed instabilities arising from military conquest and the limitations of national liberalism. Such challenges inspired progressive reformers to formulate programmatic responses, but the constraints of constitutional capacity and imagination foreclosed the national fulfillment of their goals.

THE LIMITS OF CONQUEST

The federal republic's attempts at continental mastery, in contrast to contemporaneous political modernization elsewhere, suffered a peculiar constitutional legacy. The US Constitution enumerated specific powers for the federal government and reserved other powers to the states. Government officials during Reconstruction and the Gilded Age, seeking new institutional arrangements for law enforcement, typically pursued piecemeal arrangements with private actors or deployed the few established constitutional mechanisms—such as taxation powers, the Post Office, and militarism.[7] Short-term military might and the will to dominate generally shaped federal power.

Reconstruction remade criminal law. In general terms, the Civil War and its aftermath provided new opportunities for reformers to bring criminal prosecution, which often was a private matter in antebellum America, fully under public authority.[8] More specifically, emancipation under the Thirteenth Amendment meant turning slavery into a federal crime, and enforcing the rights of freedmen faced jurisdictional resistance immediately. With the dislocations of war came surging violent crime and property crime, which white Southerners exploited to reassert authority through criminal justice.[9] While conceding to Black Americans some basic civil rights, the notorious Black Codes of 1865 to 1867 reconstituted racial caste through criminal law, newly contrived offenses, and enforcement mechanisms. Mississippi penal laws targeted Black Americans for carrying firearms, trespassing, engaging in "mischief" or "insulting gestures," speaking seditiously, or preaching without a license. The state's apprenticeship law directed "sheriffs, justices of the peace, and other civil officers" to track violators, and Black Americans insufficiently tethered to white employers were subject to "vagrancy" charges.[10]

Congressional Republicans responded with statutory and constitutional reforms to nationalize criminal jurisdiction. The 1866 Civil Rights Act designated US district courts for adjudicating "all crimes and offenses" against the Act and establishing uniformity of "civil and criminal matters."[11] As the Black Codes mounted, Congress pursued Radical Reconstruction. The Reconstruction Acts divided the South into five military districts, and the Habeas Corpus Act of 1867 empowered the federal judiciary to protect due process. Most important, the Fourteenth and Fifteenth Amendments formally inserted the federal government between the states and its inhabitants to protect civil rights. Federal troops secured Black men's voting rights, which led to the inclusion of Black persons in legislatures, sheriffs' offices, and police departments. In the long term, the Fourteenth Amendment would constrain state criminal justice powers to prevent deprivations of "liberty, or property, without due process of law."[12]

Federal aggrandizement of criminal justice power, soon after wartime, coincided with unprecedented ambitions for federal welfare unseen again until the twentieth century. The national government's Freedmen's Bureau pursued racial equity, material welfare, and economic planning in concert.[13] Benefits for veterans' families became the largest outlays of federal social spending in the entire nineteenth century.[14] That Reconstruction at its most radical pursued expansive criminal jurisdiction to protect civil rights and private property, along with racially conscious welfare and the first true entitlement system, marked a holistic enterprise of modern state building. In the nineteenth century as in the twentieth, national power was not built first through law enforcement, only later to become a welfare state. Nor was welfare the original blueprint for federal modernization, only corrupted by policing priorities at a later date. Despite libertarian imaginations of a night-watchman state deformed by later forays into social policy, and left-liberal myths of federal safety nets twisted toward reactionary ends during the Cold War, the national functions of policing and welfare arose in tandem. This dynamic was partly contingent on American federalism, but it also arose each time national leaders tried to create a central state. Local policing also integrated the social and the punitive. And Reconstruction's twentieth-century fulfillment would ultimately rely on partial nationalization of criminal justice rights alongside political civil rights.

But in the short term, federal officials lacked the resources to protect liberty—or to do much law enforcement at all. High-profile federal trials of the Lincoln assassins were wartime military commissions in their procedural expediency and lacked long-term political viability. In 1870, Congress created a Department of Justice to manage a barrage of federal litigation, but Justice was still barred from basic investigations and arrests.[15] The struggle over civil rights was characterized, not by deliberative jurisdictional competition, but instead by diffuse violence. White supremacist terror inspired the Klan Acts of 1870 and 1871, which empowered US marshals to protect election integrity against murderous violence. President Ulysses S. Grant blamed "lawless and disaffected persons" for "persistent violations of the rights of citizens," and urged local enforcement to assist in imposing order.[16] The third Enforcement Act allowed the suspension of habeas corpus, which Grant and Attorney General Amos Akerman leveraged to crush the Klan in South Carolina.[17]

Federal habeas corpus policy underscored the tenuousness of relying on expedient internal security rationales. Eventually federal habeas review of state-level criminal justice became a key mechanism for enforcing civil rights and civil liberties. But in the 1860s and 1870s the rapid changes to this medieval constitutional mechanism were contingent on volatile national politics and military might. Reconstruction accommodated a radical centralization: Historically state habeas power served to check federal detention power. *Tarble's Case* in 1871 upended this practice, building on the pre–Civil War precedent in *Ableman v. Booth*. Enforcing Reconstruction relied on novel federal habeas jurisdiction in 1867, which in turn relied on national force and will. In *Ex parte McCardle* the US Supreme Court upheld federal suspension of habeas corpus as an expediency to enforcing Reconstruction and punishing its opponents. But this centralizing trend slowed as Radical Reconstruction unwound.[18]

Organized violence activated Reconstruction but also brought it down. By 1871 several states had fallen to the violent intimidation of Democratic "redeemers." The centrality of criminal justice to Reconstruction was revealed in its unraveling. Enfranchised Blacks had populated police departments and sheriffs' offices.[19] Although uneven across jurisdictions, Black inclusion in law enforcement revealed the reliance of political legitimacy and enforcement power on military mobilization and national emergency.[20] The Southern white reclamation of institutions not only marked but constituted the end of Reconstruction. Redemption was itself a dialectical process between violence and political struggle over law enforcement.

While Redemption could be seen as the triumph of lawlessness, its violence, accompanying an effort to restrain, reform, and reclaim official organs of state power alongside racist vigilantism, ironically coincided with post-Reconstruction efforts at state professionalization.[21] Having expelled Union influence, Mississippi reasserted jurisdiction with draconian laws against minor crimes. Its prisons swelled with Black men, whom it leased out as forced laborers.[22] Prisons became central to reconstituting racial caste. The interplay between convict leasing and semi-slave conditions produced an interlocking system of power among official state authorities, the remnants of the planter class, and a new socioeconomic elite. At the same time, prisons were harmonizing with a national trend of profitable industrial prisons arising from the antebellum North. Carceral political economy, an unabashed state capitalism, eventually became targeted by the industrial laboring class, nurturing solidarity between agricultural populists and urban workers.[23] A sort of industrialized Free Soil ideology would eventually condemn for-profit prisons as unfair competition. A future political economy of prisons would ultimately garner support from the growing Northern white workforce and the white South, crucial constituencies to national reunification. For now this convergence was a long way off.

The Panic of 1873 clarified the reliance of conquest on material conditions. Economic depression coupled with violent resistance weakened Republican domination, and terror peaked that year in Colfax, Louisiana. White Southern Democrats overpowered freedmen and state militia, murdering 150 Black men.[24] In 1876 Radical Reconstruction incurred two vital losses. In *United States v. Cruikshank,* the Supreme Court rejected federal indictments for the Colfax massacre under the 1870 Enforcement Act. Although the white mob denied the victims their political rights and the right to bear arms,[25] the Court construed the Fourteenth Amendment to constrain state and not private actors.[26] The Cruikshank Case affirmed the Second Amendment as a matter of states' rights and found that individual Black men outside the auspices of the official state militia had no constitutional right to bear arms. Such decisions protected private militias and terror but also law and order of an older republican sort.[27] Also in 1876, the contested presidential election between Republican Rutherford Hayes and Democrat Samuel Tilden produced a compromise: The Republican took office, promising to end military occupation of the South. Although the troops had already largely left, federal surrender of criminal jurisdiction finally ended Reconstruction.[28] Federal retrenchment left Black Americans unprotected. In the 1883 *Civil Rights Cases* the Court overturned the Civil Rights Act of 1875, which had authorized federal regulation of private discrimination.[29] The restoration of white home rule coincided with the South's modernizing racial separation. In the 1880s and 1890s, US rates of violent crime among both white and Black southerners were some of the highest in the world. In the South, white Americans and newspapers saw the issue as a problem of Black criminality.[30] Notorious double standards meant Black defendants and convicted criminals suffered heavier fines and longer prison terms.[31]

As national leaders oversaw the rise and fall of Radical Reconstruction, they remained comparatively consistent in pursuing control of the West. To the rest of the nation and future commenters, the "Wild West" was the paragon of lawlessness. Newspaper headlines warned about "lawless cowboys" and "lawless Indians."[32] Like the South, the West indeed had more crime than the Northeast.[33] Scholars have nevertheless contested the degree of violence and its meaning.[34] Blurred lines between unruly violence and modern order ran through the pursuit of jurisdictional legibility and market rationality, an iconic epic contest sometimes collectively called the "Western Civil War of Incorporation."[35] From the teleological retrospection of the twentieth-century liberal state, this struggle above all sought law and order.

From another vantage, the West's lawlessness and law, private and public violence, played off one another to build the state. In 1883, for example, Wyatt Earp imposed upon officials in Dodge City, Kansas, to allow the Dodge City Peace Commission to take control peacefully, but the threat of extralegal violence undergirded its control. Jonathan Obert argues that vigilance committees and gunfighters served to modernize governance, when amid the erosion of republicanism and expanding market capitalism the rise of both professionalizing public and private vigilantism coincided with emergent liberal values. Obert identifies discernible gunfighter phases, marking phases of state building—from 1850 to 1875, defined by diffuse actors from buffalo-hunting regions most active in Texas, Kansas, and Missouri; and the "golden age" of gunfighting from 1875 to 1885, spurred by the cattle frontier, especially in New Mexico, Arizona, and Colorado, and featuring figures like Wyatt Earp at the Battle of OK Corral, Billy the Kid and Jesse James, and Wild Bill Hickok.[36] In the early 1890s the Johnson County War saw as many as dozens of deaths when the Wyoming Stock Growers Association invited "invaders" to subdue and kill accused castle hustlers.[37]

Although arguably constitutive of state building, violence in the West nevertheless revealed the limitations of the period's liberalism in producing order, legitimacy, and jurisdictional modernity. Notoriously, US wrestling for institutional coherence meant brutality against Indigenous people. Important details differentiated the many confrontations with the Cheyenne, Shoshone, Nez Pierce, Blackfoot, Comanche, Apache, and Lakota, but the popular and formal violence often fed each other. Raids, massacres, settlers' encroachments, and official military campaigns unfolded symbiotically. National hard power deployed in such famous military engagements as the 1876 Battle of Little Big Horn. Government assimilationists employed the softer power of coercive boarding schools and criminal law. Habeas corpus proceedings pondered Indigenous Americans' constitutional personhood and the Major Crimes Act of 1885 brought Indian defendants under federal jurisdiction. In what later became the state of Oklahoma, the federal government sponsored Indian police forces under white supervision. Up north, the Indian Office's prohibition of the ceremonial Sun Dance set the stage for another resort to naked military power, when years later panicked officials reacted to the Lakota's revivalist 1889 Ghost Dance by slaughtering hundreds at Pine Ridge Reservation in the Wounded Knee massacre.[38]

Violent contests in the West composed a tale not only of national imperialism but of the great paradoxes in the nation's proud self-conception of liberatory order. Emancipated Black soldiers became significant agents in securing and policing the frontier.[39] The territorial incorporation and statehood of Oklahoma compounded questions of jurisdictional ambiguity for many years, while also showcasing a celebrated example of post–Civil War Black inclusion in law enforcement. Bass Reeves, a formerly enslaved Black man, was widely venerated for bringing federal order to Oklahoma, arresting thousands of outlaws in his decades as a US deputy marshal.[40] In the West, even the most admirable exploits of the Reconstructed state donned the burdensome traces of conquest. In the future such paradoxes would be significantly rearranged to reconcile the region with a national liberal vision.

THE LIMITS OF LIBERALISM

After Reconstruction, the peacetime attempt to reestablish federal enforcement authority was principally a political challenge. Military mobilization temporarily pacified the South and removed Indians toward
the West, but in the North and East, the sustained order of courts, police, and jails required political legitimacy. Military conquest and civil law
require fundamentally different social dynamics. Legal and political
power arise from both coercion and consent, and military domination
privileges coercion whereas civil law prioritizes consent. Long-term
enforcement stability flourishes with a credible public ideology. A significant fraction of the conquered had to feel included.[41] Opposing lawlessness could be the common cause, but no ethos adequately united
Americans behind it.[42] Even when nativism fueled enforcement efforts
against immigrants, it mostly happened at the state and local level until
the 1880s.[43] The Civil War elevated a liberal nationalism dedicated to free
labor, social and political equality alongside industrial markets, and a balance between federal rights protection and subsidiarity. While it is
tempting to attribute the national state's enforcement failures to political
will, the national struggle against lawlessness fundamentally drew on
contradictory premises.

One conspicuous problem was corruption, which was not merely a
bug but a feature of governance at all levels. Dueling accusations of corruption exposed the partisan politicization of law enforcement. Even before the Civil War, in New York state-level Republicans and municipal
Democrats had openly constituted rival police organizations, which
fought in the streets for city control in 1857.[44] After the war, Boss Tweed
and Tammany Hall's grip on the city Democratic Party was precariously
maintained through violence.[45] The convincing bourgeois Republican
narrative of Tammany corruption was countered by accusations of corruption aimed at the Republicans and the Grant administration.[46] Through
the end of the century, urban political machines maintained control
through graft and violence. Police owed their jobs to party bosses and
threatened voters while repaying a share of their tax-funded income to
party coffers. Legitimate and black-market businesses submitted to overt
protection rackets run by the police.

State and local rackets were brazen and had the virtue of not being hypocritical. Rampant lawlessness was more ideologically challenging for liberal nationalism, the emerging ethos of Republican rule. Liberals espoused free labor, individual freedom to contract, and an economic role for the federal government that accommodated industry but did little else. They promised law and order, liberty and justice, an end to lawlessness. Their skepticism toward government power, when most consistent, applied to the criminal justice state. Britain's influential sociologist Herbert Spencer favored a "a rigorous criminal code" but worried that an "unscrupulous" citizenry would tolerate "tyrannical institutions" and "severe forms of punishment.[47] In the United States, liberal deference to federalism and industrial private property limited the efficacy and appeal of liberalism. Northern liberals bristled at southern sectionalism and the most extremist racism but remained skeptical of federal activism to protect Black Americans from private violence. National liberalism repelled both white southerners who resented free labor and Black southerners abandoned by federal withdrawal and judicial racial conservatism.[48]

In economic terms, liberalism inclined toward business and contractual conceptions of freedom. While abandoning civil rights, federal officials left workers exposed to violence and predation—and sometimes participated in the repression. Where liberalism did favor government to protect law and order, it gained a reputation as a servant of capital.[49] Classical liberalism pledged equality of the law, but constitutional interpretation seemingly tilted in favor of corporate consolidation. Beyond its jurisdictional timidity, liberalism offered few social reform ideas to entice urban workers or the agrarian South's white or Black populations.

Jurisdictional conflicts exposed liberalism's fatal shortcomings, especially in the cities, the cauldrons of industrial liberalism. Between the middle of the nineteenth century and the middle of the twentieth, as cities rode the waves of industrialization, jurisdictional ambiguities transcended federal questions. While the states' historical relationship to federal power remained controversial, cities were unambiguously creatures of state governments. But the economically and politically important cities were sites where rising capitalism most clearly implicated enforcement authority. Powerful cities competed with state capitals, most famously in New York, often over law enforcement. The struggle over local power complicated questions of federalism time and again. In the relationships between nation and state, state and city, and city and nation, each opportunity for a formal or informal tie across law enforcers introduced the potential for jealousies and competition that would undercut national consciousness or authority.

Policing and liberalism each promised to bring rationality to an industrializing world, but their efforts exposed political tensions.[50] In the mid-nineteenth century, all major northern cities adopted modern police forces, structured according to military tradition, capable of patrolling the whole jurisdiction. Police forces were a central mechanism of class construction that sat uncomfortably with liberalism, particularly its free-labor ideology. Class regulation relied on police because of their capacity and locational opportunity. On the one hand, the police protected property rights and social order, a function long seen as fundamental to the growth of a liberal capitalist state. On the other hand, police departments conducted overt urban patronage, inspiring middle-class ambivalence.[51] They helped assimilate immigrant ethnic whites, most famously the Irish, into middle-class respectability—while relying on hierarchies whose transparent patronage and extortion divided middle-class reformers, industrial capitalists, and aspirational law enforcers. In the third quarter of the nineteenth century, distrust of the police was common among bourgeois conservatives, and among the capitalist elite as well.

Federal as well as local enforcement actively policed moral and class boundaries, projects in tension with limited-government liberalism. Some of the most active policing targeted vice. Starting in 1873, Anthony Comstock's legislation used the mails to censor "indecent" materials. Exemplifying the limitations of liberalism amid dynamic urban troubles, Yale sociologist William Graham Sumner explicitly opposed policing disorder and vice. In his 1883 "Forgotten Man" speech he lamented the "public expenditure to prevent vice." The "industrious workman" was wrongly compelled to "hire a policeman to save the drunkard from himself." Sumner thought vice policing undermined natural consequences and penalized those "who have resisted vice"—the "clean, quiet, virtuous." He frankly thought "the drunkard in the gutter is just where he ought to be."[52] But Sumner recognized his position's unpopularity; most middle-class Americans favored vice policing, not only to control and help deviants but to maintain an orderly and healthy social space.

On a national scale, modern issues made industrial liberalism and domestic local policing especially divisive. After Reconstruction, President Hayes faced over 100,000 striking workers from Baltimore to Pittsburgh. Before being crushed by federal troops and local militia, the Great Railroad Strike halted transit and shipping. The 1877 confrontations brought capital onto the side of city police in jurisdictions like New York, Chicago, Boston, and Philadelphia, but with a thousand arrested and a hundred killed, the labor movement came to detest state and federal enforcement authority. The 1878 Posse Comitatus Act, restricting military enforcement of domestic law, gratified both white southerners and labor activists—strengthening the solidarity of traditional Democratic Party constituents against enforcement but in favor of reformist restraints. Congressional Democrats overrode Hayes's veto, another rebuke of the military regime that marked Republican national rule.[53]

In the coming decades crises of jurisdiction and liberalism intensified amid urban class warfare. The military continued to suppress striking workers nationwide, despite Posse Comitatus restrictions. They were sometimes joined by private Pinkertons, who relied on tax subsidies to profitably patrol whole cities. Political and labor dissidents endured vigilante and state repression at the state and local levels. More than two dozen states had adopted conspiracy statutes by 1886, the year the Chicago Haymarket riot inspired national fears of anarchism and activism. New York City workers were sentenced for "socialistic crimes."[54] As class tensions, repression, and political instability crested in the 1890s, labor violence revealed a weakness in the ideological justification of the state.[55] Increasing ideological institutionalization of class anxieties came alongside illiberal policing, as the proliferation of local anti-tramp laws punished unemployed vagrants. Persecution of political radicals, academics, and activists accompanied the new criminalization, and anarchist Emma Goldman was sentenced to a year in jail in 1893.[56] Pinkerton abuses in the 1892 Homestead Strike prompted legislation to bar them from law enforcement. After the Panic of 1893, Ohio businessman Jacob Coxey's army of unemployed marched in Washington, DC, in early 1894. Despite legal restrictions, federal troops suppressed the marchers.

In 1894 nearly 700,000 workers went on strike, topping the 610,000 in the Haymarket year of 1886.[57] President Grover Cleveland, the paradigmatic classical liberal Democrat, deployed troops in the Pullman Strike, constitutionally rationalizing this as protection of the mail. The Pullman Strike pitted labor against interstate capital but also exposed the zero-sum federalism of enforcement. Some Chicago officials were sympathetic to labor. The Reverend William Carwardine reported that local police even furnished money and goods to the workers. Democratic mayor John P. Hopkins, a former Pullman dockworker, also sympathized with the strikers.[58] Right-liberals, meanwhile, saw the Pullman Strike as an anarchistic calamity for law and order.[59]

Despite the labor repression, the later 1890s saw over a thousand strikes per year.[60] Repression exposed fissures in free-labor ideology, radicalizing some liberals while ultimately encouraging a more strident law-and-order middle class. Cleveland's strikebreaking alienated activist Eugene Debs, who supported Cleveland's liberalism over Republican Benjamin Harrison in 1892, and appreciated the Democrat's criticism of President Harrison's crackdown in the Homestead Strike.[61] But then criminal enforcement of the Sherman Antitrust Act, the first federal monopoly regulation, landed Debs in prison.[62] Most federal police power under the interstate commerce clause had targeted interstate transportation; the anti-monopoly Sherman Act was a glaring exception.[63] Tellingly, the Act's innovative constitutionalism ensnared labor more than capital. The Supreme Court's support of labor injunctions in *In re Debs* was but the most famous example of the judiciary's anti-labor bias. In prison Debs radicalized toward socialism. As the twentieth century approached, the working class had little use for federal law enforcement.[64]

PROPHETS OF ORDER

Eugene Debs's socialist conversion was not the period's only momentous ideological awakening. Chicago social worker Jane Addams responded to the Pullman Strike by criticizing both anarchic strikers and greedy capitalists. This response, condemning lawlessness across the classes, was a watershed for progressivism, whose reformers developed programmatic remedies for corruption, inequities, and liberalism's failures.[65]

We can debate whether progressivism was a variant of liberalism, or coherently ideological at all.[66] Regardless, we must reckon with the major arc of political history that follows classical liberalism to progressivism, progressivism to New Deal liberalism.[67] Unlike earlier liberals, progressives rejected free-market individualism in favor of government action, inspired by social reform, social welfare, and social science. Progressives joined organized labor, populists, and the rural South in distrusting unbridled capitalism and the robber barons basking in unprecedented wealth.[68] Most fundamentally, progressives understood society in associational terms rather than as a constellation of individuals. They shared this vantage with the republicanism of the early United States.

Yet compared to socialists, anarchists, or unapologetic reactionaries, progressives were liberals. Perhaps most important, progressives shared with older and future liberals an aim to overcome the materiality of class, guild, and fixed status. They sought harmonization of class interests through informed political economy, rather than navigating politics as a superstructure obscuring an irreconcilable clash arising from the patterns of production. They saw working-class consciousness as a lamentable mirror image of industrial greed. Unlike the rural populists, they respected all the professions, including lawyers and bankers—a pragmatism they shared with liberals.[69] This posture arose in part from progressives' own class position: Mostly northern or western, urbanized, and middle class, progressives lacked the New South's and labor's distrust of managerial elites or the national government. Thus, their supposed class-blindness obscured a privileging of the middle class as the unspoken neutral ideal around which to organize society. This sociological bias placed progressives at the midpoint between the lineage of classical and modern liberals, who tended toward the same middle-class politics.

Progressives were especially ambitious about the possibilities for reform, which in a way made it more difficult for them to reach a consensus on strategy. While adopting the traditional struggle of law against lawlessness, the progressives were categorically Manichean—they championed morality against immorality, virtue against sin, fairness against inequity, purity against contamination. Their theoretical currency sought to legitimate new modalities of crime-fighting up and down society. Their thirst for regulation and reform, from sexual practice to nature conservation, frequently relied on criminalization.[70] But progressives imagined reforms that exceeded institutional capacity. Dominant constitutional interpretations constrained their federal activism, and they achieved most within, not against, the federalist structure.[71] Without an institutional center, their criminological theories could not tether local governance and civil society to the federal state.

In seeking to harness and manage modernization, as institutions around them underwent rapid transition, progressives could not reach ideological consensus. Their totalistic goals defied strategic selectivity. They sought to reform prisons and policing—which had often been competing sites of reform since the rise of republican criminology. Thinkers since Cesare Beccaria had affirmed policing for its ability to deter crime through immediate punishment, making it an alternative to incarceration.[72] Into the twentieth century, America had yet to arrive at a law-and-order politics where reformers and crime hawks battled over both enforcement and punishment as necessarily complementary objects. Class, cultural, and regional divergences produced conflicting constituencies for the status quo, for modernization, or for radical reform. Generally, progressives divided on questions of criminalization, punishment, and disciplining vice.

Progressives could settle on some key questions of modernizing the disciplinary state. Humane prison treatment was a unifying cause since the 1870 National Congress on Penitentiary and Reformatory Discipline. Reformers broadly agreed on ending for-profit contractual arrangements. Even wholesale skeptics of prisons, especially among social workers, regarded the criminological state as a target of reform rather than a crucible of intractable class antagonism. Reformers like Thomas Osborne pursued substantive changes, but champions of the "new penology" reached for a punishment model that was untenable during severe societal conflict. Progressives effectively reformed indeterminate sentencing and parole, probation, and juvenile detention.[73] These reforms nevertheless faced a backlash while imposing discipline onto new subjects. It was hoped that the reforms would promote a harmony of interests, but there was not enough consensus on the underlying ideals.[74]

As to city policing, which was central to both criminal enforcement and the quest for social order, reformers often agreed on low-hanging fruit but diverged in the ambitions of their ultimate goals.[75] New York City conflicted with state officials and reformers and was isolated from federal authority. The state's Society for the Prevention of Crime had its offices in New York City, and corresponded with reformers like Frank Moss,[76] but the "crime prevention" vision lacked national sponsorship. Police reform stressed modernization and propriety, but modernization itself allowed abuse, as muckraker Jacob Riis famously exposed. In 1895 the Lexow Committee uncovered systematic police corruption in Tammany Hall's New York.[77] The new president of the board of police commissioners, Theodore Roosevelt, responded with significant reforms, eliminating partisan hiring and improving training.

Roosevelt soon emerged as the personification of muscular progressivism—reformist, systemic, committed to national greatness and social order—but his ambitions exceeded his record and yielded no national policing narrative. Roosevelt adopted a "new nationalism" slogan in his 1912 Bull Moose presidential run, a theme boosted by *New Republic* editor Herbert Croly. Croly, a progressive Republican, saw in Roosevelt's career America's coming of age, complete with the challenges of policing the modern city. According to Croly's *The Promise of American Life,* police had the "most essential function of all—that of maintaining order." Class harmony depended on police integrity, which determined the balance between the most "arrogant and lawless" unions and corporations alike. City governance would soon be "the most fruitful field for economically and socially constructive experimentation." Croly recognized the city's dual nature: its commercial ties linked the city "to the national economic system; but there is a minor part which is exclusively local."[78]

As central as city policing was to the progressive vision, there was no one clear path forward. In California, August Vollmer personified an influential reformism marked by academic imagination more than urban pragmatism. As Berkeley's police chief from 1905 to 1933, Vollmer drove the reform agenda—professionalization, social hygiene, social science, and the furtherance of progressive theory with a practitioner's agenda of regimentation. At the University of California, Berkeley, Vollmer created the first bureau of academic criminology, and in the police department he popularized fingerprinting and the modus operandi system and put patrol officers on bicycles. He kept abreast of technological developments—methods of criminal detection and apprehension, theories of punishment and rehabilitation, changes in legal practice, novel approaches to automobile regulation—all over the country and world, and his acolytes replicated his model in cities nationwide. He decried police departments' scandalously uneducated personnel and thought all officers should have at least a four-year degree.[79] Vollmer envisioned a perfectibility of policing while regarding typical police as utterly unworthy of their job. This elitism required optimism about reform in conflict with police modernizers who were loath to impugn the rank and file. How this professionalizing mission would achieve national purchase remained unclear.[80]

The progressives' biggest shortcomings, both ideological and institutional, concerned race. Vollmer's own record was mixed; other reformers more tepidly criticized racism or enthusiastically embraced eugenics. From the nineteenth century, scientific criminologists typically followed Cesare Lombroso's demographic determinism.[81] Modern progressives sought a rational state to manage industrial modernity, and eugenics was on the scientific cutting edge. At its peak, eugenics posited that there was genetic criminality among identified classes of white as well as Black Americans. Sophisticates pondered which people were suited to live freely and reproduce. Sterilization laws flourished, particularly in the West.[82] Anxieties about foreign contamination coincided with a new era of immigration control, from the Chinese Restriction Act of 1882 and other Asian migrant controls to the national quotas following World War I.[83] Eugenic theories dovetailed with nativism and a new nationalism that united protectionist labor activists with the rising second Klan and an increasingly ecumenically racist deep South.[84] The scientific language on criminality most conducive to Progressive thought was thus divisive and contingent on changing conceptions of whiteness. Consistent opposition to eugenics mostly came from Catholics, who were a large proportion of the "ethnic white" immigrant populations that progressives most wanted to assimilate.

Beyond ideology, progressives had no satisfactory practical answer to racist lawlessness—in part because of the paradoxical ways in which formal systems of law enforcement interacted with racial terror that, at least facially, was illegal. As modernists grasped for a sophisticated science of combatting lawlessness, lynching in particular exposed the elusiveness of defining law itself. Lynching was a formally illegal act claiming the mantle of justice. Of the approximately 3,000 lynchings that stained the Progressive Era, most were rationalized as enforcing laws against rape, physical assault, murder, or arson.[85] Many white Americans attributed the surge of lynchings and racial pogroms to the need for law and order. Sometimes white terror was defended as necessary and popular law enforcement; other times it was defiantly insisted that the law itself must yield to the higher needs of social order. Black journalist Ida B. Wells called for a public response "sufficient to stop the crusade of lawlessness and lynching," but there was no movement for a federal solution.[86] The Progressive Era also saw a rise of "race riots," pogroms directed against Black Americans. The 1906 Atlanta riot, where white anxieties fueled violence against a growing Black middle class, especially belied the promise of an improved era of race or class relations. Press reports of Blacks sexually assaulting white women inflamed gangs of thousands of white men and boys, who brutally killed dozens of Black people. State militia, motivated largely by fear of Black reprisals, halted the violence. The media blamed the Black population for the massacre. In class solidarity, the city's official report indemnified the respectable classes of both races.[87]

Insofar as progressives condemned this lawlessness, their answer was the modern state. But Black Americans were trapped between extralegal terror and institutional cruelties—both of which were nakedly discriminatory and structurally racist. Contemporaneous with progressive reforms, Southern cities codified racial separation.[88] Jim Crow segregation statutes multiplied after the 1896 Supreme Court decision *Plessy v. Ferguson*. This decision in a way marked modernity, sharing more with some progressive understandings of the law and liberalism than with classical liberalism. Responding to a lawsuit in which a private railroad business sought to integrate a dining car despite Louisiana's regulatory power, the

US Supreme Court welcomed the modern wave of southern state-level regulation over the property rights of railroad cars.[89] Contrasted with lynching, segregation was a modernizing project, the scientific application of urban regulatory power to the environmental differences between races.[90] All the former Confederate states would adopt segregation statutes by the end of the first decade of the century.

Acquiescence in the midst of pogroms, federal deference toward southern Jim Crow laws, and a new acceptance of racialized criminology in the North signaled a national convergence even as segregation statutes betrayed regional differences. Once heavily reliant on prisons known for "mass sickness, brutal whippings, discarded bodies, near starvation, rape," the New South adopted northern-style police departments around the turn of the century.[91] After *Plessy*, statistical criminology emphasized Black criminality even as eugenic conceptions of "ethnic" whites subsided. European immigrants enjoyed urban "crime prevention" opportunities denied to Black Americans. As the eugenic theorization of foreign-born criminality waned, what would survive was the fixation on Black criminality.[92]

Any national goal for reform would have to contend with the racial bargain facilitating a new reconciliation between northern and southern white elites. The early twentieth-century progressive presidencies enjoyed the "reunion" that eased interregional resentments tracing back to the 1860s. Boosted by the imperialism of the Spanish American War and mediated by both political parties, this reunion downplayed the centrality of racism in the Civil War and Reconstruction. The Democratic Party became nationally competitive, representing most of the white South and the northern working class, but the enforcement and policy patterns behind this national legitimation consistently broke the very promises of Black liberation on which nineteenth-century liberalism had first built the national state.

The racism of national reunion could not alone legitimate national power. Race continued to undercut solidarity across regions, where partisan variations tracked differences between the former Confederacy and the industrial North. The "labor question" meanwhile frustrated progressives, who used state violence and modest subsidies to discourage working-class rebellion. Repression expanded beyond activists toward political ideas, especially socialism and anarchism.[93] The waves of state violence, injunctions, and martial law continued in the early 1900s.

Labor repression underscored fractures, jurisdictional and ideological, that undermined progressive nationalism. Progressives wanted to constrain the lawlessness of all classes, but enforcers inside and outside government pursued lawless class war. The federal government itself was hardly consistent. A Department of Justice investigation into California's Wobblies uncovered little nefariousness, and a federal inquiry attributed the violence at the 1913 Paterson Strike to "police officials and the inferior courts." California governor Hiram Johnson, a celebrated progressive Republican, unleashed extralegal beatings and arrests on the city of Wheatland. Vigilante violence mounted. The infamous Ludlow Massacre of 1913 in Colorado hardened workers' resolve against state power. The year 1914 saw martial law in Butte, Montana, and the scandalous Joe Hill trial in Utah.[94] Force alone could not substitute national consensus for class divisions.

Progressives could claim some triumphs in social legislation and criminal justice. But constitutional traditionalism sometimes held national officials back even as local authorities sought their involvement. The International Association of Chiefs of Police, formed out of the National Police Bureau, hoped for information sharing across state lines, but its proposal for a National Bureau of Criminal Identification was rebuked by Congress in 1907.[95] National authority often depended on constitutional mechanisms most prone toward reactionary politics. The postal system, exploited to combat the Pullman strikers, was also the primary instrument of moral censorship. The Comstock Laws targeted the mailing of "indecent" materials, including contraceptive information. The federal version of these laws was strongest in areas with the clearest jurisdiction—in Washington, DC, and the federal mails. Anthony Comstock's authority emerged from his Post Office position, and he also spearheaded New York's Society for the Suppression of Vice. Such reactionary measures divided new middle-class reformers striving for gender equality. In 1915 feminist Margaret Sanger was indicted under Comstock law. Suffragette Mary Dennett agitated against the laws with some success.[96]

Yet the emphasis on purity and vice remained a progressive commitment especially conducive to amplifying national power. The Pure Food and Drug Act of 1906 and Harrison Narcotics Act of 1914 regulated drug production and consumption. In 1908 President Theodore Roosevelt, worried about radical disruption and hoping to build a basic enforcement mechanism, created what became known as the Bureau of Investigation (or sometimes the Division of Investigation) through executive order. In 1910 Congress passed, and President William Howard Taft signed, the Mann Act, targeting "white slavery," rationalizing federal regulation of migration by citing the ease of interstate movement.[97] The Mann Act thus leveraged the traditional constitutional rationale, under the commerce clause, of targeting interstate transportation.[98] But "the Chaotic Mann Law," as described by the *Atlantic Constitution,* produced jurisdictional confusion. The Dillingham Commission found disharmony between the multiple agencies in pursuit of "white slavery."[99] The Mann Act, relying on local policing, did produce 400 convictions from September 1912 to September 1913.[100] Corruption scandals, meanwhile, prompted statutory prohibition on Secret Service involvement in law enforcement.[101] In the longer term, the pursuit of vice control, lotteries, obscenities, and the like invited the logical question of why federal violent crime enforcement would not be acceptable. In the early twentieth century, as vehicles and railroads made crimes increasingly interstate, federal limits became more a matter of legislative choice than constitutional control.[102] The federal role in violent crime would nevertheless remain rather minor.

Meanwhile, in the most effective instruments for federal supremacy—the judiciary and national security—progressive aspirations stumbled ideologically. Progressives shared with radical labor a distrust in the federal judiciary, which seemingly embraced nineteenth-century liberalism more than ever. Starting with the 1905 decision *Lochner v. New York,* the Supreme Court was overturning state-level business regulations in the name of contractual liberty. Having mostly abandoned Black Americans through its narrow readings of the Fourteenth Amendment, the federal judiciary now focused on regulatory threats to the "substantive due process" rights of economic actors. Progressive jurists panned these decisions as activist adjudication based on already antiquated ideology. Such values also threatened to restrain the progressive social agenda and prevent criminal justice cohesion.[103] *Lochner* nevertheless in ways foreshadowed a more modern approach to criminal justice. National intervention into state procedure became the principal mechanism by which courtroom civil liberties would be affirmed.

Foreign affairs especially divided the middle-class reformers, even as significant federal expansions were often parasitic on imperialism.[104] The four presidents most associated with progressivism—McKinley, Teddy Roosevelt, Taft, and Wilson—dramatically flexed national defense powers, threatening to split pacifist and interventionist progressives and leave unstable legacies in domestic policy. Fears of hemispheric lawlessness inspired Theodore Roosevelt's interventions in Latin America. The Roosevelt Corollary to the Monroe Doctrine sought to keep "neighboring countries stable, orderly, and prosperous" and target "flagrant cases of . . . wrongdoing" through its "international police power."[105] In 1916 the Mexican Punitive Expedition under Wilson encapsulated this imperial law and order.

Domestically, the policing machinery imported from imperial experiments underscored multiple limitations for the security state. Experience from the "laboratory" in the Philippine War and occupation guided police and surveillance techniques at home.[106] August Vollmer's experience there informed some reforms in California.[107] The war modernized statecraft and new racialized conceptions of American citizenship.[108] But this military mobilization was in a venue with a uniquely ambiguous relationship to the metropole. The Philippines allowed domestic policing that had both military expediency and the pretense of domestic order. This infrastructure carried over to the mainland in anomalous ways. Such policing continued to rely on quasi-legal activities conducted by private–public partnerships—personnel with state access freed of constitutional restrictions. Ralph Van Deman, the so-called father of American intelligence, promoted and built the security state even in retirement. Such arrangements were contingent upon personality and particular bureaucratic ties. Stabilizing a modern security state required more bureaucratically entrenched personnel.

If empire divided progressives, the contradictions would peak in the late 1910s and 1920s in the nation's two greatest crusades since the Civil War—one to defeat lawlessness abroad, and the other to subdue it at home.

THE STRUGGLE FOR LEGITIMACY LOOMS over the political and legal history from 1865 to 1917. The Yankee Leviathan, advancing free labor and corporate liberalism, clashed with white supremacy in the South and industrial workers nationwide.[109] Continental mastery, management of the urban class conflict, reform movements, rising US global power, and technological breakthroughs often pushed law-and-order questions forward. Through the 1910s, enforcement capacity relied on areas with the clearest federal authority—powers arising from war, from taxation and postal authority, and from arrangements with private partnerships.[110] The ideological maintenance of this machinery was tenuous. Cooperative federalism was most effective in illiberal vice policing, which divided liberals as well as progressives. The peacetime Post Office, Pinkertons, Treasury agents, and military enforcers had limited reach and provoked distrust and resistance. No credible consolidation arose around a new federalism, a new nationalism, or a new liberalism. Cohesion around criminological policies and theory collapsed on regional, ideological, or partisan grounds. Every new political vision to unify America against lawlessness had at best abortive results.

A modern liberal state needed legitimacy for its enforcers. But large groups had good reason to distrust them. Enforcers had beaten down industrial laborers, failed to protect Black Americans, and irritated the rural white South. They were distrusted or discounted by the nation's states, its cities, its capitalists, its workers. The progressives' middle-class revolution achieved national leadership from McKinley through Wilson, yet at the height of their power they had only precarious support.

But in the late-1910s optimistic reformers would confront crises offering new opportunities for a national project for law and order. Their achievements would paradoxically jeopardize national legitimacy like nothing since the Civil War.

CHAPTER 2

"ANARCHY OR DESPOTISM"

Woodrow Wilson, visionary architect of the modern state, believed in limits to power. He had grand domestic and international ambitions, but no faith in Prohibition. President Wilson vetoed the Volstead Act, which outlawed alcohol nationwide. He viewed it an improper and futile attempt to police private behavior. Brewers nationwide rejoiced until a bipartisan congressional coalition overrode the veto.[1] The administration remained wary. On its behalf Elihu Root argued that the law was unconstitutional—an excessive exercise of wartime authority improper now that the war had ended.[2] The US Supreme Court upheld the law over a scathing dissent by Justice James Clark McReynolds, Wilson's former attorney general and a conservative Democrat. Quoting *Ex parte Milligan,* McReynolds warned that making enduring policy for peacetime amid war's exigencies was a "doctrine [that] leads directly to anarchy or despotism."[3]

Prohibition was perhaps the boldest domestic program arising from World War I, but it was not the sole wartime experiment of awesome state power. When it came to remaking the welfare state and US diplomacy, Wilson's war produced many precursors for the New Deal and World War II.[4] But concerning the effects of World War I on law enforcement capacity, the mobilization and retrenchment were especially chaotic and ungraceful. The war delivered the most intense wartime repression of dissent in American history, a repression that collapsed under the excesses of its own lawlessness. Prohibition sustained domestic state power in unprecedented ways, but not permanently, and indeed heightened the tensions between federal and state authority while exposing political paradoxes. Holding the bag were Wilson's three Republican successors, who sought to salvage these troublesome products of the waning Progressive Era. After the 1929 stock market crash and an early 1930s crime wave, a convergence of legitimacy problems spelled doom for Republican governance and uncertainty for the republic's future.

World War I, its repression, and Prohibition were the simultaneous fulfillment and unraveling of progressivism. One way to reconcile this paradox is in terms of enforcement authority. These crises brought that authority to the breaking point of its contradictions. The ambitions of enforcement long outstripped governing capacity and political will, leading to the dual threats for the liberal state: chaos and authoritarianism. Wilson recognized that wartime domestic police power would not endure forever. As a progressive southern Democrat, he brought together the political strains conducive to post-Reconstruction state building, but these endeavors would not long carry the repressive state, which marred politics in a key decade of partisan rearrangement. Just as Wilson's party never fully committed to Prohibition, the Republicans never fully believed in the federal tools to enforce it. From Wilson through Hoover ambitious experiments fueled enforcement power, but the cost was public disillusionment. The ideological, regional, racial, and socioeconomic factions polarized by enforcement powers from the 1860s through the 1910s remained at odds, but now with higher stakes for a modernizing federal state. From Wilson's war to the eve of the New Deal, law and order seemed as necessary and elusive as ever.

THE UNFINISHED STATE

In his unfinished tract "The State," antiwar radical Randolph Bourne, reflecting on World War I, identified the connection between war and state power. "War is the health of the state," he famously noted. Far from a blanket condemnation of government, the analysis drew distinctions between governance and rule, nation and politics. "The State is the country acting as a political unit, it is the group acting as a repository of force, determiner of law, arbiter of justice," Bourne explained. Referring to English monarchy, Bourne observed that "The history of the State . . . is the effort to maintain these personal prerogatives of power, the effort to convert more and more into stable law the rules of order, the conditions of public vengeance, the distinction between classes, the possession of privilege."[5] Although World War I expanded national power to new heights, much of its novel authority collapsed after the war. The American state nursed to health in the Great War suffered new afflictions by 1918, the same year the Great Influenza took Bourne's life. Like his tract "The State," America's state building remained unfinished.

National progressivism lived and died by the sword.[6] The war divided national leaders—Wilson's secretary of state William Jennings Bryan stridently dissented, former president Theodore Roosevelt predictably cheered, and Wilson won reelection in 1916 promising nonintervention, only to deploy troops the next year. Mobilization unleashed national power unseen since the Civil War, expanding the regulatory state, bringing nationalist progressives behind the first southern Democratic presidency since Andrew Johnson. Wilson maintained racial commitments to the white South, resegregating the Armed Forces.[7] Ultimately the economic regimentation became the antecedent to the domestic welfare state—the Food Administration, the War Industries Board, the War Finances Corporation, and other agencies resurrected in a new form in the 1930s.

Much of the enforced unity came through a new nationalized policing of ethnic and ideological boundaries. The security state symbiotically grew alongside nativism and conformity. Before the war, Wilson accused immigrants exploiting generous naturalization laws of pouring "the poison of disloyalty into the very arteries of our national life." He did veto a bill to erase time limits for political deportations, but Congress overrode him.[8] Extreme repression served the state in the short term but undercut political legitimacy, given the massive opposition to the war. The Department of Justice urged police to be vigilant on the eve of US entry into the war, after which the public and governmental energy against subversion exploded to a frenzy. The Army received orders to suppress acts that thwarted war preparation. The federal criminal code was expanded to prosecute peaceful dissidents and draft resisters. The Sedition Act penalized mere criticism of the war, the government, or its allies. A filmmaker went to prison for depicting British atrocities in the American Revolution—cinematic sedition now that Britain was an ally. Over a thousand were convicted under the Espionage and Sedition Laws. Such repression arrived in the name of "law and order." Eugene Debs again found himself incarcerated under a Democratic administration, this time for verbally subverting the war effort and military conscription. Once betrayed by free-labor liberals for supporting organized labor, he was now imprisoned for defending free labor against the progressive state.[9]

Another jailed dissident was Roger Baldwin, a pacifist and labor activist whose experience inspired his co-creation of the American Civil Liberties Union. The future Democratic coalition would unite progressives and labor radicals, but for now state power divided them and radicalized Baldwin. His ACLU began as a collaborative project with the progressive coalition, and he invited his arrest to test the law.[10] But as the Wilson administration proved increasingly repressive, anti-state leftist labor activists became more militant, seeing their civil liberties activism in terms of agitation and class war. Baldwin became at once more devoted to labor collectivism and more hostile to actually existing state power—a common labor activist orientation that the New Dealers would later confront.

In short, the war brought material expansion of enforcement capacity without the politics to sustain it. The security state was hardly the rational centralized bureaucracy many of its champions wanted. Mobilization masked fractures within the law-and-order coalition. Some post-Reconstruction criminal state legacies were reined in, particularly the Comstock Laws. Women activists exposed tensions within the coalition for social purity. Many women progressives supported Prohibition but opposed controls on women's reproductive acts and speech. Jurisdictional unevenness meanwhile defined enforcement and prosecution. Localities employed a patchwork of vagrancy and disorderly laws, criminal syndicalism and sedition statutes, but extralegal mob and vigilante violence marked most local repression.[11]

The security state relied on fragile relationships with private and extralegal forces. The Federal Council of National Defense, a network of patriotic organizations, endured national and state partisan conflicts. Republican states posed a particular challenge for Wilson's government.[12] The Plant Protection Section monitored industrial labor, but its regimentation was so clearly suited to war, its surveillance literally organized by the military, that it would stumble at peacetime. The paradoxes of postwar militarist mobilization tainted all the repression. On the one hand, militarism allowed anomalously wide federal latitude, so naturally security-state reverberations maintained a military character. On the other hand, the garrison state's inward reorientation would prove less conducive to the anti-interventionist 1920s.

Particularly tenuous was the reliance on vigilantism. Wartime repression both depended on and became embarrassed by its private collaborators.[13] The American Protective League (APL) enforced the draft with quasi-official ties to the War Department. The APL corralled tens of thousands of young men, mostly innocent of draft dodging, into vans and buses. By late 1918 its bureaucratic accomplices distanced themselves and confiscated the APL's badges. The New York "slacker" raids were especially shameful. "Never in the history of any civilized country," said Senator Albert Fall, "except in . . . Russia, could such acts have been committed."[14] Fall's criticism of APL lawlessness came from the political center, even the center-right. Patriotic repression had lost the middle.

The chaos and energy of wartime mobilization left their imprints after the Armistice, serving as both warning and inspiration for the next generation. Wartime confusion over criminal cases motivated later attempts to standardize enforcement machinery.[15] But leaders never fully abandoned the nationalist fervor that enabled wartime production and security. Two years after the war, the director of the Bureau of Investigation, William Burns, tried to ride its "spirit of patriotic effort and efficient cooperation." He wrote to police chiefs that the "representatives of law and order" must join the crusade as in no previous "time in the history of crime."[16]

In the early aftermath of the war such unconvincing appeals were nevertheless tempting rhetoric. War had built a forced if deceptive unity. Immediately after the war the legitimacy crisis returned with a vengeance. The Great Influenza of 1918 to 1919 revealed peacetime limits to Wilson's social state. Perhaps the war's mass death had fatigued the public, but the federal government did not even try to mobilize them. The administration targeted the pandemic on military bases but did almost nothing to coordinate with civilian institutions. Wilson apparently made zero public pronouncements about the virus. The medical community was largely sidelined. The limits of federalism were stark as state and city governments imposed ad hoc policies. Each locality had different enforcement mechanisms, with wildly diverging results, yielding no national narrative, much less policy. The flu ultimately killed more Americans than the war had. Despite the wartime precursors to the future welfare state, government was anticlimactically impotent in the first modern nationwide public health disaster.[17]

The flu took its toll deep into 1919, a year infamously plagued by disillusionment and dashed promises. Crime escalated, inflation hurt workers, strikes proliferated, racial strife swelled, and the Treaty of Versailles already seemed a failure. Boston police and steelworkers went on strike. The repression that outlasted the war was redirected and in ways intensified, but it also exposed the disjointed machinery and ideology of enforcement. States accommodated grassroots red scares with crime syndicalism, sedition, anarchy, and red-flag laws.[18] Intensified repression punctured the veil of legitimacy, particularly on questions of labor, ideology, race, and policing. The Justice Department's Red Scare and Palmer Raids arose from the Wilsonian security state, but elicited controversies that cast uncertainty on the very future of the Bureau of Investigation.[19] The Lusk Committee, working with the New York City police, invaded seventy-three Communist Party branches and fifty radical publications. Moderates decried the excesses of Attorney General A. Mitchell Palmer and the Bureau of Investigation. Felix Frankfurter, Roscoe Pound, and others called the Palmer Raids illegal and condemned the use of agents provocateurs. The 1919 May Day panic, followed a year later by an embarrassing anticlimax, hemmed in the Bureau's power and propelled the rise of J. Edgar Hoover, who, compared to Palmer, was a moderate defender of due process and restraint. The attribution of Red Scare excesses to Palmer was part of a pattern of blaming repressive legacies of Wilsonian progressivism on fringe reactionaries.[20] Labor repression meanwhile put the lie to progressive promises of harmonizing the classes. Federal injunctions hit striking coal miners in November 1919.[21] None of this seemed likely to produce unity or to be resolved through military victory. A businessman in October remarked that most "respectable citizens" he knew thought "we are on the verge of armed conflict."[22] The states would soon retake the lead in anti-sedition and anticommunist policing.

The curse of post–World War I disillusionment, scandalous repression, and the widespread flouting of Prohibition all undermined any consensus behind national enforcement authority. While undercutting Wilson's Democratic Party, these scandals adopted a different meaning in the 1920s Republican presidencies. Warren G. Harding, Calvin Coolidge, and Herbert Hoover inherited an infrastructure produced by Democratic and Republican progressives. Middle-class respectability had encouraged labor crackdowns and Prohibition, but now the conservative Harding administration oversaw the repressors in the Justice Department and the widely disrespected enforcers of the Treasury Department's Alcohol Bureau. Labor was as disillusioned with national government as ever, further alienated by the widespread nativism and fear of extremism during the 1921 trial of Nicola Sacco and Bartolomeo Vanzetti.[23] National liberalism expanded in avenues least congenial to organized workers. Strikes were frequent, violent, disorganized, and met with state repression. Labor regulation remained sparse, as in most of the Progressive Era, and the 1920s conservative administrations reflexively embraced business. Some judicial civil liberties triumphs occurred in the name of substantive due process rather than labor agitation. Nearly half of the total number of labor injunctions since the 1880s occurred in the 1920s.[24]

Alongside the labor question, the racial contradictions of lawlessness reached new heights after the war. Having served the advertised cause of democracy, Black veterans demanded better treatment, but the war delivered a perfect storm for intolerance. Nationalism and the Red Scare converged with destabilizing economic conditions to exacerbate white anxieties. Black migrants to the North found there a vitriol comparable to what they had fled in the South. Workers' violence often targeted Black strikebreakers. Lynchings rose after the Armistice, and in 1919 an epidemic of racial riots made for a long Red Summer. From spring through fall, Americans witnessed twenty-six race riots and seventy-eight lynchings, with eleven victims burned alive.[25] Black resistance reached new heights, and from both sides the strain on state law enforcement threatened legitimacy. The *Chicago Defender* exposed sheriffs in Longview, Texas, for covering up a lynching they had been unable to stop. The 1919 Haynes report explained the dual problem: "Unpunished lynchings . . . foster lawlessness among white men imbued with the mob spirit, and create a spirit of bitterness among negroes."[26]

The riots were some of the fiercest expressions of white supremacy in American history, and perhaps its bloodiest since the Colfax Massacre. They marked the uniquely heightened contradictions of interwar law and order—a last gasp of nineteenth-century mob terror in the cauldron of the twentieth-century city. After Emancipation such terror gave the lie to the state's promise to protect person and property, and evinced the persistent defining ills of the nineteenth century. Yet something new appeared in Tulsa in 1921—large-scale Black urban prosperity. Like before, the riot erupted over law's contested relationship to mob violence. Sheriff W. M. McCullough maintained that he had tried his best to stop the lynching of Dick Rowland.[27] But for the Black residents of Greenwood, whose neighborhoods had been ravaged, the local police appeared to side with the white mobs who had demanded that Rowland be turned over to them. It was rumored that the Klan ran the district court system and sheriffs' department. Tulsa police relied on nearly 500 deputized white volunteers to help maintain order.[28] Photos from the notorious pogrom became supporting materials for a federal anti-lynching bill.[29] Missouri's white Republican congressman Leonidas Dyer, working with Black Americans, had first proposed his legislation in 1918. In 1922 Democrats filibustered the bill, halting federal anti-lynching efforts for another decade.

The 1920s highlighted the paradoxes in policing the color line. Lynching, particularly spectacle lynching, escalated in the early part of the decade, as did race riots, and as did modernization of brutal police practices. At the same time, sentiment was starting to turn and the line between legal and extralegal white supremacist violence became a focus of reformers seeking clean distinctions for a rational future. But efforts to clarify some lines made other lines blurrier. Jim Crow segregation was at once the polite alternative to lawless lynching and its progressive urban counterpart. Segregation statutes relied on state and local enforcement, rationalized as being more civilized than the unpredictable foil of racial terror. Law and lawlessness justified and constituted each other in an unstable dialectic. Ambivalence between order and chaos was mirrored in the national constitutional system. Federal officials did little to directly facilitate state segregation, and virtually nothing to deter it. Northern and southern police departments meanwhile resembled one another in racial makeup and racist policing. New criminological language also allowed for affinities across regions. Whereas segregation statutes and city ordinances hardened regional distinctions, cities and national discourse harmonized professionalization and racism, modernization and brutality.[30]

Brutality repelled respectable criminologists and gave reformers pause about local police. Legal theorists saw the "third degree" police interrogations as a breach in modernization—even as other civil liberties seemed anachronistic impediments to a smooth-running state. Just as segregation was seemingly preferable to lynching, streamlining due process appeared better than vigilantism and torture. Reformer August Vollmer believed in a more highly functioning justice system, saw actual personnel as falling short, but meanwhile supported unleashing its power in the courtroom. The quality of personnel presumably would eventually improve with the expansion of criminal justice power.[31]

The clarifying of some boundaries obscured other aspects of criminality and national belonging. The criminalization and brutalization of Black Americans helped consolidate American whiteness, which at first reinforced ecumenical nativism. This revealed enforcement tension in relation with vigilante terror. The Democrats were the party of Jim Crow white supremacy, but racial animus had complex partisan correlations. The second Klan often dominated southern Democratic machines, but in the North had more Republican influence, targeting Catholic and Jewish immigrants. As foreign nationals were ensnared in 1920s repression, immigration control and ideological panic made them easier to marginalize. But an America embarrassed by its own wartime conduct made even the repression of foreigners conspicuously ugly. Progressive nativism—cultivated at least passively by reformers, suffragettes, and presidents—became fixated on eastern and southern Europeans, culminating in the 1924 Immigration Act. Nineteenth-century nativism had generally relied on social pressure, assimilation, and local enforcement. National immigration control had arisen in the last century, targeting Asian migration, but the systematization, quotas, and enforcement of 1924 still marked a departure.

In the longer term, nativism exposed racial contradictions. Perhaps the very success of immigration enforcement opened a window of assimilation that helped relax the nativism against ethnic whites. It also coincided with intensifying perceptions and theorizations of Black criminality. The most deterministic eugenics would eventually lose respectable supporters, suggesting that a popular law-and-order politics could accommodate both facially race-neutral approaches and explicitly racialized conceptions. The 1920s struggles over nativism further unsettled the civil libertarian logic of progressives. In *Meyer v. Nebraska,* which overturned a state prohibition on teaching German, the Supreme Court's *Lochner* jurisprudence empowered the central state to overcome the nativist impulses of parochial rule.[32]

For over a decade, the Red Scare, immigration enforcement, and a weak Bureau of Investigation kept the security state on life support. The problems became attributed to the conservative 1920s rather than the aftershocks of high progressivism, so the Democrats could remake themselves. Nowhere else did progressive energy for expanding enforcement produce a problem for legitimacy—and nowhere else did the success of the prophets of order become a weightier albatross for both them and their successors—than with alcohol.

TURNING LAW AND FEDERALISM UPSIDE DOWN

From the end of World War I to the beginning of the New Deal, Prohibition above all defined the new expanse of the federal government. Prohibition aspired to secure every household and jurisdiction, but instead brought enforcement contradictions to their ideological and institutional climax. Jurisdictional problems had marred vice policing since the Mann Act. During this period of "vice-crime federalism," from 1909 through alcohol Prohibition, jurisdictional issues were messy.[33] But Prohibition raised the stakes. The national promise to strike lawlessness at its root instead fueled distrust in the law. The promise for new cooperation between federal and state government yielded an upside-down federalism that came at every jurisdiction's expense.

Those who might have called themselves progressives found themselves divided. Contingent coalitions had delivered the Eighteenth Amendment. Prohibition was, as John Allen Krout remarked in 1925, "the final expression of a fundamental change . . . more than a century in the making."[34] Temperance politics proliferated in the antebellum urban North and returned with greater force at the dawn of the twentieth century. Whereas antebellum Whigs had emphasized social pressure, the new Prohibitionists respected the force of law. This revolutionary social movement complicated the regional dynamics of progressive activism and opened politics to new possibilities. The South had experimented with liquor bans during the Civil War. The Prohibition coalition united southern conservatives, western progressives, respectable WASP Yankees, and women outraged about drunken men beating their wives and children.[35] Women dominated the activism by the late nineteenth century, hoping to shutter saloons and reduce domestic abuse. These "Home Defenders" aimed generally "to regulate pleasure and alter masculine behavior."[36] The Women's Christian Temperance Union organized through the Prohibition Party, whose portion of the national vote peaked at 1.91 percent in 1904.[37] The Anti-Saloon League later became the nexus, its leaders disproportionately representing the middle-class Northeast.[38] But by 1917 only four of the twenty-six dry states were in the North—the remainder were west of the Mississippi or south of the Mason Dixon Line.[39] This coalition's political volatility undercut partisan coherence. Andrew Volstead, the Republican congressman and namesake of the Prohibition law, co-sponsored early 1920s progressive legislation to protect farmers' cooperatives from antitrust regulation. Some lifelong Prohibition Party members meanwhile eschewed the Eighteenth Amendment as a vehicle for the Republican and Democratic stranglehold.[40]

Due to its complex political history, Prohibition inflamed controversies over national authority while realigning solidarities, but above all it sharpened long-standing enforcement contradictions. Prohibition promised policy modernization, harmonization of progressive social values, familial tranquility, and general respect for law. Prohibitionists predicted a new, preventive approach to crime and social dysfunction, where scientific governance cut off domestic violence at the source. They promised enforcement beyond the vagaries of bureaucratic stagnation. Prohibition agents would ascend through expertise and commitment, not through favoritism or the arbitrary Civil Service. Prohibition promised finally to end the lawlessness tracing back to the nineteenth century.[41]

In reality, Prohibition produced lawlessness all the way down. Closing down saloons had been a much more modest undertaking, relying on local regulatory power common in Victorian cities. Banning all alcohol sales nationwide required a much more invasive, multipronged strategy. Enforcing the Volstead Act demanded governmental cooperation and an agreeable population. Democratic "wets" never believed in the law's justice and the Republicans vowing normalcy after World War I never accepted the jurisdictional implications of the national ban. President Harding had whiskey served at his regular poker nights. Prohibition worsened and exposed law enforcement uncertainty, systematic corruption, and violence. It introduced new opportunities for organized criminals, who often enjoyed public admiration rather than universal opprobrium.[42] The trope of Prohibition turning people against the law was so resonant, it became a policy argument analogy. Nicholas Butler warned that anti-evolution statutes encouraged disrespect for the law just as Prohibition had.[43]

Prohibition was a twentieth-century possibility that depended on nineteenth-century systems of enforcement. It is doubtful the national government could have achieved it politically or institutionally before the Great War. Wartime bans on alcohol in Washington, D.C., helped inspire the Eighteenth Amendment. Technological modernity helped justify new criminal powers in other areas, such as the Dyer Act of 1919—named after the same congressman who proposed anti-lynching legislation—which enabled states to pursue automobile thieves across state lines.[44] The Treasury Department, which had been barred from participating in

Justice Department enforcement following a fraud scandal, obtained new powers.[45] In 1922, Dyer convictions accounted for 43.74 percent of convictions pursued by the Bureau of Investigation. The Supreme Court upheld the Act in 1924.[46]

Yet Prohibition, with which the Bureau was not much involved, still drew heavily on the ad hoc machinery common since the Civil War— Treasury agents, citizens groups, jurisdictional ambiguities, patronage. Prohibition exposed the modern state's failure to curb even its own lawlessness. Treasury and Justice became embroiled in conflicts over disorganization. The Justice Department handled prosecution but was barred from conducting arrests. Freed from Civil Service constraints, Treasury was lousy with patronage but low budgets and understaffing limited enforcement. Prohibition clogged the judiciary, producing almost two-thirds of federal district court cases in the late 1920s.[47]

Far from fostering inspirational federal–state relations, Prohibition turned traditional federalism on its head. Whereas federalism formerly had signified the rivalry between national and state authority, Prohibition created something more unworkable—an upside-down federalism where authority transformed from the prize to be won into the liability to avoid. The Eighteenth Amendment vaguely gave Congress and the states "concurrent power to enforce" Prohibition.[48] Drug enforcement and the Mann Act had also produced such jurisdictional ambiguities, but not at the level of Prohibition.[49] Federal spending on Prohibition enforcement was never adequate to the task.[50] The Treasury Department's Prohibition Unit had 1,550 field agents, far more than J. Edgar Hoover's Bureau, but did not convincingly coordinate local police. National politics prevented a true revolution in federalism. President Coolidge once tried to empower state and local police to cross borders to enforce Prohibition, but this met with a bipartisan backlash.[51] Meanwhile, charged with cooperating as never before, but without the commensurate resources or public support, federal and state authorities often dodged responsibility. Catholic Maryland barely lifted a finger in enforcement. Democratic New York was initially reluctant, leaving the Treasury the task of policing the border with America's biggest city as well as with wet Canada. Tammany Hall opposed Volstead outright, but New York soon passed a Mullen-Gage Enforcement Law, a local version of Volstead.[52] The unprecedented aspirations of Prohibition, far from bringing federal and local officials into eager cooperation or friendly competition over arrests and prosecutions, enabled impotent and corrupt authorities to flee responsibility for repeated failure.

As upside-down federalism contributed to greater lawlessness, calls abounded for yet more national resolve. Onlookers recognized that Prohibition spawned pathologies—the racketeering scourge was the "offspring of prohibition."[53] Crime warriors had a national vantage in attempting to root out the local, the corrupt, the lawless. Into the next decade, some even suggested building upon the Prohibition model, extending federal jurisdiction into murder, homicide, robbery, burglary, kidnapping, extortion, coercion, arson, larceny, and conspiracy, while leaving sexual offenses to the states.[54] Although upside-down federalism created confusion, corruption, and a scramble to avoid responsibility, some prominent voices favored a constitutional amendment to widen concurrent jurisdiction, nevertheless aware of such possible complications as double jeopardy. (The idea was that those "guilty of more serious crimes" did not deserve such protections.[55])

Yet far from being a workable model, the upside-down federalism of Prohibition was only the most conspicuous jurisdictional quandary for law enforcement. When J. Edgar Hoover took over the Bureau of Investigation in 1925, confusion reigned. There were redundant criminal identification functions, some being transferred to the International Association of Chiefs of Police.[56] By the early 1930s, America had an especially decentralized policing system—approximately 30,000 separate police agencies without a single centralizing federal record depository.[57] Hoover had especially prioritized information collection and forensics, interests he shared with August Vollmer along with a mutual respect.[58] At the decade's end the Bureau stepped toward national leadership by inaugurating its criminal statistics program.

Throughout the 1920s, tensions among cities, states, and federal authorities climaxed. State and federal officials eyed each other with suspicion. And meanwhile local politics suffered the bad reputations of city police forces. Police tended to be seen as poorly trained and implicated in corruption and criminality; the ideal officer, symbolizing progress itself, remained the goal. In 1928 Uthai Vincent Wilcox wrote that the policeman was "the emblem of the city and of modern civilization." The Greek etymology of the term "city," *polis,* meant that "A *polis*-man is a city-man in the literal sense." But too much responsibility fell on the lamentably distrusted police officer.[59] Urban police forces not only provided social mobility for the working-class men they hired as officers but also often protected capitalist interests, yet classist bourgeois reformers looked askance at the rank and file. Reform groups vigilant about wiping out local vice and crime often found themselves in direct conflict with the police. The New York Society for the Prevention of Crime (NYSPC) was a thorn in the side of local police, even when winning over politicians and reformers. And those favoring modernizing incarceration were still a distinct lot from police modernizers. As the venue of the last gasps of Victorian New York City machine politics, police became a wrinkle for Democratic organizing.

Policing during Prohibition highlighted challenges to urban reformers, adding to their social engineering ambitions while straining institutions. The NYSPC, which on paper was opposed to all urban vices, immediately noted the limitations of Prohibition. It was "not strange that the letter of the new law is not immediately observed by all," given the common use of alcohol "since the beginning of history." The problem, however, was lack of will to enforce law that ran "counter to our personal whim or weakness." The dysfunction of law and order was visible with police "in particular" and "municipal administration in general," due to "laxity and corruption" and low morale. The NYSPC's strategy for combating corruption meant policing the police, inviting accusations of entrapping officers. The organization had worked with Fannie Greenspan, an alleged sex worker, accusing police of having arrested her for four alleged solicitations that "*never* occurred." Coupled with institutional jealousies was the legacy of liberalism, embattled rather than tempered by recent radical trends. For the NYSPC, Prohibition's stumbles were a damning indictment of America's "exaggerated individualism." Not a proud product of the nation's republican and classical liberal past, this individualism was "created and stimulated by the . . . radical agitator and malcontent." The precarity of law increased with the war's "reliance upon force and chance, which breed recklessness."[60] Policing conjured the remaining ills of an antiquated liberalism that progressives had failed to truly reform.

And so, the problems of the city and upside-down federalism obstructed enforcement of the social order. Upside-down federalism turned a zero-sum game into a negative-sum game and elicited various ideological criticisms. Progressives and socialists pointed to corruption; constitutional conservatives lamented unworkable nationalization. Enforcing Prohibition exposed fractures across conservative and progressive ideologies.[61] The contested legitimacy of law threatened the political stability of the two parties. That Republicans took over at the moment of Prohibition's constitutional codification complicated the emerging identity of conservative politics. Republicans notoriously provided little funding and federal oversight, and reformers thus had a convenient scapegoat for social dysfunction for which their own forbearers were largely responsible.[62]

Prohibition's unpopularity also flummoxed Democrats. Prohibition was both the grand culmination of bourgeois progressivism and anathema to the Democratic base, which had championed the right to drink since its clashes with antebellum Whigs. The Democrats identified the problems of legitimacy and lawlessness in the early 1920s but vowed to make Prohibition work. In the 1920 presidential election both Democrat James Cox and Republican Warren Harding were reluctant to divulge their enforcement plans, frustrating the Anti-Saloon League.[63] Ultimately Cox signaled moderate support for the Eighteenth Amendment, a question "as dead as the issue of slavery," and pledged full commitment to enforcement.[64] Cox and his running mate Franklin D. Roosevelt lost to Warren Harding. In 1924, Democrat John Davis ran against Harding's and Coolidge's reputation of cronyism. Davis related law and order to his identification as "a progressive . . . [who] cannot see a wrong persist without an effort to redress it." He lamented an impotent executive branch and a vigilante atmosphere, in which "administration of the law" had become a matter "little different from those of private vengeance." The answer resided in steadfast "enforcement of the law, and all the law," whether against "wealth that endeavors to restrain trade and create monopoly" or against liquor. Officials failing to enforce Prohibition should be held in contempt. Davis denounced the lawless social conflict undercutting political legitimacy. The "solidarity of the great war" had yielded to "a chaos of blocs and sections and classes and interests, each striving for its own advantage, careless of the welfare of the whole."[65]

Talk of national unity and the rule of law could not conceal the widespread violence and lawlessness, the corruption from top to bottom. Enforcement was conspicuously uneven, targeting the poor and people of color. In the legal black hole of upside-down federalism, enforcement sometimes fell to vigilantes, a haunting echo of World War I.[66] Lawlessness abounded in both the flouting and the enforcement of the law. In September 1924, New York judge Alfred J. Talley was quoted condemning America's high murder rate in an article titled "The Most Lawless Nation in the World."[67] In 1926, in testimony before a Senate committee, he attributed a doubling of homicide rates, and rampant corruption and crime, to the impossibility of enforcing Prohibition.[68]

Americans agreed that Prohibition's shortcomings could not be ignored, but sharply disagreed on the remedy. Some rethought their positions and others became more vigilant. Irving Fisher had opposed Prohibition but told Congress in 1926 that he had "radically changed" his "attitude," and advocated "increasing the legal machinery" and only "fuller enforcement" would bring "real personal liberty."[69] In 1929 the Bureau of Prohibition moved from the Treasury to the Justice Department. That same year Assistant Attorney General Mabel Willebrandt conceded that her policy unleashed lawlessness. She condemned the "wholly unwarranted . . . killing by prohibition agents," decried the hypocrites drinking while they enforced Prohibition. But she proposed strengthened enforcement, better coordination between Justice and the Treasury, more controls on industrial alcohol, tightening the border with Canada, and abolishing patronage.[70]

Willebrandt, "First Lady of the Law," embodied this difficult time for both progressivism and the Republicans. Her presence in ways brightly captured the reform spirit as she had championed the hodgepodge of early-century progressive causes. She opposed Prohibition personally but supported strict enforcement for the sake of legal integrity. At any rate, Prohibition soon became her albatross. It had promised a middle ground of order between extremes and between different class interests. But instead of producing a middle ground between anarchy and despotism, it produced a mixture of both—the sort of fusion of lawlessness and mobilization that could be organized in a coherent, politically viable manner during warfare, but not during peacetime. America was in a state of pacifist militarism, drained from war but lackadaisically mobilized, and it needed rationalization under new structural and ideological patterns. Many progressive reformers, seeking more humane conditions for prisons or police reform, had staked their lot with Prohibition and lost credibility.

A newer breed of liberals meanwhile tried to find a practical compromise between idealism and draconian punitiveness. The 1920s, the first half of the interwar period, dug deep into the wounds of America's pacifist militarism. And then the market crash of October 1929 ripped off the scab.

AN UNCONVINCING WAR ON CRIME

In the first years of the Depression, the volatility of upside-down federalism facilitated political realignment. Even by 1928, Democratic Party ambivalence began breaking in favor of a coherent criticism of Prohibition. The national platform still ambiguously stressed states' rights while condemning the Republicans' "flagrant disregard" for the Constitution and pledging to make "an honest effort to enforce the eighteenth amendment" along with other federal law.[71] But the convention nominated Al Smith, who took "bribery, corruption, lawlessness" and "disrespect for all law" as consequences not of inadequate enforcement but of Prohibition itself. He claimed William Howard Taft and Woodrow Wilson as good progressive company in this view—allowing Democrats a reform narrative that disowned Prohibition's chaos. Wilson had said that one "cannot regulate the morals and habits of a great cosmopolitan people" through "unreasonable restrictions upon their liberty and freedom." Smith vowed to enforce the law but also promised a democratic reconsideration and to try to relegate it to the states.[72] Republican Herbert Hoover's victory over Al Smith pleased Dry America, but he inherited an enforcement machinery with an ambiguous fate, contested in increasingly partisan terms. His pyrrhic victory won him a convergence of crises that had been germinating for generations, inflamed by the 1929 crash and the ensuing Great Depression.

The Democrats faced their own legitimacy crises. In 1928 Franklin Roosevelt, who gave the nominating speech for Al Smith, won New York's gubernatorial election, but Democrats lost several traditionally reliable southern states. At the time, President-elect Herbert Hoover was massively popular, including among Democrats, and Roosevelt himself called Hoover "an old friend."[73] With the Mullen-Gage law already repealed, Roosevelt nevertheless entered office facing lawlessness, which he approached with humanitarian reform and toughness. He found himself caught between the corruption of Tammany Hall and critics to his left and right. Demands to investigate corruption brought him to the precipice of his power. The 1907 Moreland Act empowered the governor with investigations but only for state activity. For local investigations Roosevelt largely depended on the special assistant attorney general, but this process needed specified allegations, nuances that the critical press did not always appreciate.[74] Eventually a Tammany-aligned district attorney passed on some corruption indictments, and Roosevelt delegated responsibility to Republicans—the state's attorney general and a Supreme Court Justice—relinquishing an opportunity for political consolidation.[75]

In his first term Governor Roosevelt strove for balance amid tumultuous controversies over crime. Roosevelt's approach was informed by an affinity to scientific criminology. He valued Sheldon and Eleanor Glueck's work on troubled juveniles.[76] From the mid- to late 1920s, some of the most connected criminologists began gravitating toward what would become Roosevelt's core team. Columbia academic Raymond Moley spent years on crime studies, including the well-known New York Crime Commission, and in 1926 he tried to get Vollmer involved in a National Crime Commission on police.[77] Moley also collaborated with future New Deal official Justin Miller, who took a position at Duke Law School, and they both cheered Roosevelt's 1928 campaign.[78] Moley, Vollmer, and Miller represented liberal reform conducive to Roosevelt's politics—aspirational and pragmatic, hopeful that institutions would become vigilant against lawlessness, including inside their own walls.[79]

Moley's ideas would become familiar in the New Deal. He wanted to give prosecutors more power and flexibility, supported Miller's work on reforming juries, and was skeptical of grand juries.[80] Moley championed probation and informed Roosevelt on questions of parole.[81] In contrast to academia's sociological criminologists, this new crop approached the crime problem holistically and valued all levers of state power. Moley's emphasis on government administration left leading social-scientific criminologist Edwin Sutherland unimpressed.[82] Moley envisioned a multidisciplinary and centralized institution: criminological outfits at Harvard, the University of California, the University of Chicago, and Northwestern lacked the reach of a "super-institute." He wanted a fully integrated understanding of crime—causes, prevention, treatment, enforcement—informed by studying law, administration, sociology, and psychiatry.[83]

Governor Roosevelt implemented his idiosyncratic criminological vision through reform. In late 1929, prison riots rocked his state. Roosevelt discouraged journalists from interviewing prisoners, lest they publish inaccurate "gory details," but he conceded the need for "better prison accommodations." He was ambivalent about New York's draconian Baumes laws, which mandated life imprisonment upon a fourth conviction. They were exercised "harshly and unjustly in some cases, though perfectly rightly and justly in other cases."[84] Roosevelt's lieutenant governor, Herbert Lehman, also mildly criticized the laws for ignoring "criminal tendencies." The problem was "not that of crime, but the criminal," best pursued through "intelligent coordination of all agencies."[85]

Prohibition-era politics was a war of attrition, and Roosevelt predicted the issue would soon fluster Republican rule.[86] He was cautious about his own public pronouncements.[87] He believed Al Smith had "every wet vote in the country" but could not win enough "middle of the road votes."[88] Roosevelt's adviser Louis Howe, looking ahead to national politics, urged a middle ground through the logic of states' rights and freedom to experiment. Roosevelt should pay lip service to temperance and cheer the abolition of the public saloon, while condemning the ineffectual nationalization foisted upon the country.[89] Roosevelt's attempt at this balance earned Walter Lippmann's criticism.[90] The Democratic Party felt the costs of this ambivalence. The 1930 New York state platform called for repeal but New Yorkers were uncertain about the policy course.[91] Roosevelt won reelection with a tepid slogan, "Bread, Not Booze."[92] In his second term Roosevelt focused on reform more than Prohibition. Corruption scandalized New York City, its courts, and its police department. The Hofstadter Committee identified framings, false imprisonments, and systematic injustices. More than a thousand witnesses were called. In 1931 Roosevelt removed some of the implicated officials. Biding his time soon paid off.

The year 1931 would bring big talk against crime. A year before, in reaction to a crime wave, President Hoover had deferred to the states: "Every single State has ample laws," the president insisted. "What is needed is the enforcement of those laws." In 1930 federal aid to states was limited.[93] That year, of 87,305 federal prosecutions, 57,000 were related to Prohibition, 8,000 were in the District of Columbia, 7,000 concerned immigration, and 3,500 involved drugs. Most Bureau of Investigation pursuits leading to convictions were for the National Motor Theft Act or Mann Act.[94] Hoover's attorney general, William Dewitt Mitchell, disowned the balance of the problem, estimating that organized criminals violated ten state statutes for every federal statute they transgressed.[95]

But in 1931 Herbert Hoover's response to racketeering coalesced around what the press called a "war on crime." Federal innovations included ensnaring bootlegger Al Capone through tax law.[96] To some degree, the new national role amounted to greater attention to the "war" the states and localities were already waging. Attorney General Mitchell reiterated to the American Bar Association that the states were shirking their enforcement responsibility.[97] In 1931 the federal government released its most comprehensive law enforcement study ever, a bipartisan affair. Roosevelt had hoped Howe would lead the Commission.[98] The job went to Republican and former attorney general George W. Wickersham, who himself aspired to more national centralization than proved politically viable. The National Commission on Law Observance and Enforcement, known as the Wickersham Commission, gave unprecedented national attention to crime and punishment, an admission of a law-and-order crisis. Fourteen volumes covered alcohol prohibition; criminal statistics; prosecution; deportations; federal child offenders; the federal courts; criminal procedure; penal institutions, including probation and parole; crime and the foreign born; lawlessness and law enforcement; the cost of crime; crime's causes; and the police.[99] The Commission centered on Prohibition—its results, enforcement structure, obstacles, and high casualties among enforcers and civilians. It identified uneven enforcement as the central problem. James Britt, chief counsel of the Prohibition Bureau, recently transferred from the Treasury Department to the Justice Department, told Wickersham that the United States could repeal Prohibition or else double down, which would require loosened Fourth Amendment restrictions on searches, at least 5,000 officers, and a $25 million budget.[100]

The findings on police exposed the resentments and limitations vexing upside-down federalism. Vollmer produced volume 14, a plea for systematic police reform. Consulting new research, including questionnaires from 575 cities, Vollmer's report sought "universal underlying causes" behind the "general failure of the police" to manage crime and be "intelligible to every citizen." Its conclusions—that politicization afflicted chief positions, that departments suffered inadequate personnel, that police had too many duties—cohered with Vollmer's thinking throughout his career. Vollmer pointedly criticized departments in San Francisco, Chicago, Detroit, and elsewhere for politicization and graft.[101] The press widely reported Vollmer's criticisms. Page one of the *New York Times* aired accusations that police departments coddled gangs and suffered from "incompetence" and "inadequate equipment."[102] The *Los Angeles Times* relayed Vollmer's observation that urban police chiefs lasted about a year and a half.[103] It editorialized that a more "efficient" department need not "be unduly expensive" and blamed "the taxpayers for not voting" to fund equipment.[104] Local authorities protested Vollmer's national report. Before its publication, New York's Edward Evine complained that "most of the deficiencies" did not apply to his city.[105] After publication came more backlash. Chicago's mayor resented accusations of unintelligent personnel, saying that the Chicago "police force, as I know them, are of average intelligence." The former Indianapolis mayor resented Vollmer's criticism that he hired his tailor as police chief.[106] While exposing fissures in war-on-crime federalism, the report revitalized reform sentiments. Roger Baldwin sought a movement to "rid of the police brutalities and abuses which the Wickersham Commission so vividly exposed."[107] Moley replied that the courts would either "recognize the right of the police to use the third degree" or else stop it.[108]

Both Roosevelt and Hoover had to respond, but the governor had less to answer for. Roosevelt scrambled to address the description of New York's particular dysfunction. He castigated his major cities' police commissioners for weakness against "the gang element" and demanded "recommendations for the elimination of shootings, machine guns, [and] hold ups."[109] Hoover meanwhile had a nation full of problems. He vowed more enforcement, neglecting most findings of the commission he initiated.[110]

Hoover's last full year in office brought a crescendo of troubles. Prohibition was competing with the Depression as a campaign issue.[111] The Depression in ways fed the war on crime and dampened the romanticization of gangsters.[112] Kidnapping was especially significant in undermining federal legitimacy in securing society. Reports of abductions exploded in the years where Prohibition and Depression overlapped. Tools useful to bootlegging—and hiding liquor—proved useful to hiding abductees. Syndicates of kidnappers plagued the country. Speakeasies made for easy, underground victims, and soon wealthy and prominent persons were being kidnapped for ransom. This seemingly more indiscriminate phenomenon frightened the public, as there were 2,500 reported cases between 1929 and 1932.[113] In the spring of 1932, after newspapers publicized the abduction of the twenty-month-old son of Charles and Anne Morrow Lindbergh, the kidnapping panic spread, and Hoover pushed federal authority to new limits. In May he announced the activation of federal "law enforcement agencies and the several secret services" while conceding no federal "police authority in such crimes."[114] In June, Hoover signed the Federal Kidnapping Act, also called the Lindbergh Act, and created federal jurisdiction for interstate abductions, but left the material and constitutional limits ambiguous.[115]

Prohibition had worn out its welcome and was weighing down the new war on crime. By 1932 the Democrats clarified their anti-Volstead posture. Smith had begrudged Roosevelt for not making the election a referendum on Prohibition.[116] Some Roosevelt supporters, like New York social worker Lillian Wald, still favored Prohibition.[117] More Democrats wanted to end it. They agreed on a national effort against the crime Prohibition had unleashed. When Roosevelt accepted the nomination in July, unlike John Davis, he enjoyed a growing national consensus. Unlike Al Smith, he represented the center of his party's Prohibition politics. He applauded the convention's clarity: It "wants repeal" and America "wants repeal" and so "the 18th Amendment is doomed." The states should nevertheless keep their rights to restrict alcohol and "rightly and morally prevent the return of the saloon."[118]

Roosevelt struck a balance where Hoover could not. The incumbent attributed lawlessness to "our dual form of government and constitutional provision" for "independent but coincident action." Hoover was right about that. But Hoover rejected repeal and unconvincingly urged each state to handle crime "as it may determine."[119] Amid the political volatility of 1932, Roosevelt's answer was more coherent and bridged a new Democratic politics to the party's traditional liberalism, even beyond states' rights and the right to drink. Roosevelt's running mate meanwhile accused Hoover of taking America down the "road to socialism."[120] Roosevelt advocated a 25 percent cut in federal budgets and salaries, and international trade over protectionism. Roosevelt's Prohibition position harmonized Wilson's wet progressivism with nineteenth-century urban commitments to individual freedom. Hoover could not survive the legacies of Prohibition, which he was stuck defending and many were abandoning. The Women's Organization for National Prohibition Reform featured women reformers who decried the Noble Experiment's collateral damage. Lifelong Republican progressives now backed Roosevelt. The American Federation of Labor supported reform.[121]

Discontent with the economy was meanwhile rising. Labor repression had subsided in the late 1920s. Now, under Herbert Hoover, local insurrection and criminal-syndicalism laws proliferated.[122] Economic strain contributed to a significant experiment in interwar immigration enforcement, which also revealed weaknesses in federalism and enforcement machinery. The early 1930s repatriation of Mexican Americans—as many as hundreds of thousands of them—was not measured by a central database, and hence was illegible to any one legal authority. How many were forcibly seized or self-deported to avoid extreme discrimination and coercion is unclear. It was an effective but lawless mass deportation, and it is unknown exactly how many of the deportees were US citizens.[123]

Depression anxieties and Prohibition fatigue converged in the demands of the Bonus Army veterans of World War I. Unemployed and feeling abandoned, they called for Prohibition's repeal.[124] When they marched on Washington in July 1932, calling for early disbursement of their benefits, Hoover first entertained a compassionate response.[125] He then became convinced of Army Chief of Staff General MacArthur's approach. Hoover ordered federal troops to suppress the protests. Attorney General William Mitchell claimed the targets were the "criminal, communist, and nonveteran elements," and not the "many thousands of honest, law abiding men."[126] The administration was humiliated by both the chaotic clash between law enforcement and the Bonus Army and defections among the government's ranks. Washington's superintendent of police condemned Hoover's evacuation order. He offered to resign rather than "turn my police force into a military organization."[127] In later hearings he contradicted the administration and military's assessment of the situation.[128]

The Republican Party, which had arisen alongside the national government to conquer the South and the Plains, had lost enforcement command over the nation's capital.

By November 1932 the ideological and institutional crises of law and order had peaked. Close to the election, Hoover again accused the Democrat of ignoring lawlessness. Campaigning in progressive Madison, Wisconsin, Hoover blamed Roosevelt for mishandling the gangster problem.[129] Within a week Roosevelt carried forty-two states. An internal study found twenty-six newspapers with a combined circulation of 1,995,800 named Prohibition as a chief factor in the election result.[130]

FROM 1917 TO 1932, the United States undertook serious law enforcement experiments, most of them fleeting. Progressive visions for national domestic power finally manifested, if in distorted form. More than earlier liberalism, this vision sought state maintenance of social order and criminal justice reform, but the vision capsized under its own overreach. Repression and Prohibition sowed distrust in enforcement. Combating lawlessness abroad and at home nationalized the once-diffuse threats of anarchy and despotism. The motley crew of Prohibition advocates did the unthinkable—approaching lawlessness from the bottom up—but their policies multiplied the contradictions of law and order, federalism, political legitimacy, and ideology. The early 1930s rise in organized crime alongside the Depression brought urgency to long-standing problems. Having spanned from Armistice to 1933, Prohibition typified the disorganized hubris that culminated in an unconvincing war on crime.

Rising lawlessness greeted Roosevelt as he became president. Repealing Prohibition was a necessary but insufficient part of his reform mandate. Voters demanded relief from the Depression and the surge of robberies and kidnappings. In the longer term, federal legitimacy was at stake. To build this legitimacy meant law and order, a previously unseen national unity, and a new politics of liberalism. Roosevelt's vision had to overcome deep political, ideological, institutional, class, regional, and racial divisions. It had to succeed where Reconstructionist and Gilded Age Republicans, Grover Cleveland liberals, progressive reformers, and Prohibitionist presidents had failed. To finish building the state imagined by Randolph Bourne would require a new domestic war with extraordinary support, waged by the right leaders at just the right time.

PART II

PERFECTING THE MACHINERY,

1933–1934

On a Wednesday night in the middle of February 1933, Giuseppe Zangara was in Miami to murder Franklin Roosevelt. He missed the president-elect but shot five people, killing Chicago mayor Anton Cermak. Zangara came from New Jersey carrying a newspaper account of the McKinley assassination. He hoped to "kill every President . . . kill them all . . . kill all the officers," the police later reported. Maintaining his composure, Roosevelt instructed the Secret Service to intervene and shield Zangara's life from the violent mob.[1]

Roosevelt became president the next month amid an epidemic of lawlessness. Prohibition had brought black markets, disrespect for the law, and corruption, and publicized kidnappings and bank robberies scandalized the economically depressed country.[2] But the outrages of 1933 obscured a much deeper problem. Federal authority turned on its institutional and political capacity to enforce the law. Intractable conflicts over this authority had shaped politics for all of living memory. Although Roosevelt had won the presidency with his party's biggest landslide, he needed to address the legitimacy crisis to realize his domestic ambitions. The conspicuous criminality at the junction of Prohibition and the Great Depression forewarned two threatening possibilities: Roosevelt's mandate might collapse, as had the credibility of every previous coalition seeking order since the Civil War, or the early 1930s might deliver a settlement that was stable but sharply illiberal. A month after being caught between an assassin and a mob, Roosevelt hoped to navigate the nation between the criminality that the public feared and the temptation to overreact lawlessly.

In 1933 Roosevelt's team found its bearings and asserted federal authority over lawlessness. Roosevelt and Attorney General Homer Cummings worked across ideological and institutional lines to create a new consensus around crime control. Calls for extremism raised the stakes while widening the possibilities for action and making the New Dealers appear relatively moderate.

The next year Roosevelt's team translated their program into a groundbreaking reformation of the federal enforcement state. It is easy to take modern government for granted, but it was deeply shaped by both the New Deal and the modernization of law and order. Rather than automatically arising from the confluence of activist liberalism and the early 1930s crime panics, Roosevelt and Cummings's political accomplishment was both highly contingent and profoundly deliberate. They sometimes referred to their challenge in the first two years as the refinement of America's law enforcement "machinery," and they proved up to the task. By the end of 1934 the war-on-crime coalition had resolved the fundamental nineteenth-century quandary for American authority and signaled the beginning of a new era in liberal politics and governance.[3]

CHAPTER 3

"THE BASIC IDEA OF DEMOCRACY"

During the month when Roosevelt took office, audiences cheered an American dictator on the silver screen. In *Gabriel over the White House,* bankrolled by William Randolph Hearst, actor Walter Huston portrayed President Judson Hammond, a do-nothing allegory for Warren G. Harding or Herbert Hoover who awakens to his nation's needs and embraces his awesome power. Responding to attempted impeachment, Hammond dissolves Congress and establishes martial law. Responding to attempted assassination, he deploys new federal police forces, convenes military commissions, and lines up bootleggers for summary execution. The film captured the political moment. A *Chicago Daily Tribune* critic declared: "If Mr. Roosevelt ever folds up or runs out of ideas—there seems no likelihood of it—I'm all for drafting Mr. Walter Huston as President Extraordinary and giving him free hand to do just what he does in this picture."[1]

The film's depiction of mobilization against both economic depression and criminals was salient. Americans clamored for vigilance against industrial reactionaries and lawbreakers, and politicians recognized the political stakes. As with the progressives who sought to tame the unruliness of rich and poor alike, the New Dealers inherited class anxieties. Herbert Hoover also feared corporate greed's ideological ramifications. As a lame duck, Hoover told Attorney General William Mitchell that the scandalous failures of federal regulations contributed "more to the growth of Communism and Socialism in the United States than the efforts of all the followers of Karl Marx and Lenin in the world." Worse than infamous bootlegger Al Capone were "banksters who rob the poor," and these "traitors to our institutions and national ideas" undermined "confidence [which would] break down the whole system."[2]

In addition to his economic mandate, Roosevelt had a mandate against lawlessness. Homicide rates peaked in 1933, up nearly 20 percent since the Depression began.[3] Crime would dominate the news for the next couple of years.[4] The international press highlighted the Roosevelt administration's plans for the "crime wave"—to "wipe . . . out" the "enemies of the public."[5] Impatience with Prohibition and anxieties about the corruption and crime it bred fueled political and institutional volatility. Roosevelt could not ignore these challenges. When Giuseppe Zangara, who tried to murder Roosevelt and killed Chicago's mayor, received a death sentence, the judge used the opportunity to advocate national firearms laws, a matter handled by the states.[6] Inside and outside government came strident demands for new federal action.

Roosevelt's commanding victory, the surrounding atmosphere of political extremism, and a broadening conception of lawlessness meant policy uncertainty and opportunity. But longer-term challenges of legitimacy, stretching back to Reconstruction, still endangered the course for federal power. Fortunate circumstances made Homer Cummings attorney general. His approach to transforming legal authority helped to redefine liberalism and create a new coalition, which by year's end showed unprecedented promise for law and order and the modern liberal state.

A COALITION'S GENESIS

Prohibition generated organized crime and corruption, which worsened during the Depression, and Roosevelt's team knew they could not instantly fix these problems. Prohibition's critics consistently argued that it fed underworld profits, violence, and political malfeasance. They pointed to the "sharp increase" in kidnapping and racketeering.[7] They argued that Prohibition's futility spurred disrespect for the law. Such criticism invited a coy response. Former Anti-Saloon League stalwart and Democratic congressman William D. Upshaw asked Roosevelt rhetorically: If flagrant illegality discredited Prohibition, why not repeal kidnapping statutes to reduce kidnapping?[8] Such glibness aside, dry Americans posed an incisive question: Whatever Prohibition's counterproductivity, disrespect for the law now included violence and property crimes, so how would anti-Prohibition groups address these problems? Having argued that enforcement of the Volstead Act encouraged crime, the new administration's wets softened their promises of what legalization would accomplish. Roosevelt adviser Louis Howe signaled that ending Prohibition might indeed increase crime, as bootleggers shifted to "blackmail, kidnapping and counterfeiting," problems local government could not handle alone. One letter to the Washington Post quipped: "Now that the wets believe repeal to be imminent it is astonishing to note their almost daily repudiation of the golden promises of yesterday."[9]

The crime problem soared in the years shared by Prohibition and the Depression. A conspicuous uptick in gangsterism followed the 1929 economic crash. The gruesome Lindbergh kidnapping remained unsolved when Roosevelt took office. Larger-than-life robbers and bandits made national headlines that punctuated the last years of dry America, and neither anti-Prohibition logic nor the limits of federalism seemed a sufficient explanation. The Barker-Karpis Gang, led by Fred Barker and Alvin "Creepy" Karpis, associated with Ma Barker, conducted robberies and kidnappings starting in 1931. In May 1933, "Handsome" John Dillinger was paroled from Indiana state prison, and in June he began a string of high-profile stickups. The Dillinger Gang, including "Baby Face" Nelson, robbed banks into the next year. Other celebrity outlaws included George "Machine Gun" Kelly, Frank "Jelly" Nash, and Charles "Pretty Boy" Floyd. The papers colorfully depicted the violent and thieving escapades of Bonnie Parker and Clyde Barrow up and down the central United States.[10]

Lawmen were no match for these lawless personalities. The Bureau of Investigation was weak and controversial, personified by J. Edgar

Hoover since the previous decade. Hoover had his fans: Endorsements for reappointment came from police officials and George Wickersham, the Republican former attorney general whom President Hoover had entrusted with the national crime commission. The American Institute of Criminal Law and Criminology and the International Association of Chiefs of Police also supported J. Edgar Hoover, as did retired police chief August Vollmer, the nation's top police reformer. Hoover's other endorsements reflected regional and partisan diversity—Democratic congressmen John L. McMillan and John J. McSwain from South Carolina and John McCormack from Massachusetts; Republican congressmen Harry Estep from Pennsylvania and William Lemke from North Dakota; Michigan representatives Claude E. Cady, a Democrat, and Jesse Wolcott, a Republican; Democratic senators Hubert Stephens from Mississippi and William King of Utah; and Republican senator Gerald Nye from North Dakota.[11]

But J. Edgar Hoover also had detractors. Although credited in the 1920s for his moderation compared to A. Mitchell Palmer, Hoover was associated with right-wing repression. Now Hoover faced the electoral triumph of exuberant liberals. In the longer term, a symbiosis between Hoover's FBI and the New Deal would shape the trajectory of the American state. But first historical contingency intervened to bring Hoover and other personnel from the Republican 1920s into Roosevelt's government. Roosevelt first picked as attorney general Montana senator Thomas J. Walsh, an embodiment of Democratic Party progressivism. Walsh criticized the Palmer Raids and investigated Harding's Tea Pot Dome scandal. He supported Wilsonianism abroad, women's suffrage, child-labor restrictions, and Prohibition, which he vowed to enforce vigorously so long as it was law. Walsh disliked and planned to replace J. Edgar Hoover, whose Bureau had spied on Walsh during the Tea Pot Dome investigations. But on March 2, 1933, while on a train to Roosevelt's inauguration, Walsh died suddenly and mysteriously.[12]

Roosevelt asked Homer Cummings, a high-profile Democratic associate from the Wilson years, to delay his trip to become governor general of the Philippines, and temporarily run the Justice Department. Cummings agreed, eventually to become the permanent attorney general until 1939. He was thoroughly loyal to Roosevelt and the Democratic Party and was fond of J. Edgar Hoover. A former prosecutor, Cummings had anti-crime credibility, free of the taint of Prohibition. He won the respect of reformers in 1924 when, despite a confession and murder weapon, he undertook to exculpate Harold Israel, a vagrant accused of murdering a priest. He considered it "just as important for a state's attorney to use the great powers of his office to protect the innocent as it is to convict the guilty."[13]

Cummings saw his role as historical, an important chapter in a grand legal story tracing from the seventeenth century and the American founding through the Civil War and Progressive Era challenges. This historical sensibility animated his speeches and writings, including a sweeping historical treatise coauthored in 1937.[14] Cummings also understood the short-term urgency of problems he inherited in 1933 when he took over the Justice Department, which faced basic questions including its size and scope—each of its subdivisions had become "as large, even as important, as the whole Attorney General's office was a generation ago."[15] He had seven assistant attorneys general, about a dozen divisions, as well as directors of Prohibition, the Bureau of Investigation, and the Bureau of Prisons. Federal attorneys faced an explosion of activity. Thanks partly to Prohibition, district courts had 126,363 cases for the year ending in June 1932—up from 22,541 in 1914.[16] Jurisdictional ambiguities mounted, and demands of austerity imposed on Cummings to cut costs.[17]

The uncertain future of the Justice Department and J. Edgar Hoover spoke to something deeper. Cummings recognized his immediate challenges and the long-term problem of political authority as having intimately intertwined roots. About a month into the job, Cummings gave a speech in Bridgeport, Connecticut, that explained this greater context—imbalanced budgets, taxes burdening industry, and a political system unsuitable to modernity. The "heritage of liberalism" marked by restrained government had served America well, but anachronistic legal principles now obstructed progressive reform. Underneath the political battle lines lay deeper social and institutional problems. America's "governmental machinery," Cummings lamented, had fallen "out of adjustment."[18]

Cummings was on point to invoke the history of liberalism. Two of his party's key constituencies, the white South and urban labor, remained skeptical of national power. Prohibition's failures tainted progressivism, whose middle-class managerialism sat uncomfortably with the rural South and working class. Attitudes about government and its machinery both needed "adjustment" to accommodate Cummings's agenda. But although he believed liberalism needed to evolve, the day's political extremism presented a threat. Cummings and Roosevelt sought balance while governments and intellectuals flirted with communism and fascism.

Calls for radical change in crime policy underscored the delicacy of this problem. If lawlessness indeed warranted swift, bold remedies, a warlike stance seemed appropriate. In the waning shadow of World War I, policy initiatives still waved the banner of national security. In his first inaugural speech, Roosevelt called for "broad Executive power to wage a war against the [economic] emergency, as great as the power that would be given to me if we were in fact invaded by a foreign foe."[19] The Justice Department's fusion of national security and criminal justice accompanied the New Deal's general fluidity of policy categories. In June Cummings readied for Roosevelt a list of military prisoners, "deportable aliens," and convicts under the Espionage Act.[20] Another tabulated list came out the next year.[21] The two spent their first seasons in office contemplating amnesty for World War I draft violators and categorizing aliens subject to deportation. Cummings later furnished a list of seventy-two persons eligible for deporting.[22]

Roosevelt and Cummings promised to stretch definitions of federally actionable criminality. State governments would pursue the usual targets with federal assistance. Men of color and poor vagrants would in practice constitute the bulk of the criminal classes. But organized crime allowed the inclusion of ethnic whites, while the roving bandits included assimilated white, working- and middle-class deviants terrorizing middle America, a group of miscreants that could, frighteningly, come from anywhere. The New Deal rhetorically added to these groups those whose economic malfeasance violated public trust. Combatting all lawlessness would be a mainstream concern for American security and welfare.[23]

STATE OF SIEGE

A comprehensive approach to securing the nation enjoyed broad appeal. Many Americans saw crime as an existential threat and clamored for a militant, more literal war on crime. Alongside his radical economics, Detroit's Father Charles Coughlin advocated a crackdown. While he blamed Prohibition for intensifying organized crime, Coughlin, moved by the Lindbergh kidnapping, called for a campaign "to eradicate the gangster."[24] Concerning his crime plans, Coughlin indicated that 2,800 telegrams would arrive at the White House.[25]

Indeed, beginning in 1933, letters tackling crime from many angles inundated the administration. Personal letters to Roosevelt urged the creation of a new federal police force.[26] The president received proposals for routine weekly searches of private homes, and "death without a jury trial" for those carrying unregistered guns. The cities needed to be "purified by a great leader, a fearless man, with . . . a forceful hand."[27] One pamphlet, "Uncle Sam Start after Crime," suggested a declaration of war, mandatory and strictly regulated universal bearing of arms, with those carrying illegally deemed guilty until proven innocent. Fifty thousand good men died for world peace in the Great War, and America should not "hesitate to sacrifice, if necessary, double that number of our worst men for the sake of peace here at home."[28] The *Tulsa Tribune*'s Richard Lloyd Jones drew another parallel, to the Sioux executed during the Civil War: "When Indians kidnapped and massacred our bold pioneers on the frontier we put the army to work to capture and punish violators of our laws," he reminded Roosevelt. "Today kidnapping is growing alarmingly and our army is idle." Instead of wasting time playing golf, Cummings should direct the War Department against the kidnappers.[29] Such extreme proposals exceeded Roosevelt's vision for liberalism, which was to accommodate progressive activism while maintaining deference to constitutional stability, property rights, civil liberties, and due process.

The administration navigated an atmosphere of grassroots mobilization, differentiating vigilantes from welcome volunteers. Overeager citizens groups offered to enlist themselves in martial regimentation. The American Citizens' League fancied itself a semi-militaristic organization, opposed to communism and committed to the new economic controls of the National Recovery Act. Roosevelt, consulting the group's bylaws, expressed provisional approval.[30] The Crusaders, a citizens group, hoped Roosevelt would remotely join their mass meeting at Carnegie Hall in June.[31] Joseph Nelson at the NRA Chicago Compliance Board vetted a new voluntary association modeled on the wartime American Protective League.[32] The Grand Commander of the Protective Order of Police wanted Roosevelt's endorsement, which J. Edgar Hoover cautioned against.[33]

One challenge was reconciling liberalism and organized labor during fierce unrest. Labor radicalism extended to and arose from problems of law and order. The federal government had historically opposed labor radicalism, but the New Deal brought new possibilities, including a federal government less captured by industry than the states were. Appeals for flexing power came in conflicting directions. Workers saw false accusations and convictions as major weapons of capital. The Socialist Party of America cited the "Wickersham investigations" in pleading with Roosevelt "to intercede on behalf of justice."[34] Racial politics drove other cries for nationalization. The National Equal Rights League demanded that federal troops protect the Scottsboro defendants, Black teenagers falsely accused of rape in Alabama, to "avert a racial massacre."[35]

While the Justice Department eschewed the boldest demands, its relative moderation should not obscure the moment's radicalism. In August Roosevelt told James Moss of the US Flag Association that he "heartily" endorsed its "crusade against crime," a "patriotic undertaking" worthy of "the support of all loyal citizens."[36] The attorney general spoke more explicitly that month before the Daughters of the American Revolution: "We are now engaged in a war," said Cummings, "with the organized forces of crime."[37] This "real war" posed an "open challenge to our civilization."[38] Stauncher rhetoric came from Joseph B. Keenan, assistant attorney general in charge of racketeering, in a Chicago speech, excerpted in a *New York Times* article, titled "Federal War on Crime." Keenan related anti-crime vigilance to the New Deal: "Just as the present administration . . . has courageously faced the serious economic and social problems, it will move in every lawful manner to exterminate that group of people who . . . prey on the helpless public [to] earn their livelihood, even to the point of luxurious existence."[39] The militant war on crime's place within the New Deal became a common theme. The Flag Association touted Cummings's program as "the first scientific, concrete and practical plan."[40] Although discouraging the Association from using letterhead suggesting presidential endorsement, the administration agreed on modernized state power.[41]

In addition to the press, citizens, admittedly a self-selected sample, wrote to the administration and let their concerns be known. Many such letters became available to criminologist Raymond Moley, who undertook a major survey into crime's causes and factors, particularly racketeering, which would serve as a flexible and useful concept in the war on crime. A close adviser to Roosevelt, Moley was present at the police interrogation of his attempted assassin.[42] Moley's approach characterized New Deal criminology. He compiled bibliographies and input on different theories of racketeering—including environmental factors, social isolation, outdated statutes, strains on legal instrumentalities, machine politics, governmental disorder in foreign countries, and unscrupulous lawyers.[43] Theoretical but pragmatic, Moley's undertaking would echo in the Justice and Treasury Departments' criminological studies throughout the 1930s. In the short term, the purpose of Moley's efforts became distorted as his research traversed the grapevine. Press reports gave many Americans an impression that Moley was heading a new federal agency or serving as grand strategist against all lawbreaking.[44] The unsolicited letters to Moley, Roosevelt, and Hoover help contextualize the boundaries of an emergent war-on-crime liberalism. Many Americans were eager to work with Moley, to suggest extreme measures or panaceas, and their desperation only made the dramatic escalation pushed by the war-on-crime coalition appear measured and necessary.

Many Americans offered their services. Some hoped to work directly with Moley or contract with him. One man offered to build infrastructure.[45] Prospective crime fighters advertised their qualifications. Walter Dixon, the Grand Commander of the Protective Order of Police, touted his experience.[46] Another man boasted his PhD in social statistics and psychology.[47] John Doyle openly appealed to partisan patronage—"I'm a triple 'A' Democrat"—and asked to join the "Secret Service Department."[48] Moley and his assistant dispatched routinized responses denying any need for additional personnel.[49]

The ghost of Great War mobilization haunted many letters. A former military intelligence official decried the poor coordination between national and local policing.[50] One Samuel Johnson, who had commanded international military police in Vladivostok, Siberia, to maintain "law and order amongst the large criminal population," offered his "police service" and "crime prevention work."[51] Transnational comparisons abounded: Other countries would "laugh" at "our utterly careless disregard for the enforcement of our laws."[52] Recalling World War I, some proposed reviving the cooperative efforts of repression. Alfred G. Clark informed J. Edgar Hoover he had a network of 30,000 in the war, through business, civic, and social organizations, and suggested these "snitches" could again prove useful. Hoover referred Clark to Detroit's special agent in charge and sent the idea to Keenan.[53] There was a blurry line between a reasonable collaborative idea and a reactionary throwback to the Red Scare. The administration was skeptical of an Indiana man's offer that his Nathan Hale Fellows could educate the public on the Constitution and also "stamp out Communistic activities—Racketeering—and lawlessness."[54]

Crime was commonly depicted as a warlike crisis justifying a commensurate militarized response. One letter said that criminals should be "hunted down" and executed for kidnapping, racketeering, and bank and highway robberies.[55] A Los Angeles jailor suggested deploying "Federal police" and forcing defendants to face court martial. Those deemed guilty would be shot the next day.[56] Ominously, one letter suggested that an Alaskan prison camp would be useful in a potential war with Japan.[57]

Appeals to militarism sometimes emphasized the importance of history. Concerned citizens saw themselves as championing progress, conscientious of national modernization—suggesting nothing either unprecedented or reactionary. Amid the era's constitutional innovations, the "crime menace" amounted to an "invasion," which would justify suspending "habeas corpus." Despite seeming "far-fetched," the United States had engaged in a "more serious stretch of imagination" and "'got away with it.'"[58] Identifying a dilemma as formidable as what "confronted Lincoln," one man suspected that nefarious "men of ample means," particularly those of French, Italian, and British extraction, were funding crime. Those who were in "open and armed rebellion" should be "exterminate[ed] by death or by imprisonment."[59] After Prohibition, thousands "with no regard for law and order" would be free, and a "new deal" for the "situation" meant "martial law against kidnapers"—federal judges with kidnapping jurisdiction modeled on jurisdiction over "Oklahoma and Indian territories."[60]

Americans often demanded that modern lawlessness required nationalization. National police should handle not just interstate crimes, but local lawbreaking. The cities, citadels of civilization, needed disciplining. Americans long decried urban disregard for the Eighteenth Amendment, and demanded federal correction as in the strikes of 1877 and 1894.[61] Thomas Galway suggested full federal control over police; strident discipline of their public behavior, drinking, eating and personal habits; and automatic suspensions and tribunals for disobedient police.[62] Brute force, guided by military progressives, was the winning formula. Emergency legislation would cleanse the cities—with current tax revenue "Smedley Butler would have cleaned up Philadelphia some years ago."[63]

Other proposals, more legalistic and surgical, still pushed the boundaries of constitutional tradition: A near-total ban on firearms to cut crime by 75 percent;[64] identification schemes for the criminal class or even all Americans; prisoner reports to authorities every six months;[65] income reports to drain black markets.[66] More than one letter suggested outlawing negotiations with kidnappers, enforced by a federal takeover of communication lines and mails for families of abducted victims.[67] Preventing ransom could "eliminate all incentive for kidnapping."[68] Perhaps family members notified of an abduction should themselves be subject to severe federal supervision.[69] One suggested sterilizing every inmate to create a "world of super-men," a "NEW DEAL" and "New world."[70]

Several claimed to possess a secret formula for abolishing crime. Some offered to divulge their secrets once brought on board.[71] One man had a "plan to considerably decrease" crime but could not do it justice in writing.[72] One James Clark, self-fashioned as the "World's Greatest Scientist," said that ending meat slaughterhouses would reduce human reliance on fire and save humanity.[73] The inventor of the "Davis Cashier Bandit Protection" offered his device to stop daily holdups.[74] Some concerned citizens were savvy enough to know that that their unique expertise would raise doubts. One man, identifying city slums as the *"incubator of all crime,"* reassured Moley he was not "some crank, with 'an ax to grind.'"[75] Francis McCady, advocate of a new "American Secret Police," was also "not a crank."[76]

Such single-minded proposals were a world apart from Moley's institutional and holistic Brain Trust approach. Generally, the very idea of a panacea was anathema to Moley, who straddled academic disciplines and appreciated all the social levers of law and order. It likely frustrated or at least amused Moley to learn that criminality could be diagnosed so reductively. The problem was the "criminal lawyer."[77] Or perhaps the "alliance between crime and politics."[78] Or maybe criminals had become "too smart for the ordinary police."[79] One teacher just knew the problem was teachers who drank and smoke, who should instead be made "free from radicalism and immorality," to ensure good citizenship.[80] Another offered, modestly, that a new postage stamp campaign would lift American morals.[81]

WAR-ON-CRIME LIBERALISM

The correspondence received by the administration, even in the demands for extremist solutions and panaceas, hinted at new parameters for Roosevelt's "liberal" approach to crime. The diversity of letters promising a silver bullet contributed to the recognition of a multifaceted problem, and most letter writers had some piece of the truth. Many of those flirting with ideas beyond the ken of liberalism shared overlapping concerns. Most relevant, the extremism of opinion was reframing a developing New Deal response. What once seemed radical now seemed like compromise. While "public sentiment could condone universal marshall law," Wiley Jones suggested sterilization, modernized drivers' licenses, pardon reform or abolition, a Scotland Yard–style police force, removing police from politics, and enhanced federal authority. Constitutionally he justified these innovations through the welfare clause and Justice Story's "liberal interpretation to meet any and all contingencies."[82]

Some rather impassioned pleas expressed an aspiration that law and order could serve the most vulnerable Americans. This egalitarian theme was politically important. One recurring formulation framed lawlessness as economic injustice, prodding the New Dealers for their moderation. A man predicted that despite promises to combat "white collar rackets," the administration would give tycoon "[J. P.] Morgan a clean bill of health."[83] John Fox condemned Standard Oil and urged the administration to "prosecute the Big Crook as well as the small one," to ensure "respect for law."[84] Racial lawlessness also came to Moley's attention. The secretary of the Scottsboro Boys Defense Club called "lynching . . . one of the most dastardly crimes in this country" and said the sheriff appeared to be "working hand in glove with the lynchers."[85] Not all economic egalitarians were racially conscientious. One who wished to deport all "undesirable aliens" and even strip "undesirable naturalized citizens" of their citizenship to deport them also hoped the government would stop bowing to "industrial [and] financial position and influence."[86]

Moley's correspondence did include suggestions foreshadowing the new liberal synthesis. Alameda County district attorney and Republican Party leader Earl Warren took aim at law enforcement decentralization, police and prosecutorial ignorance, and politicization. He recommended state-level bureaus of investigation, state police, and police schools, more federal Department of Justice studies, increased interstate jurisdiction, loosened extradition law, uniform criminal legislation across jurisdictions, deportation for criminal aliens, fingerprints, anticorruption efforts, and a ban on machine guns.[87] Emil Elis promoted regional crime districts through compacts, uniform criminal legislation, criminal procedure reform, and a presumption against wealthy people without a visible lawful occupation.[88] Some had long wanted a "clearing house of investigation," a reorganizing of federal enforcement authorities, and for the Department of Justice to take over drug enforcement.[89] In the early New Deal such reorganization schemes often circulated, which were somewhat bold but not nearly as revolutionary as what some in the public demanded. One of the ideas was to create a new centralized Department

PROPOSED ORGANIZATION OF FEDERAL POLICE AGENCIES

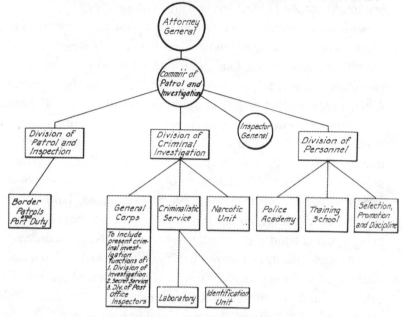

Figure 3.1   Proposed Organization of Federal Police Agencies, ca. 1933. Raymond Moley Papers, Hoover Institution Library & Archives, Stanford, CA.

of Justice, unifying investigative and policing functions, drug control, and training under one bureaucracy (Figure 3.1).

Ironically, the energy for militaristic mobilization ultimately served a rather legalistic liberalism. This ambitious agenda could claim the virtues of mainstream Americanism, continuity with tradition, and progressive hope. In a speech to the American Bar Association titled "Modern Tendencies and the Law," Cummings explained how centralization, through the New Deal and its war on crime, would ride the logic of the evolution of law. This development would fulfill America's promises. Local government had proven insufficient—and so came the demanded National Recovery Act, Agricultural Adjustment Act, and national remedies for problems historically "thought the proper subject of local control—racketeering, kidnapping, and the whole problem of crime." Cummings denied accusations that the New Deal was uprooting American traditions. There was "no resort to force or fear; no repression of dissenting thought or criticism." There were "New laws and new powers!—yes," but an expansive reading of government's role was indeed "based upon traditions and ideals fundamental in Americanism—leadership, justice, moderation, co-operation, unity, confidence, faith, enthusiasm." Such principles were "as old as America, as old as the basic Idea of Democracy, and by them we shall find our way back."[90] War-on-crime liberalism would become a distinct part of both the Democratic Party agenda and the nation's bipartisan consensus.

This liberalism harmonized repression and the welfare state, both of which Cummings personified. New visions of repression extended to national penitentiary expansion and the first federal civilian maximum-security prison.[91] Five months into office, Cummings informed Keenan that there was a need for "special prison for racketeers, kidnappers, and others guilty of predatory crimes." He envisaged this new facility "in a remote place—on an island, or in Alaska"—to shut off "constant communication with friends outside."[92] A week later Bureau of Prisons director Sanford Bates wrote back, having favored relocating "perhaps one hundred of the most desperate men in each Atlanta and Leavenworth" to avoid embarrassing public protest, and now suggesting Alcatraz as suitably located for "desperate or irredeemable types of individuals."[93] Cummings arranged with Secretary of War George H. Dern a "revocable five-year permit" to use "Alcatraz Island and the War Department installations."[94] The *Washington Post* hailed the development: "The welfare of society demands that criminals of this type" be allowed "no escape," and that they be locked up where they cannot "contaminate prisoners serving sentences for minor offenses."[95]

Cummings's appreciation for such unapologetic state power strengthened his coalition. It bonded him to J. Edgar Hoover at a key moment of agency reorganization. A reshuffling of the Justice Department combined the Bureau of Investigation and the Bureau of Prohibition into the Division of Investigation. Hoover remained at the helm, but the New Dealers were truly driving the changes.[96] Indeed, Cummings advocated for a well-armed Division of Investigation more adamantly than did Hoover himself, who prioritized administrative and technical skills over firearms in his hiring. Hoover allowed, but did not encourage, his agents to arm themselves. But on June 17, 1933, an attempt by gangster Vernon C. "Verne" Miller to free Frank "Jelly" Nash from federal custody after he had escaped from Leavenworth resulted in the deaths of Nash and four law officers. This debacle, the Kansas City Massacre, convinced Hoover of the need of more firepower, but Cummings had even grander ideas in mind. In July Cummings announced a "war" on crime and the retention of Hoover.[97] The next month, upon catching the Kansas City Gang's Harvey Bailey, Hoover thanked Cummings for his support. Working for Cummings was "an inspiration," and Hoover confidently affirmed "that the entire personnel of the Division of Investigation will bend every effort to carry out its duties in a matter that will be a credit to your administration." Hoover's intimate loyalty meant he could conceive of "no demand which you can make upon me, officially or personally, with which I will ever fail to comply."[98]

Despite their affinities, Cummings, unlike J. Edgar Hoover, was an unmistakable New Dealer.[99] Some even saw him on its left flank, and because of his progressivism there was some resistance to his appointment. Chief Justice Charles E. Hughes, wrote Cummings, feared he would "shake the foundations of the industrial world."[100] Frank Murphy praised Cummings's speech "Education, Science, and the New Deal" and hoped for a "well organized" campaign of "those close to the President to preach the gospel of the New Deal."[101] In combining repression and welfare, Cummings's philosophy mirrored the holistic and pragmatic liberalism of Roosevelt. The attorney general recognized that his legislative agenda followed trends of modern governance, where public interest regulation needed to advance with the times. But he doubted that subjecting "the individual" to more "regulation and supervision than in the past" marked a "shift in our fundamental political philosophy." Cummings recognized the "essential freedom for the individual," only insisting that the greater "complexity of our civilization" required more regulation of "the individual . . . for the general good."[102]

An emphasis on anticorruption also brought criminal justice into the New Deal vision, which targeted the "unholy alliance between venal politicians and organized bands of racketeers."[103] Cummings's Justice Department spent its first four months investigating electoral corruption in Pittsburgh, producing indictments and local praise of the "Federal police forces."[104] Joseph Keenan investigated racketeering in New York City, considering "the maximum use of the Federal authorities."[105] After an appeal of a costly Pennsylvania trial in a Prohibition graft case spared seventy-one defendants from punishment, Cummings nevertheless applauded the disruption of "one of the most corrupt political machines" and the "large sums in income taxes" gathered.[106]

Cummings's New Deal commitments and active Justice Department entrenched him in an administration pushing constitutional boundaries. He considered law "not a mere body of precedents" but a "living, vital, growing theme."[107] Roosevelt would consult Cummings on important appointees.[108] Cummings aided Roosevelt in the slippery redefining of liberalism in both partisan and nonpartisan ways. The attorney general considered partisan priorities and innovation in legal thought when it came to Justice Department and judiciary appointees. He took seriously the input of Roscoe Pound, the pioneer of sociological jurisprudence.[109] Cummings also noted a prospect's activism in the Democratic National Committee. He cared about ideology as well as a "well written and progressive opinion."[110]

Cummings's legalistic approach to social and crime policy jibed with the New Deal blurring of policy lines. His was comfortable with a regulatory regime that embraced criminalization as a tool—out of convenience or state-building design.[111] Lawyers from the National Recovery Administration (NRA) and Justice Department worked together, using the 1907 Criminal Appeals Act to allow direct appeal to the US Supreme Court when a district court stayed indictments on grounds of a statute's constitutionality.[112] Roosevelt advisor Louis Howe saw the NRA's famous Blue Eagle as a symbol to inspire a public "organized movement" whose citizens would join "juries [that would] convict rather than face public scorn of chicken-heartedness of their part."[113]

As attorney general, Cummings constantly pondered constitutional and legal limits. He stressed the need to police the jurisdictional "twilight zone" that federalism left ungoverned.[114] Virtually every day he considered shifting boundaries of federal power. This made him exceedingly important to all domestic policy. Cummings became the lead authority of New Deal legal thought. He chimed in on food and drug legislation.[115] The administration consulted him on executive orders and statutes.[116] He fielded jurisdictional questions about courts in the Canal Zone, the Virgin Islands, and China, which Cummings worked to transfer under the Justice Department.[117] He contemplated whether courts qualified as an "executive agency" for purposes of reorganization.[118] Cummings routinely asked to publish these opinions.[119] Of course, he deliberated on the legal significance of repealing the Eighteenth Amendment.[120]

The attorney general did not rubberstamp everything—he argued against the legality of parts of Roosevelt's Federal Alcohol Control Administration executive order.[121] He did not want the NRA code authority directly under General Hugh Johnson.[122] Even these exercises in interpretive restraint often affirmed presidential authority. Cummings favored expansive executive power, arguing that the authority to confiscate gold inhered in the "broader powers vested in the President himself."[123] He read statutes liberally, arguing that the National Industrial Recovery Act authorized Roosevelt to create the Commodity Credit Corporation.[124] The Federal Emergency Relief Act similarly gave Roosevelt broad authorization.[125] Cummings found extensive statutory power for executive agencies like the Agriculture Department.[126] Eventually Roosevelt authorized agencies with jurisdictional questions to consult Cummings directly.[127] Cummings even became a major authority on how to legally appropriate money.[128]

AS PRINCIPAL LEGAL ARBITER, Cummings pushed federal limits while elevating his office's prestige. He eased the redefinition of liberalism and the war on crime in mutual symbiosis, all while accommodating institutions long jealous of one another's authority. His integrated vision smoothed relations across institutions and managed systemic volatility. On gold hoarding, Cummings urged Roosevelt to allow Treasury time to distribute regulations to Federal Reserve member banks.[129] The Treasury sometimes raised questions, anxious about the changing institutional landscape. Reorganization meant Cummings wanted to transfer Internal Revenue's general counsel to the Department of Justice's Tax Division.[130]

Great uncertainty loomed in the last days of Prohibition. Winding it down threatened the Treasury's enforcement powers, and Cummings wondered how to deal with the persisting racketeers.[131] But on December 4, 1933, America was wet again. Cummings and Roosevelt had new leeway to shape the future of the war on crime. Having spent ten months finding their bearings, the New Dealers adopted novel approaches to the short-term crises and set the track for long-term reform. In the next year their war-on-crime coalition's triumph would become undeniable.

CHAPTER 4

"FEDERAL BULLETS"

A s historians have recognized, 1934 was a big year for the federal war on crime. Perhaps *the* big year.[1] Prohibition ended and yet law-enforcement mobilization had just begun. In his annual message to Congress on January 3, Roosevelt predicted that legalization of alcohol would "give material aid" to "new forms of crime which came from the illegal traffic in liquor."[2] He called on the "strong arm of the Government for [the] immediate suppression" of "banditry, coldblooded shooting, lynching and kidnapping."[3] A week later Cummings boasted of the past year's successes and warned that law enforcement would not de-escalate after Prohibition. In a National Radio Forum address on January 10, Cummings hailed the Justice Department's "unparalleled volume of work" in providing legal opinions, reviewing "new legislation and executive orders," and pursuing "civil activity, including gold hoarding, National Recovery Administration matters, tax cases, land condemnations, customs matters, and the vast realm of government litigation." Describing alcohol control as both punitive and regulatory, Cummings argued that even with the repeal of the Volstead Act, Washington would "protect the dry states from the illegal importation of liquor."[4]

The crime spawned by Prohibition and the regulatory burdens of legalization introduced new demands and opportunities for enforcement. In 1934 homicides remained at about double the 1900 rate and continued to occupy headlines.[5] With Prohibition over, Roosevelt and Cummings could reshape the politics of law and order. Their political strategy often amounted to leveraging the extremes to redefine the center. Many worried that legalizing liquor would bring anarchy. Congressman Francis Shoemaker pined for the "morale" the nation had "before prohibition," and hoped for a return to this "civilized state."[6] Roosevelt and Cummings drew on this moment of volatility and anxiety to transform America permanently. They advanced radical changes, which they framed as both broadly popular and distinctively their own—both necessary for national legitimacy and yet discernible in its partisan themes. In 1934 they achieved unprecedented federal legislation and institutional stabilization, exploiting wide opportunities for actors across the crime-fighting state to take on responsibilities without getting in each other's way. These institutional and ideological achievements marked the consummation of a war-on-crime coalition that would set the trajectory for the American liberal state.

LAYING DOWN THE LAW

The attorney general exploited the opportune moment to pursue wide-ranging legislation. In 1933 Congress had federally criminalized activities in certain federal jurisdictions that had previously been actionable under state but not federal law.[7] The 1934 proposals went much further. A total of 105 crime bills were considered.[8] In April, Cummings introduced his "Twelve Point Program" to the Daughters of the American Revolution, situating current crime problems in the historical sweep: The "suppression of crime had become a national program of the first magnitude," costing billions annually. Corruption contributed through an "unholy alliance between venal politicians and organized bands of racketeers." Crooked lawyers delayed justice. The lawlessness problem paralleled foreign threats to national security. A century earlier, "the chief concern was the common defense against foreign aggression and savages." Now it was "common defense against organized, anti-social activities extending beyond state lines." Facing jurisdictional uncertainty, Cummings hoped to nurture relations among states, restrict firearms, prioritize crimes against federal officials, and streamline criminal procedure.[9] Some of the boldest proposals did not pass in 1934, namely on criminal procedure, a pet project of Cummings, who hoped to weaken habeas corpus and alibi defenses.[10] Although Cummings succeeded in blunting the statute of limitations for second trials, he could not pass his proposal to ease restrictions on spousal testimony.[11]

Nevertheless, Cummings's legislative achievements in the spring and summer of 1934 were some of the most radical expansions of national power in US history. Relatively little controversy allowed the smooth passage of many breathtaking statutes (see Table 4.1). Amid the public demand for action, the proposed legislation revealed dramatically shifting boundaries of debate. By casting themselves as standing between anarchy and despotism, Cummings's legislative supporters could fundamentally alter government while claiming moderation. As Congressman James Ruffin observed, the "strong clamor for the Federal Government to step forward" included "suggestions" of "martial law" and "military action." The proposed nationalization of "the entire police power from the States" went too far, but serious measures were needed.[12] The consequent legislation redefined national liberalism by consolidating consensus around supposedly unobjectionable proposals, reconfiguring federalism while accommodating the states, and shifting the balance between the federal government and individuals when it came to enforcement and weaponry— an undeniable if incomplete move toward a monopolization of legal violence.

Cummings had dependable congressional allies, such as Senators Henry Ashurst and Royal Copeland, who crafted legislation.[13] The Senate advanced legislation in clusters with little resistance. One bundle was simply called "sundry bills prepared by the Department of Justice known as the 'antigangster bills.'" On May 3, senators summoned several bills without objection. One congressman predicted, a bit overoptimistically, that "the entire program of the Attorney General will be enacted into law." The urgency was palpable: Never before had "such an organized body of men" undertaken "grave crimes" as in the "last 2 or 3 years." By the second

Table 4.1 Key Crime Legislation Passed by the 73rd Congress, 1933–1934, with Ratification Dates

Legislation and Date Signed	Effects
1933	
H.R. 5091, Public No. 62, June 15	Allows crimes on federal territory outside federal criminal jurisdiction to be punished under state jurisdictions
1934	
S. 2461, Public No. 117, March 8	Allows the Supreme Court to prescribe rules for post-verdict criminal proceedings
H.R. 7748, Public No. 180, April 30	Provides time limits for certain actions taken against criminal indictments
S. 2460, Public No. 217, May 10	Modifies statute of limitations to allow new indictments when indictments are found defective or insufficient within the prescribed time
S. 2080, Public No. 230, May 18	Provides punishment for killing or assaulting federal officers
S. 2249, Public No. 231, May 18	Asserts interstate authority over extortion conducted via telecommunications
S. 2252, Public No. 232, May 18	Enhanced Lindbergh Act: Death penalty for injured victims of kidnapping, with presumption of interstate crime after one week of kidnapping
S. 2253, Public No. 233, May 18	Prohibits interstate fleeing to avoid prosecution or testifying
S. 2575, Public No. 234, May 18	Criminalizes instigation of riot and escape in federal prisons, committed by penal employees and others
S. 2841, Public No. 235, May 18	Establishes death penalty for robberies resulting in deaths at banks that are members of Federal Reserve system or insured by the FDIC
S. 2845, Public No. 246, May 22	"National Stolen Property Act": Extends Motor Vehicle Act to punish interstate transportation and receipt of stolen goods worth over $5,000
H.R. 7353, Public No. 293, June 6	Allows interstate compacts to prevent crime
H.R. 9370, Public No. 295, June 6	Establishes $25,000 awards for aid in capturing federal criminals, with attorney general discretion
S. 2248, Public No. 376, June 18	Protects commerce and trade against violence, threats, coercion, or intimidation
H.R. 9476, Public No. 402, June 18	Empowers designated Division of Investigation agents to make arrests and carry firearms
S. 822, Public No. 414, June 19	Enhances certain restrictions on mailing poisonous drugs
H.R. 9741, Public No. 474, June 26	"National Firearms Act": Requires registration of machine guns and sawed-off shotguns and rifles, establishing regulation and enforcement with penalties up to five years imprisonment, essentially banning new production and distribution of these classes of weapons

Source: *Statutes at Large of the United States of America,* vol. 48: *March 1933 to June 1934* (Washington, DC: US Government Printing Office, 1934), 152, 399, 648, 772, 780–783, 794, 909, 910, 979, 1008, 1063, 1236.

week of May, after some back and forth between the House and Senate, a bicameral conference compromised on half a dozen bills, quickly sent for Roosevelt's signature.[14]

Some proposed legislation rapidly fortified the criminal justice system itself against pronounced threats or made subtle but serious reforms. Bills protected federal officers against violent acts and penalized disruption and rioting by prisoners, which had been a scandal since the 1920s. One bill provided the US Supreme Court with rule-making authority in criminal proceedings with guilty verdicts.[15]

Other legislation extended criminal justice powers deeper into American life. In relying on interstate commerce for constitutional validation, Cummings's legislative agenda resonated with New Deal regulatory philosophy. Banking laws nationalized the struggle against robbery. With S. 2841, Congress aimed to punish some offenses against banks operating under US authority or as members of the Federal Reserve system.[16] Cummings championed S. 2248 as an "antiracketeering statute based on the interstate commerce power" that built on the Sherman Act. The bill removed the conspiracy requirement to target criminal behavior found to be "affecting, burdening, hindering, destroying, stifling, or diverting trade or commerce or any article or commodity moving or about to move in trade or commerce."[17] Another bill, S. 2249, federally criminalized extortion by "telephone, telegraph, radio, or oral message."[18] These last two bills frustrated the American Federation of Labor, which worried that the legislation might discriminate against workers, but their successful passage relied on an interstate commerce reading that evoked New Deal liberalism.[19]

While interstate federal power sometimes broke new ground, legislation was framed in terms of past precedents and aimed for broad support. Ratified federal power generally promised to complement rather than override the states. One initiative amended legislation from 1909 and 1929 to forbid mailing drugs.[20] Some of the most significant legislation built on recently tested federal authority, such as an expansion of the Lindbergh Act, and S. 2845, an extension of the Motor Vehicle Theft Act to apply to other forms of property.[21] With S. 2917, Ashurst pushed for congressional recognition of interstate compacts to coordinate against crime.[22]

Roosevelt masterfully took credit for this popular legislation on behalf of his new liberalism. On May 18 a posse—Cummings, Ashurst, J. Edgar Hoover, and Assistant Attorney General Joseph Keenan—surrounded the president as he signed a slate of legislation and, at Cummings's urging, gave a statement.[23] In the escalating offensive Roosevelt pledged "no relenting" and invited the public to support "law enforcement and gangster extermination." Paying deference to Hoover's struggle with America's infatuation with gangsters, Roosevelt condemned "efforts to romanticize crime." This emphasis on turning the culture against lawlessness and toward the central state unified social reformers and conservatives. Even as Roosevelt emphasized the pursuit of interstate robbers, he struck a note of egalitarianism, promising a "broader program . . . to curb the evil-doer of whatever class."[24] Congress and the president for the first time significantly extended federal authority in a bipartisan effort to address crime as a general cultural and social problem rather than haphazardly reacting to the moment's peril.

Arguably even more revolutionary legislation passed the next month. In June Congress literally tipped the balance of firepower toward the federal government. The Justice Department had virtually no powers of enforcement or investigation until the twentieth century, and since its beginnings in 1908 the Bureau of Investigation (now under the Division of Investigation) had been weak and controversial, its trajectory precarious. The administration's war on crime, more than endogenous forces within Hoover's agency itself, propelled it to new heights. Cummings strongly supported empowering the Division under J. Edgar Hoover. The attorney general wished to boost its budget to $700,000 but would willingly compromise.[25] One recommendation from the states' governors would give the Division new personnel. Senator Copeland criticized the Bureau's heavy presence of attorneys. It would be "an absurdity" for "20 lawyers . . . from Chicago" to deploy "into the woods of northern Wisconsin" to hunt John Dillinger. Although Cummings wanted "a thousand men," Copeland considered at least one hundred a good start.[26] The June legislation, H.R. 9476, ultimately authorized Hoover's "Assistant Directors, agents, and inspectors" to "serve warrants and subpoenas" and "to carry firearms."[27]

Hoover's expanding bureaucracy received vindication in July, when his agents captured and killed the notorious gangster John Dillinger, who had broken out of an Indiana jail in March. Also in July the Bureau, at Roosevelt's encouragement, found new public relations support in a strengthened Hays Code, which censored motion pictures, including their depictions of law enforcement.[28] It not only empowered the Division but clarified its role after years of uncertainty. Hoover's outfit, which for years had been the subject of contention and almost powerless, had a new stamp of permanence.

As Congress armed Hoover's Division, it passed comparably ground-breaking legislation to disarm criminals. Firearms control was a bipartisan priority that united crime warriors and economic reformers. When he spoke to the Daughters of the American Revolution, Cummings explicitly complained that national power was being outgunned by the lawless. On April 19, 1934 (the anniversary of the battles of Lexington and Concord), he had given a "conservative" estimate that there were "more people in the underworld carrying deadly weapons than there are in the Army and Navy of the United States."[29] In addition to resonating with law enforcement, the firearms issue reinforced New Deal logic. Roosevelt ally W. G. Shephard condemned a greedy industry that provided "machine-guns and revolvers . . . to any one who can afford them," hoping the United States would "put [its] thumb on [its] gullet . . . until that industry ceases to breathe.[30] Roosevelt connected gun control and economic regulation in October 1933 in urging that National Recovery Act codes restrict machine gun sales.[31] Gun control strategies for the next year focused on regulations and taxes. Copeland argued for licensing manufacturers and retailers, fingerprinting gun owners, tagging guns with serial numbers, and forbidding the purchase of ammunition for firearms the buyer could not legally own.[32] The plan under H.R. 9741 would register firearms and tax targeted models out of regular use.

The debates produced legislation that restructured firearms policy around a new and broad consensus that firearms restrictions need not threaten American traditions. Original drafts confronted resistance. Sports and hunting organizations worried that their pastimes would become prohibitively expensive. Others feared that restricting handguns would jeopardize self-defense at home. New Deal stalwart Robert Doughton, chairman of the House Ways and Means Committee, took such concerns seriously and removed pistols and revolvers from the legislation. Most on the Committee thought that handgun use for "protection . . . should not be classed with criminals, racketeers, and gangsters" and that no law-abiding gun owner should be "compelled to register his firearms and have his fingerprints taken."[33] Sporting groups withdrew their opposition, but progressive activists and women's groups protested the backsliding. Others feared that the law might preclude state controls and taxes, but these concerns quickly abated. Taking handguns out of the legislation deflated the controversy, and one senator interrupted a floor speech to move to pass the House version, promising the speech could continue after the law passed. The Senate ratified the National Firearms Act on June 18.[34] It was a constitutional milestone. Whereas a constitutional amendment had authorized Congress to ban liquor, the first federal gun law claimed authority in federal taxing power, modeled after the Harrison Narcotics Act of 1914.[35]

Despite falling short of Cummings's vision, the prohibition of certain classes of firearms was significant.[36] Its wide acceptance by conservatives and liberals signaled impressive consensus. They agreed over a policy area that for most of US history, before and after, provoked sharp division. The New Dealers' compromise, moderate by their standards but radical in its historical sweep, maintained harmony in the war-on-crime coalition. More important, the national government had penetrated personal firearms ownership at the same time as it was expanding its domestic enforcement capacity. June 1934 was a remarkable step toward the creation of something representing an actual national state with a monopoly on legal force.

STRIKING BALANCE

In addition to far-reaching legislation, Roosevelt and Cummings spent mid-1934 focused on their executive branch, reconciling needs within their coalition. This meant bridging long-standing institutional divides and finding middle ground between competing factions. Collaboration across institutions began in August 1933, when Roosevelt transferred Assistant Secretary of State Raymond Moley to conduct the Justice Department's crime survey, a transfer "from one department to special duties in another . . . believed to be without precedent."[37] May 1934 saw the report's first installment. As Moley noted, the organized crime problem necessarily extended to the "broad aspects of criminal law enforcement generally," embroiling government offices at various levels and departments. Moley had consulted diverse voices, from Joseph Keenan and J. Edgar Hoover to Chicago Crime Commission director Colonel Henry Barret Chamberlain and Alameda County, California, district attorney Earl Warren.[38] Yet after a survey so broadly considering causes and remedies to lawbreaking, Moley settled on the liberal synthesis. He warned of the "danger of autocracy or bureaucracy,"[39] and reaffirmed the New Deal center, especially on federal power. Moley's report identified the "very nature of our Federal union" as a constraint while invoking "considerable opinion in favor of enlargements in Federal criminal jurisdiction." Ultimately the report threw its weight behind Cummings's legislative program.[40]

Reconciling the law enforcement needs of Treasury and Justice, which had long been adversarial, posed deeper challenges. Partisan polarization and strong personalities had driven wedges between some New Dealers and Treasury, still marked by the legacy of former treasury secretary Andrew Mellon, a quintessential Republican. Narcotics Bureau head Harry Anslinger, Mellon's nephew-in-law, provoked deep distrust among Democrats, who spent the early New Deal trying get rid of him and his Bureau.[41]

Politics and policy guided Roosevelt's reconciliation of such tensions. Roosevelt retained Anslinger time and again, pacifying the turf battle. The Treasury Department continued to target bootlegging through taxes and regulation, and prosecutions of smuggling and alcohol violations persisted. Cummings and Roosevelt's Treasury secretary, Henry Morgenthau, ably cooperated through this tense time of institutional shuffling. On March 10, 1934, Roosevelt signed an order jointly designed by Justice and Treasury to consolidate Treasury's taxation enforcement organs. The order abolished the Bureau of Industrial Alcohol and the

Office of Commissioner of Industrial Alcohol and transferred their powers to the Commissioner of Internal Revenue. The order undid a 1930 measure that had transferred Prohibition functions to Justice.[42] It helped that the New Deal war on crime provided so much work for everyone. Cummings's department, hustling through his ceaseless plans, lost no importance when abdicating functions to Treasury.

By September, Treasury had its own modernized international role in criminal law. Every week representatives of the relevant divisions convened in the Committee on the Coordination of Treasury Activities for the Prevention of Smuggling. In these meetings, the Coast Guard, Alcohol Tax Unit, Customs, Narcotics Bureau, and Secret Service updated one another on the protection of America's territorial integrity.[43] They were especially focused on the messy aftermath of Prohibition. Repeal reduced smuggling, but tax evasion and narcotics continued to pose challenges.[44] International cooperation loomed on the agenda, particularly collaboration with the Canadian Preventive Service.[45] Officials braced themselves as states began repealing their liquor laws, scrutinizing the "character" of liquor license applicants. Morgenthau's men discussed cooperation with state officials near divisions in Boston, New York City, Norfolk, Jacksonville, New Orleans, San Francisco, and Seattle.[46] Anslinger's star rose at these meetings. He encouraged colleagues with his charitable "interpretation" of government search powers, describing how to keep legally problematic raids off written records.[47]

While the Treasury enjoyed new enforcement prestige, the Justice Department, even beyond the Division of Investigation, received its biggest makeover in 1934. New pardon applications were established in the spring.[48] In May a fresh official seal appeared.[49] Most important, Justice finally got its own permanent building. Although Herbert Hoover had laid the cornerstone in his last weeks as president, Cummings's agenda energized the new building with activities commensurate with its size. The New Dealers gave the Justice Department's coming of age an appropriately grandiose dedication on October 25, 1934 (see Figure 4.1). The Navy band's live music, ranging from "In Ole Virginny" to "Stars and Stripes Forever," suited the interregional diversity of the New Deal coalition.[50] The ceremony's organizers arranged 2,917 seats for spectators to the dedication of the $10 million building. Cummings narrated

the genealogy of his office and department. "During the greater part of its 145 years of existence," reflected the attorney general, "the legal department of the United States has been a government wanderer with no local habitation of its own . . . for more than half that period, without an authoritative name." Justice had once been housed within the Treasury building, half a mile removed from the law library. Cummings described the pathetic absence of institutional memory, as attorneys general would come to find little to guide them. As Albert W. Fox wrote, the new building stood "symbolic of twentieth century growth of the government's legal machinery"; its comparison to the department's "past crude facilities" was akin to "comparing a modern automobile with an old horse-drawn wagon." Its 20,900,000 cubic feet could house 12,000 people and accommodate an impressive law library.[51] October 1934 was indeed a long way from the days when Justice occupied several floors of the Freedmen's Bank Building. Roosevelt sent a statement honoring the Justice Department's functions now falling "under one roof."[52]

Along with balancing institutional needs, Roosevelt and Cummings confronted the grassroots tensions pulling on the enforcement state. Roosevelt enlisted the right flank of his coalition to guard against both outer extremes. The Division of Investigation and the Justice Department

Figure 4.1   Dedication ceremony for US Department of Justice building, October 25, 1934. Reproduced from U.S. Department of Justice, "The Robert F. Kennedy Building: Celebrating Art and Architecture on the 75th Anniversary, 1934-2009."

monitored James True, singling out his "Industrial Control Report" and identifying his statement of "America First" as pernicious, years before it became the slogan of a large isolationist contingent.[53] Hoover in turn signaled his loyalty to the center by voicing concern about the right-wing "Crusader White Shirts" in Chattanooga.[54] Such vigilante groups sought alliances with the federal state as during World War I. Closing ranks against the fringes, the war-on-crime coalition pursued a vigilantly liberal center in law enforcement.

The moderation and legitimacy of the enforcement state relied on a strategic reluctance to intervene in politicized acts of disorder, while maintaining at least a symbolic liberalism against lawlessness. Cummings reviewed the fraught historical uses of federal troops in domestic affairs—in Arkansas and Colorado in 1914 and West Virginia in 1921—and circulated the list among his team.[55] On the labor question, there were serious considerations in both directions—the New Deal state might protect capital against lawless strikes, or the war on crime might target chaotic social reaction. The mayor of New Orleans pleaded for federal intervention to protect property. Antitrust assistant attorney general Harold Stephens argued against intervention, believing riots improbable.[56] Organized labor also clamored for intervention, usually unsuccessfully. Although generally resistant to such pleas, Cummings kept abreast of the San Francisco labor strikes that summer.[57] The New Dealers were nervous about the incendiary politics, having received warning from a trusted lawyer that "radical agitators and Communistic leaders" ran the San Francisco Longshoremen's Union, but also that Upton Sinclair's extremism would deliver California to the Republicans. That particular state was an irritant, and even indicted a Federal Emergency Relief Administration field representative, an indictment that administrator Harry Hopkins pressured Roosevelt and Cummings to quash.[58] Ultimately Cummings took a firm stand against the radical left, congratulating Justice for not intervening on behalf of labor, and indeed calling it "a serious mistake" not to "vigorously pursue all avowed Communists and deport those who are subject to deportation." In September others requested intervention in a Rhode Island strike, but J. Edgar Hoover cautioned against it.[59]

The unions' mere attraction to federal police power, however unrequited, marked an unmistakable shift. Roosevelt's predicament of reconciling liberalism and organized labor at a time of unrest and radicalism extended to, indeed arose from, the problem of law and order. His administration gestured toward the possibility that the federal government might prove less captured by industry than the states were. Although activists like Roger Baldwin of the American Civil Liberties Union expressed skepticism, others held out hope.[60] Some radicals found promise in New Deal economic rhetoric. F. J. Gorman, chairman of the strike committee of the United Textile Workers of America, identified state militia mobilization against strikers in the South, and hoped for federal reinforcements on their side.[61] Federal restraint in these affairs was likely the best either labor or industry could realistically expect, but each side of the class conflict wanted to believe that the New Deal state would protect and serve them.

If labor became increasingly vital to the New Deal coalition, the Democratic South, profoundly skeptical of federal law enforcement, needed reassurance. Protests against lynching exposed the breach. After Roosevelt named lynching as a threat to American "security" in his January 3 address, some members of Congress repeatedly proposed federal bans on lynching but were never successful.[62] The White House pressured its partisans to stop the anti-lynching legislation. Roosevelt's advisor Louis Howe explained that federal criminalization would "create hostility to [the] other crime bills."[63] Black Americans hoped that Roosevelt might eventually combat lynching, but Jim Crow Democrats were confident he would not—a balancing of conflicting hopes the New Dealers navigated for the rest of the decade.[64]

In the week before the November election, Cummings had in mind law-and-order politics as he stumped for his president. In Stamford, Connecticut, where he was once mayor, Cummings promoted the New Deal against accusations of dictatorship. He lauded the war on crime as part of the liberal agenda—both of which he defended against "reactionaries." As Cummings explained, detractors always resisted the march of progress, from the Louisiana Purchase to the Federal Reserve, and they similarly dismissed the modernizing "genius of the New Deal," its "application of science" and "doctrines of co-operation." Calculation and planning had guided the Agricultural Adjustment Act, the National Recovery Act, the Home Owners Loan Corporation, the Civilian Conservation Corps, the Civil Works Administration, the Farm Credit Administration, the "cleansing of the public service," and the "campaign against crime"—all "undertaken as matters essential to a healthy national life."[65]

The November election vindicated Roosevelt and Cummings. Howe's shrewd guidance to avoid the lynching issue served the law-and-order program, which in turn served the Democrats. For the first time since the Eighteenth Amendment's ratification, federal enforcement issues did not inconvenience the incumbents or frustrate the Democratic Party. Democrats gained nine seats in each house, a remarkable midterm triumph for a sitting president's party. Cummings had helped, branding the war on crime as both distinctly liberal and American common sense. Writing to a representative of the Tennessee and Mississippi Sheriffs and Peace Officers Association, Cummings drew a connection to law enforcement in securing New Deal America in both the partisan and nonpartisan sense. The Association had endorsed "Cummings' and Hoover's war on crime." Despite requests to send agents to protect the polls, Cummings had declined, confident that the case for reelection had extensive appeal.[66]

CALL TO ORDER

In December 1934 Cummings convened a striking diversity of personalities at his National Crime Conference. Participants legitimated each
other and their multipronged campaign against crime. Law enforcers
offered credibility to the holistic welfare approach, and reformers celebrated police and prosecutorial power. The press covered the conference
extensively. The front page of the *New York Times* published Roosevelt's
speech and devoted much of its second page to related issues, listing the
seventy-three organizations and officials represented at the conference
and crediting law enforcement for catching seventy-four kidnappers and
793 narcotics violators.[67]

Roosevelt was the indispensable attraction. Cummings considered the
president's presence so important that he scheduled around it.[68] The event
was postponed, and its opening timed in the evening, to accommodate
the president.[69] The traditionally local issue of crime was now a national
matter; Roosevelt branded the war on crime as an endeavor distinct to
his politics yet deserving of national unity. Across politics, American
leaders should give support and detractors should be marginalized. Interstate commerce of stolen goods and illegal drugs made the problem
national. Roosevelt praised Justice Department cooperation with state
and local governments. Social welfare and social science would guide the
anti-crime campaign. Protection from "the lawless and the criminal
elements" was a "component part" of his larger plans, like "feeding
and clothing the destitute" and securing "agricultural, industrial and
financial structures." To go beyond "mere repression" of crime, "scientific research, highly trained personnel, [and] expert service" would coordinate "home, school, church, community and other social agencies,
to work in common purpose with our law enforcement agencies." The
Justice Department had suffered "unscientific administration and lack
of public support and understanding" along with poor local interagency
coordination, with "heartbreaking results." Roosevelt's holistic strategy
would draw on "every crime-preventing, law-enforcing agency of every
branch of Government" and sincerely address "great crimes, lesser crimes
and little crimes." Roosevelt lamented that "public opinion" was still
unprepared.[70]

The conference provided constant opportunities for coalition members to air their mutual admiration. Everyone praised Cummings. Harvard criminologist Sheldon Glueck celebrated his department for "becoming the symbol of efficiency in [criminal] apprehension and prosecution."[71] J. Edgar Hoover credited Cummings for bringing to his office "an indefatigable spirit and an appreciation of the practical side of criminal investigative work."[72] The editor Fulton Oursler thanked Cummings and Hoover for "winning some important battles" in what he called "an actual civil war."[73] Prison Bureau chief Sanford Bates flagged Cummings's "enlightened leadership."[74] Republican Harry Anslinger, Treasury's most famous law enforcer, followed suit. After years of polarization by party, institution, and Prohibition politics, the infrastructure controversially leveraged against dissent and alcohol was taking aim at narcotics. Anslinger touted Treasury's record, including 450 narcotics deportations, and gratefully acknowledged the "complete cooperation" from Cummings, the district attorneys, and J. Edgar Hoover and his subordinates. Coordination in a recent drug bust had proven the "perfection of this machinery."[75] Cummings reciprocated the fondness in the atmosphere, grateful to be "renewing old friendships and . . . establishing new ones." His coalition's "willingness to cooperate" made it all possible. While offering his own vision, he pressed the crowd to "quickly reach common ground." The crime crisis required all hands on deck, all institutions, modern science, and an "extension of federal power."[76]

Cooperation would reconcile progressive and scientific criminology to the repressive momentum of the anti-gangster war. Glueck railed against police abuses and antiquated patrolling methods, and compared the "patchwork of inconsistencies" in American legal development to the "lack of central planning and control that characterized the military efforts of the allies until the coming of [Ferdinand] Foch and centralized command." Glueck quoted Cummings on the "glorification of the criminal classes" and condemned popularization of "the gangster . . . as a hero with good qualities of mind and spirit, while the police officer is represented as a mean or heartless individual, glutted with authority and stupid in the performance of his duty."[77] Cultivating positive impressions of lawmen unified criminologists, Roosevelt, J. Edgar Hoover, and Hollywood filmmakers governed by the new censorious 1934 Hays Code.

The ecumenical conference welcomed lawyers famously critical of New Deal economics. Scott Loftin from the American Bar Association announced that "life, liberty, and the pursuit of happiness" required security against "the criminal element," as he echoed Roosevelt's calls for scientific expertise and interstate coordination. Whereas the Wickersham Commission had produced little policy, the ABA was pushing meaningful reforms, particularly at the state level, with help from the Social Science Research Council, American Psychiatric Association, National Crime Commission, American Medical Association, American Prison Association, International Association of Chiefs and Police, and American Law Institute.[78] With ABA support, William Draper Lewis promoted the Institute's model Code of Criminal Procedure.[79] Such experts and reformers had long played a role in state building, but they would gain more traction in the New Deal.

On federalism, most opinions gravitated toward a middle ground between anachronistic subsidiarity and despotic consolidation. The federal government would accommodate states, each adopting different degrees of centralization. Gordon Dean championed interstate compacts, anticipated in the Constitution but rarely used, which allowed federal involvement "without any concessions" from "states rights."[80] Under the Constitution, Anslinger argued, only a Uniform Act harmonizing state policies could prohibit drugs nationwide.[81] Keenan criticized inaccurate press reports that the New Deal "deprived" the states of "their traditional control of crime." He conceded that changing conditions since 1789 required interstate innovations but upheld the primacy of local authority.[82] This formulation would characterize 1930s war-on-crime federalism—all levels of government activated around a liberal center as an alternative to illiberal extremes.

Within the consensus existed nuanced disagreements, such as on jurisdictional questions. Earl Warren bemoaned the "decentralized system" and called for state departments of justice, predicting that enforcers would "gladly submit to their supervision.[83] Former Ohio attorney general Gilbert Bettman, however, warned against the bureaucratic and antidemocratic implications of centralization. He touted the county as "the historical unit of government," and cautioned about state-level corruption. Why "expect that higher ideals pervade state than county affairs?" Pointedly he invoked the unnerving consolidation of near-dictatorial power in Louisiana under its demagogic senator: "How about Huey Long?"[84] Selective deference to the states accommodated southern delegates: North Carolina governor J. C. B. Ehringhaus thanked Cummings "on behalf of the Governors of the several states" for balancing federal and state power.[85]

More intense dissent appeared outside the conference, where picketers from the NAACP protested Roosevelt's failure to combat lynching, which had surged in 1934. Picketers were arrested and the president refused to give a hearing. The *Chicago Defender* credited the delegates for condemning unlawful "methods" in "industrial conflicts and racial antagonisms."[86] But the conference had "roundly scored" all the "minor infractions of the law" while neglecting the "real monster" imperiling the "progress of Christianity and civilization." Alluding to the doomed project of Prohibition, the paper regarded "this highly-publicized meeting as just another 'noble experiment.'"[87] Along with Black Americans, labor activists would soon register skepticism. That same month an ACLU event on "Civil Liberties under the New Deal" offered a broad understanding that included jury trials and the rights of American Indians.[88]

Despite these important caveats, Cummings's conference maintained impressive political unity around a daring and comprehensive approach—preventive and repressive, scientific and messianic, humane and unapologetic, aspirational and pragmatic. Those involved in punitive approaches gave deference to the preventive and vice versa. Some speakers related crime to broader problems in culture and society. Earl W. Evans lamented declining respect for the law and argued that the most important thing in a "war without cessation" against crime was "eternal war against sin."[89] H. V. Kaltenborn criticized radio shows.[90] Grove Patterson and Stanley Walker criticized shoddy newspaper coverage.[91] Charles W. Hoffman of the Cincinnati Juvenile Court located crime's "origin in childhood."[92] Katharine Lenroot, chief of the US Children's Bureau, wanted juvenile law that could adapt to "our concepts of idleness, vagrancy and nomadism," and promoted Civilian Conservation Corps employment of troubled youth.[93] Anslinger touted the Public Health Service, the Treasury Department's rehabilitative narcotics farms, and the need for the "Penal and Correctional method" to "be supplemented by medico-social work."

We need "humane treatment . . . continued by supplementary assistance."[94] Prison Bureau director Sanford Bates affirmed probation, as not "everyone can be put in prison."[95] James A. Johnson, the warden of Alcatraz, argued against "too much punishment," which "may be worse than none at all," and called for prisons to be "bettered, improved, modernized, humanized," so the "finest prison we can build will stand as a monument to neglected youth."[96]

With such recognition of societal factors, the war-on-crime coalition was nevertheless enthusiastic about repressive power—dramatically amplified in 1934, when J. Edgar Hoover celebrated the state violence that Cummings encouraged him to unleash upon organized crime. The newly empowered Division of Investigation with the "cooperation of city, State and National law enforcement agencies" was finally crushing the domestic enemy:

> John Dillinger, the flag-bearer of lawlessness, is dead, killed by Federal bullets. "Pretty Boy" Floyd, who for years laughed at the law—lies in his grave, dead of gunshot wounds inflicted in open battle by our Special Agents. The career of "Baby Face" Nelson is over; he died of seventeen bullet wounds while two of the finest men I ever knew, gave their own clean lives that they might serve society by ending his filthy one. Wilbur Underhill no longer carries the name of the Tri-State Terror. He, too, is gone, as well as such men as Homer Van Meter, Tommy Carroll, and others. That is progress.[97]

"Federal bullets" meant federal "progress." Hoover's bloody expeditions completely jibed with the New Deal vision. He cheered the new jurisdictional coordination: the "campaign against crime depends as much upon the county sheriff as upon the police of the largest city." He decried the "wealth and privilege," the "deference to political pull," that had corrupted American justice. He celebrated social science, fingerprinting, forensics, and crime labs. While he said the criminal only understands one threat—the "certainty of going to the penitentiary"—and while he called criminals "vermin" and his agents "soldiers," he celebrated rehabilitation, reform, and crime prevention. "Given the right kind of respect for law," many potential Dillingers, Floyds, and Nelsons could "become good citizens." But should social reform fail, the others could have every confidence that Hoover's Bureau would wage "a war to the death."[98] And Cummings gave him the guns and bullets to do it.

BY THE END OF 1934 the New Deal and war on crime had already begun transforming America. The "First New Deal" of 1933 and 1934 had laid new foundations for political economy. The Emergency Banking Act and Glass-Steagall Act brought new financial regulations. The administration set gold prices under the Gold Reserve Act. The National Industrial Recovery Act spawned sweeping corporate and labor standards and created the Public Works Administration to revamp infrastructure nationwide. The Agricultural Adjustment Act modernized farming policy and imposed controls on commodity prices. These and many more changes relied on new and newly respected mechanisms of enforcement. The Securities Exchange Act of 1934, for example, provided many new powers for prosecutors and the attorney general.[99]

The war on crime, meanwhile, had greatly expanded the criminal code, the Bureau of Investigation, and the federal role in incarceration. As for its short-term effect on crime, the quantitative impact was hard to assess. Bureau of Investigation statistics revealed mixed results. Per capita crime was peaking when Roosevelt took office. From 1932 to 1933, robberies and auto theft rates had fallen, but the rates of aggravated assaults and larcenies crept upward. From 1933, the last year of Prohibition, to 1934, non-negligent homicides continued to fall, as did robberies, burglaries, and auto thefts. More rapes were reported in 1934 than in either 1932 or 1933, but non-negligent homicide rates were down.[100]

Regardless of the short-term effects on crime, in qualitative terms, the war-on-crime coalition was undeniably strong. Facing an organized crime panic, an atmosphere of political extremism, and the volatile process of winding down Prohibition, Roosevelt and Cummings achieved broad support across partisan and institutional lines for their activist law-and-order agenda. Unprecedented legislation modified federal relationships to the states and individuals, serving a new liberal consensus around governance. The consensus accommodated great diversity in approaches, interests, and agencies. Under Cummings the Department of Justice obtained more power than ever, and the post-Prohibition Treasury Department gained new responsibilities as well. Across the criminological community, welfare workers, conservative lawyers, police practitioners, and academics backed a distinctively New Deal program with stunning ecumenical resonance.

Roosevelt later recalled that as president he immediately knew that "the Federal legal and administrative machinery for the detection, prosecution and punishment of crime required complete overhauling," and undertook to do exactly that.[101] This was no temporary fix. The illegitimacy that peaked as he took power had deep roots. For nearly seventy years, partisan, regional, racial, and class divisions, and institutional jealousies thwarted the consolidation of the core powers of a modern central state. Having won with promises to end Prohibition, Roosevelt salvaged, expanded, retooled, and legitimated federal enforcement machinery, producing the stability that politicians since Reconstruction sought and failed to achieve. This accomplishment was no automatic confluence of liberal politics and crime-fighting inertia. It required deliberate coalition building in fortunate conditions.

The New Dealers popularized law and order and placed its reforms at the center of their agenda. Their war on crime became a national fixture and a partisan brand. Law enforcement mobilization, long fatally divisive, was now good politics. It would never again be the same, and neither would liberalism or the American state.

PART III

THE WAR ON CRIME CONSTITUTION,

1933–1941

From Reconstruction through Prohibition, constitutional federalism imposed the great institutional limit on national enforcement. Federalism and its challenging contours were products of politics as well as law. Efforts to conquer the Plains, occupy the South, wage wars, and suppress labor offered opportunities for federal mobilization, but national power generally retrenched after these fleeting undertakings. Partisan and ideological divisions obstructed settlements between national aspirations and state and local power. In the 1920s the upside-down federalism of Prohibition further strained interjurisdictional relations, as authorities blamed one another for the experiment's failures and corruption. Lynching and racist law enforcement brought the post-Reconstruction jurisdictional predicament into sharper relief, as New Dealers struggled to maintain their southern base while gaining support from Black Americans with very different hopes about enforcement power. The New Dealers succeeded by building new relations across the scales of government. From the 1930s on, the federal and state governments could expand their criminal-justice powers in complementary ways, even if sometimes with contradictory purposes.

This structural transformation came alongside a parallel consensus in legal thought. A new politics of federal power reinforced new ideas about the law. No less than Roosevelt's economics, anti-crime policies pushed the boundaries of legal and constitutional interpretation. These interpretive novelties served a political function—smoothing relations across jurisdictions, partisan camps, and even racial divisions to ease state building at all levels. Different groups long distrustful of enforcement now welcomed law and order. Dramatic changes in crime policy—diluting due process protections, federal-state collaborations, criminal code and policing expansion—required a retooled federalism and new constitutional rationalizations distinct from the Prohibition era. Despite diverse views, New Deal legal theorists and the American Bar Association's conservative thinkers largely supported constitutional accommodation of new powers with respect to crime.[1] Regarding crime, some disagreements were substantive, but most were largely rhetorical. Conservatives stressed deference to tradition while championing expansive national power, whereas liberals reversed the emphasis, urging modernization while renouncing full nationalization.

Both the importance of the new consensus and a clue as to its historiographical neglect can be found in the year 1937. That year Roosevelt and Cummings lost their controversial bid to pack the Supreme Court with additional liberal justices to reliably uphold New Deal legislation.[2] The controversy illustrated a larger clash between constitutional liberalism and its conservative critics. The showdown and greater conflict dominated 1930s legal debate, upstaging the consequential consensus over criminal law. Indeed, it was also in 1937 that national marijuana prohibition, without a constitutional amendment, marked a staggeringly new broad acceptance of federal police power. Reflections on 1937 constitutionalism still fixate on the abortive court-packing rather than the enduring drug policy. Yet even in the shorter term, marijuana control nurtured a new jurisdictional agreement after the divisive traumas involved in enforcement of the Volstead Act. In the long term, federal drug control would drive some of the century's most consequential state building. Alcohol prohibition had undermined the legitimacy of all levels of policing. But drug control, from the international to the local, became a bipartisan effort to reinvigorate law enforcement and its vast and intimate reach into social life.

The same year senators unified around marijuana prohibition they rejected a House bill making lynching a federal crime. Texas Democrat Tom Connally filibustered the Gavagan-Wagner Act, which even many liberals critical of lynching agreed extended federal power too far. The lynching controversy highlighted not only a major fracture within the New Deal coalition, but also the paradoxical ways in which both sides mobilized conflicting racial politics in support of state building. William J. Donovan, Coolidge's former assistant attorney general in charge of criminal prosecution, had assailed court packing as a threat to American "rights."[3] These "rights" included those of white southerners, whose private freedom of racial discrimination the US Supreme Court had been "courageous" to protect. But Donovan also applauded the Court's protection of Black defendant rights in Kentucky, West Virginia, Alabama, and Mississippi.[4] Donovan was confronting New Dealers with the cardinal paradox of their imagined coalition, whose rivalries traced the defining constitutional predicament since the 1860s—the contest over southern criminal jurisdiction and civil rights. Crucial to the coalition was the maintenance of simultaneous, conflicting hopes—white southerners wanted the federal government to countenance local white supremacy, and Black Americans and racial liberals hoped for intervention. The war on crime was a central venue of this contradiction. For years the New Dealers did almost nothing to stop lynching through federal power, even as they gestured toward strengthened national civil rights enforcement. Eventually zero-sum federalism would reemerge, pushing forward questions of civil rights. Yet in the 1930s every level of the carceral state, and indeed the New Deal state itself, obtained energy from the paradoxical consensus.

Scholars have observed that, despite the absence of formal amendments during the Roosevelt administration, the period's significant changes in judicial interpretation and public attitudes allowed for the triumph of a de facto New Deal Constitution.[5] But less appreciated is that amid the decade's anomalous legal conditions, a parallel shift in opinion and practice gave rise to a War on Crime Constitution, which channeled significant political questions—divisions between New Dealers and constitutional conservatives, enforcement ambiguities after Prohibition, the fundamental racial dilemma of southern politics—toward radically restructured law and order. Its reconfigured contradictions were obscured for years and would ultimately return to undercut political legitimacy. For now, the transformations of law and federalism served government power at a new peak of legitimacy, in ways fundamental to the modern liberal state.

CHAPTER 5

THE ANTI-CRIME CONSENSUS IN LEGAL THOUGHT

The 1930s are hardly remembered for legal consensus. Roosevelt's 1937 court-packing initiative is indeed immortalized as a battleground in a national struggle over social policy. This tale typically overshadows any constitutional discussion of crime. And yet Roosevelt held that his court-packing and crime agendas shared progressive principles. In defending his judicial reforms, the president argued that economic regulation should follow "the same general direction" as the "great advances" in criminal procedure. He identified "a veritable conspiracy" of legal professionals exploiting "technicalities of the law" and the "conservatism of the courts" to obstruct "social and economic reform."[1]

Looking back, the divisions and backlash Roosevelt identified seem an almost pure proxy for the period's politics. Roosevelt's 1937 setback tracks the general difficulties he faced in the late 1930s, and arguments over the judiciary underscored political factions. Court packing divided New Dealers and radicalized some outsiders. In drifting from the New Deal, Raymond Moley insisted he remained a progressive and liberal. The sin of court packing was its break with traditional norms. While the proposal remained "within the letter of the Constitution," Moley noted, King George III also had violated "no written words" when the Declaration of Independence "charged him with wrong and oppression." As with the presidency's customary two-term limit, the Court's integrity was "sealed in blood."[2] Moley regarded opposition to the scheme as a laudable appeal to "true liberalism."[3] For Moley, Roosevelt's intentions were secondary. The threat, as he told Joseph O'Mahoney, was a "mixture of FDR's itch for power and the strange and un-American . . . purposes of some of his followers."[4] Progressive Republican Hiram Johnson conceded that perhaps Roosevelt "would not be Dictator," although he confided to "doubt this very much."[5]

The politics of this debate over constitutional interpretation is better remembered than the New Deal's connection to criminal law and enforcement. Politics also commanded the discussion in its time. Cummings, like Roosevelt, saw the legal struggle as political. Legal conservatism was a creature of political conservatism. Cummings's adaptive legal philosophy challenged reactionary traditionalism, a clash "between those who take a liberal view and those who take what is called a conservative view of the law."[6] One of Cummings's key partners in the court-packing proposal was Carl McFarland, his co-author of *Federal Justice,* who likewise saw a cohesion to their whole legal agenda of modernization. Robert Jackson similarly decried the American Bar Association's anachronistic "Old Deal" understanding of the Constitution "not as a source of power to advance the general welfare, but only as a document of limitation." The very "progress of government," Jackson held, "lies in the direction of carrying law and order across the frontiers of anarchy."[7]

Yet the political and legal stories become disjointed on questions of crime, obscuring the origins of postwar law and order. Legal scholarship has followed Cummings and Jackson in framing but not in full substance. Focused on welfare state legitimation, histories have allowed political rhetoric to overshadow the consensus on crime and punishment.[8] These issues nevertheless drove enduring constitutional changes for enforcement authority, civil procedure, and federalism. The anti-crime consensus in legal thought allowed a constitutional reimagining that was remarkably consequential in the long term, if masked by the time's partisan divisions. It was in the 1930s that legal thinkers laid the groundwork for constitutionally legitimating wars on crime and the modern government that waged them.

THE OTHER DUE PROCESS

Interwar anxieties about criminal procedure raised fundamental questions. In the 1923 case *Moore v. Dempsey* the Supreme Court affirmed the right of an Arkansas Black man to a trial free of mob intimidation.[9] In 1932 the Court further extended federal oversight over state courts. *Powell v. Alabama,* the first of three famous cases challenging the state conviction of nine Black teenagers falsely accused of raping two white women, reproached Alabama for neglecting their right to counsel. Justice Sutherland's majority opinion affirmed that this Sixth Amendment right bound the states through the Fourteenth Amendment. Justice Butler dissented from this "extension of federal authority into a field hitherto occupied exclusively by the several States."[10] Such federal protections in state court multiplied after *Powell.*[11] These landmark cases complicate reductive explanations of the Court's ideology. In *Moore v. Dempsey,* conservative judges Willis Van Devanter and Pierce Butler sided with Oliver Holmes's majority, while conservatives James McReynolds and James Sutherland dissented. In *Powell v. Alabama* the four conservatives divided again, but along different lines. Justice Van Devanter joined Sutherland's opinion, whereas McReynolds gave Butler his sole concurrence. These "Four Horsemen" famously repudiated New Deal legislation, inspiring the 1937 court-packing idea. The Court's eventual ratification of economic regulation typically marks the end of the so-called Lochner era, when activist conservative judges interpreted the Fourteenth Amendment "due process" clause to overrule state regulations.[12] Despite conflating different issues, especially federalism, "substantive due process" prevails among tropes narrating the 1930s clash over legal thought.[13] Yet in the original due process—procedural defendant safeguards—the fault lines sometimes defied conventional politics.[14]

Indeed, the loudest opponents on economic "due process" shared remarkable agreement on the other due process—legal protections for the accused.[15] Prohibition's failures underscored the urgency for reform. The

Wickersham Commission recommended altering double-jeopardy statutes, interstate witness summoning, and use of force in arrests. After the 1931 commission, liberals and conservatives argued for reform in different terms but mostly converged on policy substance. On balance Roosevelt and Cummings exploited this agreement to strengthen prosecutorial advantages in federal and, most effectively, state courts. They leveraged the consensus to serve both crime policy and liberal judicial reform. Although usually prosecutions resulted in convictions without trial, New Deal liberals and constitutional conservatives most fretted about the guilty evading conviction.[16] And so as substantive due process struggles waned, procedural due process consensus set the agenda.

The New Dealers inherited and adeptly leveraged this consensus and an ongoing campaign of state-level reform. The American Law Institute (ALI), committed to publicly accessible common law, completed its model code of criminal procedure in 1930 and soon began petitioning states through its Advisory Committee on Criminal Justice. Despite feeling snubbed by the Roosevelt White House, which broke the tradition of hosting ALI's principals and their wives, ALI director William Draper Lewis emphasized their shared dedication to modernizing the criminal law.[17] George Z. Medalie, a Republican and former judge appointed by Hoover, championed this consensus against "archaic and antiquated criminal procedure," applauding the ABA and Cummings's "law enforcement program" and championing passage of ALI's "radical procedural improvement" in the states.[18] In 1934 the ABA registered strong support. It distributed 1,450 questionnaires on criminal law, including on the Model Code, sponsored by the ABA.[19] Across rural and larger communities, criminal procedure reform was the highest priority among nine possible concerns, including politics and racketeering.[20] One ABA meeting focused heavily on crime. The organization recommended state and local bar association committees on criminal procedure reform, policing, and prosecution and favored the ALI's reforms on alibis, testimony, and jurors.[21] In law journals, scholars criticized insufficient centralization as well as prosecutors who dismissed too many cases and made vulgar errors that freed the guilty.[22]

Starting in the early 1930s the ABA's meetings and journal showcased prominent dissent against New Deal constitutionalism while devoting serious attention to crime. In April 1934, while pushing his far-reaching crime legislation, Cummings told a bar association gathering that "no question confronting the American people . . . [is] of more immediate and vital consequence [than crime]."[23] Bar members welcomed this viewpoint. Cummings's twelve-point program included tweaking statutes of limitations to allow re-indictments and generally took aim at due process. Some such proposals failed in 1934: allowing testimony between husbands and wives, weakening habeas corpus, compelling advance notice for alibi defenses, and allowing prosecutors to comment in open court about defendants' refusal to testify.[24] Even the failed proposals found ABA support.[25] Delegates at the 1934 Crime Conference advocated several of them. Other proposals included alternate jurors, allowing some indictment by information as a substitute for the grand jury, and making nine out of twelve jurors adequate for most trial convictions.[26]

Most substantive legal changes happened at the state level, where the ABA and ALI did the heavy lifting and whose progress the administration favorably monitored. At the same time the administration recognized that states often mimicked federal constitutional restrictions on prosecutorial powers.[27] Nationally coordinated state reform was a key component of war-on-crime federalism, both in making policy and in building relations. While they showed less consistency on punishment reform, states mostly moved in concert in criminal procedure. In 1932 Louisiana consolidated multiple offenses into singular trials. Rhode Island made indictments harder to quash on technicalities.[28] An *ABA Journal* piece titled "A New Deal for Justice" applauded the Oklahoma Supreme Court for adopting rule-making authority.[29] Legal scholars praised Ohio, Michigan, and Wisconsin for restricting the alibi defense.[30]

Despite this consensus, conservatives and progressives stressed different reasoning. The Justice Department characteristically claimed a middle ground even as it postured against conservatism. Special Assistant Justin Miller advocated easing convictions to advance civilization while opposing "third degree" interrogations and the "prevalent" reliance on "more and longer imprisonment." He criticized both the "partisan advocate of the rights of the state" and the reflexive "defense of the underdog" through "antiquated . . . procedure," and condemned the lawlessness of both the "shyster lawyers and the lower type of police officers."[31]

Cummings proclaimed cohesion between criminal procedure reform with living constitutionalism, legal modernization, and progressive governance. He believed reflexive deference to procedural rights threatened freedom. Seemingly nodding to legal discourse jealous of "substantive" over procedural rights, Cummings predicted that reforming procedure would "vindicate and enforce substantive rights." Procedure was "mere machinery" that could "delay justice" when overly burdensome.[32] Clumsy procedure amounted to ceremonial anachronisms weighing down the march of history. Indeed, scrapping these vestigial protections of the guilty was one of the modern leviathan's civilizing duties. Recalling William Howard Taft's past efforts as colonial administrator to ban headhunting in the Philippines, Cummings told a Judicial Conference that "weird old rituals of primitive peoples were convenient for the medicine men of those early days; but no one would justify them today."[33] Recapitulating their fixation on corruption, Cummings condemned defense attorneys in "close contact with the criminal classes," who exploited "cumbersome and archaic procedural rules" to delay trials while witnesses disappeared and who filed repeated "appeals upon frivolous grounds" that shielded the guilty.[34] Confronting the "lawyer criminal," Cummings disputed the sacred "first duty . . . to his client," and advocated fast-tracked disbarment hearings.[35]

Throughout the discourse rang an attribution of overbearing due process protections to outdated antigovernment tradition. In front of a North Carolina social service gathering, Cummings belabored the long litany of rights, as if to convey the burden: "the right to counsel, the right to a day in court, the right to a jury trial, the right to have witnesses subpoenaed in his behalf, the right to be tried only upon an indictment found by a grand jury, the right to bail, the right to employ the writ of habeas corpus, the right of the presumption of innocence, the right to be present at his own trial and to be faced by the witnesses who testified against him, the right to be convicted only upon proof beyond reasonable doubt, the right of appeal and the rest of the elaborate [protections]." He did not favor outright abolishing these rights but blamed excessive worry about convicting the innocent for strangling justice. Addressing social workers, Cummings related criminal procedure reform to a modernizing liberalism.[36] Legal historian Pierre Crabités, whose New Orleans and Paris civil-law training nurtured a criticism of America's burdensome exceptionalism, applauded French judges for their role as interrogators while still protecting the accused. Anti-state American culture, formed by "sturdy pioneers" who "sympathized with the 'underdog,'" too often decided "'not guilty' in apparent defiance of the evidence." This national "sense of fair play," not politics, corruption, or cowardice, was the problem.[37] Some due process traditionalists accepted the exceptionalism premise. Responding to arguments that high-quality jurors minimized oppression, Republican lawyer Otis F. Glenn solemnized the long common-law history of protections against self-incrimination.[38]

While many legal progressives supported criminal procedure reform and some legal conservatives opposed it, prominent critics of living constitutionalism generally backed Cummings's crime agenda. They quibbled mostly about the reasoning. Chief Justice Charles Evans Hughes, a Republican appointee and moderate skeptic of New Deal economics, decried the delays in trials and appeals preparation. Hughes suspected "no greater reproach to the administration of justice" and cited the complaint of Attorney General Mitchell, a Republican, that "months and even years" passed between guilty verdicts and appeal proceedings while "the accused have been at large on bail."[39] Other legal conservatives argued that Prohibition's wrongful expansion of federal authority imposed burdensome technicalities on the states. ABA president Clarence E. Martin hoped states would assert and enhance prosecutorial powers. America was "a crime breeding and criminal protecting nation," weighed down by "legal rules in the trial." The "presumption of innocence" produced protections innocent people did "not need." Martin wanted to abolish appeals of right, to stop paroling second offenders, and for states to simplify indictments, mandate jury service, and allow nine out of twelve jurors to convict in noncapital cases.[40]

Despite differences in emphasis, the New Dealers and their critics' agreement in criminal procedure generally carried over to the war on crime. In August 1936 Cummings expressed to Roosevelt his pleasant surprise about a Los Angeles ABA meeting. He expected "an anti-Roosevelt meeting," but instead received a "great deal of praise" for the anti-crime program.[41] Later that year he braced himself for "a rather chilly reception" at a New York meeting, but instead the applause "amounted to an ovation" —the "Liberty Leaguers" had less support than they had anticipated.[42]

Through criminal procedure reform, Cummings pulled the administration to the front of the parade of legal transformation. His war-on-crime coalition now included the New Deal's most venerated legal critics. His war-on-crime federalism accommodated ambitions at all levels of government. In its ideological and structural contours, certainly over the long term, this leadership, more than any specific reform, created the War on Crime Constitution.

THE OTHER POLICE POWER

Questions of criminal procedure implicated and indeed complicated ongoing questions of federalism. Some critics of strong due process protections saw jurisprudential centralization and harmonization as the problem. The protections in the US Constitution's Bill of Rights were in the long process of being effectively but inconsistently extended against state governments, which had their own constitutional protections and traditions of judicial interpretation sometimes modeled after the federal Constitution and federal court interpretations.[43] Following federal trends could restrain state governments by, for example, preventing them from appealing criminal acquittals.[44] Champions of weakened due process concluded that state constitutions might have to be formally amended.[45] Political scientist J. A. C. Grant argued that the extension of common law protections to America's federal system, especially in areas of concurrent federal and state enforcement, allowed Bill of Rights provisions against self-incrimination, unreasonable search and seizure, and double jeopardy to become "shields of the guilty."[46] Critics of the "incorporation" of the Bill of Rights within the states sometimes argued for amendments to the federal Constitution. In 1938, a former assistant attorney general in Minnesota advocated amendments to dilute the Fourth Amendment's restrictions on search and seizure and the Fifth Amendment's protections against self-incrimination.[47]

Others who lamented burdensome due process protections placed the blame not on state governments following national trends, but rather on the outworn legacies of decentralization. Cummings saw unreconstructed federalism and due process anachronism as twin evils, spawned in the depths of outdated tradition. He sought to modernize and centralize criminal procedure, including by empowering the Supreme Court to make rules for criminal procedure within the federal district courts, which had traditionally followed state and local customs.[48] In philosophical terms, Cummings understood that hostility to oppression had long constrained national power as well as criminal prosecutors. Cummings opposed "the more 'static' members of the bar" who worried about the "legal aspects and implications" of new policies, and he maintained that the New Deal did not mean a "new social order" but instead treated "ideas and principles as living and vital things"—yielding a dynamic constitutionalism that transcended such tropes as "'economic law,' 'fundamental liberty,' 'equality of opportunity,' and 'social justice.'" Cummings postured as a moderate skeptical of total nationalization for local problems like "racketeering, kidnapping, and the whole problem of crime." But the peacetime emergency of crime required new powers just as World War I produced new powers concerning the "Selective Service, Espionage, the War Industries Board, the Food Administration, the Control of Railroads, Industrial Mobilization." American recalcitrance, now exacerbated by technology and an unruly "heterogeneous population," allowed a jurisdictional "twilight zone" where criminals eluded federal and state enforcement.[49] Automobiles, interstate abductions, and robberies highlighted the threat. Only national coordination could traverse the "natural corridor" that left "unpoliced and unprotected" an "unholy sanctuary of predatory vice." The "concurrent enforcement" of Prohibition accentuated the "twilight-zone," forcing the issue of antiquated federalism.[50]

While Cummings criticized conservative legal thinking, conservatives generally agreed with his lamentations of the twilight zone, where criminals found escape from police power. In constitutional literature, the term "police power" typically refers to a jurisdiction's general regulatory authority. Lochner-era judicial disputes had often pitted federal judicial activism against state-level police power, as conservative federal judges overrode progressive regulations through "substantive due process." But in the 1930s increasing agreement coalesced behind the other police power—the power of states to arrest and prosecute suspected criminals.[51]

Raymond Moley noted in March 1934 the "considerable opinion in favor of enlargements in general criminal jurisdiction."[52] Questions remained as to the federal government's precise role. Justice Department spokesman Gordon Dean saw the question of jurisdiction for "a given type of criminal conduct" as one of the "fundamental problems [for] any systematic program of crime repression."[53] The New Dealers were inspired by nationalist imaginings. Roosevelt found "extremely interesting" an article by English theorist Harold Laski that criticized America's cumbersome amendment process and expressed the hope Roosevelt would "remake the . . . Constitution" into something to which the "document of 1787 will bear no substantial resemblance."[54] But Roosevelt never supported full nationalization. A new broad consensus advocated action from all levels, but even ardent centralizers stopped short of unitary government.[55] Although conservatives and liberals quibbled over jurisdiction, and Cummings championed "progressive control of crime," there was bipartisan agreement on Cummings's federalism plans.[56]

The New Dealers positioned themselves between the extremes of nationalism and states' rights, a position that appeared reasonable in contrast to advocates of extreme centralization. Congressman Ruffin pointed to the public demand for full nationalization.[57] Ruffin called such revolutionary change unacceptable, while lamenting the status quo of federal impotence. Cummings's Justice Department repeatedly affirmed the states' importance. Pointing to the Senate Committee on Crime and the Special Division on Racketeering and Kidnapping, Cummings denied that he had intentions to nationalize crime control or to "invite local organizations to turn over their problems to the Federal government." Senator Copeland and Justin Miller favored more centralization than J. Edgar Hoover or the local police did, but New Deal liberal rhetoric emphasized moderation. In his 1934 National Crime Conference address, Joseph B. Keenan called "absolutely untrue" a respected periodical's assertions that federal legislation had "definitively revised the traditional American policy."[58] August Vollmer generally favored centralization with more ambivalence toward police nationalization. He was sure that "centralization and nationalization" in Cuba's police forces was positive.[59] He admired the federal Justice Department as an interstate coordinator and a model, and he agreed with Hoover that a "national police hookup [would] strengthen [enforcement]."[60] But while he found one "proposal" for national police "unquestionably sound," he prioritized "centralization of all police activities in each state."[61] He also worried that "a federal police force would be a dangerous experiment" and relayed the Wickersham Commission's description of national police as unconstitutional.[62] Vollmer's protégé Orlando Wilson echoed these subtleties. Wilson objected to plans for a "federal, state, municipal cooperative police system" as defying "the founders of our constitution."[63]

As with criminal procedure, legal conservatives differed in reasoning and emphasis but agreed on the general reform trajectory. Clarence E. Martin described Prohibition's repeal as an admission to federal limitations, and he opposed a federal Child Labor Amendment modeled on the Eighteenth Amendment. Although he celebrated "the structure the Fathers" had crafted, which restrained "nationalizing and socializing" tendencies,[64] Martin agreed that states and national powers should expand and coordinate. Americans demanded federal vigilance against "criminal conspiracies" with "no regard for state lines or national boundaries." Martin regarded the Mann Act as balanced, although he thought the states needed to do more. Against the "inhuman" evil of child labor, he declared, "No [state] laws can be too stringent," but national overreach threatened to substitute "state socialism for social justice."[65] John Dickinson observed a jurisdictional mess that gave lawbreakers "immunity from arrest and punishment." He defended the Mann Act, the Fugitive Felon and Witness Act, the federal bank robbery laws justified under *McCullough vs. Maryland*, the National Firearms Act, and the Pure Food and Drug Act, but criticized federal interference in states' policing their own borders.[66] Circuit Judge John J. Parker, a Calvin Coolidge appointee, explained that conservatives "lose substance by clinging to form" whereas progressives "lose substance in their desire for change of form." Parker acknowledged "sovereign powers reserved to the states" and opposed "state socialism," but cheered federal checks on "inefficient and corrupt" states and welcomed the "definitive passing of the laissez faire theory of government."[67]

Crucially, federal escalation did not mean retreat by state officials. Crime powers at all levels centralized and expanded, often complementing each other. The states took inspiration from the national war on crime, and attention to street-level offenses nurtured new federal respect for the locals, whose footwork enabled coordination. National energy drove state energy through informational commissions and compacts. Texas governor James V. Allred, a Democratic New Dealer, won office condemning his predecessor's generous use of clemency. "War has been declared against the lawless elements of Texas with the inauguration of a new State administration," the *New York Times* reported.[68]

Crucially, the federal government facilitated interstate coordination.[69] The Interstate Crime Commission (ICC) made recommendations to assist the states. Uniform state laws offered support for interstate "close pursuit" cases, and a Uniform Act on Interstate Extradition would prevent escapes from justice. Proposed Indiana–Illinois legislation allowed out-of-state supervision of parolees and probationers. Summoning witnesses across states was also considered. Other recommendations included state-level bureaus of criminal identification, and fingerprinting for automobile purchases and for drivers' licenses.[70]

Federal officials were proud of their support for states. J. Edgar Hoover credited Cummings's coordination for the successful pursuit of oil magnate Charles F. Urschel's kidnapper.[71] Justin Miller called continuing coordination weaknesses "the most striking discrepancy" as each jurisdiction pursued "a campaign of its own, of greater or less intensity, without much regard for the others."[72] The 1934 Interstate Compact Act gave "blanket congressional consent in advance to all compacts entered into by any two or more states in the field of the 'prevention of crime and the enforcement of their respective criminal laws and policies.'" Gordon Dean emphasized that states' rights sensibilities should acknowledge "corresponding state duties," rendering the "compact statute . . . a direct challenge to the states." Agreements entailed pursuing officers, witness coordination, joint agencies, and interstate detainee supervision. The Fugitive Felon Law banned fleeing from a state to avoid testifying. By February 1935 Congress had approved approximately seventy compacts.[73]

Beyond coordination, governors followed Washington's lead to centralize and expand their own capacities. The 1930s were indeed especially consequential for state centralization. In 1934 Massachusetts governor Joseph Ely, a conservative Democrat, proposed centralizing the police.[74] Multiple models of state centralization existed. As of 1935, Arizona, Arkansas, California, Colorado, Florida, Georgia, Illinois, Indiana, Michigan, Minnesota, Nebraska, New York, North Carolina, North Dakota, Oklahoma, Pennsylvania, Texas, and Utah were deliberating on procedure reform, state departments of justice, unification of law enforcement agencies, or state police.[75] Whereas there were no state police agencies before the twentieth century, by 1941 all states adopted at least highway patrols, and over half had state police forces—approximately twice the number in both categories from a decade before.[76]

At the same time, state government also provided one cautionary tale of illiberal authoritarianism, nearly inviting significant federal intervention against state police power. Senator Huey Long, working through his proxy governor back in Louisiana, was despised by Roosevelt for his combination of dictatorial powers and a more radical social welfare agenda than the New Deal. The American Newspaper Publishers Association depicted Long's promiscuous use of secret police without warrants, censorship, and martial law as a plan to "Hitlerize the state and nation," and Roosevelt also worried that Long's "share the wealth" campaign would pose a third-party challenge. As the Bureau of Investigation spied on Long, federal officials who were petitioned for redress of Long's oppression were in a bind. Employing substantive due process rationales for undercutting Long's violation of Louisianans' property rights would seem to affirm Lochner principles. The House of Representatives investigated Long's violations of fundamental rights, and the New Dealers even pitched an idea to activate the Constitution's "guarantee clause" ensuring a republican form of government, overriding Louisiana's state police powers and putting the New Deal state firmly on the side of centralized liberation. But Long's assassination made the issue moot.[77]

New York governor Herbert Lehman's war on crime meanwhile mirrored Roosevelt's more liberal approach. Lehman hosted a large 1935 conference, "Crime, the Criminal and Society," airing myriad reform proposals from his own idea of universal fingerprinting to Republican former US attorney George Medalie's proposal that attorneys general be appointed rather than elected.[78] Cummings took notice.[79] The New York Times referred to Lehman's "war on crime," pointing to his sixty-point law-and-order program, including a state-level Department of Justice modeled after Washington's.[80] Describing the atmosphere fostered by

Thomas E. Dewey, Lehman's special prosecutor who embraced secrecy, cooperation with police, and federal assistance, the *Times* reported that "what he is doing now very much suggests the beginning of a war."[81]

Less in sync with Roosevelt's agenda than New York, California demonstrated the flexibility of war-on-crime federalism. California pursued centralization with a state department of justice but resisted interstate coordination. State regulatory boards and the agricultural department cooperated. Criminal justice took over traffic control. Police methods and due process underwent modernization. "California has always been advanced in its attitude toward crime," as Judge William A. Beasly put it.[82] But California was also a site of resistance. In October 1933 the San Francisco Police Commissioners protested the use of Alcatraz as a federal prison. They bristled at hosting "criminals ... considered too dangerous" for other US prisons. The "presence ... of the associates of such convicted criminals" would bring "prejudice" against the city.[83]

California's Republican governor Frank Merriam typified a conservative approach to centralization alongside skepticism about interstate cooperation.[84] He used the state militia during the 1934 San Francisco waterfront strike, approved state exclusion of migrants "likely to become a public charge," and in 1935 favored centralizing state roads.[85] He agreed with Vollmer on centralization and professionalization, and they both attended a March 1935 Western States Anti-Crime Conference, but they diverged on interstate cooperation. Vollmer suspected that his 1932 support of incumbent C. C. Young against Merriam irritated the governor,[86] but the friction arose on substantive policy. In 1936 Merriam gave slow responses to Vollmer's questions about the ICC.[87] In February he asked Merriam to convene western governors to "consider the transient problem," pointing to the rise of crime from October through April "due to the influx of these migratory adolescents" and "professional criminals."[88] Merriam was skeptical, seeing California's "transient situation ... [as] different from that of the other Western States."[89] He passed Vollmer's concerns to the legislative bureau, but effectively killed the dream of interstate coordination.[90] Merriam supported some bills at Vollmer's urging but generally disappointed him.[91]

In the longer term, Vollmer's vision would gain traction among California Republicans. California's attorney general, Earl Warren, whom

Vollmer recommended to Merriam for the ICC, embraced liberal war-on-crime federalism. A Republican, Warren said a consensus recognized "altogether too much crime," which "no one knows and understands . . . as a whole."[92] If America "were no larger than California" with "natural and political boundaries" like in Europe, "our major crime problems would fall of their own weight." Warren outlined four proposals—regarding federal centralization, state centralization, the status quo, and more federal supervision—and called his own the reasonable path. National centralization was "not the American way" but each state needed its own department of justice, as the ABA recommended.[93]

THE CONSUMMATION OF WAR-ON-CRIME FEDERALISM

Given its high stakes, it is understandable that the 1937 court-packing showdown overshadowed questions of crime. Since 1933 a conservative judiciary impeded Roosevelt's domestic program. One proposed remedy was a constitutional amendment requiring that a federal law could be overturned only by a Supreme Court supermajority.[94] Research found that 12,001 to 3,475 Americans would support constitutional changes to ease the way for Roosevelt's agenda.[95] Upholding the administration's retreat from the gold standard in 1935, the Supreme Court nevertheless overturned the Railroad Pension Act and the National Industrial Relations Act that same year, and parts of the Agricultural Adjustment Act in 1936.[96] The Court upheld federal and state social legislation around 1937, when Roosevelt announced the court-packing plan. The *ABA Journal* cautioned against "an All-Powerful Central Government with the Rights of the States Subordinated."[97] To criticize the plan, legal conservatives appropriated liberal rhetoric on individual rights and civil liberties. Former US attorney Donovan, a Republican who vigorously enforced Prohibition, argued that Roosevelt's plan threatened "minority rights"—including habeas corpus for Chinese immigrants, German immigrant rights to teach their language, Catholic rights to religious schools, and free speech for political minorities.[98] Cummings and Roosevelt in turn related court packing to their efforts to streamline criminal procedure.[99]

But even as the court-packing controversy peaked, consensus over crime powers was being consummated in policy and culture. In October 1937 the *Washington Post* hailed federal, state, and local coordination, trumpeted the end of jurisdictional "jealousies," and lauded new federal resources like the FBI's G-Men (government men) and Alcatraz.[100] The paper's front page announced that together federal and state officials achieved "a 'New Deal' in America's war on crime."[101] While the federal judiciary increasingly deferred to state economic regulation, it sometimes upheld state assaults on criminal due process. *Palko v. Connecticut* affirmed Connecticut's law allowing appeals to not-guilty verdicts.[102] Americans welcomed the unprecedented federal powers unleashed by the 1934 revolution and heighted prosecution of liquor violators, car thieves, narcotics addicts, counterfeiters, forgers, and postal violators. The public sometimes had an exaggerated understanding of national authority. Americans mistook a Senate subcommittee studying crime as "a kind of super-police" with prosecutorial power, requesting "all types of investigations, into all kinds of wrongs," ranging from "the internal affairs of municipalities" to "alleged unconscionable mortgage foreclosures."[103] Instead, the Senate subcommittee took a serious but mostly passive interest in the multijurisdictional problem of crime. It detailed firearms control including merchant licensing, interstate movement of stolen property, interstate traffic and automobile sales regulation, fingerprinting, proposed legislation to prohibit felonious fugitives from conducting interstate commerce, racketeering, the Lindbergh law, increased Sherman Antitrust penalties, various criminal code changes, poultry regulation, and proposals for harsher evidentiary requirements and three-fourths majorities to convict defendants in noncapital cases.[104]

Perhaps the starkest example of a New Deal program enhancing cooperative federalism in enforcement arose in the Tennessee Valley Authority (TVA). From its beginning, the TVA pushed the frontiers of federal security and policing. TVA office buildings had limited access and required new security agents. To police the Norris Dam, the TVA created security forces, including college-educated "junior guides" who performed protection and public relations functions. The guards had clerical duties, working with maps and staffing the library, proofreading and assisting with reports, labels, and folders. The creation of police functions from scratch followed an ad hoc trajectory. The original TVA law did not authorize a force with general policing power. Financing the police force was a challenge unanticipated in the appropriations process, and officials considered diverting Norris operating accounts budgets to fund the novel operation.[105] The ramshackle TVA public safety service would not earnestly yield to modernization until the eve of World War II.

In hoping to assist the rural South in modernization, the TVA lacked clear enforcement authority, exemplifying the nation-state's growing pains. The TVA's contingent construction of law and order illustrated the ad hoc qualities of law-enforcement federalism even at the New Deal's peak. The TVA allowed a federal law enforcement agency developed from nothing—along with polities and communities created and modernized by federal planning in the heart of the old confederacy. Attempts to se-cure the Valley relied on piecemeal relationships with federal and, more important, state officials. To guard officials carrying money, the TVA re-quested highway patrol chaperones. Some officials aspired to profession-alize and bring TVA police in line with the contemporaneous moderniza-tion of policing. In September 1936 the question arose of professional leave for safety officers to attend the Wichita, Kansas, police school.[106]

Perhaps no other venue of federal state building better underscored the uncertainties of jurisdictional authority. On the one hand, the TVA was the crown jewel of New Deal political legitimacy in the rural white South, particularly the contested upper South. If ever there was an op-portunity for national authority with minimum deference to local pieties, this was it. On the other hand, the spirit of law-and-order federalism both elevated the aspirations of a unitary enforcement authority and reinforced the subsidiarity of America's patchwork jurisdictional past. Until the decade's end, the TVA relied on the good graces of state officials in Ten-nessee, Kentucky, North Carolina, Georgia, and Alabama. In the mid-1930s they were still considering improvising methods to empower their safety officers across jurisdictions. Ideas included deputyships from the county sheriff in Cherokee County and authorization from the US deputy marshal. Perhaps, it was hoped, one marshal per police force would be sufficient.[107] Seeing US marshals or county sheriff deputization as comparably plausible approaches underlined the new federalism, where enforcement power was no longer a zero-sum game between parochial interests and grand national aspirations.

At the same time, the fledgling TVA public safety service, grappling for jurisdictional certainty and parity with other professionalized forces, embodied war-on-crime liberalism. Policing the Tennessee Valley required skills and tasks that drew on different facets of New Deal statism. In late 1936 a circulated report determined officials' priorities for the safety service's functions. Policing functions were broad and extensive. Officers patrolled the Valley on foot and by car, maintained order among employees and visitors, protected property, regulated traffic and disciplined violators, helped keep cars safely maintained, aired complaints from visitors about others' conduct, cooperated with law enforcement across jurisdictions, and undertook "crime prevention by proper education" for the camp's children. They prosecuted criminal cases and compiled evidence to present to judges and justices of the peace. But they also administered social functions not typically categorized as policing: greeting and guiding visitors, working on fire prevention, inspecting and maintaining infrastructure, and carrying out first aid and telecommunications activities.[108] As of April 1937 a characteristic analysis found that policing and traffic together constituted 40 percent of the job, guide duties 25 percent, and fire response and maintenance 15 percent each.[109] Supplying information, dealing with fire hazards, protecting property, maintenance, and violations ranked highly as internal priorities.[110]

By 1937 expansive commerce clause readings accommodated escalating national action.[111] J. Edgar Hoover traced this interpretive evolution to the White Slave Traffic Act of 1910.[112] But the interpretive plasticity swelled under Cummings, yielding apparent successes on the ground.[113] Bank robberies dropped 37 percent in 1933 and kept falling in 1934 and 1935.[114]

The legislative revolution had meanwhile slowed after the 1934 barrage of new criminal laws, and less exciting legislation in 1935 reformed Alaska's criminal code and targeted mail fraud and robbery of custodians of government property.[115] In late 1936 Cummings recommended more federal laws—extending the Firearms Act to include pistols, revolvers, rifles, and shotguns; easing punishment for violations on the high seas; extending the National Stolen Property Act to include embezzlements and counterfeited securities; penalizing fake kidnappings, extortion letters sent to oneself, and the receiving of trafficked women. On criminal procedure, Cummings wanted to give US commissioners trial powers over petty offenses on Indian reservations; empower prosecutors to take deposition in criminal cases; abolish appeals for interstate removal proceedings; compel advance notice for alibi defenses; confiscate felons' firearms; parole the mentally afflicted; establish indictment by grand jury; and allow spouses to testify, prosecutors to comment on defendants' failure to testify, and Circuit Courts of Appeal to revise sentences. Cummings wanted US marshals to take disbursement duties from the Treasury and limit interest on claims against the government. He would enhance war-on-crime federalism by aligning federal death penalty processes with the states in which the crimes took place. In December Roosevelt called Cummings's whole slate of recommendations "excellent."[116]

Despite the failure of most of this legislative program, and even amid late-1930s fractures over constitutional interpretation and social policy, some major federal crime statutes passed with little debate. One big precedent was the 1934 National Firearms Act, which used taxation power to effectively outlaw automatic weapons. In 1936 the Supreme Court unanimously upheld the Act in *Sonzinsky v. United States,* rejecting a challenge that the law was an unconstitutional regulation in the guise of taxation.[117] In 1937 federal marijuana prohibition, also achieved through the tax power, came with an unceremonious voice vote (whereas federal prohibition of alcohol had required a constitutional amendment).[118]

Cummings's push for expanding firearms control helped to consummate war-on-crime federalism. Beginning with New York's Sullivan Law in 1911, states increasingly regulated firearms, but only New York required a license simply to own a handgun. By 1938 forty-five states banned concealed carry of firearms or required licenses for lawful use, and twenty-two states adopted licensing and taxing schemes. Thirty states required dealers to maintain detailed records of all firearms sales.[119] Several states passed the Uniform Firearms Act, endorsed by the ABA, and the Uniform Pistol Act, which restricted firearms, encouraged target shooting, and provided the National Rifle Association with an effective monopoly on target-shooting pistol procurement from the government.[120] Cummings hoped to go further than many states with comprehensive registration. He compared America's homicides, disproportionately committed with firearms, to much lower rates in Canada, England, and Wales, and reasoned that whether Americans had "five million" or "ten million" handguns, "the number is large—too large."[121] Just as the *ABA Journal* resounded New Deal opinions on crime, it aired support for gun control. One article worried that technology, having reduced criminality, now aided it. For centuries governments had suppressed crime with "firearms and artillery" that criminals could not afford, but "recent inventions have somewhat reversed these comparative advantages."[122]

Striking a familiar note, the Justice Department asserted a moderation between extremes. Justin Miller opposed national firearms bans, saying they required searches that trampled the Fourth Amendment and confiscations that offended the Second. He conceded that manufacturers and "rifle associations" obstructed registration and licensing proposals, but maintained that 1934 had mostly exhausted US "jurisdiction . . . under the Constitution."[123] Cummings carefully differentiated his new regulatory ambitions from the effective 1934 ban on machine guns through taxation. He told Roosevelt a registration scheme would be a "potent weapon" for "law enforcement" and impose only reasonable burdens on lawful owners.[124] A Justice Department press release promised that the new law would barely inconvenience the law-abiding. The 1934 Act had already registered "18,000 machine guns and machine rifles, 16,000 sawed off firearms, [and] 700 rifles," and although in some ways "small weapons are even a greater menace than machine guns," a measly one-dollar tax on firearm transfers would impose "no serious financial burden." Invoking vehicular registration, an important policy development in recent decades, the Justice Department insisted that the "honest and law abiding citizen" would suffer "far less hardship by the proposed enactment than by the existing requirement that he register his automobile."[125] Congress passed, and Roosevelt signed, the Federal Firearms Act of 1938, which restricted weapons transfers but fell short of Cummings's original plan.[126] The National Rifle Association supported the measure.[127]

As Cummings approached retirement, he was proud of but not fully satisfied with his criminal justice accomplishments. Cummings did not see his most ambitious 1936 criminal procedure reforms pass, but federal authority nevertheless advanced considerably. War-on-crime federalism thrived as the national judiciary showed increasing, if uneven, interest in state court proceedings.[128]

Cummings spent his second term as attorney general trying to ride the inertia that propelled his crime and judicial reform, invoking past reforms to justify new ones in a changing legal bureaucracy. Cummings pointed to the overworked federal courts clogged with "fifty thousand undisposed of cases."[129] District court cases involving criminal charges rose from 19.5 percent on July 1, 1936, to 21.3 percent on June 30, 1937.[130] In 1938 Cummings urged further criminal procedure reforms. He sought to permit defendants to waive indictment by grand jury and "to consent to prosecution by information." He pressed for advance notice for alibi defenses, freedom for prosecutors to comment on defendants' failures to testify, and extension of the Criminal Appeals Act to afford more appeals by the government.[131] He encouraged Roosevelt to show Congress a letter boasting of "great steps forward. . . . in judicial reform" while allowing space for "protection of substantive rights and adequate, but not extravagant, judicial review." The district courts had already undergone broad "reform of civil procedure" that could now extend to "the several Circuit Courts of Appeals."[132] Under Arthur T. Vanderbilt, the ABA backed Cummings on the new court rules, the bill for additional judges, and the creation of an administrative office for the federal judiciary.[133]

Cummings ended his tenure widely praised for his work on criminal procedure and interjurisdictional cooperation. He thanked his situational allies at the ABA.[134] New ABA president Frank Hogan expressed disappointment about Cumming retiring—despite their disagreements, Cummings's Justice Department showed great "ability and impartiality" and a "high degree of efficiency."[135] Roosevelt thanked Cummings on the last night of 1938 for guiding the Justice Department "through a difficult period." Cummings helped make "the homes of America" safer, reduced "interstate crime," and made "great strides . . . in improving judicial procedure."[136] An official press release credited his expansion of the FBI, creation of the National Police Academy, modernization of prisons, enhancement of his office's litigation power, and passage of an omnibus judges bill. It praised Cummings for transforming federalism. The states had gone "without facilities or power to reach interstate criminals who operated in what Attorney General Cummings terms 'No Man's Land' between state and federal jurisdiction." The 1934 changes in criminal law constituted the most "far reaching reforms since 1789." So far none of Cummings's laws were "held invalid by any court."[137] (The next year, although the Supreme Court rejected a Second Amendment challenge to the Federal Firearms Act, a 7-1 decision reversed parts of the Act on Fifth Amendment grounds.[138] The Act's registration requirement had compelled people either to admit to lawbreaking or to risk conviction for possessing an unregistered weapon.[139])

Despite the praise Cummings enjoyed in the late 1930s there was some growing dissent on some issues, which was ominous for the momentum for reform. Cummings's visions for administrative law included a distinct role for criminal enforcement, and here the consensus broke down. In June 1935 ALI president Cornelius W. Wickersham, son of George Wickersham, warned that the regulatory state was intruding into "an infinite number" of areas, "imposing restrictions, obligations and duties, many of which are enforcible by criminal penalties."[140] Charles Wyzanski, a future district court judge appointed by Roosevelt, believed that administrative law could "satisfy the constitutional mandate of 'due process'" despite the "unworthy criticism" from such reflexive anti-regulation voices.[141] On the other hand, Cummings's close associate Carl McFarland, hoping for more administrative law theorization, later struck a more realist tone, conceding that "no law and no procedural system can eliminate the improper use of the vast power of the state." The "oppressive use of tax investigators, securities investigators, antitrust investigators, postal inspectors, and others against a single disfavored person, or corporation, or industry, or class—or the threat of ruinous criminal proceedings or civil actions under strained interpretations of law and evidence"—could occur under any "form or structure of government. That problem is not one of laws but of men."[142]

The inertia for criminal procedure reform also found new dissent, foreshadowing future coalitional fractures. Pendleton Howard, a law school dean, chided the dominant view that blamed "interminable delays and continuances" on legal procedures' "failure to 'adapt'" and "antiquated judicial machinery." Howard argued that Roosevelt had already overseen "more wholesale and constant tinkering" with criminal law and criminal procedure than ever seen before, and crime commissions had already gutted appeals and the "sanctity of [the] jury."[143] ACLU general counsel Osmond K. Fraenkel presciently called liberals shortsighted and "naïve" for wanting to abolish judicial review. Without it, "repressive and arbitrary acts of government would be much freer from correction." It was in "minority rights [and] civil liberties, that constitutional restraints have their greatest significance and judicial review its real value."[144] In 1940 a major criminological journal argued that weakening due process barely inconvenienced serious criminals but gravely threatened "youthful, inexperienced, and oftentimes doubtful offenders."[145]

More strikingly, Roscoe Pound, father of sociological jurisprudence, worried that New Deal modernization had gone too far.[146] In 1934 Pound took a moderate stand on criminal procedure not dissimilar to Justin Miller's, condemning third-degree interrogations while supporting loosened Fifth Amendment restrictions on prosecutors commenting on defendants' failure to testify—a protection that "ceased to have any basis in the seventeenth century" and no longer aided "the innocent.[147] The next year Pound criticized the extent to which prosecutors were pressured to "assent to pleas of guilty of lesser offenses" and he called for looser rules for extradition and interrogation.[148] In 1936 he warned that the "decrying of the bill of rights" would only grow louder while maintaining that criminal law reform was necessary given the "administrative side of punitive justice."[149] Pound agreed with Cummings on harmonizing the law to facilitate a national welfare state.[150] But by 1939 he worried that the administrative state would wreck due process. He extended to criminal procedure the arguments for common-law rulemaking in civil procedure.

Common-law rules were more adaptive and more accessible for judges to apply holistic approaches quickly in consultation with the bar, whereas incurious legislatures cared little about detail and procedural changes. To those who worried that the courts would "bear too hard upon accused persons," Pound attributed criminal procedure erosions to the Department of Justice, that "great prosecuting bureau." He called for more scholarship and criminal law treatises to withstand the mechanical anti-intellectualism of the growing administrative leviathan he had made his career championing.[151]

Cummings ultimately had more success with centralization of rule-making than with his biggest plans to streamline due process protections. Even after retirement Cummings remained dedicated to the cause, bemoaning a disparity: The Supreme Court's rule-making power extended to equity, admiralty, bankruptcy, copyright, and, since 1935, criminal cases after verdict. But the Court still needed an expedited criminal procedure, from arrest to verdict, to "speed and simplify the administration of justice."[152] Cummings's Justice Department collaborator Alexander Holtzoff lamented that criminal cases were "covered by a strange admixture of federal statutes, state statutes and rules of common law." Volumes on criminal procedure were available but there existed no "complete body of procedural rules." It was up to the federal legislature to make changes.[153] In 1939 Cummings stressed the urgency for rule-making reform legislation.[154] The bill passed eventually and Roosevelt gave Cummings the pen he used to sign it.[155]

Ultimately the Supreme Court sometimes used this power to protect defendants, sometimes to empower prosecutors. By 1940 the critics of Supreme Court rulemaking feared an imbalance between speedy prosecution and protecting the "multitude of uncounseled 'little people'" to minimize the "risk of hasty conviction of the innocent. For many defendants, criminal justice is already too speedy."[156] Having done so much to shape due process, federalism, and police power in the 1930s, Cummings left it to future generations to fine-tune the liberal state's powers against crime. Legal minds would argue for weaker or stronger due process protections, often at both the federal and state levels.[157] But for the rest of the century all levels of government would generally expand their reach into the "natural corridor" of the lawless, thanks to the consensus in legal thought that Cummings had nurtured.

DESPITE THE 1937 CLASH over the Supreme Court, legal liberals and legal conservatives enjoyed remarkable agreement on crime. Through different premises they arrived at a practical consensus. Pushing for federal procedure changes in 1938, Cummings hailed law as a "living, breathing, vital thing, and not merely a rule of conduct."[158] This living constitutionalism differed from, yet complemented, the conservatives' impulse to update traditional enforcement powers. By the late 1930s some fractures in the consensus portended later twentieth-century debates, but the outlines for a multijurisdictional, bipartisan, and cross-institutional struggle against crime were firmly in place. In regard to criminalization, prosecution, and anti-crime cooperative federalism, we can find striking the consensus between liberals and conservatives, whether in the 1990s, 1960s, or 1940s.[159] In fact, this consensus was as foundational as the oppositional politics around New Deal economics, serving both sides since their modern inception in a dialectical competition over unleashing the state against criminals. The Roosevelt administration's particular role in this legal consensus was constitutive of its larger political legacy.

It is true that Cummings never fully delivered his federal criminal procedure revolution. This vision, which he and the president understood as constitutionally progressive and liberal, promised even more advantages for the prosecutorial state than the New Deal could deliver. But the general consensus behind expanding federal criminal powers remained even if at times its activities slowed. Significant federal criminal laws indeed passed in the late decade. Aside from the Federal Firearms Act, notable legislation in 1937 and 1938 clarified policies for federal death penalty using state accommodations, modified the nation capital's juvenile courts, allowed the attorney general to join the international criminal police commission, and reformed appellate jurisdiction in Hawaii and Puerto Rico.[160] New laws targeted the impersonation of federal officers and fraudulent claims against government along with damage and theft of government property.[161] Due process protections were even weakened slightly as Congress abolished appeals in certain habeas corpus proceedings.[162]

In the longer term, perhaps the most significant change in criminal law arrived in the 1937 Marihuana Tax Act. Even though eventually the mid- to late-1930s consensus on gun control and criminal procedure would fracture, when it came to building a multijurisdictional police state and a broad political coalition, through such initiatives cooperative federalism proved enduringly essential to twentieth-century governance. Chapters 6 and 7 will reveal how two policy areas—drug control and southern treatment of Black Americans—demonstrated the enduring significance of war-on-crime federalism in the making of modern government.

CHAPTER 6

WORSE THAN MURDER

Making the War on Drugs

n July 1933 in Lexington, Kentucky, an inaugural cornerstone was placed to mark a new kind of national detention facility. Officials situated the first federal narcotics farm, instituted for both voluntary and coerced treatment, in the sweep of US global leadership. The United States had led the world against the drug "danger"—guiding opium prohibition in the late nineteenth century, spearheading a conference in Shanghai in 1905 and at the Hague in 1912, and delivering anti-narcotics treaties in 1925 and 1931. The narcotics farm followed this tradition of "control, management, and discipline" aimed at the "safekeeping of the individual and the protection of American communities."[1] Domestic security and diplomacy, repression and rehabilitation, converged in Lexington.

The New Deal embraced and expanded federal drug control. Beyond narcotics farms in Kentucky and Texas, the Roosevelt administration led global anti-trafficking efforts and extended the reach of domestic drug police. These undertakings pushed constitutional limits, leveraging treaty obligations to persuade state legislatures to ratify model drug legislation. The constitutional adventurism peaked when Congress passed the Marihuana Tax Act of 1937, outlawing cannabis throughout the United

States.[2] Unlike alcohol prohibition, this national crusade had no supporting constitutional amendment, but instead passed by voice vote before Roosevelt unceremoniously signed it. Within five years the administration that had vowed to end alcohol prohibition started the modern war on drugs.[3]

Historical accounts tell a drug war story mostly distinct from the New Deal.[4] They often showcase Harry Anslinger, chief of the Federal Bureau of Narcotics, as an obsessive conservative holdover from the Herbert Hoover administration,[5] who stayed in power thanks to powerful allies, and despite deep disagreements with Roosevelt's politics.[6] Histories often point to reactionary xenophobia, racism against Black and Hispanic people, and a moral panic about marijuana's "sweeping march" against which Anslinger activated the nation in sensationalized struggle.[7] Nevertheless, scholarship shows his mission unfolding within the continuities of broadly supported domestic and international agendas.[8]

Anslinger's indelible influence indeed flourished alongside the New Deal crime policies. As the head of a key Treasury Department enforcement agency, he was a principal figure in the war-on-crime coalition, reconciling the operations of Henry Morgenthau and Homer Cummings. Like J. Edgar Hoover, Anslinger was racist and reactionary in ways that became increasingly conspicuous during his long tenure within the rising liberal state. But in the 1930s Anslinger's agenda in fact brought him closer to the liberals.[9] The classism and racism that defined his mission also characterized New Deal drug policies outside his direct control. While many white Americans anxiously associated drugs with Black, Hispanic, and Chinese populations, such bigotries hardly deterred progressive and liberal drug warriors from exploiting the propaganda.[10] Anslinger and the New Dealers also shared other values, including global-mindedness. International agreements not only strengthened national boundaries, satisfying xenophobic fears of drugs as alien contaminants, but brought enforcement uniformity across national lines.[11] The 1931 Geneva Convention, time and again, was the crucial rationale for maintaining the Narcotics Bureau and encouraging state-level legislation.

New Deal liberalism and Anslinger's operations served one another and brought war-on-crime federalism its largest enduring policy achievement. Urging state marijuana bans in 1931, Anslinger conceded that the federal government could not impose such policy.[12] Six years later, New Dealers entrusted him with groundbreaking national power. The story of Roosevelt's retention of Anslinger points to the drug war as a co-authored composition. Despite differences over liquor, after alcohol prohibition Anslinger could cooperate with New Dealers to maintain Treasury's enforcement role and launch modern drug control as a founding commitment of the new liberal state.

GLOBAL-MINDEDNESS AND WAR-ON-DRUGS FEDERALISM

Alcohol Prohibition's unwinding brought difficulties and opportunities for the Treasury Department's enforcement machinery. Instead of pursuing a laissez-faire liquor policy, Treasury targeted bootlegging through taxes and regulation. Legal liquor dealers, in turn, became a regulated industry negotiating for influence. Morgenthau's Treasury Decision 4429 imposed a tax on spirits, required at customs houses. One spirits dealer argued for a streamlined taxing system to cut the costs of legal imports and undercut bootleggers' arbitrage opportunities.[13]

Relegating alcohol control to regulation, the administration found more uncompromising campaigns against intoxication elsewhere. Roosevelt himself was an established drug hawk. As New York's governor he backed the idea that states would pass Uniform Narcotic Drug legislation championed by Richmond Hobson, the "Father of American Prohibition." Narcotics control united Hobson and other Democrats despite disagreements over alcohol.[14] In its first years the administration faced significant questions of restructuring, budgets, and personnel. It quickly expanded the Treasury's enforcement role through interagency coordination against smuggling.[15] But Roosevelt's election also made possible big structural changes. The Narcotics Bureau, constructed ad hoc in 1930, carried some Republican baggage. Republican Harry Anslinger was married into the family of Andrew Mellon, whom Democrats despised for his fiscally conservative policies as Treasury secretary. New Deal restructuring and partisan animus counted against Anslinger's fiefdom. Whether to retain him was a weighty question, as had also been the case with J. Edgar Hoover.

Despite all this, Anslinger shared a drug vision with New Deal Democrats. Their mutual values overcame partisanship and saved the Narcotics Bureau's independence. Anslinger's global-mindedness, humanitarian interventionism, and holistic criminology better fit Cummings's ethos than did the views of less progressive or more isolationist Republicans. These common commitments, not merely his conservative connections, saved and empowered his Bureau and helped build the modern war on drugs.

The common ground became clearer after alcohol legalization. Anslinger had been a hard-liner at the Bureau of Alcohol, favoring incarceration for consumption.[16] But his Narcotics Bureau now cooperated smoothly with such other bureaucracies as Indian Affairs and customs consulates.[17] He enjoyed the respect of J. Edgar Hoover, who promised to help in "every possible way."[18] Oscar Ewing believed Anslinger had the backing of "every social agency interested in anti-narcotic work," including the Bureau of Social Hygiene, as well as Mrs. Hamilton Wright, widow of the famed opium commission mastermind.[19] Anslinger also brought value to the administration through his public relations skills and cordial connections with journalists and civic organizations ranging from the American Association of University Women to the Lions Club.[20] Prestigious academic institutions invited him to give lectures.[21] C. H. Thienes from the University of Southern California Pharmacology Department told Anslinger that if "all branches of government were as efficient as yours, tax payers would have little cause for complaint."[22]

Anslinger also enjoyed a reciprocal fondness and respect with the pharmaceutical industry, to whose challenges and developments he paid close attention.[23] Industry groups like the National Association of Retail Druggists and the American Drug Manufacturers Association invited him to speak.[24] Anslinger shared a legislative vision with the American Pharmaceutical Association, which opposed efforts to replace him, pointing to his "real desire to co-operate with the public health professions." They valued him for keeping "unnecessary and burdensome regulations" in check and for backing the Uniform State Narcotic Drug Act.[25]

The Wholesale Druggist Association also supported Anslinger.[26] F. W. Russe of Mallinckrodt Chemical Works told Roosevelt that Anslinger served the New Deal goal of credible governance. Roosevelt's "energetic, courageous and far-seeing" legislation had "universal approval" and restored bipartisan faith in government's "integrity and efficiency." Despite having "financial" interests in weak enforcement, Russe reassured Roosevelt that Anslinger would govern with integrity.[27]

Anslinger liked the "druggists," who "cooperate . . . much better" than doctors.[28] He had strong disagreements over treatment with physicians, who often bore the brunt of drug enforcement.[29] In Hollywood, Dr. Edward Williams oversaw a program that furnished maintenance doses to addicts, which according to Anslinger "aroused universal condemnation from here and abroad."[30] Edward's brother Henry Williams called Anslinger's hard-line response more draconian than "Soviet Russia or Hitlerite Germany," saying it had no place "in the land of the New Deal."[31] Henry suspected that Anslinger's harsh enforcement was meant to turn people against Roosevelt, and argued that drug policy should be taken over by the public health service "where it obviously belongs."[32]

But in fact, the New Dealers largely agreed with Anslinger, particularly on controlling narcotics through constitutional innovation. Progressive reform, guided by global concerns, united Anslinger and the liberals, and Anslinger was committed to working around constitutional constraints to modernize drug policy.

Anslinger proudly personified global-minded governance. Since at least Teddy Roosevelt's time, opium control aspired to "international scale." The Opium Advisory Committee of the League of Nations oversaw opium manufacture in Turkey, Yugoslavia, Japan, and Russia.[33] American ships engaged in confiscations, and the Narcotic Drugs Import and Export Act imposed regulatory penalties against those who evaded criminal court.[34] Anslinger associated himself with the strategic marriage of international soft and domestic hard power.[35] He was an honorary member in the International Police Chiefs Association.[36] An autobiographical blurb touted his time at the American consulates in Europe, South America, and the West Indies, from 1918 to 1929, and as a delegate to the League of Nations opium advisory committee, before becoming assistant commissioner of Prohibition in 1929 and head of Narcotics in 1930.[37]

Anslinger and the liberals had a mutual collaborator in Richmond Hobson, the Democrat heading the World Narcotic Defense Association (WNDA).[38] In November 1933 Hobson issued Recommendation XII, hoping Roosevelt and Congress would create a Council for Applied Education and systematically investigate economic crises, crime, and social disease. A proposed Department of Social Reconstruction would feature many welfare bureaus—for narcotics, alcohol, health and hygiene, lawlessness and crime, national and international economic problems, and education and social relations with a division on child welfare. Hobson predicted Russia and East Asia as the next fronts in "the Narcotic War," and lamented the long list of aloof countries—"Afghanistan, Australia, China, Japan, Siam; Abyssinia, Liberia, Union of South Africa; Austria, Estonia, Finland, Latvia, Luxemburg, Norway, Greece, Russia, San Marino, Yugoslavia; in America: Honduras, Panama, Argentina, Bolivia, Columbia [sic], Paraguay, Venezuela." Hobson wanted the United States to send commissioners to Latin America, East Asia, and Europe, a proposal Roosevelt considered impractical. But the administration respected Hobson's organization. In 1935 Cummings asked Roosevelt to contribute to the association's radio address.[39]

International commitments helped secure Anslinger's job within the New Deal state on multiple occasions. In 1933 Roosevelt faced a difficult choice regarding Anslinger's future.[40] Democratic partisans saw Anslinger as a threatening remnant from the previous administration.[41] His defenders stressed his foreign experience and diplomatic alacrity, and his expertise on the big smuggling issue.[42] Under Secretary of State William Phillips called Anslinger the "supreme authority" on narcotics.[43] Anslinger never faced a serious controversy for being more of a drug hard-liner than the administration. He was in fact warned not to advocate amnesty for drug dealers.[44] One man, criticizing Anslinger's connections to the "Mellon family," suspected a Republican conspiracy to promote weak enforcement in order to incite an anti-Roosevelt uproar.[45] Detractors continued to demand Anslinger's replacement, but their alternatives often appeared too partisan or political.[46] Anslinger's many connections proved politically and strategically valuable. Cummings took them seriously, and Anslinger's allies passed him intelligence on attempts to undercut him.[47]

The precarity of Anslinger's job coincided with a general uncertainty in drug policy.[48] Policymakers were considering questions like codeine deregulation.[49] The restructuring of federal agencies was still a live issue, with circulating proposals to absorb the Narcotics Bureau into another bureaucracy.[50] Federalism remained a big question. Anslinger recognized the need to strike the right balance. He liked the idea of a central investigative unit but believed most enforcement should remain local.[51] To save the Narcotics Bureau, he stressed not domestic commitments but "treaty obligations." The 1931 Geneva Convention required each signatory to maintain independent narcotics agencies. Anslinger argued that merging narcotics control with the Bureau of Internal Revenue would violate the mandate. He insisted he was "arguing for a principle and not for a job."[52] Richmond Hobson circulated resolutions echoing the argument.[53] Along with Hobson, a group of 17,000 retail druggists rallied with a petition that opposed reorganization.[54] After the under secretary of state inquired about the proposed merger, an April memo within Treasury declared "no intention of abolishing or merging" the Bureau, given treaty obligations.[55]

Having saved the Narcotics Bureau, Anslinger wanted to increase its size and prestige. But owing to Roosevelt's mandate for 15 percent salary reductions and general budget cuts, Anslinger's Bureau lost $400,000 from its $1,400,000 budget.[56] At the same time, former liquor enforcers hoped for jobs in the shrinking agency. Louis Ruppel, the Narcotics Bureau's deputy commissioner, faced more than 200 unemployed Volstead enforcers seeking work.[57] Soon after the budget cuts came a reversal. Senator William McAdoo saw narcotic enforcement as having "grave importance" and sought more resources to combat drugs in California.[58] Roosevelt received advice on the need for more personnel and asked the Director of the Budget for input on appropriations.[59] Louis Howe, who saw austerity as an opportunity for "big house cleaning," nevertheless acceded to hiring more customs agents on the Pacific Coast. Howe eventually signaled a Narcotics budget increase for 1935 by $150,000 up to $1,194,899.[60] Drug control broke against the austere tide of the early New Deal.

Diplomatic relations allowed the Narcotics Bureau to thrive. Facing an international drug trade, US leaders sought foreign cooperation, even urging the Soviet Union to enforce opium conventions.[61] The State Department authorized Anslinger to attend the Seventeenth Session of the Opium Advisory Committee of the League of Nations.[62] He was the administration's main international expert and closely monitored Canada's pedestrian troubles, including injection infections, codeine control centralization, and doctors who allowed heroin abuse.[63] The Bureau worried about opiates from Japan, where pharmaceutical houses were diverting narcotics.[64] Japan offered opportunities for interagency and international cooperation, as seizures from Japanese peddlers in California brought together the Customs Bureau and Narcotics Bureau.[65] The United States appealed to Japanese narcotics efforts to "remove some of the criticism" when it came to opium abuse.[66] Even Anslinger's crude racism celebrated international participation, not nativist isolation, as he called Japan's opiate official Shiko Kusama "the best Jap I know."[67] Anslinger paid heed to social knowledge, taking seriously Egypt's report attributing illicit narcotic market success to governmental neglect.[68] He kept abreast of narcotics literature distributed in Calcutta.[69]

Even his pet issue of horse racing allowed Anslinger to draw on international interests for domestic policy. The drugging of racehorses, along with industry bookmaking, angered him.[70] He received undercover dispatches on the use of stimulants and narcotics,[71] spoke at the National Association of Racing Commissioners,[72] and followed reform proposals including saliva tests and closer monitoring.[73] His *Esquire Magazine* article "Hopping Horses" received wide attention.[74] He tracked horse drugging from France to Canada. In correspondence with William Randolph Hearst, whose newspapers publicized the problem, Anslinger pondered how to suppress horse drugging "in accordance with legislative and treaty commitments."[75]

Horse drugging aside, the leveraging of treaty obligations toward domestic regulation became more relevant in policing human consumption. This diplomatic rationale for policy secured Anslinger's place and became drug policy's leading example of war-on-crime federalism. Anslinger valued every government level—from the global down to the local—and his constitutional innovations became valuable to Roosevelt and the future of drug policy.

The supposed internationalism typically returned inward. The 1934 Uniform State Narcotic Drug Act provided model legislation for states, beyond that permitted at the national level. Through this legislative campaign, Treasury and Narcotics expanded their reach in the guise of respecting treaties. The Uniform Act could promote nationwide marijuana bans without federal statute, circumventing the "difficulties which arise out of our Constitutional division of sovereignty."[76] The Uniform Act became a reinforcing rationale for an independent Narcotics Bureau, creating state-level work for the Bureau to coordinate. Hobson assured Roosevelt that the law would "throw into the fight, the full organized Police power of our country."[77]

The Uniform Act enjoyed broad support across many relevant associations. The forty-second Annual Conference of the Commissioners lent its approval.[78] The grassroots Anti-Narcotic Society in San Francisco eagerly asked for extra copies.[79] Whatever disagreements existed between doctors and pharmacists, the American Medical Association (AMA) and the Druggists Association agreed on the Act.[80] A pamphlet titled "Why the Legislatures Should Enact the Proposed Uniform Narcotic Drug Law"[81] boasted support from the Conference of Commissioners on Uniform Laws, the ABA, the House of Delegates of the AMA, the National Drug Manufacturers' Association, the National Association of Retail Druggists, the National Kiwanis, the General and State Federation of Women's Clubs, the City Federation of Women's Clubs, and the National Parent-Teacher Congress.[82]

The Narcotics Bureau had been selling the Uniform Act to the states even as Roosevelt awaited his inauguration.[83] Narcotics agents refined, rehearsed, and repeated the pitch during his first term: The AMA supported the law. It would combat blackmail and fraud and channel confiscated assets into state coffers. It would harmonize federal and state authorities and end the drug enforcement "twilight zone." Most important, the Hague agreement required American compliance.[84] As of February 1935, Uniform Act legislation had passed in Nevada, New York, Florida, New

Jersey, Virginia, Rhode Island, South Carolina, Kentucky, and Louisiana.[85] Hobson brought his organization behind it. He took an intimate interest in each state's passage, and circulated arguments calling for uniformity.[86]

Not all states accepted the legislation, often because they found their own laws adequate, whether or not federal officials agreed.[87] The Washington State Assembly's model included rationing for addicts.[88] California, for its part, needed little motivation to strengthen enforcement.[89] Anslinger agreed with state senator Dan E. Williams that California's laws were sufficient.[90] The governor pocket-vetoed two model laws while supporting the rest.[91] Alabama's hesitancy, on the other hand, came from a place of anti-federal principle.[92] Despite support from the governor and the state medical association, and a unanimous resolution from the state pharmaceutical association, state health officer J. N. Baker obstructed the legislation.[93] Described as "a Virginian and a stickler for States Rights," Baker thought Alabama had an "efficient and satisfactory narcotic law" and did not need "outside guidance or interference."[94] He maneuvered to get the Narcotics Bureau representative removed.[95] Anslinger sided with his agent against Baker, who had voting on the issue indefinitely postponed. Hobson was frustrated by Baker's seeming ignorance in thinking cannabis and marijuana were different drugs.[96] Anslinger pointed to congressional directives that the states cooperate with Treasury; twenty-seven states passed the bill without medical opposition.[97] In September the bill finally passed in Alabama.[98]

Through 1934 and 1935, Anslinger's dexterity with federalism made him a valuable asset despite partisan rancor and controversy. In late 1934 Anslinger called a suspect a "ginger-colored n*gger."[99] The racist language provoked an "avalanche of protest."[100] Despite this outward bigotry, Roosevelt stood by Anslinger. Whatever their disagreements on racial politics and rhetoric, they agreed on policy. In a prepared 1935 statement, the president urged the states to incorporate the Geneva Narcotic Limitation Convention prohibitions to give their "people far better protection . . . against the ravages of the narcotic drug evil." It would assist federal "promotion of the welfare of our people and the peoples of other lands."[101]

THE NEW DEAL TREASURY'S DRUG WAR

Outside of the Uniform Act campaign, the Treasury pursued other col-laborative avenues of regulation. Anslinger coordinated with Treasury agencies at regular meetings on smuggling. The smuggling committee served as a testing ground for drug control militarization and institu-tional integration. Much of the effort aimed at ensuring that importers did not flout the regulatory regime of the new legal alcohol market. The committee communicated with Britain about smuggling.[102] Different nations had different standards. Holland and Germany had very few restrictive duties, whereas Belize and Puerto Rico were under heavy scrutiny.[103] Bootleggers, attempting to circumvent taxes, duties, and reg-ulations got creative. In Milford, Connecticut, two stills were caught re-cooking denatured alcohol.[104] Japanese steamships were suspected of carrying opium.[105] Even small amounts of contraband drew attention. The Rockland Tax Unit reported sixty-six bottles of untaxed beer.[106]

Anslinger enlivened the committee meetings with his input, charmed representatives from across Morgenthau's Department, and happily apprised them of Bureau operations.[107] New Dealers shared Anslinger's assumption that cutting off supply, his principal strategy, could work. Reports of black-market alcohol selling for 34 cents a gallon in New York elicited disbelief, given estimated production costs at 50 cents excluding infrastructure.[108] Anslinger boasted US progress against opium and pro-posed that preventing poppies from flowering would stop the drug.[109]

The committee observed crime coordination unfolding under the Treasury. In mid-1936, field representatives from the Coast Guard, Se-cret Service, Customs, Narcotics, the Intelligence Unit, and Alcohol Tax Unit met in St. Paul, Seattle, San Francisco, Los Angeles, Denver, Kansas City, New Orleans, and Jacksonville.[110] Despite some shortcomings, the collaboration encouraged calls to continue. In 1936 Morgenthau chided the Commission of Internal Revenue and the heads of Coast Guard, Cus-toms, Narcotics, and Secret Service for failure to "cooperate properly with each other" and investigators outside Treasury, include state, mu-nicipal, and foreign officials.[111]

Concerning alcohol smuggling, at least, the Treasury was pleased by its progress. By late 1935 the West Coast saw little smuggling, although some contraband leaked in through Maine.[112] By October 1936 reports commonly found zero smuggling in Boston.[113] Japan posed difficulties in Hawaii because Japanese steamships carried excessive cargo, personal furniture crates, and boxes, and no infrastructure could store and examine it.[114] Anslinger cheered the seizure of twenty-two pounds of morphine on a Japanese motorboat, the largest capture in several years.[115]

In addition to these antismuggling meetings, the Treasury Department undertook other regulatory strategies, often with Anslinger playing at most a peripheral role. In three areas—tax collection, the regulation of coca extract content in cola products, and treatment facilities—Morgenthau's bureaucracy incorporated coercion and soft power in its multifaceted efforts.

The power to tax is the power to destroy, and the Treasury's most awesome power lay first and last in its taxing authority. Tax cooperation across jurisdictions was limited. Federal use of local tax laws was discouraged. An official called it "inadvisable from a tax-collection standpoint" to "harass" suspects with New York tax laws because New York might get the money first. In any event, the governors of New York and California historically rejected cooperating with such efforts.[116]

The Narcotics Bureau proudly assisted in the use of tax evasion tools against drug offenders.[117] Anslinger and the Commissioner of Internal Revenue shared intelligence on violators of the Harrison Narcotics Act with conspicuous black-market wealth—sometimes "undoubtedly far in excess of the amounts which they reported."[118] Tax collection unified the whole structure of narcotics enforcement, and Anslinger's subordinates kept him abreast of violations. District supervisors furnished lists, long and short, vague and specific, of possible violators. Large dealers were generally prioritized, along with those suspected of also breaking gambling and alcohol laws.[119]

As the Narcotics Bureau's tax activities became routine, so did procedures. In March 1936 Anslinger issued Circular 384, ordering the reporting of "every" narcotic violator suspected of "a large or unusual income" to local Special Agents in Charge. New York City responded with a long list of suspects. Too many improvements on a house could trigger a federal investigation, as could a tipoff from informants working at the local drug store. Intelligence of corruption went to the FBI. By 1937 Internal Revenue and the Treasury itself wanted direct access to the Bureau's valuable tax reports.[120]

Accustomed to regulating narcotics through taxation, the Narcotics Bureau now used drug investigations to collect "substantial amounts" of revenue. Even smaller forfeitures of $4,000 here or $2,800 there occasioned internal boasting. By August one Narcotics official exclusively managed tax violations. Narcotics officials were strategic, rejecting a proposal to threaten addicts with taxation to capture dealers, since the addicts would probably not know major dealers. The racial disparities of drug enforcement extended to tax collection as immigrants, and especially deportees, found themselves ensnared. Chinese nationals in particular became suspect and even relatively small amounts, under $500, could implicate an entire Chinese-owned bank. Yee Long found himself arrested in violation of the Harrison law and the Narcotic Drugs Import and Export Act. The reported amount was exaggerated by a factor of ten. The goal of revenue extraction proved flexible, as collectors took payment in Chinese currency and jewelry.[121]

Beyond taxation, the Treasury regulated drugs in other ways. One of its missions was to keep soft drinks soft. Coca-Cola's formula had originally included cocaine, and the company relied on federal public relations help. The company offered to "reimburse" Congressman Robert L. Ramsey's expenses for generating a federal report certifying that Coca-Cola contained no narcotics or opium.[122] Consumers had been writing to the Internal Revenue Department or Department of Agriculture, worried about Coca-Cola's habit-forming qualities, its caffeine contents, or possible narcotic ingredients. The Narcotics Bureau cared about cocaine but was uninterested in "remaining alkaloids" and directed such questions to the Food and Drug Administration.[123]

An international export question exposed tensions in legal positivism, corporate relations, and interagency collaboration. Legislation from 1930 allowed limited importation of coca leaves for medical use, which were then destroyed under Narcotics Bureau observation. Merck & Company imported the java variety and Maywood Chemical imported the Peruvian variety. Maywood also had license to import "special" leaves to de-cocainize. The Harrison Narcotics Act allowed an exception for de-cocainized coca leaf derivatives that were no longer psychoactive. But while de-cocainized leaves were permitted in the cola formula, no such exemption existed in the Narcotic Drugs Import and Export Act from 1922, which completely prohibited trade of any extractive, including Coca-Cola's Merchandise No. 5 (coca leaf extract). After Canadian interception of Coca-Cola, Anslinger discussed the application for coca leaves with Maywood Chemical. Maywood insisted that exporting Coca-Cola with Merchandise No. 5 would not alter the demand for cocaine, which already outstripped the need for residual de-cocainized leaves. In September officials reasserted the export ban on Merchandise No. 5.[124]

Coca-Cola petitioned for reconsideration, now arguing that US law inspired the Geneva Convention of 1931 in the first place. Ensnaring the company would contradict the "reiterated statements of responsible statesmen in committee hearings." The 1936 Report of the Bureau of Narcotics conceded that Coca-Cola was not narcotic. Coca-Cola decried as incoherent the law's finding that "this non-narcotic flavoring extract" would be "encouraged" for "all our own citizens" but "would become a 'narcotic drug'" upon export.[125] The Treasury Department finally allowed an exception. The vice president of Coca-Cola thanked Anslinger for his "good will" and vowed to support "the Bureau that has been so well developed under your distinguished leadership."[126]

The Narcotics Bureau's implementation of the coca leaf rules sometimes hurt Coca-Cola's competition. Questions arose over the destruction of leftover leaves for a discontinued product. The Bureau mulled over questions of extracts as interstate commerce but usually Anslinger found no violations using de-cocainized leaves. One mysterious extract turned out to be from chestnut leaves. An investigation into Browne Corporation's Brownie Cola and Sparkling Kola discovered de-cocainized leaves originating with Merck. Sometimes Narcotics officials asked the Food and Drug Administration to investigate violations of the Pure Food and Drug Act. Coca-Cola often complained about knockoffs, and one of its competitors unreservedly asked the Bureau for help in procuring cocaine extract. Typically, the Bureau would gently remind companies of the law.

One entrepreneur had a hard time understanding that the Bureau would not help him obtain the formula from Merck.[127]

Perhaps the narcotics farms best embodied Treasury's soft power—and its limits. Many Americans had clamored for such an institution.[128] The first farm, in Lexington, Kentucky, was planned under President Hoover and scheduled to open in April 1935. A second farm would open in Fort Worth.[129] Federal penal and medical officials had to approve the applications.[130] One of William Randolph Hearst's newspapers championed narcotics farms in every state.[131]

The narcotics farms especially encapsulated both the coercive and the rehabilitative mechanisms of New Deal penology. Roosevelt applauded their "new and most helpful direction."[132] Both federal narcotics convicts and American-born voluntary patients were eligible, and Anslinger advocated more voluntary admits. The therapeutic state and carceral state came together as Surgeon General H. S. Cumming collaborated with district judges, narcotics agents, US marshals, US attorneys, and penal officials. Millicent Gardner Morison thought the farms would prove that "drug traffic can and will be eradicated." Others, like George V. Achilles, criticized the rehabilitative focus. Achilles reviewed a thousand cases and concluded the farms were wasteful, preferring hard time in isolation at the Caroline Islands, and life imprisonment for repeat offenders.[133] Another hard-liner advocated sterilization for addicts.[134]

The farms' duality of punishment and rehabilitation caused practical problems. Undercover operations sought violations. Sometimes a small fraction of volunteer candidates would enroll, prospective patients had trouble paying, and poor offenders opted for jail to avoid the narcotics farm fee. Anslinger also found narcotics agents luring addicts into assisting enforcement efforts with promises of treatment, a practice he forbade.[135] Confusion arose as to the narcotics farms' purpose and structure. The press labored to dispel the myth that the farm actually cultivated narcotics. Surgeon General Hugh S. Cumming wanted a name change to avoid the connotation.[136] Its jurisdictional complexity created bureaucratic confusion.[137] Anslinger repeatedly informed members of the public that the narcotics farms were under the Public Health Service's jurisdiction.[138] Sometimes narcotics agents accidently sent patients to the narcotics farm.[139] Middlebrooks circulated a reminder that the rules mandated deference to the Public Health Service.[140] Officials hoping for special favors ran into stifling paperwork.[141]

Conceivably, the narcotics farms' greatest legacy was making drugs a federally legible issue. Addicts were defined by habitual use of opium, cocaine, marijuana, or peyote. By including marijuana, the narcotics farms signaled a national recognition of illicit drugs broader than federal criminal law.

MAKING A FEDERAL CASE OUT OF MARIJUANA

In 1936 Anslinger faced major hurdles, and yet the ingredients were present for an unprecedented expansion of national drug enforcement. That year Anslinger failed to convince the nations at the Illicit Trafficking Convention to ratify an international opium prohibition.[142] New Dealers meanwhile contrived a new scheme to destroy his agency. But diplomatic experience, innovations in federalism, and ambitious policy goals would soon secure Anslinger's role in the administration once and for all. Morgenthau applauded Roosevelt's executive order targeting the narcotics trade.[143] The Treasury secretary reportedly attributed to narcotics "greater importance than . . . any other laws" under his jurisdiction.[144] The Treasury Department had pushed the boundaries of taxation power in drug control, and thanks to the narcotics farms marijuana was a nationally legible subject.

These resonances once again saved Anslinger's office, this time through an inflorescence of national power. The immediate threat was another reorganization scheme. New Deal lion Robert L. Doughton—the House Ways and Means chairman who introduced the National Firearms Act and shepherded Social Security to passage—now aimed his influence toward destroying Anslinger's Bureau. He sponsored H.R. 10586 to bring the Bureau along with the Treasury's Alcohol Tax Unit, Internal Revenue Bureau, and Customs enforcement, into the fold of the Secret Service.[145] Morgenthau's support of the idea suggested the serious threat to Anslinger's power.[146] Anslinger and his allies again brandished treaty obligations against reorganization. But now they had a new menace du jour—marijuana use nationwide—which ultimately united Anslinger and Doughton in the most significant constitutional rupture in drug policing.

The reorganization legislation had many detractors. The National Woman's Christian Temperance Union and the Federation of Women's Clubs voiced their opposition.[147] Among the industry voices protesting the change was the American Pharmaceutical Association.[148] A representative from the Washington Association of Retail Druggists called it a "potential danger to the pharmacists."[149] Anslinger's allies pushed to remove his Bureau from Doughton's reorganization bill.[150] The usual suspects made the usual arguments: reorganization would violate the 1931 Geneva mandate, embarrass America before the League of Nations, and undermine relations with the medical profession.[151] The WNDA railed against H.R. 10856.[152] An internal letter warned about national humiliation and undercutting the "structure thus far erected for international control."[153] Hobson directly wrote Doughton, stressing treaty obligations and the Uniform Narcotic Act and asking for a chance to voice opposition.[154] In March Hobson lobbied the president and warned that it would "do violence to the cause of humanity against its deadliest enemy" and "strike down the historical leadership of America . . . the very soul of humanity's warfare against this enemy."[155]

But now the Narcotics Bureau's partisans had new ammunition—marijuana. A February circular warned that this "dangerous drug" had only "recently . . . attracted wide attention," and the Narcotics Bureau needed to balance enforcement and "legitimate business interests."[156] That same month publisher Charles E. Tuttle identified the Doughton Bill as an obstacle in facing this "especially menacing" scourge.[157]

In April an illustrious international audience took up the issue. The Mayflower Hotel in Washington, D.C., hosted a celebration of the anniversary of the 1931 Geneva Convention on narcotics.[158] Delegates represented the Irish Free State, the Minister of Yugoslavia, the Italian Embassy, Lithuania, and everything ranging from Europe's totalitarian right to the US New Deal's left. Nazi ambassador Hans Luther touted Germany's ratification of the Opium Conventions and creation of "an official control office . . . to concentrate all endeavors" against drug abuse. America's political spectrum was well represented; J. Edgar Hoover sent a message and pro-labor Democrat Robert Wagner "most heartily" wished "every success" to the WNDA. The executive secretary of the National Education Association affirmed his group's devotion to this cause of "democratic civilization." Speaker of the House Jo Byrns stressed that "treaties" and "international cooperation" were "absolutely necessary, but "national legislation and regulations" were needed, while recognizing that the "dual system of government" required that "domestic police power" remain "under the control of the individual states."[159]

The big new agenda item was the "menace of marijuana." American Federation of Labor president William Green condemned nefarious dealers who "hook even our school children with their destructive Marijuana cigarettes, with heroin and other powerful drugs." He announced "organized labor can be enlisted 100% in the fight against dope" and would give Hobson its "fullest cooperation." Mrs. Hamilton Wright urged "wholehearted cooperation" for this international problem. She praised the twenty-nine states that passed Uniform laws and urged that "all states and communities should act IMMEDIATELY" against marijuana.[160]

Beyond the conference, marijuana now appeared to transcend local concern. Officials fretted about Mexican imports.[161] One woman worried about the "invasion" reaching "Milwaukee High Schools" and distressing rumors "that reputable tobacco companies" would nationally market pot.[162] The National Police Academy was warning about cannabis.[163] Marijuana abuse was undercutting national security and military morale. Navy sailors were indulging in it, soldiers on the coast smoked, and military police in Hawaii found enlisted troops carrying it.[164] By 1936 most states banned marijuana but its enduring attraction was hard to overlook. One man in Mississippi had gone from writing Anslinger to offer his services in suppressing it despite being unsure it was illegal, to embracing the drug's "sublime influence" three years later, boasting that "no act of man or god can displace" this plant that made life a "[Garden] of Paradise."[165]

National efforts to encourage state bans sometimes invited mixed messages. One mother told Eleanor Roosevelt that marijuana ruined her son's life.[166] Anslinger could point to *American Magazine*'s famous issue "Marijuana: Assassin of Youth." In a hearing he told Pennsylvania senator James Davis that "one cigarette" could give the user a "homicidal mania, probably to kill his brother."[167] Officials blamed marijuana for vicious crimes, including child rape.[168] But other authorities were more skeptical, including a Narcotics Bureau official who thought it comparable to tobacco, coffee, and tea.[169] One doctor warned that a strict law might harass physicians.[170] Some psychiatrists, in order to counter the criminal defense of incompetence, ironically insisted that marijuana did not cloud moral judgment.[171]

Regardless of jurisdictional messiness or mixed messages, constitutional tradition so far kept the marijuana issue with the states. In late 1936 the WNDA planned a new Uniform law campaign updated to include marijuana.[172] Collaboration with the states remained a powerful argument for maintaining the national infrastructure.

National marijuana prohibition, however, would go further to secure the Narcotics Bureau. Yet even war-on-crime federalism, at least as so far developed, would not legitimize an outright national ban. In 1935 the Narcotics Bureau in fact opposed two bills to extend interstate and foreign commerce powers to marijuana transportation bans.[173] In early 1936 Anslinger met with a Columbia professor along with officials from the State Department, the League of Nations, and the Foreign Policy Association, to discuss "every angle" for a ban. The interstate commerce clause seemed insufficient. They considered *Missouri v. Holland*, a 1920 Supreme Court case affirming the 1918 Migratory Bird Treaty Act against a Tenth Amendment challenge, pondering smuggling authority under treaties with Canada and Mexico. They held that regulation would have to accommodate the medical industry, who despite a "small medical need for marijuana" agreed to do without.[174] But Anslinger had served New Deal war-on-crime federalism, and it now returned the favor. Cummings's

1934 National Firearms Act became the legislative model.[175] Congress still wondered if regulation, without a taxation rationale, was legitimate, and Anslinger himself doubted the constitutionality.[176] At congressional hearings, he nevertheless eagerly emphasized interstate marijuana flow.[177]

Global-mindedness had protected Anslinger's job and elevated the marijuana issue—but it was New Deal constitutionalism that ultimately gave the Narcotics Bureau long-term stability.[178] Indeed, it was Robert Doughton, who had introduced H.R. 6906, the Marihuana Tax Act, and now relayed the "unanimous" support of the committee. Forty-one states had banned marijuana, and now the federal law passed with a unanimous voice vote. Doughton began 1936 aiming to scrap Anslinger's Narcotics Bureau and ended 1937 with its most consequential mandate for enduring power—far beyond Anslinger's justifiable hopes.[179]

As with alcohol, marijuana prohibition combined federal and state enforcement—but this time the cooperation would be amicable for many years. In the Act's first three months federal officials identified 250 violations, 221 seizures, and 223 arrests. Federal and state officials confiscated 6,401 marijuana cigarettes, 667 pounds of dried marijuana, 33.5 pounds of seeds, and 70,000 plants.[180] In the first conviction, Denver judge J. Foster Symes sentenced Sam Caldwell to four years in a penitentiary. He condemned marijuana as "the worst of all narcotics—far worse than the use of morphine or cocaine." It turned men into "beasts." The judge had "no sympathy" for dealers and looked forward to giving "the heaviest penalties."[181]

As national narcotics officers coordinated with police departments, federal scrutiny of petty details underscored its unprecedented reach. Anslinger intimately monitored street-level violations and even Morgenthau sometimes received such details.[182] The state apparatus devoted itself to snitching. A deputy clerk of court disclosed that he was once in a band in Peoria, Illinois, where people smoked pot.[183] Undercover agent John H. Orth reported on those he lived among over a prolonged period, frequently depicting smokers as benign. A "Puerto Rican woman, about 22 years of age" became "very hungry" and ate "double the amount of the normal person" when smoking. A young white man who enjoyed the drug thought himself a great publisher. A Cuban would smoke and fall asleep in the nearest automobile, which bothered no one "except possibly the owner of the car." Orth described a forty-year-old Greek man who spoke quickly when high and a "group of colored men" who smoked "several" joints each, then "appeared to be happy and laughing at the stories told" while playing pool, which did "not seriously annoy anyone else."[184] Federal marijuana enforcement eventually scaled up and became impersonal, but for now enforcers took interest in subjects they often knew as harmless.

The federal and state governments never approached full enforcement. Perhaps the relatively fringe usage of marijuana, and its benign effects, initially made the failures to stop it less conspicuous than with alcohol. Early on officials doubted the drug's severity. Edward A. Murphy reported giddy and restless users, found the withdrawal symptoms almost undetectable, and pondered whether alcohol drinkers had more problems.[185] Others suggested that the propaganda films exaggerated effects "to make lots of money."[186]

On the edge of policy consciousness, the constitutional revolution also provoked little legal scrutiny. Despite long-standing constitutional doubts, Anslinger embraced legal positivism after the ban passed. In response to charges of sensationalist propaganda, Anslinger noted that all forty-eight states agreed with him and that Congress made it illegal. The League of Nations Committee of Experts moreover associated marijuana with "murder, brutal assault and other crimes of violence," and Egyptian authorities reported an epidemic in the hospitals.[187] In 1938 Anslinger credited enforcement for reducing the number of addicts to about 50,000 and suggested that more personnel could wipe out marijuana in Minnesota.[188] Critics note Anslinger's about-face on the ban, but once the New Deal state embraced the war on marijuana, his place was secure.[189]

Anslinger did not have to twist the liberals' arms. Marijuana was the common cause that bound him to Doughton, to the narcotics farms, to the New Deal war on crime. Within the administration he was a hard-liner on alcohol, but Anslinger was never really an aberration on other controlled substances. Indeed, Anslinger sometimes recommended pardons for drug offenses.[190] Roosevelt, on the other hand, generally resisted clemency. He considered drug crimes "the worst of all crimes except murder," and perhaps even "more severe," going beyond the taking of "the life of a fellow human being" to destroy "the mind of the individual and make his future life intolerable for the good of his own soul."[191] While murder was and has remained primarily a state issue, drugs were threatening enough to invite one of the New Deal's greatest and most enduring expansions of federal power.

ANSLINGER MAINTAINED THAT DRUG CONTROL was not exclusively an enforcement issue, but the New Deal made punishment the norm. This was not entirely by design. In 1939 Assistant Surgeon General Lawrence Kolb called addiction "an evil that has been with us always" and conceded that although addicts were usually "unstable neurotic or psychopathic people," many addicts lived "normal, useful lives." Kolb supported Lexington's narcotics farm and lamented the thousands of addicts in prison "where their real needs were neglected." Marijuana, however, was especially "harmful when continually taken," even if it was milder than most drugs when used moderately.[192] Anslinger and Kolb agreed that punishment was inappropriate and often tragic, but Kolb argued that the "extensive machinery" needed to sort them out did not exist.[193]

With marijuana, what began as a therapeutic interest of the national narcotics farms became a program of criminalization. More generally, drugs marked the future of federal policing under the modern liberal state. Alcohol Tax Unit employees envied the job security of their Narcotics counterparts, who enjoyed Civil Service protections. In March 1938, Chicago alcohol enforcers lobbied the president directly for permanent Civil Service status, but the Treasury and Civil Service Commission recommended against the change. The agents had come through the Works Progress Administration and never navigated the competitive Civil Service procedure. Denied civil service, alcohol agents faced rumors of Treasury reorganization. The Reorganization Plan No. III, ratified in April 1940, abolished the office of the Federal Alcohol Administration.[194] Marijuana had saved Anslinger's Bureau; no such blessing appeared for alcohol control. By 1940, Treasury enforcement yielded average sentences of around 700 days for drugs, about twice as long as alcohol penalties.[195]

Anslinger's 1930s activities unfolded in parallel and in concert with Roosevelt's war on crime. Despite partisan divisions, his usefulness to liberal plans saved his job and bureau multiple times. The New Deal state's perfection of Treasury machinery—its weaponization of taxation, cocaine regulation, and narcotics farms—complemented Anslinger's own work. His global-mindedness and constitutional innovations made him an indispensable member of the war-on-crime coalition, and in the end the New Deal's revolutionary constitutionalism reciprocated. The drug war would shape America's destiny. In January 1942 a narcotics official in Alabama mused about stricter drug penalties, now that the state health official J. N. Baker, who obstructed the Uniform Narcotic Act, had died.[196] The Deep South, long resistant to federal encroachment, would become an enthusiastic partner in federal drug policy. Unlike alcohol prohibition's upside-down federalism, the supercharged war-on-drugs federalism bound federal and state power in longer-term harmony. The limiting factors would be politics and sheer carceral state capacity, both of which would soon accommodate drug enforcement beyond Anslinger's wildest imagination.

CHAPTER 7

SOUTHERN STRATEGIES

In February 1938 Walter White, secretary of the National Association for the Advancement of Colored People (NAACP), sent an anguished letter to Nebraska senator George W. Norris. Norris's speech opposing a federal anti-lynching law was a "most painful blow" for White. The senator's otherwise progressive record compounded the betrayal.[1] A prohibitionist who nevertheless broke with his Republican Party to support Al Smith, Roosevelt, and the New Deal, Norris changed his affiliation to independent in 1936.[2] Now he and White reenacted a conflict that reached back from the nineteenth-century rise of national power: Norris warned that the anti-lynching law would awaken "the slumbering beast of the Reconstruction period"—reviving acrimonious divisions between North and South, Black and white. The South was, according to Norris, handling racial difficulties "magnificently" on its own. But for White, lynching proved that the "beast of race hatred" had never even "taken a cat-nap," as millions of Black and white Americans endured a "state of terror" that made the "Reconstruction period" seem "almost like a pink tea." For White the terror surpassed the "symbol" of lynching and undermined basic living conditions and the welfare liberalism shared by White and Norris, whose Tennessee Valley Authority electrified the upper South. While admiring the TVA, White observed that a man found little security in an "electronically lighted home" if he could be seized "as easily as from a cabin lighted by candles and burned to death."[3]

The split between White and Norris revealed deep tensions in New Deal liberalism's relationship to race and federal power. In the middle third of the twentieth century, the Democratic coalition's strongest supporters included white southerners and, increasingly, Black Americans, who energized national state building with ultimately incompatible civil rights goals. If in future generations Republicans pursued a "southern strategy" of luring traditionally Democratic white voters, an earlier southern strategy was the Democrats' challenge to maintain this voter base while gaining the support of Black citizens and civil rights activists. This strategy largely succeeded for decades, bringing the most formidable coalition in twentieth-century politics behind the growth and modernization of government.

Facilitating this unlikely coalition was the unique moment when America's governing structure and ideological formations were undergoing transformation, allowing different groups to harbor conflicting hopes about the future while cooperating in the present. In considering the white South's reclamation of influence and trust in the federal government, historians have stressed the theme of national "reunion"—an interregional detente starting around the early twentieth century that included a de-emphasis of the racial motivations behind southern secession, a whitewashed revisionism of Reconstruction, a northern neglect of Black civil rights, an exuberant unity behind imperialism, and the elevation of such southern Democrats as Woodrow Wilson to the pantheon of respectable progressivism.[4] A possible framing of the Democratic Party's puzzle from the 1930s onward is the necessity to maintain that national camaraderie of reunion to tame white reaction while gesturing toward the promise of Reconstruction to ensure Black and liberal support.

Common explanations stress economic and labor policy as assuaging these conflicting factions, and sometimes relate this delicate balancing to the restructuring of federalism, after which intensifying civil rights enforcement eventually guided the coalition's collapse.[5] Scholars have recognized the anti-lynching cause as a major challenge for civil rights activism, liberal politics, and constitutional modernization.[6] While many white supremacists long saw lynching as a method of law enforcement, even some racist state modernizers often saw mob violence as a threat to a more orderly form of social discipline. In the longer term, national law enforcement would become a significant tool in civil rights enforcement. Attorney General Frank Murphy's Civil Liberties Unit, which opened in 1939, showed interest in reviving the promises of Reconstruction, and the commitment would grow more serious in the 1940s and beyond.[7] The Justice Department and even J. Edgar Hoover's FBI would pursue cases of police misconduct, peonage violations, lynching, and voting suppression with greater rigor.[8] Less emphasized is how intimately this political story interweaved with the New Deal war on crime even through the earlier 1930s, and the crucial role of Black activists in reforming federalism and liberalism.[9] Along these lines, war-on-crime federalism allowed white supremacists and Black liberationists to maintain incompatible visions for the rising liberal state, while building federal and state enforcement power. Keeping southern Democrats in the coalition relied on federal support for local law and order, including its apartheid. Simultaneously, Black activists finally saw hints that the federal government would eventually vindicate civil rights against state-level oppression and local complicity in anti-Black lawlessness. New Deal sensibilities moving down the registers of government persuaded civil rights hopefuls that even local enforcers would sometimes protect them. In short, for white southerners federal sponsorship of local policing legitimated the national war on crime; for Black Americans, the national war on crime offered some evidence of legitimate local policing.

Some reassuring trends distinct from the New Deal were unfolding in the early 1930s. The unquestionably important Scottsboro cases shaped the following decades of jurisprudence touching on Black subjugation. But the federal judiciary itself offered no overdetermined trajectory for civil rights. In the shadow of Scottsboro, law enforcement and activists adjusted to shape the policy worlds they inhabited. The cases' exposure of coerced confessions, threats of mob law, and a tainted trial and jury pool fueled reform efforts against racial lawlessness—national activism against lynching and police brutality—and for strengthened due process protections. While New Deal crime warriors favored streamlining criminal procedure, it was thanks to these cases that the bare-bones protections that promised to make the system less nakedly racist would become part of the liberal consensus. Yet these cases also revealed the limits of federal action against racist local oppression. They moreover reinforced hope in the reformability of law enforcement power that would prove an unreliable ally at best. The overturning of egregious injustices encouraged the NAACP to focus on cases it deemed most worthy and viable.[10] The administration's uncertain posture toward federal jurisprudence meanwhile provided opportunities for opposing constituencies to project their hopes onto the future of the New Deal state.

During Jim Crow, Black Americans made momentous decisions, as individuals and in social movements, in navigating the space between openly racist law enforcement and the terror of white lawlessness. Traversing this world sometimes meant resistance and sometimes collaboration. Scholars have long described Black activism against lynching and have recently shown how Black Americans worked with policing to pursue community ends and help shape social narratives.[11] Beyond having a defensive or reactive posture, Black activists in the New Deal era pushed the criminal system toward a more inclusive future. From picketing Cummings's 1934 crime conference to exposing contradictions in the war on crime, the NAACP redefined criminal justice as a civil rights issue and a key venue for vindicating Reconstruction. Over time the reconstructed government would yet sustain racial tensions. Its reformed liberalism would thrive on its newly reconstituted paradox: it would be an officially colorblind, nonpartisan, patriotic, and ecumenical effort to finally confront some of the worst anti-Black lawlessness—but simultaneously it would accommodate the radical, egalitarian, left-leaning Democratic project that unified workers' rights, civil rights, and law and order. The NAACP's own southern strategy would also contribute to the aspirations of liberalism and the structural transformations of the law-and-order state.

THE CRUEL LIMITS OF FEDERAL LAW

Amid the heated anti-crime rhetoric in 1933, white crime warriors sought the NAACP's blessing. In September the US Flag Association asked Walter White to attend a National Crime Conference, calling the crime crisis as severe as any since the Great War.[12] NAACP leaders would willingly join, provided the crisis would be construed broadly to include the racist lawlessness inside and outside legal institutions. Along with White the NAACP's assistant secretary Roy Wilkins and lawyers Thurgood Marshall and Charles Houston aimed to make civil rights legible as law and order. White supremacy made a mockery of law, and federal failures to stamp out racist lawlessness in the former Confederacy endangered lawful liberty everywhere.

From the end of Reconstruction until recently, Black Americans had little reason to trust federal enforcement much more than southern institutions. Now the volatility of federalism allowed the NAACP to consider jurisdictional questions strategically. Although Scottsboro made a robust federal role appear promising, sometimes northern state governments still seemed preferable. In a 1933 murder case Virginia sought extradition of George Crawford from Massachusetts, inviting questions of whether a state should depend on federal constitutional guarantees to apprehend fugitives while flouting such guarantees to due process. Crawford insisted that he was in Boston during the crime.[13] But the NAACP relied on federalism, not innocence, arguing that a state "cannot appeal to and nullify the constitution at the same time." The NAACP appealed to "patriotic New Englander[s]" to resurrect the antebellum spirit of personal liberty protections against fugitive-slave authority: "Boston citizens" had a new "opportunity to follow in the footsteps of William Lloyd Garrison, Wendell Phillips," and the "Abolitionists that made New England famous throughout the entire world."[14] The NAACP marshalled legal arguments from the post–Civil War constitutional tradition—the Fourteenth Amendment, the *Slaughterhouse Cases,* and *Ex parte Virginia.* In addition to channeling these memories, the on-the-ground maneuvering to protect Crawford seemed tactically quaint. Their lawyer, with news of an impending rendition warrant, scrambled throughout the morning to stay ahead of the federal agent, shopping jurisdictions for a habeas corpus writ without time to spare.[15]

Extradition cases were an exception.[16] In the main the post-Scottsboro NAACP championed federal intervention against private and state lawlessness. The glaring evil was lynching. For decades mob vengeance, primarily and increasingly targeting Black Americans, was attributed to, if not always excused by, "growing distrust in the promptness and efficiency of the law." After years of slightly subsiding, lynching surged in 1933 and 1934, as federal anti-crime rhetoric also swelled. Most Americans abstractly opposed lynching and supported government action. By early 1934, Alabama, Indiana, Kansas, Kentucky, Virginia, and North Carolina banned lynching as a specific crime.[17] Old Right journalist H. L. Mencken, whose piece "The New Deal Constitution" lambasted Roosevelt and even satirized his abuse of "due process," nevertheless supported a federal response to lynching.[18]

In such an atmosphere New Deal leadership was strikingly ambivalent. Southern senate Democrats mostly succeeded in resisting federal interference throughout the decade. But against this reactionary posture liberals emitted flashes of hope. In late 1933 Walter White, having asked Roosevelt for an "an emphatic pronouncement . . . against mob law," thanked him for a "magnificent and unequivocal condemnation of lynching," appreciated by "twelve million negroes and many millions of whites." Colorado senator Edward Costigan, whose switch to the Democratic Party marked larger trends in partisan realignment, co-sponsored an anti-lynching bill with pro-labor senator Robert Wagner, decrying mob threats to "orderly justice." He predicted "the end of free government on this continent" if "such blind and menacing lawlessness" was tolerated.[19] One activist resolution condemned lynching as a "direct challenge to governmental authority" and a "disgrace to our American civilization."[20] A supporter of the bill called it "an attempt to end barbarism in America." Eleanor Roosevelt arranged discussions between the president and an anti-lynching delegation.[21] The Democrats thus gave some hope, year by year, that they would ultimately protect Black Americans' rights. To be sure, disappointments punctuated the gestures. The First Lady once warned that the NAACP would dislike Roosevelt's current thinking, while suggesting he might change his mind.[22] But even the discourse signaled a new political importance of Black Americans, who were abandoning the Party of Lincoln.[23] Over time anti-lynching politics ironically came to define the New Deal coalition even as one of its major constituencies opposed federal remedies.

The casting of lynching as pure lawlessness had paradoxical implications for the developing liberal coalition. NAACP activists adopted their own rhetorical war-on-crime liberalism—including familiar admonitions that law-and-order pragmatism would forestall extremist threats. In response to lynchings in Scottsboro, the NAACP warned that "The Negro . . . is going to be forced to fight back like a cornered animal" and this "rising militancy" would mean "blood shed if a halt is not called to mob murders."[24] Lynching as lawlessness even brought some credibility to southern Democratic governments. State-level efforts suggested that even southern states might counteract the worst horrors. Illinois congressman Arthur Mitchell denounced this "lawlessness peculiar to the United States" but was encouraged "that Virginia's 1928 law had stopped lynching since." As Louisiana's governor Huey Long boasted, "For 2 years . . . not one, white or black, has been lynched." His administration ensured "an observance of the law on both sides, and offered no pardon for those who took 'revenge of the law' in their hands."[25] On the other hand, lynching's lack of official legal legitimacy gave cover to federal inaction. Lynching was a private crime, illegible under the federal Constitution since the 1870s and still illegible under the War on Crime Constitution, especially under Cummings. As he revealed in his tract *Federal Justice,* Cummings was aware that Reconstruction had carried enormous stakes and also that it had "brought upon the Department of Justice tremendous criticism."[26] While his Justice Department had some concern for civil rights, it respected a federalism that deemed lynching lawlessness a local issue.[27]

In October 1934 the gruesome lynching of Claude Neal shocked many Americans into demanding federal action. As described in northern and southern newspapers and by an NAACP investigator, it was one of the most heinous racist killings in living memory. Yet while particularly monstrous, its details must have seemed familiar. Twenty-three-year-old Neal was accused of murdering Lola Cannady, a white woman whose father owned the farm they all worked in Jackson County, Florida. Neal confessed under private interrogation, signing his name with an "X," according to an FBI report decades later. After the confession the sheriff, fearing a lynching, sent Neal to Chopley, Florida; then by boat Neal was taken to Pensacola and over the border to Alabama. A white mob conspired to intercept him. Thirty cars gathered at the Brewton, Alabama, jail and forced a janitor to break Neal out. He was brought back to Mariana, the scene of Lola's death. In the morning, newspapers and the radio announced that the lynching would occur at 8 p.m.[28] A note summoned "all white folks" to bear witness.[29]

What was planned as a spectacle lynching attracted thousands. The unwieldy crowd threatened to throw the ritual into chaos. The "Committee of Six" in charge feared that a white person might get shot. The *Baltimore Sun* gave a breaking update: "Lynching Put Off for Fear of Disorder: Mob Asks Crowd to Depart So It Might Kill Negro in Peace." The "Committee of Six" was torturing Neal deep in the woods, having promised that the Cannady family would get their own chance. If the crowd thinned, the public lynching might still commence. The sheriff, satisfied things were under control, told the governor not to send troops.[30]

Fearful of the bloodthirsty crowd they invited, the "Committee of Six" themselves undertook the execution after about ten hours of torture. They sliced Neal's sides and his stomach, burned his body with red hot irons. They would hang him until within a gasp of death, bring him back to the ground and torture him more. They removed Neal's fingers and toes. A participant told an NAACP investigator that the men severed his penis and testicles, forced him to eat them, and "say he liked it."[31]

Claude Neal was dead by the time he was delivered to the Cannady family house. They had readied knives and sharpened sticks but now they could only defile his corpse. A woman plunged a butcher knife into Neal's heart. They drove cars over his body, and photos and body parts circulated as souvenirs.[32] "They done me wrong," complained Lola's father George Cannady. He was supposed to "have the first shot."[33] Neal's body dangled from a tree by the courthouse, a warning to those who challenged white rule. But the mob were unsatisfied. They tried to lynch another Black man and threatened the Black population to leave.[34] Gangs terrorized the whole town, beating Black men, women, children.[35] After the mob threatened to kill Claude's mother and aunt, destroying their property, the women were jailed without charge "for safe keeping." The lawless and racist state probably saved them from a worse fate.[36]

The Neal atrocity brought new support to anti-lynching legislation. A promised spectacle had lured thousands to watch, illustrating the broad populist support for white supremacist terror. Yet the crowd overwhelmed even the lynch mob leaders. The pretense that lynching was a necessary evil to maintain justice never seemed less credible. The NAACP tried to determine whether Neal even murdered Lola and found conflicting rumors.[37] The next year the Cannady father was sentenced to five years for attempted murder in a case that further cast doubt on the story of Lola's death. "Yes, judge, I am plumb crazy," he said.[38] But Claude's guilt or innocence could not alone make sense of the surreal horror, reported in real time by modern media. The *Cleveland Call and Post* labeled the killing "unbelievable, ghastly, grisly, nauseating bestiality, probably unequalled in all the history of lynching."[39] The NAACP called it "one of the two or three most horrible lynchings in the history of America or the world."[40]

It was indeed a monstrosity. But what made it especially conspicuous was the timing. Its instantaneous press coverage, a confluence of radio modernity and medieval barbarism, happened a month and a half before Cummings's crime conference. Neal's death exposed the lie in the war on crime and its federalism. Despite New Deal promises of perfected enforcement, the NAACP credibly decried the "complete failure of the state and county machinery."[41] This lynching appeared ripe for federal action under early 1930s statutes. Neal was abducted across state lines for the purpose of murder. Royal Copeland, co-author of an amendment to expand the Lindbergh law, thought his legislation applied to the Neal kidnapping. William Pickens noted that if Neal's killers escaped justice, the federal government should "apologize to the relatives of the Dillingers and the Floyds, and to dismiss all pending cases against petty criminals of the kind." The NAACP prepared a comprehensive argument for using the Lindbergh law, citing Keenan's insights and the South's inability to police itself even if it wanted to.[42] Walter White explained to Cummings that federal power must extend to such crimes when so conspicuously "advertised twelve hours in advance." The NAACP emphasized that in Roosevelt's twenty-one months in office, mob violence claimed forty-five lives.[43]

The virtual exclusion of the NAACP and lynching from Cummings's December conference underscored the hopes and limitations of New Deal law and order. Keenan seemingly gave activists the runaround when they asked to be included. NAACP officials decided to picket. Their approach underscored a paradox of civil rights liberalism—it was both racially neutral and racially conscious. Sometimes framing lynching as a colorblind question of justice, Wilkins also remarked that white allies could not see things "through our eyes." The picketers sifted through pointed slogans—"When IS Kidnaping Not Kidnaping / When Victim Is Black?"; "Cummings Bluffed by Mobs?"; "Al Capone Got 11 years / Lynchers Get Cheers"—including a description of Cummings as attorney general of three-quarters of America, and Judge Lynch as attorney general of "the rest."[44] After Roy Wilkins and three others were arrested for illegally picketing, sixty NAACP supporters and Howard University students protested, quietly standing with small signs pinned on their clothing (see Figure 7.1). The conference issued what the NAACP called an "almost meaningless resolution" against "methods of dealing with industrial conflicts and racial antagonisms" that departed from "orderly and lawful procedures."[45]

At year's end the NAACP and American Civil Liberties Union (ACLU) dispatched a memorial to the president. Signatories backed the Costigan-Wagner bill. A note from a University of Chicago academic called lynching "the most outstanding National crime."[46] Arguments situated anti-lynching legislation in the canonical Western traditions against lawlessness, and so federal action would offend neither "English law" nor the "statute of Winchester." Even Hammurabi's code "contained the germs of some of" Costigan-Wagner.[47] The memorial condemned the "killing and burning of human beings by mobs" as a "reproach upon our nation throughout the civilized world." It urged treating lynching with the federal attention kidnapping received. Northern governors and mayors, university presidents, and other civic leaders endorsed the memorial along with scattered officials from the South. It resonated with southern clergy, doctors, and academics.[48] Civil rights activists aimed to divide the South's reactionaries and liberals.

Figure 7.1   Howard University students and anti-lynching activists protest at 1934 Crime
Conference. Bettmann/Getty Images.

Changes in opinion on federal anti-lynching measures correlated with
shifting views on federalism. Some rationalized their opposition as they
called the South a backward, hopeless, essentially foreign place. Samuel K.
Wilson claimed that he had no "sympathy" for "mob violence" but that
"too much federal legislation" already existed and would miscarry in
"backward southern communities" that were "not in favor of the law."[49]
On the other hand, Georgia bishop Frederick Reese explained his own
evolving constitutional thoughts. He used to think it a "mistake to relieve the states of responsibility," but prosecutorial failures convinced him
to support federal intervention despite fears it could produce conflict.
Reese reasoned that federalism was "seriously impaired" already by federal funding to states.[50] Hypocrisies in war-on-crime federalism invited
this kind of novel argument. It was confounding, Charles Beard observed,
for congressmen to "support and vote for the recent acts thrusting federal intervention into the ordinary criminal processes of the states, and
then declare the anti-lynching bill unconstitutional."[51]

In 1935 and 1936 anti-lynching activists sharpened their constitutional arguments, mostly in ways consistent with law-and-order liberalism. An NAACP circular responded to states' rights arguments by contending that states lost sovereignty by accepting federal aid. To opponents calling the legislation a Force Bill singling out the South, the reply was the law applied everywhere and many southerners supported it. Responding to fears of unchecked rape, the rejoinder came that only a sixth of lynching victims were accused of rape—as if to concede some of the premise legitimating vigilantism against serious crimes. Some argued that the bill financially penalized good people in lawless counties, and the circular's response was they needed more incentive to press reform. And while others argued that states still mostly managed gangster crimes, lynching meant "the complete breakdown of law enforcement machinery" and undermined "the authority of the State and the United States." Lynching meant "open anarchy."[52]

Cummings, for all his constitutional flexibility, stubbornly rejected such arguments. His input was valued—Costigan solicited his appearance before the Senate Committee on Lynching—but his expertise perhaps served as cover for inaction.[53] In rhetoric mirroring Cummings's self-conscious historical sensibility, anti-lynching law advocates expressly reflected on the historic constitutional moment. In the wake of Scottsboro, it was time to act.[54] But Cummings's doubts frustrated civil rights hopefuls. After the lynching of Elwood Higginbotham in Oxford, Mississippi, Walter White lobbied the president, who sympathized but punted the question to Cummings.[55] The attorney general remained unmoved on the constitutional question.

Putting aside new legislation, Walter White continued to press Cummings on using kidnapping statutes for interstate lynchings. He asked for "the theory of law." While the NAACP did not oppose "activities against banditry or murder," he questioned whether it was worse to "steal from banks" than to "steal the body of a human being for the purpose of putting it to death without authority of law."[56] In 1936 the Supreme Court decided *Arthur Gooch v. United States,* arising from a nondeadly interstate kidnapping of two police officers. The Court interpreted the Federal Kidnapping Act to include "material benefit" other than "ransom or reward." In reference to the "still broader construction of the statute urged in some quarters" to include "interstate abductions for the purpose of murder," Cummings nevertheless concluded that the Court's opinion did not implicate lynchings.[57] Also sharing his constitutional reasoning with a receptive Roger Baldwin,[58] White protested Cummings's standard. "Are officers of the law offered the protection of the Department of Justice while private citizens are denied this protection?" White asked Cummings. To White it appeared that the "Department of Justice protects white persons who escape a murderous assault while it ignores a Negro citizen who is killed."[59]

Roosevelt's first term continued giving hopeful signs. Americans petitioned for federal help against anti-Black discrimination laws concerning a movie theater in Chester, Illinois.[60] The administration considered placing in the federal judiciary Black Americans, such as James A. Cobb.[61] The Justice Department was especially open to Black judges on an "experiment[al]" basis, such as in the Virgin Islands.[62] But Black activists were frustrated on the lynching issue. By the mid-1930s the demand for action became a plea for securing democracy. White met with Roosevelt in July 1936 and discussed the "broad issues dealing with lawlessness," including the 10 percent of Americans with "tendencies toward fascism." Since Costigan-Wagner would not pass, they sought to "integrate that crime" of lynching with "the whole subject of lawlessness," including through a Senate investigation. Roosevelt, aware of the "powerful . . . Negro vote" and Republicans' "vigorous effort" to win it back, suggested that the NAACP cynically accept money that Republicans were spending on the effort: "We are all talking about sharing the wealth—my advice is to take the money and vote for [my] administration." In 1936 the NAACP asked both parties to include anti-lynching planks, along with calls for enfranchisement, "economic and educational justice," and "legal rights" in court.[63] Roosevelt's equivocation on lynching proved electorally shrewd, just as in 1934. The Democrats won a growing share of Black voters without alienating their white southern base.

LIBERALISM AGAINST ANTI-BLACK LAWLESSNESS

Outside lynching, the NAACP combatted local lawlessness—especially at the hands of officials—and sought redress from all levels of government. But where there was opportunity there was also disappointment.

Just as white supremacy thrived in the civil-rights vacuum between national and state power, state governments hosted similar dynamics. The
ambiguities of jurisdictional pluralism frustrated Charles Houston when
a Missouri official wrote that the state government had no "function . . .
to investigate and prosecute crimes committed in the various counties."[64]
And yet the NAACP committed itself to refining law and order toward
more racially just ends, an undertaking that brought the organization and
the liberal state closer together in vision.

Scottsboro brought attention to the possibilities and urgency of stem-
ming state oppression of Black Americans. This goal conspired with
Depression-era austerity and anti-lynching campaigns to narrow the
NAACP's focus on criminal cases. Anti-lynching activism reinforced a
hopeful posture toward the criminal justice state's future while consuming
limited resources. Energy expended to direct enforcement power against
white lawlessness came at the expense involved in helping victims of legal
repression.[65] Choosing worthy causes, in both its strategic and ethical dimensions, nurtured a pragmatic liberalism. In its criminal defenses, the
NAACP privileged the seemingly innocent over the seemingly guilty,
blatant racism over less provable disparities, and unambiguous constitutional violations over facially legal instances of abuse. The NAACP's
approach became vigilant against lawless oppression and strategically
narrow in defining racism, while it willingly pursued avenues of favor and
patronage to ease injustice in marginal cases. Despite its strategic limitations and long-term frustrations, the NAACP's liberalism was not so
humble given the trajectory of racialized law since the Civil War. It aimed
to fulfill Reconstruction's promise of what the law could achieve.

By working to affirm the dignity of legal process, the NAACP sometimes rejected cases where lower courts had followed the law's letter or
where defense counsel appeared competent. When a "reputable Negro
Attorney in Baltimore," whom Marshall knew personally, had defended
Richard Hammond, Marshall found the case suboptimal for NAACP
consideration.[66] This emphasis on proper procedure sometimes produced
a paradox where ideal cases resulted when legal counsel was incompetent but not too incompetent. As in other modern litigation, the order of
operations mattered. Where complaints had not been raised at the proper
time, the NAACP saw little prospect for redress.[67] Houston reminded a
Texas lawyer that the Supreme Court would not consider constitutional

issues that attorneys failed to raise during state proceedings. In addition, cases had to show that jury exclusion was "solely because of race."[68]

The magnitude of injustice made the NAACP's process of rejecting cases especially bitter. "To tell the truth," Wilkins lamented, "we haven't the money to fight any kind of case, but there are some what we mightn't refuse."[69] Houston regretted not rescuing "every Negro who is threatened with injustice."[70] But scarcity of resources hardened the criteria for worthwhile cases.[71] In the early Depression the NAACP refused to defend people who were already imprisoned.[72] By the mid-1930s the criteria stressed injustice based "solely because of [a defendant's] color" with there being at stake "some fundamental citizenship right of colored people."[73] In November 1936 the assistant special counsel named two criteria: clear unjust "discrimination based on race or color" *and* the potential to "set a precedent for the protection of Negroes as a group."[74] Evidence of Black exclusion from juries specifically because they were Black was the most fruitful angle. Anything that elicited specific precedents in *Norris v. Alabama* was promising.[75] Unfortunately, victims of court injustice had a difficult case in jurisdictions where "Negroes have served on juries in recent years."[76] Sometimes racist enforcement was too subtle, particularly when disparities appeared to result from inequities in arrest patterns.[77] In February 1936 Charles Houston had emphasized a third criterion: innocence. The NAACP could not "defend every colored person who gets in trouble," only those appearing "innocent" and "threatened with persecution on account of race or color."[78] In one extradition case, a Mrs. Willie Fleetwood faced trial for killing a Black man. Houston explained that without "some evidence of race discrimination" and "evidence of oppression" the NAACP would not "interfere in cases of Negroes against Negroes."[79] By the middle of World War II, Marshall routinized these criteria: innocence, injustice based clearly on race or color, and the "possibility of establishing precedent."[80]

Forced to follow narrow criteria, NAACP officials vented their frustrations. Under financial strain their priorities toughened their stance toward Black Americans they regarded unhelpful. Houston placed some blame on Black Americans "and their friends" who only gave a combined $50,000 a year, noting that most "who complain loudest when we do not help them were never members of the Association before they got in trouble."[81] He later complained of those who "spend money for their pleasures, but not for their rights."[82] NAACP officials had the least patience for the seemingly guilty. One NAACP lawyer said that the extensive criminal record of one man, including "offenses involving sexual perversion," rendered his case and that of his less experienced accomplice "beneath the dignity of the principles of the N.A.A.C.P."[83]

But some cases compelled the NAACP to stretch its own criteria and accommodate strategies outside formalistic exercises. Occasionally the NAACP offered small sums to support cases in which they did not "actively participate."[84] Between successful challenges and total defeat lay a middle ground, sometimes through patrimony and favor. Mercy appeared through negotiation and compromise. One client pleaded guilty for a life sentence, figuring that at his age any likely lesser punishment "would amount to a life sentence in effect." He would have "more freedom" in a penitentiary than waiting "in a jail cell." His lawyer wanted reassurance that "we made a trade to his advantage."[85] The NAACP found ways to offer support outside formal avenues, suggesting clemency for a seemingly guilty man because in Maryland the prejudicial "death penalty seems to be for Negroes alone."[86] But the NAACP observed limits to seeking mercy at the edges of formal process. One lawyer in Tampa recommended that his defendant strategically plead guilty, hoping for relief from the pardon board. An innocent verdict, he feared, could incite lynching. The NAACP could not endorse the approach, instead encouraging the governor to protect against lynching threats.[87] Such pleas offered opportunities to work with southern officials, especially Democratic politicians. The NAACP asked governors for help in sympathetic cases even absent innocence or clear-cut racism.[88] They relied on state governments and state militia to guard against mob violence. This encouraging intermittent contact with Democratic governors in the South broadened the imagined horizons of policing in a racialized society.[89]

Assorted cases encouraged the NAACP's hopes in the efficacy of the criminal justice system. Committing to a case required such hope. The organization sought official penalties for public deprivations of civil rights. The occasional conviction of a particularly egregious police officer encouraged optimism. In 1939 one Alabama police officer was found guilty of abuse. The Personnel Board of Jefferson County, Alabama, touted its vigilance against lawlessness: "This Board does not approve of police officers attempting to administer punishment to law violators. Such persons should be placed under arrest."[90] Sometimes criminal processes seemed the only means for policing bad counsel. Houston's only advice to a man who pleaded guilty to rape was to consult the "attorney general of the state, bringing charges against your lawyer."[91]

The NAACP also recognized that some Black Americans saw law enforcement as protection, however imperfect, against private tormenters. Black Americans asked the NAACP for help finding assailants, both Black and white. One man requested assistance against a "Chicago gangster that killed" his brother who was "defended by powerful Negro business men in Atlanta."[92] After a "group of Italians" beat a Black man nearly to death, Wilkins was asked for help getting an investigator to "see that the Italians are punished as the police seemed very hostile to the Negro."[93] Threats of white mobs reinforced NAACP efforts to reach out to local government seeking protection. When a few hundred whites threatened two Black youth, North Carolina's governor received pleas for protection.[94] The NAACP called for prosecution and punishment after a Black worker was beaten in Tampa.[95]

At the same time, local enforcement vagaries foreshadowed a new reckoning of jurisdiction. Vagrancy skirmishes had the potential to develop into state-level oppression. In Maryland, after the shooting of a Black cannery worker who said, "Ah the hell with the chief of police," a riot ensued, inflicting suffering on the Black population.[96] The mayor warned unemployed Blacks to "get out of town" or be arrested for vagrancy. In the incident, law and order divided left and right. A *New York Post* piece observed that Maryland conservatives—in a "lather lately about the danger or dictatorship, the suppression of American political institutions, individual rights, States' rights and so forth"—noticeably ignored the police beating, abusing, and killing of Blacks.[97]

The Stafford Dames case encapsulated the complex and multifaceted liberalism in NAACP hopes for inclusion within the law-and-order coalition. Someone shot a Miami police officer. Dames, a Black nineteen-year-old altar boy, was trying to enter the Catholic Church where he had been a member for six years. Mistaking him as a fugitive, police shot and killed him. Police apparently planted a gun to make him look menacing. The NAACP at first responded conservatively with appeals to the party apparatus, white Floridians, and government oversight. The NAACP hoped to marginalize the police as rogue agents and turn white Americans against them. The ACLU urged a "thoroughgoing investigation" so as to avoid the "Scottsboro reputation" for Florida. Activists pressed for more state regulation of local police. The ACLU and NAACP hoped the imperfect and biased legal process might rein in the worst offenders in enforcement. William G. Fennell argued for a civil suit, regardless of the futility of its judgment, "because careless policemen deserve warning of consequences." The ACLU and NAACP were determined to find an effective criminal justice solution to a criminal justice problem. They sought to prosecute police for "criminal negligence and reckless disregard" of human life. Casting the police as lawless showed some promise even with a racially unsympathetic white populace. Anti-police sentiment from the *Miami News* indicated popular white dissatisfaction with the Dames case despite lacking particular concern for Black suffering. Judge Raleigh Petteway, running for governor, gestured toward support for criminal and civil action against the police.[98]

The failures of these official channels to offer redress emboldened activists and sharpened the radical edge of Black law-and-order liberalism. Law offices deemed Dames's death as "not necessarily malicious." Dames's father was told to drop the cause or else pursue a civil suit against the city. The police responded to activists' measured calls for justice by red-baiting. The police chief lashed out at the ACLU, an organization "90 percent communistic," for stoking Black resentments and causing "further unrest" to build another "Scottsboro Case."[99] In these years communists—including those in the Communist Party USA and affiliated southern organizations and fellow travelers—did much of the heavy lifting in civil rights activism, and opposition to civil rights often took the form of reactionary anticommunism.[100] In the longer term, liberalism would straddle the divide, programmatically anticommunist while offended by the unmeasured and crude anticommunism of the American right. Such moderation would characterize the cautious trajectory by which liberalism would accompany the civil rights struggle.

The NAACP and ACLU's determination to frame the Dames cause as opposition to rogue lawlessness, and the bureaucratic and reactionary responses to it, helped to harmonize the activists across conciliatory and radical tendencies. Their demands for justice could entertain thoroughgoing critiques of systemic inequities while demanding the modernizing state to marginalize the worst white supremacist offenders. A question was whether to treat blatant injustices as the exception to a refinable system, or as representative of structurally inexorable evils. This puzzle was especially intelligible in geographical and jurisdictional terms. Perhaps the problem was Miami, where the same police who killed Dames had committed another second-degree killing. However bad an apple Miami was, Wilkins hoped to tie the Dames case to the "general lawlessness in Florida," to show how "brutality, lynching and all that grows out of it work against all people as well as Negroes."[101] Marshall had a larger scale in mind: to identify Miami as one "example of injustice and oppression, . . . throughout the South."[102]

A related question was whether to point to such injustices to motivate all Americans based on neutral principles, or instead to mobilize the racial justice movement leftward. On the one hand, the red-baiting reaction to ACLU involvement inspired appeals to the organization's increasing emphasis on civil libertarian neutrality. Activists found reassurance in the ACLU's ecumenical approach to rights. That the ACLU would "even defend the rights of a fascist or a member of Hitler's party," and was "only interested in civil rights which should interest every citizen, white and colored," was meant to reassure Dames's father that the organization could withstand accusations of ideological opportunism. At the same time, solidarity for Dames came principally from groups that skewed Black and left-wing: Black groups like the Greater Miami Civic League, Ministerial Alliance, Negro Merchants Association, Adelphian Club, Dade County Academy of Medicine, the Miami Branch NAACP, Legal Defense Control Committee, Colored World War Veterans, Young Business Men's Club, Universal Negro Improvement Association, International Longshoremen's Association, Hodcarriers and Common Laborers' Union—and left-leaning white groups like the Miami branches of the Workers' Defense League and the Workers' Alliance of America.[103] As with other facets of the liberal struggle against lawlessness, its potency and limitations resided in its simultaneous appeal to the universal and the particular.

REUNION AND RECONSTRUCTION UNDER
WAR-ON-CRIME FEDERALISM

Many Black Americans and their allies hoped that increased oversight would spur even local law enforcement to stem white supremacist violence. Racial reactionaries had other reasons to back local policing and the federal attention it brought. While prioritizing different understandings of "lawlessness," the competing racial visions reinforced war-on-crime liberalism. Before the 1940s break toward increasing federal civil rights enforcement, later intensified by the politics of World War II and the Cold War, the distinct 1930s conditions laid a groundwork for anomalous state building.[104] New Deal crime policy managed the improbable feat of maintaining the politics of reunion while revitalizing the promise of Reconstruction. It never fully committed to combatting lynching, but the Roosevelt administration did assert jurisdiction over the southern states, against antebellum legacies of racial control, while bringing the federal and state governments closer to having monopolies on legal violence that even some southern politicians could support.

With Reconstruction's collapse, a great federal weakness was in reconciling aspirational constitutional will with legal capacity against private violence. The Justice Department's direct engagement with the Klan proved short-lived. Violence in behalf of white state sovereignty, but not under official auspices, was deemed federally illegible in 1876's *United States v. Cruikshank* decision. Private discrimination was deemed similarly untouchable in the 1883 *Civil Rights Cases*. But in the 1930s, federal policing of exceptional racist violence could accommodate state government priorities. In 1936 in the Eastern District of Arkansas, peace officer Paul Peacher faced charges for violating section 443, title 18, of the US Code, the statute against slavery, by abusing the peonage system. He had convinced the mayor that eight Black Americans were vagrants and that he had a county convict-leasing arrangement. At least some of the eight were clearly not vagrants, at least one owned a home, and Peacher had no such legal arrangement, but for twenty days he forced them to labor on his leased land. The Justice Department met with sympathetic locals, including a socialist gubernatorial candidate and representatives from the Southern Tenant Farmers Union.[105] Although Special Assistant Brian Mc-Mahon suspected the union of opportunistically raising money on the scandal, a confluence of interests among organized labor, civil rights activists, and federal enforcement produced a civil rights watershed.[106] Despite local support, Peacher was unanimously indicted.[107] Victims testified to being beaten and deprived food for days.[108] Under the judge's pressure, an initially deadlocked jury convicted Peacher on all charges, and he was sentenced to prison time, deferrable through a $3,500 fine. The Farmers Union took credit for putting pressure on Roosevelt in an election year.[109]

In convicting Peacher of slavery, the federal war on crime followed through on some of the most basic national promises of the 1860s. The *Chicago Defender* declared it a "complete victory for the Race."[110] The *Little Rock Gazette* ominously wondered what "would have happened if the federal government had not gone in?" The *Afro-American* recognized the political timing but called the conviction a "feather in the cap of slow-going" Cummings, who, after refusing to use kidnapping statutes against lynching, had perhaps finally "awakened from his slumber." With a new federal law, the paper optimistically predicted that the "federal government could wipe out lynching in one year."[111] Under Roosevelt, the party of the Southern Confederacy was steering a new national enforcement of Reconstruction, all while reinforcing local state sovereignty. Peacher's actionable sin was that he exaggerated his official authority and usurped the exploitative prerogative of government. Cummings hailed the conviction as a "distinct victory for law and order."[112] In 1938 the Justice Department prosecuted two more cases under the 1867 Peonage Act.[113]

In another situation involving unsettled nineteenth-century problems of labor rights and civil rights, the NAACP defended Angelo Herndon, a Georgia man who became ensnared by a slave insurrection law for having distributed material demanding better labor conditions. The all-white jury in 1933 recommended mercy.[114] But under the anachronistic law, Herndon received an eighteen- to twenty-year sentence. The Georgia

Supreme Court upheld conviction, finding no federal question involved. The US Supreme Court upheld the law, against a dissent from justices Benjamin Cardoza, Louis Brandeis, and Harlan Stone.[115] But after initially affirming his sentence to a chain gang, in 1935 the Court issued a stay of sentencing. Throughout 1935, a broad group of activists challenged Herndon's treatment and the law itself. The American Federation of Labor called on organized workers everywhere to oppose the law. A number of habeas and appeal proceedings eventually brought the case back to the US Supreme Court in 1937.[116]

The Herndon case captured the reoccurring ambiguity of whether such injustices would mobilize reformers to define liberalism in a bipartisan or a particularly left-leaning Democratic sense. The miscarriage of justice was egregious. It was conservative Owen Roberts who granted a stay of execution.[117] The activists saw the case as a momentous bookend to nearly a century of struggle predating the Civil War. The case reinforced hopes in the criminal justice state, its ultimate reformation toward Reconstruction with the abolition of a literal remnant of slavery—reaffirming free labor together with the First Amendment in ways both racially and ideologically neutral and in distinct furtherance of left-liberal values. On the one hand, "widespread interest . . . by all classes" could mean "agitation for social reform."[118] But on the other hand, the Herndon case especially motivated concerned minorities, Jewish activists, and the ACLU. The case demonstrated that legal rights were not truly politically neutral. Herndon saw his cause as a "fight against Negro discrimination and growing fascist reaction."[119] In April 1937 the US Supreme Court overturned Georgia's insurrection law. Roberts joined the Court's liberals, against the conservative minority, to pen the opinion. Much like the Court's upholding of the Wagner Act, the case was seen to pit progress against reaction. Herndon celebrated the decision's "heavy blow" against "the Jim Crow oppression of the Negro people" and the "evil and cruel oppression of all workers."[120]

But even as flashes of hope refracted within war-on-crime liberalism, new developments in federalism served to reinforce the old racial order, both where federal power expanded and where it mostly allowed states to act unencumbered. The paradoxical racial implications appeared in three areas with truly innovative federal experiments in jurisdiction—Indian policy, the Tennessee Valley Authority, and local police torture.

The first innovation concerned an issue separate from and as old as that of policing Black America—the question of Indigenous Americans, whose plight since the nineteenth century turned on distinct dynamics. National consolidation, while sometimes protecting Black Americans against parochial and state oppression, was often more unambiguously dire for Native Americans. While largely a result of western conquest, their subjugation was a southern issue since the 1830s removals from the Southeast to Indian Territory—much of which merged with Oklahoma Territory. Its Native inhabitants suffered white supremacy but also the shame associated with secession, given the territory's Confederate allegiances. From Reconstruction through Oklahoma's statehood in 1907 and into the 1930s, federal officials grappled with jurisdiction—usurping criminal jurisdiction from the tribes in the Major Crimes Act. Most contentiously, the federal government remanded jurisdiction over "restricted" children and minors to white supremacist Oklahoma Courts. Oklahoma's racial coalition was as paradoxical as Democratic Party dynamics between Black Americans and white southerners. While white Oklahoma was solidly Democratic, Indians voting in 1932 turned out 90 percent in favor of Roosevelt.[121] The 1934 Indian Reorganization Act, often called the Indian New Deal, rearranged federalism to accommodate Indian self-governance nationwide, reversing the allotment system and decades of assimilationist experiments.[122] The 1934 Act spawned legacies of Indian law and tribal sovereignty throughout America.[123] In Oklahoma, however, the home of more Indians than any other state, racial politics were more complex. Opposition to recognizing communal Indian land holdings came from both whites and the more assimilated "progressive" Indians of the Five "Civilized Tribes."[124] Eventually the 1936 Oklahoma Indian Welfare Act passed, bringing a jurisdictional balance for radically different constituencies.

The second innovation exposing racial paradoxes was the federal project dearest to Senator Norris's heart. As Walter White conceded, Norris deserved applause for the TVA, the most massive and celebrated federal undertaking directly aiding the rural South, which nevertheless was inadequate consolation to those suffering lynching terror. In pedestrian terms the TVA encapsulated conflicting New Deal messages to Black Americans, many of whom were materially aided by electrification despite its entrenching of discrimination. The establishment of the TVA expropriated Black homeowners to make room for white workers. Thousands of families suffered a racialized displacement, their homes confiscated through eminent domain. Among those harmed were a significant community of independent farmers: two-thirds of East Tennessee's Black Americans worked their own farms, compared to one-third in other rural areas. The relocation turned middling property-owning Black farmers into landless wage earners, and those enforcing relocation were uniformly white.[125] TVA labor conditions and racially regressive hiring practices worried the NAACP. White unionization often conspired to prevent the hiring of Black workers.[126] Majority rule, a major principle of labor self-organization, was racially weaponized.[127] A September 1938 hearing considered numerous grievances against white officials' discrimination and disciplinary actions. A few cases of disciplinary action against Black workers were deemed too severe, but generally the hearing concluded that there was insufficient evidence of discrimination and racial harassment.[128]

A potentially important way the TVA reinforced white supremacy was in the national reliance on states' law enforcement authority. Even as the TVA became a federal laboratory of experimentation for local policing, it depended on local and state enforcers. Having uprooted established Black communities and practiced discrimination within, the TVA introduced jurisdictional innovations that entrenched relations between national enforcement and the Jim Crow South. Such cooperation was consistent with other southern patterns of war-on-crime federalism. By legitimating southern policing through compacts, subsidies, and intelligence sharing, the war on crime offered a consequential parley in the spirit of national reunion. Empowering the Jim Crow police state could not help but support reactionary local governance, from its unequal enforcement of criminal law to the implementation of segregation statutes.[129]

Third, police brutality and torture further demonstrated the de facto federal acquiescence in state government oppression. Given the legacies of white mobs and lynching, southern apartheid could resemble a pursuit of legal modernity. Even as many opposed federal interference, interwar southern elites, politicians, and law enforcers turned against lynching. Stamping out lynching would serve their monopolization of legal force—which often meant the monopolization of violent, even lawless, white supremacy. They welcomed this modernization even if skeptical of federal guidance in the transition. Historians show how in this period, incarceration, executions, and extralegal police brutality and torture effectively socialized racial violence, transferring from the mob's rough justice the prerogatives of white domination.[130] At the same time the federal war on crime and the rising security state sought national standards, with some gestures toward reining in the worst southern excesses. The Wickersham Commission had identified torture as particularly acute in the South, where the water cure was imported from the Philippines for use against mostly Black Americans. Until World War II, however, federal scrutiny of southern policing would remain limited. The US Supreme Court practiced some scrutiny, most famously in *Brown v. Mississippi,* overturning a murder conviction obtained purely through torture. But police were not investigated or scrutinized directly until about 1940, even as their departments enjoyed new status and resources from the FBI's training school. For most of the 1930s southern police and sheriffs enjoyed a free hand to define and tame lawlessness—both of white mobs and Black suspects—with their own sorts of brutalities. The NAACP took up police torture as a major issue, with limited success.

In war-on-crime federalism, white supremacist modernizers had little to fear even as Black Americans saw flashes of hope. Outside the South, reactionaries gave assurances that the transforming federal government would for now allow the white South to manage its lingering peculiar institutions. Walter White described one congressman's sadly predictable lynching posture: he was "all for the protection of Idaho potatoes but doesn't think that human lives should be protected by the Federal Government."[131]

The irreconcilable visions of the NAACP and the Jim Crow South found rapprochement in a strange way when Walter White essentially supported the nomination of Hugo Black to the US Supreme Court. The Alabama senator was a loyal New Dealer who opposed conservative obstruction of social legislation and used his senatorial power to investigate Roosevelt's critics.[132] He was also a former member of the Klan, which helped propel him to the Senate. Senator Black later disassociated himself from the Klan, but he helped lead the filibuster of federal lynching legislation in 1935.[133] As late as June 1937 there was hope he would come to support it.[134] Controversy swelled in August, when Roosevelt announced Hugo Black as his first nominee to fill the seat of retiring conservative Van Devanter. Mainstream and Black American journalists criticized the nomination. A *New York Amsterdam News* editorial condemned the senator's record on civil rights along with his willingness to confiscate property "without ever dreaming of 'due process of law.'"[135] The *Chicago Defender* decried the elevation of this "arch-enemy of our race."[136] The United Colored War Veterans protested the appointment.[137] The Senate confirmed his nomination over only sixteen objections.[138] The Justice Department responded to the furor with a press release insisting that Hugo Black's "record of public service" and electoral successes for state and national office "made his suitability beyond question."[139]

One charitable interpretation entertained by some NAACP activists was that Senator Black opposed racial reactionaries in principle but prioritized New Deal economics: "The 'economic royalists'" would do all "in their power to defeat Black because of his economic liberalism," and to defend this agenda he had to tread carefully.[140] Hugo Black's appointment divided Black American activists, but some hoped it provided potential leverage. White suggested stressing the controversial appointment to embarrass Alabama's governor into addressing abuses by sheriffs.[141] Another urged that the NAACP should "make it very clear" that it was "none too pleased," so as to "capitalize subtly" on it, so that Roosevelt might even feel shamed into supporting anti-lynching legislation.[142]

Lynching legislation divided Democrats into the next year. NAACP activists protested the elevation to the US Supreme Court of Hatton W. Sumners, who opposed the legislation but was outraged that lynching undermined Mississippi law and order.[143] But the NAACP would never see Roosevelt sign the law. Theodore Bilbo, a loyal Mississippi New Dealer, led the 1938 campaign against the Costigan-Wagner Act, warning it would "open the floodgates of hell in the South. Raping, mobbing, lynching, race riots, and crime will be increased a thousandfold" as the land flooded with "the blood of the raped and outraged daughters of Dixie"[144] and with the blood of the Black perpetrators brought to justice. Federal action would cause more lynching, in other words—a perverse twist on the pragmatic considerations in building law and order. Even though they could not have been further apart on federal lynching policy, Bilbo and the NAACP both predicted heightened lawlessness if their warnings went unheeded. The ecumenicism of war-on-crime liberalism and war-on-crime federalism for now kept them behind the same party as it modernized enforcement up and down the rungs of government.

THE STRANGE CAREER OF ANTI-BLACK TERROR helps explain the paradoxes of Black activism during the liberal war on crime. The enormity of lynching made the campaign against lawlessness attractive to the urgent cause of Black freedom. NAACP activists could point to anti-gangster vigilance in the North and argue that the South needed help against lynching.[145] Walter White told A. Philip Randolph he was encouraged by Roosevelt's proposal to direct the FBI to investigate lynchings. But he recognized larger stakes in the debates over political economy. Lynching was pushing "the reactionaries of both major parties . . . into one camp" and the "decent and liberal ones . . . into the Roosevelt camp."[146] An NAACP study identified economic anxieties and jobs scarcity as major factors exacerbating race relations.[147] The AFL saw anti-lynching as part of the New Deal promise to "Negro Workers and under-privileged white workers." The Unknown Soldier Post of the American Legion called lynching a violation of "the true spirit of Americanism."[148]

The NAACP's participation in this framing was far from passive. Its activities contributed enormously to both the practical and the idealistic sides of liberalism and its relationship with law and order. The twentieth-century triumphs and shortcomings of Black inclusion within the liberal coalition thus had foundational origins before World War II. The pragmatism, compromise, and hope achieved real gains and identified real limitations. Once on the bench, Hugo Black was regarded an NAACP ally. In 1940 the organization considered asking his "confidential advice" on a major Birmingham case.[149] The First Lady again expressed interest in anti-lynching legislation.[150] Against the mere flashes of hope offered by Democrats, Republicans offered even less. They opportunistically pushed for a vote when the present Democrats overrepresented the South, aiming to exploit the Democrats' contradictory constituencies, but the move appeared cynical.[151] In 1940 senators once again filibustered an anti-lynching law.

Roosevelt's expanded machinery could both stem racial oppression and enhance it. The federal government began new civil rights interventions. A reduction of lynching coincided with states tightening their grip and bringing racial oppression, both legal and extralegal, under their own auspices—muting the stakes of conflict within the New Deal coalition's sharpest contradiction long enough for World War II and Cold War mobilization to become relevant avenues of civil rights agitation. State-level police modernization in some ways curtailed racial lawlessness, and in other ways monopolized it under the color of law.

In a sense Senator Norris correctly identified an impolite return of Reconstruction-era politics, which threatened the uneasy peace from the age of reunion. The Progressive Era's marginalization of people of color, the liberal white silence as thousands succumbed to pogroms, would no longer suffice even if the wholesale abandonment of racial control collapsed the coalition. Roosevelt's liberalism could not resolve the Reconstruction-era fractures, but it accommodated them within a new settlement for another generation. Federal jurisdictional innovation encouraged Black activists even as federal power refortified prejudicial policing. Policing the most egregious American legacies—enslavement and lynching—came alongside state monopolizing of racial violence. In the 1930s the bar was so low, the constitutional trajectory so indeterminate, the political alignments so contestable, that the New Deal's racial contradictions could, on net, invigorate political legitimacy.

Eventually the state-building inertia would test the patience of the factions. Federal civil rights enforcement would repel a key Democratic constituency and Black Americans would openly resist the racial repression that war-on-crime federalism set in time-release motion. For the time being, the New Deal contained these potentially explosive fractures. The same Treasury Department that abandoned the inequitable war on alcohol was building a modern drug war whose racial disparities would define the late twentieth century. The same FBI that was beginning investigations of lynching and police torture was supporting state intelligence operations that would become weaponized against civil rights.[152] And, in a topic undertaken in Chapter 8, the same welfare state abolishing for-profit prison labor was building up the institutions that decades later posed one of the harshest setbacks for Black liberation—modern mass incarceration.

PART IV

DISCIPLINE AND WELFARE,

1933–1941

Racial politics did not mark the only paradox in midcentury liberalism. The tensions between the social state and the carceral state characterized much of the New Deal order. In waging war on crime, the Roosevelt administration would expand infrastructure, aggrandize the criminal code, and amplify the brute force against gangsters, while giving unprecedented attention to holistic visions for crime control. These visions drove much of its engagement with institutions across jurisdictions and social life. Attorney General Homer Cummings, law enforcement elites, and academics knew that federalism and tradition constrained national police power, a recognition that only intensified their emphasis on intellectual leadership. Indeed, as with racial justice, even when idealistic aspirations failed to achieve their goals, the aspirations themselves illuminate the ideological contours that served to legitimate the rising liberal state.

Criminology and penology had major, if underappreciated, roles in building 1930s liberalism. Justin Miller, former dean of Duke Law School and an advisor to the Justice Department, spearheaded ambitious agendas on "crime prevention" as well as penal reform that harmonized policy goals across the welfare state and the various scales of government. Miller's work with the Works Progress Administration's Survey of Release Procedures brought federal resources behind an unprecedented defense of probation and parole. His work on the Attorney General's Advisory Committee on Crime sought to create a "crime prevention" bureau that bridged the academic community to police nationwide. Miller and others in Roosevelt's Justice Department, led by Cummings, broadened the vision of prevention and rehabilitation to include the repression associated with prisons, policing, and the FBI. In New Deal penology, the goal of integrating welfare with discipline brought about an expansion of both, while promoting new cooperation between federal and state institutions. In New Deal criminology, the goal was more theoretical, and the more idealistic their ambitions, the more welfare leaders pondered new avenues of punishment and control. In these areas, much like in jurisdiction, the New Deal moved the game beyond the zero-sum. Discipline and welfare were not adversarial approaches but instead mutually reinforcing. In both its practical outcomes and its theoretical aspirations, the synthesis between these approaches would shape the trajectory of American governance and also the future of liberal law-and-order discourse.

CHAPTER 8

BUILDING CARCERAL LIBERALISM

Alcatraz represents the ultimate in isolation," wrote former Attorney General Homer Cummings. "And yet, oddly enough, it lies in the very midst of the busy, hurried life of the bay region." In the mile and a half between the island prison and San Francisco drifted "tiny boats" and "great ocean liners." The port linking America's west to East Asia overflowed with the bustling of commerce and the "hum of life." The inmates endured a bitter juxtaposition: "life" was "so near, but liberty so far."[1]

It was 1939, and Alcatraz was under attack. The assault came from within, as American newspapers and even Attorney General Frank Murphy, Cummings's successor, questioned the prison in theory and practice. The retired Cummings defended the prison's uncompromising discipline while affirming its enlightenment spirit. Despite crude comparisons to France's penal colony, Alcatraz was no "American 'Devil's Island.'" Where misguided critics condemned a "place of brutality . . . a throwback to the Middle Ages," misguided supporters believed "murderers and kidnappers . . . deserved such 'brutal' treatment." Cummings sought to correct both extremes, championing Alcatraz as a model of both humanity and control.[2]

While it has long captured popular imagination, Alcatraz sits uneasily among scholarly treatments of the New Deal.[3] General histories barely mention it—or prisons at all.[4] Yet surging incarceration characterized the Depression decade. From 1930 to 1940 the federal inmate population rose from 12,964 to 19,260, and the state inmate population climbed from 107,532 to 146,325 (see Figure 8.1). Although federal incarceration reached a summit under President Herbert Hoover and even receded in 1934 and 1935, by 1938 the figure rebounded and the Roosevelt administration could claim unprecedented numbers of persons under federal supervision, including probation and parole (see Figure 8.2). Meanwhile the New Deal sponsored prison construction in the states where the increase, disproportionately in the South, easily offset the volatility at the federal level. In 1939, the year Cummings defended Alcatraz, imprisonment broke new records. Despite expectations that legalizing alcohol would reduce incarceration, the combined state and federal prison population reached 179,818 in 1939. That year, 137 out of 100,000 Americans were serving sentences in captivity, up from 111 in 1932 (see Figure 8.3). This per capita figure would not be reached again until 1979, forty years later, as the era of mass incarceration began in earnest (see Figure 8.4).[5]

The New Deal story rarely integrates these carceral trends.[6] Alcatraz is a curiosity confined to the gangster era. Prisons hardly register in welfare state histories, despite the Works Progress Administration's direct

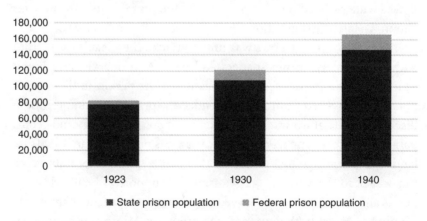

Figure 8.1   Federal and state prison populations in 1923, 1930, and 1940. Data source: *Historical Corrections Statistics in the United States*, Table 3-2, 29.

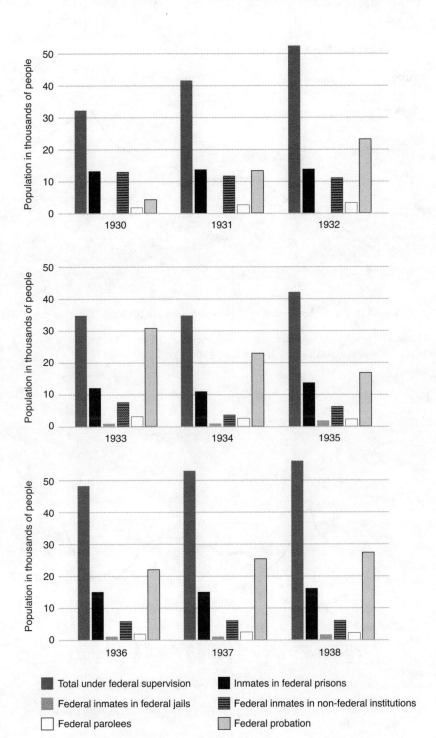

Figure 8.2　Numbers of persons under various forms of federal supervision, 1930–1938.

Data source: *Survey of Release Procedures,* 5:310.

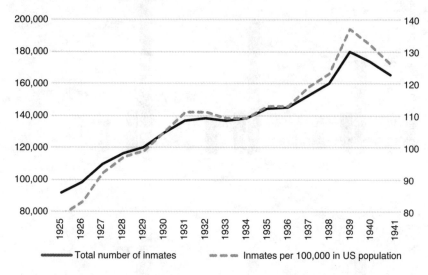

Figure 8.3   Combined federal and state prison population, 1925–1941. Data source: *Historical Corrections Statistics in the United States,* 1850–1984, Table 3-7, 35.

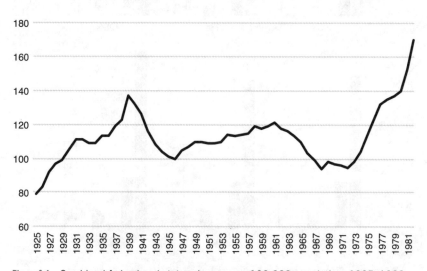

Figure 8.4   Combined federal and state prisoners per 100,000 population, 1925–1982.
Data source: *Historical Corrections Statistics in the United States,* 1850–1984, Table 3-7, 35.
This graph uses more inclusive figures from 1976 onward, which may slightly exaggerate the later prison surge compared to the 1930s.

role.[7] Carceral historians have, however, gestured toward the political legitimation of 1930s crime fighting.[8] In considering New Deal incarceration, scholarship has tended toward two approaches. One approach interprets the New Deal as the end of a long nineteenth-century prison labor story. Challenging once-dominant interpretations, associated with Michel Foucault and David Rothman, that emphasized bodily and spiritual discipline, Rebecca McLennan showed how antebellum and Victorian penitentiaries prioritized productive, profitable labor, before succumbing to a postindustrial prison model in the interwar period.[9] Others have focused on national solidarity with activists to separate prison labor from the market economy, exemplified by Roosevelt's Prison Industries Reorganization Administration (PIRA).[10] The second interpretive approach is retrospective, depicting the late-twentieth-century carceral state as a retreat from New Deal liberalism, or as an expression of liberalism as actualized in the 1940s security state.[11] A stress on postwar rupture suggests that the New Deal, supportive of rehabilitation and labor reform, was an abortive or ineffective obstacle to contemporary prison growth.[12] Thus is New Deal incarceration separated from both the early 1930s and the much later iteration of the war on crime.

Perhaps because it unfolded at key junctures in the complex histories of liberalism, federal power, law enforcement, and penological ideas, the New Deal is more manageable as a bookend than as a coherent period of transformation. McLennan has suggested the importance of the 1930s, when Sing-Sing warden Lewis Lawes's 1920s model of "penal managerialism" spread from New York across the northern United States, displacing the economic priorities of productive labor.[13] This interpretation invites more consideration of the Roosevelt administration's national penological undertakings, its implications for liberalism and federalism. But if prisons freed from profit swelled, perhaps Foucauldian models of discipline applied better to the state-building liberalism of the New Deal than to the fiscally conscientious liberalism of the nineteenth century.[14] And although historians recognize postwar developments that do not inexorably follow the New Deal, the literature suggests important carceral state roots in 1930s modernization.

The tale of postwar incarceration, flowering into mass incarceration, must reckon with the New Deal's carceral program. The Roosevelt administration's policies complicate attempts to understand the origins of mass incarceration, including its white supremacy, since federal and state trajectories fit discordantly with each other even as they pointed toward a modern form of racial discipline. Although carceral populations were disproportionately Black before the New Deal, the disparities would become much more apparent in the decades after New Deal reforms. In any event, race was unlikely at the top of New Dealers' minds as they pursued carceral expansion. They sought first and foremost to harness the punitive and reformist infrastructure already in place, and to hasten its modernization on both fronts. Their modernization goals were aspirationally colorblind and plausibly even racially egalitarian insofar as they sought to give more attention to crimes associated with white Americans, while still building on the penological trajectory of the Jim Crow South and discriminatory North. The Roosevelt administration attempted simultaneously to find the balance between highlighting the racial and class disparities that parole and probation could ameliorate while crediting southern governments whose release procedures it wished to defend against naysayers.

This chapter identifies New Deal penology as the cauldron in which strains of earlier intellectual and institutional development formed the foundation of the modern carceral state. Like the Progressive Era's New Penologists, New Deal authorities denied any association between their prisons and *brutality*. This term arose repeatedly as a foil to their proclaimed devotion to *humanity*. Along with humanity New Deal penology stressed individualized correction. As with the penal managerialism of Lewis Lawes, the New Deal penologists stressed *discipline* to maintain order within prisons and beyond through parole and probation. But the New Dealers also inherited the Hoover administration's short-term problems and long-term institutional trajectory. From 1929 to Roosevelt's inauguration, America's bloated prisons appeared a conspicuous microcosm of larger deficiencies—economic depression, crime panic, and social disorder. The Hoover administration responded with a temperamental *carceral conservatism*, prioritizing order above reformist impulses. Others took this carceral conservatism further, alleging that parole and probation coddled criminals and endangered the public. National power and politics offered both opportunities and challenges for Roosevelt. The states dominated incarceration, highlighting the importance of federal leadership in setting examples with its own prisons and in its interaction with the states. Even where the federal government could not adopt the rehabilitative approach to which national officials aspired, the states became an ideological and cultural model.

With their experiment at Alcatraz, the New Dealers took discipline even further than their predecessors. With their Survey of Release Procedures, they defended parole and probation against critics. Roosevelt, Attorney General Homer Cummings, Prison Bureau director Sanford Bates, and Justice Department official Justin Miller, despite their disagreements, worked to reconcile the numerous demands putting strain on the prison system. Within two terms the New Dealers met their daunting challenge: to manage the radically transforming penal landscape while integrating the trends of reform and addressing the crises of law and order. They built *carceral liberalism*—influenced by the New Penologists' emphasis on humanity and the disciplinarian program of northeastern penology—while both empowered and constrained by operating on the national scale. To maximize stability, carceral liberalism observed the somewhat consensual relationship between federal and state authorities. Roosevelt could not apply one formula mechanically. Instead of a grand strategy, carceral liberalism was an exercise in managing the paradoxes of discipline and rehabilitation. This meant understanding how state prison authorities administered their systems, embracing incarceration, rehabilitation, parole, and probation in symbiosis. The paradoxes within Alcatraz, within the Survey of Release Procedures, and within the national sponsorship of state prisons brought each project of carceral liberalism more tightly into the whole.[15]

INCARCERATING THE DEPRESSION

Roosevelt became president at a transformative time for penological ideas as well as institutions. Both the reform spirit and the drive to expand incarceration transcended party. Roosevelt retained Herbert Hoover's Prison Bureau director, Sanford Bates, who embodied the dualities of punishment and rehabilitation, of interwar policy continuity and reform.

The personification of northeast penal progressivism, Bates saw the "battle against crime" as requiring "one master motive controlling all operations."[16] As Boston's commissioner of penal institutions immediately after World War I, he had "discovered that these prisoners were human beings." Bates headed the Department of Correction of Massachusetts for nine years and served the Justice Department under Assistant Attorney General Mabel Walker Willebrandt, a dedicated enforcer of Prohibition despite her personal reservations.[17] He took pride in prison labor policies that "organized" incarceration on "an intelligent and progressive basis." His time at the Department of Mental Diseases convinced him of the importance of "crime prevention" and the correctional system's "adaptation" to each particular criminal's "individual needs." He was a radical critic of all pretrial detention,[18] but saw no conflict between discipline and rehabilitation. As he recalled telling President Calvin Coolidge, prison labor could be "both deterrent and constructive."[19] Although Bates first took charge of the nation's prisons under Republican rule, his ideas fit better with Roosevelt, whose attention he attracted along with that of Homer Cummings.[20]

Roosevelt's own gubernatorial experience exposed him to reformism even more ambitious than Bates's. Roosevelt embraced the model of Warden Lewis Lawes of New York's Sing-Sing prison, whose "penal managerialism" stressed a holistic welfarist approach of democratizing prisons.[21] During the state's high-profile prison riots, particularly at Auburn Prison, the national press credited Sing-Sing's relative order to Lawes's progressive-minded rejection of draconian punishments.[22] Roosevelt also found Sing-Sing inspiring. In December 1929 Roosevelt articulated his broad penological vision.[23] He demanded a balance of "adequate punishment" as well as "the treatment of prisoners" that would allow them "to resume their places in the community." He urged a slate of reforms— more prisons, improved facilities, and modernized parole and probation systems. Roosevelt wanted to bring "good conduct time" back to "improve the morale of the prisoners of the State." In January 1930 the New York legislature unanimously approved Roosevelt's bill appropriating $750,000, much of which targeted overcrowding and some of which funded better inmate meals and clothing.[24]

But as president, Roosevelt could not simply apply New York's model to the nation. In addition to constitutional constraints, he inherited a carceral system in momentous and unwieldy transition. Indeed, his generation witnessed a breathtaking ascendance of federal penal institutions from practically nothing, a profound development Cummings and Mc-Farland later examined with seriousness in their treatise.[25] Before 1929 there were only three federal penitentiaries, all founded well after Reconstruction—McNeil Island, in Washington; another in Leavenworth, Kansas; and a third in Atlanta—as well as a national men's reformatory in Chillicothe, Ohio, and a women's institution in Alderson, West Virginia. The Federal Bureau of Prisons only opened in 1930.[26] Federal procedures for release were even more novel. After the US Supreme Court in 1916 restricted judicial suspension of sentences, legislation produced modern probation and parole systems. Before 1930 there were few designated federal probation officers. Parole was first issued by prisons and penitentiaries, then by parole boards giving relief to federal prisoners in state institutions.[27]

Meanwhile, the numbers of persons under penal control multiplied. By June 1933, there were 12,148 people living in federal institutions, excluding jails, which housed another 1,043, and another 7,590 federal prisoners resided in nonfederal institutions. Federal parole accounted for 3,306 people, another 106 were on conditional release, and 30,870 were on federal probation. The vast majority of prisoners lived in various state correctional institutions—industrial penitentiaries, labor camps, and "experimental institutions." The number of state inmates climbed by 140 percent from 1904 to 1935, and from 107,532 to 126,258 in the short period between 1930 to 1935.[28]

Roosevelt's team faced both a long-term structural shortcoming and an urgent national emergency. In the long term they sought to manage the continuity of reform toward a politically sustainable trajectory, to accelerate the evolution of correctional structures and ethos, up from a dark past of repression, brutality, and corporate profit, and toward a future of rehabilitation and enlightened public interest.[29] But most immediately the Roosevelt administration inherited from its conservative predecessors an emergency of public order. Prison riots and the crime wave of 1933 to 1934 prompted them to embrace and expand upon the unforgiving carceral repression of their conservative predecessors.

The need for prison order struck at the very integrity of carceral governance. Unprofessional guards fired guns recklessly. From February through July 1933 at least half a dozen Leavenworth guards were reprimanded for sleeping on the job. In December Leavenworth officials fired on a plane operated by the Department of Commerce that flew close to the ground. The Bureau of Prisons agreed to advise "guards [to] be more discreet in firing upon unidentified planes."[30] Some prison guards were found helping inmates escape.[31] Recalcitrant prisoners remained an irritant. In November 1933 about 500 Philadelphia police helped suppress a riot in Eastern State Penitentiary.[32] In 1935 eleven prisoners died during escape attempts in Louisiana; in addition, seven died in Texas, four in Mississippi, two in Alabama, and one in Arkansas.[33]

The New Dealers offered new assets to secure order. They introduced legislation to target conspiracy to "cause any mutiny, riot, or escape"; to prohibit any "tool, device or substance designed to cut, abrade or destroy" the material of prison buildings, along with any "narcotic drug" or "weapon"; and to restrict correspondence between inmates and the outside.[34] New criminal codes ensnared new interstate informants, a triumph of war-on-crime federalism. Bureaucratic integration flourished, as J. Edgar Hoover alerted the Bureau of Prisons to rumors of escape plans. Surgeon General H. S. Cumming touted the "relations" between the Public Health Service and the Bureau of Prisons to be "so harmonious" that he regretted the tensions arising when a warden caught a public health official with a prohibited inkpad.[35]

New Deal penology embraced the duality of order and equity, discipline and fairness. Bates stressed the "importance of equal treatment for all" in relieving tensions among prisoners.[36] Leavenworth officials hoped a "uniform rule" on personal property might minimize resentment and envy. Particularly worrisome was the "privileged treatment" that staff rewarded some inmates. Inmates could nevertheless complain about favoritism. For their part, guards perceived as being too cruel or draconian also frustrated order. Acting Deputy Warden Albert Singer noted that Leavenworth inmates especially disliked one guard who undercut morale by forbidding guitar playing after 7:30 p.m. Poorly disciplined guards could upend prison tranquility. The philosophical question of collective punishment further posed practical obstacles to achieving order within a modern prison state determined to lessen and not fuel social dysfunction.[37]

The urgency for order prompted New Deal innovations that qualitatively and quantitatively constructed the carceral state. In qualitative terms the administration pioneered a harsh disciplinary theory at Alcatraz, the first federal maximum-security penitentiary. Its architect, Homer Cummings, basked in its outsize cultural significance. In August 1933 he suggested a remote "special prison" for the most "desperate or irredeemable" prisoners, transferred from Atlanta and Leavenworth.[38] He considered Alaska, the Aleutian Islands, and the isles off Florida, then settled on Alcatraz, a military army installation since 1854, once a prison in the Indian Wars.[39] There prisoners would not receive the scandalous special treatment Al Capone enjoyed at Atlanta US Penitentiary.[40] Alcatraz soon symbolized the modernizing Justice Department and Cummings's authority: judges could not sentence convicts to Alcatraz; only Cummings's discretion could transfer them to Alcatraz. In August 1934 Cummings touted the late-night operation that discreetly brought prisoners, unaware of their destination, by train to the West Coast just in time for him to mark the historic commencement.[41]

Alcatraz captured the conflicts within the new carceral liberalism. Sanford Bates was skeptical of its merciless design, which clashed with the high-progressive penology of social workers and emphatic practitioners. Bates asked August Vollmer for advice on personnel for Alcatraz, but recognized that the project would not appeal to him personally, given that it would not offer "great opportunity for rehabilitation work."[42] Yet Alcatraz also indirectly served as a pressure valve for conspicuous systemic failures. Men attempting to escape Fort Leavenworth with smuggled firearms were transferred to Alcatraz, which Warden Frederick Zerbst said "lessened the tension greatly."[43]

Alcatraz revealed internal contradictions. Conceived as a prison for the irredeemable, by September 1934 it included thirty-two holdover military prisoners, sexual offenders—both so-called deviant and violent—including a "moron" who "may not have wit enough to go straight."[44] Another fourteen were attempted escapees and "agitators" from McNeil Island. Eight people came from the Lorton Reformatory in Washington, D.C., and seven from Leavenworth.[45] One "agitator and trouble maker" was there mainly for associating with "dangerous and bad criminals."[46] Another transfer from McNeil Island was serving twenty-five years for postal violations because he encouraged others "to get in trouble while at the same time staying out of trouble himself."[47]

The "hardened" prisoners nevertheless served the rationale of unforgiving discipline. High-profile inmates included Al Capone; members of the Purple Gang, the Barker-Karpis Gang, and the infamous gangs of Roger Touhy, Bugs Moran, and Irish O'Malley; accomplices and associates of Harvey Bailey, Machine Gun Kelly, John Dillinger, Baby Face Nelson, Bonnie and Clyde, Al Spencer, and Frank Nash. Notorious kidnappers counted among them.[48] Inmates endured strict regulation—days scheduled down to the minute, with two eight-minute rest periods. Prisoners were allowed very few possessions and had the most restrictive visiting hours in the federal system. Alcatraz utilized alcoves previously used as dungeon cells.[49] Recalcitrant prisoners found themselves in solitary confinement.[50]

Beyond strengthening punishment, the pursuit of carceral order implicated prison labor, on which Roosevelt's team expanded and innovated upon their predecessors' work. Hoover administration officials tabled a 1929 proposal for "prison camps" in national forests, expecting prison populations to decline after Prohibition. As the prisons nevertheless swelled, the New Dealers revived the idea.[51] Responding to the prison population growth, Bates in 1935 called for "constructive means of utilizing the energies of our inmates." Forest prison camps could mandate "a reasonable amount of work." The Forest Service, preoccupied with Civilian Conservation Corp (CCC) programs, was unmoved, but deliberations for a federal detention farm in Kentucky's Cumberland National Forest persisted through 1936.[52]

In prison labor the New Dealers offered their other important qualitative contribution to disciplinary theory. War-on-crime federalism
brought new energy to the campaign against private profits in prison
labor, tracing to the 1880s abolition of the contract labor system and reforms in New York and beyond. President Hoover contributed to this
effort through Reconstruction Finance Corporation (RFC) restrictions
and the 1930 Hawes-Cooper Act, banning sales of prison goods on the
open market beginning in 1934. As prison industries closed, states scrambled to reorient their operations. The Roosevelt administration harnessed
this energy while affirming the disciplinary role of labor. The RFC and
the principles of the Hawes-Cooper Act carried forward in the National
Industrial Recovery Act, and the Prison Labor Authority's commercial
codes encouraged new prison labor standards across the states. The
Ashurst-Sumners Act of 1934 imposed criminal penalties on the illegal
interstate transfer of prison goods. The Ulman Committee, named after
Joseph N. Ulman, with participation from criminologist Frank Tannen-
baum, pressed the National Industrial Recovery Board (NIRB) to support
aid to states for the transition away from private contracts and toward
"state use" for all products of prison labor.[53] The Supreme Court repudiated the NIRB, and so Roosevelt, urged to carry the state-use mission
forward, issued an order in September 1935 creating the Prison Industries
Reorganization Administration (PIRA) to perform studies and investigations, recommend appropriate prison labor projects, and recommend
"loans or grants" to state governments.[54]

PIRA revealed the opportunities and challenges of federalism. Mobilization linked both administrations grappling with long-term problems
exacerbated by the Depression. But Roosevelt's ambition went further to
reveal the delicate navigation that federalism required. Congress frustrated PIRA by ignoring its requests for more aid to states. With its
small budget, a couple dozen personnel, and limited authority, PIRA had
relied on agencies like the WPA, the Bureau of Labor Statistics, and the
Public Health Service, for information and funding. PIRA could not force
its services onto states and so only worked where "invitations were
extended through governors." Yet this consensual arrangement likely
strengthened interjurisdictional relations. By May 1937 PIRA could report
serious interest from seventeen states, signifying geographical diversity.

PIRA had a foothold in Delaware, Maryland, Pennsylvania, and Vermont in the east; in the heartland and southward in Indiana, West Virginia, Tennessee, Arkansas, Georgia, and Kentucky; and farther west—in Texas, Oklahoma, Utah, Wyoming, New Mexico, Oregon, and California.[55] In 1937, as PIRA's Gustav Peck urged Congress to extend funding and expressed concern about the perils of prison idleness, he hailed PIRA's "lifting of states with the lowest standards to a better level, and the willingness of these states to adopt systems of rehabilitation."[56]

While PIRA recognized the constraints of subsidiarity, its advisory arrangement emboldened its vision. Acknowledging the "widespread opposition to the use of prisoners on road work," tainted by the "unsavory reputation of the chain gang," PIRA nevertheless championed the "wise and constructive use of prisoners for the better types of highway work, and on conservation work such as forestry, drainage and soil erosion projects."[57] PIRA accepted that "public indignation at the brutal treatment of prisoners" under convict lease had led to its abolition, but insisted on the need for hard labor. Finding labor outlets was a "difficult task" and state use would "not alone solve the problems of idleness." PIRA suggested prison labor on "public roads, farms, forestry and soil conservation projects for the benefit of the state."[58] While PIRA had important pre–New Deal antecedents, its distinctive contribution to carceral liberalism was the exploitation of war-on-crime federalism to legitimize national power and push the frontiers of prison discipline.

The New Deal state meanwhile fueled a quantitative expansion of carceral institutions. The Public Works Administration, a creature of the National Recovery Administration, undertook the construction of prisons and jails at both the national and local levels. Through 1939 the PWA provided over $14 million to the Federal Bureau of Prisons, more than its assistance to the Post Office or to the Departments of Agriculture, Commerce, or Interior. A PWA publication lamented the failure of federal prisons to meet the government's penological standards and boasted of having financed "75 Federal prison projects . . . including new correctional institutions for short-term Federal prisoners in Colorado, Connecticut, Kentucky, Texas, and Indiana."[59] At the local level the PWA provided $24,478,700 for "126 nonfederal prisons and jails," emphasizing a "tailor-made" approach to the "needs of the community" for jails no less than schools and bridges. Upon learning of the pitiful lack of a court-house Gainesville, Missouri, the object of a nationally known editorial cartoon, the PWA approved $16,380 for a courthouse and new jail. The PWA elsewhere replaced "disgraceful" jails and "cramped" police head-quarters. Poor Barton County, Missouri, received assistance replacing its Reconstruction-era jail, lousy with "wet and moldy" cells, "rats, and mice." The PWA graced Barton County with a "modern $36,363 struc-ture," and proudly improved prison infrastructure at Sing-Sing, Auburn, Joliet, and Atlanta.[60]

Even more important was the WPA, which approved a $1.1 million improvement at Alcatraz[61] and indeed furnished labor and funding to the building and renovation of 760 penal institutions—a fraction of the 40,000 buildings constructed and the 85,000 improved by the agency, but a considerable impact on the carceral state.[62] At the federal level, WPA workers built the National Training School for Boys from 1935 to 1937, employed 222 workers on Bureau of Prisons projects in June 1939, and ac-counted for $51,974 of Bureau spending through June 1943.[63] The WPA also collaborated: with the CCC to build a juvenile correctional camp; with the Federal Emergency Relief Administration to improve a Framingham, Massachusetts, reformatory; and with the Federal Art Project in reno-vating the grounds for California's Whittier State School for Boys.[64]

Most WPA carceral construction enlisted cooperation with states and localities. In its first few years, WPA labor built a jail for Somervell County in Glen Rose, Texas; assisted with jail renovations in Rutland, Vermont; helped improve Rikers Island and a civil prison in Brooklyn, New York; built a second addition to the Baca County Courthouse Annex in Spring-field, Colorado; and undertook major renovations of the Contra Costa County jail in Martinez, California. In 1936 the WPA helped renovate a detention facility in the Municipal Building in Pennsauken, New Jersey; provided $5,802 to jail construction in Kingfisher County, Oklahoma; and provided funding for a jail in Santa Cruz, California. In the late 1930s the WPA erected a new jail in Carbon Hill, Alabama; helped expand the Lincoln County jail in Canton, South Dakota; constructed the Trinity County Jail in Groveton, Texas; built the Peoria Jail in Arizona; and trans-formed the Victorian décor of a jail in Carlsbad, New Mexico, into an early Spanish aesthetic. In 1940 the Jefferson County Jail in Monticello,

Florida, received WPA support, and as World War II raged the agency helped construct a Maries County courthouse and jail in Vienna, Missouri. From Ellicott City, Maryland; Pineville, Kentucky; and Jasper, Alabama—to Montrose, Colorado; San Francisco, California; and Lahaina, Hawaii—the WPA revamped the detention state from sea to shining sea.[65]

VINDICATING REFORM

Along with expanding incarceration, the New Deal mounted an unprecedented federal defense of rehabilitation. The Survey of Release Procedures examined parole, probation, and pardon, and performed the first comprehensive study of the states' prisons and release mechanisms. The program began with an intellectual aspiration, but served to test war-on-crime federalism. In the end it also underscored the New Deal's penological contradictions.

Cummings feared public backlash against the rising use of parole and probation.[66] In January 1935 he called "for a nation-wide examination" of these issues "vitally related . . . to the proper administration of criminal law."[67] The Survey authors appreciated their place in a long institutional evolution, which began in 1790 with "the most revolutionary step in the whole history of punishment for crime" when incarceration displaced corporal punishment.[68] The Survey self-consciously came at the end of four discernible eras—the new republic's practices in incarceration, the domination of the Pennsylvania and Auburn prison systems from 1830 to 1870, the reformatory system from 1870 to 1900, and the "custodial, punitive, and industrial" era of 1900–1935. The new reformers sought to purge the system of private profit and augment the reliance on custody with the strategic use of release.[69]

The Survey encapsulated the collaborative principles of New Deal federalism and political economy. It was diagnostic, seeking to understand and learn from the nation's lower jurisdictions.[70] The Survey asserted federal leadership in rehabilitation discourse while showcasing the states as policy models and resources for its defense of rehabilitation "in a spirit of experimentation."[71] It also sought to integrate labor and

crime policy across agencies. Roosevelt's November 1935 authorization
of work projects provided the funding. He instructed Treasury Secretary Henry Morgenthau to earmark $14,112,442 from the Emergency
Relief Appropriation Fund for hiring "white-collar" workers off the relief rolls. From this a sum of $1,424,298—over 10 percent—was reserved
for the "Survey of Methods of Dealing with Persons Found Guilty of
Crime." A quarter of the money went to individual states. Later funds
were disbursed to state administrators answering to state and regional
directors.[72] Future funding flowed through the Works Progress Administration, which also supplied labor. While announcing Dr. Barkev
Sanders as the Survey's technical director, Cummings highlighted both
the WPA goal "to employ white-collar workers now on relief" and the
Justice Department goal of studying "methods of releasing prisoners
from courts and penal institutions."[73]

Cummings entrusted Justin Miller, dean at Duke Law School and head
of the Attorney General's Advisory Committee on Crime, to manage the
survey at the Justice Department. Miller stressed redemption and welfare, a challenge when "so much emphasis is being given to the repressive phases of crime control."[74] His commitment to rehabilitation had
exempted juvenile offenders from a CCC policy that barred convicts.[75]
Miller hoped that "public opinion" would favor "a well-rounded program
of crime control."[76]

The study was intellectually ambitious. Within eleven regions, justice
officials examined eighty-eight state prisons and reformatories, personally visiting eighty-two of these, and studied releases from 1928 through
1935. Statistical supervisors compiled data. The Survey aimed for a comparative digest of state-level policy, a case history analyzing data on relationships between offenses and releases, an analysis of successful parole
discharges, an outline of tentative probation standards, and an evaluation
of the efficacy of release methods. They hoped for a "prediction study" that
could make policy forecasts.[77]

This intellectual ambition, devoted to long-term goals, nurtured a
humility about immediate reform. Miller discouraged "suggestions for
improvement as applied to any particular state system."[78] The advisory
committee kept quiet about recommendations before publication. Survey
author Howard Gill pondered giving suggestions on parole quotas and

psychiatric needs, but Sanders cautioned against "snap judgments and broad generalizations" that might provoke institutional jealousies.[79] Internal discussions emphasized larger structural goals. A circuit judge hoped to defeat "outmoded social and legal views" and replace "a socially correctional for the revengeful point of view."[80] There was elsewhere some hope to extend the exercise to the "penal colony question."[81]

The Survey required extensive data collection and the experts to analyze it.[82] Advising the program were penological heavyweights Thorstein Sallin, Edwin Sutherland, Joseph Keenan, and Federal Board of Parole chief Arthur D. Wood.[83] Regional supervisors would optimally have graduate training and competence in correctional institutions, probation law, custody practices, management principles, architectural and personnel requirements, classification techniques, medical services, psychiatry, education, employment, recreation, religion, and moral training. An ideal supervisor would possess that intangible alacrity, that sense of "what constitutes a good indeterminate sentence and parole law."[84]

But the expert intellectuals had to navigate institutional realities, bureaucratic logistics, labor priorities, and a thicket of national and state authorities. In spirit there existed a solidarity across institutions. Bureau of Prisons parole executive Ray Huff backed a federal study in theory and Justin Miller valued the cooperation from wardens and superintendents. But ironically, shared values sometimes revealed redundancy, such as when Miller was considering a PIRA member as an advisor and realized the ambiguous contours of these institutions' work.[85] PIRA's work overlapped with the Survey's, and a PIRA official admitted than he could not "even pretend to know . . . the President's intentions" in considering these investigations.[86] One senator conflated the Survey of Release Procedures with a "Crime Prevention Bureau"—a separate project of Miller's that did not actually exist.[87] An American Prison Association official could not easily discern "the alphabetical parade and the various groups coming into the now popular field of crime treatment."[88] National leaders feared duplication with state WPA and Treasury records.[89] Ironically, avoiding extraneous data compilation created extra work.[90] After a long national neglect of penology, the frenzy of bureaucratic activity now entrenched confusion.

Despite its geographic ambitions, the Survey suffered from an East Coast and national parochialism. The leadership's vast majority lived east of the Allegheny Mountains, and western states pleaded for more representation.[91] An Illinois parole official hoped his valuable knowledge of middle America would not be overlooked.[92] Overbearing approval processes encumbered requests for funding and to move a regional headquarters from Seattle to Portland.[93] National officials meanwhile distrusted precinct captains, whose possession of intimate details allowed a "tremendous power for oppression" and "extortion and blackmail."[94]

The states, for their part, responded unevenly to the Survey. Oregon officials were impressed by representative Ray Huff, but other states feared federal domination.[95] One state board demanded that it approve all personnel and scheduling and that records stay onsite, threatening to "terminate the study" at its discretion.[96] Some states were hesitant to reveal "confidential" case history; an official called it a "breach of confidence" to let WPA workers read parole records.[97]

Miller saw a fundamental tension in the New Deal's dual aims—between the Justice Department's intellectual purposes and WPA's labor goals. Justice officials did value WPA involvement, hoping its workers would relieve them of tedious labor. Sanford Bates wanted WPA workers, not probation officers, to serve as paymasters.[98] As for the scientific side, criminologist Sheldon Glueck declined to advise the Survey, doubting the value of entrusting "technical" research to "an army of the unemployed." Miller appreciated this "critical comment" and shared Glueck's bias for elite expertise.[99] Miller mused that moving $25,000 from relief workers to expert administration would be harmless, while a transfer of "any . . . amount" in the other direction would "cripple us very, very seriously." Seeing WPA workers as "very short of the class of employees necessary," Miller requested exemptions from WPA hiring rules.[100] Sanders and Miller wanted to fingerprint everyone on the relief rolls to keep criminals away from a survey that "relates to criminal justice."[101] J. Edgar Hoover initially balked at providing FBI manpower for this fingerprinting, which local police undertook instead.[102]

But from the WPA's perspective, the Survey was its subordinate subsidiary, funded through the Emergency Relief Appropriation Acts of 1935 and 1936 on the condition that WPA workers occupy most jobs.[103] The WPA had its own constraints, as funding covered regional directors and field supervisors but not state supervisors.[104] WPA had to maintain a "maximum of employment in all localities" while accommodating "flexibility in state plans."[105] Miller acknowledged these constraints of federalism, but Justice officials from the beginning struggled under WPA budgetary restraints.[106] Knowing that 1935 appropriations would expire after June 1936, Justice officials gambled on securing funding as they went.[107] They were accustomed to shuffling funding creatively. Although WPA dollars came with some flexibility—5 percent of allotments for transportation and relief personnel could be transferred[108]—rules precluded funding for "routine departmental tasks" like clerical help.[109] Joseph Keenan could not move Helen Fuller from the Lands Division to the Survey Payroll.[110] And Miller preferred to consider the WPA's tight work schedules "suggestive."[111]

In June 1936 the WPA asserted its financial control when Corrington Gill requested that $900,000 be returned to the agency, which would disburse funds as needed.[112] After Bates was reluctant to request an extension,[113] Cummings intervened, stressing to Gill his understanding of the project's economic importance: Relief workers would receive 73 percent of the funds. In the bigger picture, crime was economically harmful and "more adequate criminal statistics" could help combat the "growing public sentiment against parole and probation."[114] Cummings hoped his high-minded progressive priorities would overcome WPA's bureaucratic requirements.

After the Survey was rescued by the 1936 Emergency Appropriation Act, it soon fell behind schedule. Disparities across WPA guidelines for workers' hours, new reductions in hours, confusing WPA rules, and "unpredictable circumstances" caused delays. Budgeted hours for relief workers had fallen from 166.6 to 140 and then down to 96 in late 1936.[115] Quarantines and prison riots slowed things down.[116] Michigan and Illinois suffered delays in their survey work.[117] In November, Stuart Rice, the acting chairman of the WPA's Coordination Committee of the Central Statistical Board, warned Miller that time was short. Miller complained about budgeting restrictions as he wanted to hire Wayne Morse, an Oregon law professor, who could not take the job for $3,600. Miller also identified political skepticism among states suspicious of federal motives and "almost invariably . . . horrified" to trust sensitive records with relief workers, so work had to be conducted onsite.[118]

Budgeting cuts converged with coordination problems to cause frustration. Miller hoped to attract top experts on short notice to a November 1936 conference on the same weekend the executive committee of the Prison Association of New York was holding a long-planned meeting that competed for attendees. Reimbursing attendees proved difficult and rules against financing air travel discouraged attendees from the West. The conference could not afford to publish proceedings, and budget constraints reduced the next conference, two days after Christmas in Chicago, to a dinner affair with limited reimbursements.[119]

And then there were threats due to labor conditions. Some workers' grievances mirrored Miller's desire for flexibility. Miller wanted maximum salary exemptions to accommodate a "supplementary payroll."[120] Administrative workers wanted the annual leave and vacation days afforded by other government jobs.[121] Sanders and Miller recognized that restrictions on leave would undercut morale.[122] Miller worried that planned hours reductions might inspire "radical elements within the labor group" as workers complained about payday inconsistencies, lunch times, and night shifts. They wanted more transparency in job descriptions and promotion. In 1937, junior coders, card- and keypunchers, calculator machine operators, tabulating machine operators, and editors made 60 cents per hour, while their senior counterparts made 76 to 80 cents—26.7 to 33.3 percent more. Some workers demanded pay commensurate with the work they said they were already doing. A Workers Alliance chapter demanded clearer pay brackets and a third-party arbiter from the National Labor Relations Board to adjudicate disputes. The Workers Alliance also decried "unfair discrimination based on race, color, creed, political, fraternal or other such classification," and worried that "negro workers cannot qualify for certain higher classifications." Black workers demanded access to the Department of Justice restrooms of their choosing, and to the cafeteria. One worker, Orval Miller, demanded back pay for work beyond his pay schedule, the difference between $58 and $72 per month. Although his supervisors took his grievances seriously, Sanders dismissed him as a "shyster and chiseler," according to Morse.[123]

New challenges emerged in 1937, especially after Miller left in February to join the US Board of Tax Appeals.[124] Morse, wishing to ensure that the first volume was "thorough and scholarly," urged Cummings to provide a larger staff and called the July 1 deadline unrealistic.[125] The academic cycle proved challenging in the fall when two professors had to leave the project to return to their universities. Meanwhile the committee struggled to budget the Survey's printing, even considering Leavenworth prison labor while hoping for WPA funding.[126]

Budgetary shortcomings, beginning in late 1936, forced the Survey to narrow its scope. It now seemed that the questionnaires were "too large and complex" for wardens to manage and yielded data unsuited for statistical analysis.[127] Cummings abandoned his hopes to extend the Survey to Hawaii.[128] By March 1937 dramatic cuts required a reduction in fieldwork and the coordinating committee was unimpressed with the progress.[129] In April the executive committee revised the schedule to close statistical units by April 17 and continue coding and editing until June, with a contingency plan to furnish data to academia if funding terminated.[130] WPA worker requirements forbade the Survey from cutting fieldworkers unless it cut administrative staff. Survey leaders asked Hopkins for regulatory exemptions.[131] Cummings again intervened, writing to Stuart Rice, the acting chairman of the coordinating committee of the Central Statistical Board of the Works Progress Administration. Cummings reminded Rice that for two years the Justice Department had accommodated bureaucratic requirements, and that since 1935 the "assumption" was that "sufficient extensions of time and funds" would allow completion, despite the WPA's labor priorities. Cummings insisted challenges like the lack of uniformity across states were predictable, but Rice insisted on further attenuating the program. Cummings stressed that field units could not close by April 17.[132]

Despite such setbacks, the survey studied 9,000 federal parole outcomes by mid-1937. Even under austerity pressures, its architects remained determined to create a "first-rate" study. Throughout 1938 the five-volume project continued as the committee oversaw more revisions, entertained more questions about its specific uses, fielded more requests for author extensions, and listened to anxieties about their progress.[133]

The published *Survey of Release Procedures* reports grappled toward a delicate balance. They aimed to defend and celebrate the processes of parole, probation, and pardon already underway, especially at the state level. Simultaneously the reports sought to look forward and identify areas for improvement. The national government posed as the indispensable leader, which meant distinguishing itself as uniquely appreciative of the progress in motion.

To grasp the tensions that federalism brought to carceral liberalism, it helps to examine an area whose importance was only beginning to gain federal attention—the problem of race. In terms of disproportionate incarceration rates, racial disparities—especially in state prisons—shrunk in the 1930s, an anomaly compared to trends in the Progressive Era or in the 1940s and postwar period, when the extreme racial inequities became more pronounced.[134] Perhaps the New Dealers had little informed reason for realizing that this would happen. In their enthusiastic defense of rehabilitation, the Survey authors were sensitive to racial inequities, especially in parole, and they took care to publicize this recognition without undercutting the state systems they sought to vindicate. The Surveys were assessing a reformist architecture often segregated by race and, especially outside the South, sometimes cognizant of race for reasons of equity. The Washington, D.C., parole board had a "prominent Negro educator and author to represent his race."[135] In Illinois, "negro districts, supervised by negro agents" had "overlap" with "white districts."[136] In New Jersey, parolees were supervised by people of the same gender, and "negro men and one negro woman supervise negro parolees."[137]

On occasion the Surveys counteracted certain racist assumptions. This effort was not always especially visionary. At a time when eugenic criminalization of ethnic whites had largely yielded to the emphasis on Black criminality, volume 2 of the Survey noted that "many studies have concluded that foreign-born whites are less liable to resort to crime than native-born whites."[138] The same volume drew attention to racial disparities. Yet while the publication appeared aware that race consciousness, particularly in the South, did not always aim toward equity, it exposed "unjust" racial discrimination in a way that affirmed southern officials' integrity. A South Carolina former governor noted that he frequented the penitentiary soliciting parole applications, because white men could gain access, while "a negro was seldom given any opportunity."[139] Some attempts at humanizing discrimination's victims resorted to cultural caricatures. Volume 3 of the Survey, focused on pardon, observed that executive mercy could ameliorate conditions where people endured unreasonably equal standards: "Racial minorities of a lower or different cultural standard may preserve attitudes [legal] in their former times." The report concluded that certain punishments "according to our behavior-patterns, would be absolutely legal, but scarcely just to them."[140]

The embryonic racial commitments of federal carceral liberalism motivated a search for anti-Black discrimination in release statistics. Volume 2 of the Survey scoured the available racial statistics of probation processes for the District of Columbia, Missouri, Maryland, and thirteen states outside the old South—Arizona, California, Colorado, Illinois, Kansas, Minnesota, Massachusetts, New York, Ohio, Pennsylvania, Rhode Island, Vermont, and Wisconsin—and relayed a marked but perhaps unexpectedly subtle disparity: Black probation violators "totaled 1,062 cases (47 percent), and of these, 530 (23 percent) resulted in revocation," whereas "white probation violators numbered 4,727 (36 percent), and of this number 2,253 (17 percent) had their probations revoked." A 17 percent white revocation rate was not trivially lower than the 23 percent Black revocation rate, but perhaps less disparate than anticipated. These discrepancies nevertheless drove attempts to rationalize, understand, or critique. While a "cursory glance" at statistics might yield "no reason to believe that Negroes universally violated probation more often than whites," volume 2 clarified that a "more intensive study shows that" the statistics were indeed generally "unfavorable for Negroes." Yet the Survey's statistical work revealed "no significant difference between the outcome of native-born whites and Negroes" once on probation. One possible implication was that whatever racial disparities between white and Black criminality, the system was successfully locating the reformable percentage of each race. Any continuing disparities were contingent on local circumstances—statistical noise within the nationally triumphant system of reform. As a whole, volume 2 affirmed that "Negroes, as a general rule, [appeared no] more apt to violate the terms of release." Apparent disparities "may have been due to local conditions instead of being attributable to a greater tendency toward criminality."[141]

To be sure, volume 4, on parole, found true disparities through statistics. Looking at more than "half the institutions . . . a significantly small proportion of Negroes were paroled."[142] Yet, as if to show that reform could overcome even these disparities, volume 4 noted that "in at least three institutions" in Ohio and Pennsylvania, Blacks were paroled "more often" than whites, a suggestion "that discrimination . . . was not universal."[143] Moreover, "only . . . certain sections of the country" demonstrated severe disparities.[144] Controlling for parole violations categorized as "new offenses" brought racial parity: "Thirteen percent, or 10,072 whites, had their paroles revoked for violations by new offenses, as contrasted with 15 percent, or 2,260 Negroes."[145] As with probation, the Survey touted its success as both a diagnostic of racial disparities and proof that progress was occurring.

In general the Survey's treatment of race balanced carceral liberalism and war-on-crime federalism. Its defensive appreciation for state and local release systems meant vindicating their triumphs while evincing sensitivity to room for improvement. It meant showing the need for both federal and state cooperation. In one telling passage, volume 4 indicated that carceral nationalization would not necessarily produce racial equality. In federal systems, "white persons were more likely to be granted parole . . . than were [persons] of minority races."[146] (The Survey did not spend much time considering whether low recidivism rates among released Black Americans suggested that lower thresholds had put them in prison in the first place.)

Aspiring to demonstrate racial progressivism in action, the Surveys had to openly publicize disparities in systems outside federal reach—just one of several tensions the whole undertaking had revealed. As the Survey finished up and approached publication, the ironies of carceral liberalism fused in a curious synthesis. While pursuing national appreciation for state governance, federal administrators faced suspicious state authorities. Hoping to unify relief work and a defense of rehabilitation, Miller and Cummings became flustered by labor disputes and WPA priorities. Setting out to marry criminological discipline to the humanism of the social state, the Justice Department fell behind schedule and became obstructed by cold bureaucracy. Rather than affirming a unity of reformist purpose, the Survey of Release Procedures revealed the complexities of war-on-crime federalism and the New Deal state's contradictions. Perhaps most ironically, the Justice Department's punishment bureaucracy had to overcome the WPA's welfare bureaucracy to make its case for rehabilitation. Thus, the racial paradoxes in the New Dealers' rehabilitative vision followed their general propensity to rearrange but not extinguish the contradictions of American incarceration.

DISCIPLINE WITHOUT BRUTALITY

The New Deal's simultaneous aggrandizement of carceral capacity and attention to rehabilitation served to construct carceral liberalism. In the early 1930s, Roosevelt deployed his bold ideas through the jurisdictional complexity that he inherited. Along with its national ambition and constitutional humility, carceral liberalism balanced radical reformism with disciplinary pragmatism, and so by the late 1930s a discernible program arose, combining discipline with a rejection of brutality. The conceit of humane incarceration promised to make the carceral state more palatable even as it expanded. Whether in defending repression in terms of its opposite or leveraging state power as a critique of itself, Sanford Bates, Homer Cummings, and Howard Gill each articulated different facets of this new paradoxical program.

Bates's 1937 *Prisons and Beyond* offered one reconciliation of the tensions. Bates championed scientific understanding of every prisoner, the abolition of county jails, restorative justice, and a "more or less permanent" isolation of "incorrigible criminals" from society. He wanted effective parole and probation—a humane regime of "constructive discipline" that avoided "brutality on the one hand and sentimentality on the other." Hardly a work of reactive expediency, Bates's tract depicted the prison as a social constant, a fixture of the future, its core functions eclipsing historical particularity. Bates optimistically anticipated technocratic discipline, which had already defeated the draconian vagaries of antiquity. With "the failure of the British colonial penal ventures" now behind, "we have discovered much about sanitation, hygiene, and protective medicine," Bates enthused. The world was made smaller by the "telegraph and radio" and there remained "no inherent reason why a prison colony should be a place where cruelty abides." Bates enthusiastically envisaged the "prison of the future!" freed of the need for "silent, lonely" guards carrying firearms "at great expense to the taxpayers," for the "institutions" might be "protected entirely by science."[147] Bates's prison was liberated not only from history but also from materialist political economy, with disciplinary "public-work projects, labor camps, and opportunities for individual or group service" shorn from such considerations as unfair competition with free labor.[148] Prison labor's purpose was to provide prisoners with meaningful work.

Bates rejected brutality but eschewed the very notion of leniency, defending reform on disciplinary grounds. Restitution would prevent lax justice. Inmate psychiatry did not imply coddling. Bates's ideal deputy warden was an "absolute monarch" who must "decide as justly as he can" whether inmates violated rules so as "to mete out punishment. He must be neither too soft nor too harsh." Even Bates's defense of parole venerated the punitive state. Far from lessening reliance on punishment, parole would augment and ensure it. Parole violations had loose standards of due process that could easily ensnare the guilty and afford "a higher degree of protection to the public." Parole thus meant longer prison sentences.[149] In sum, Bates's harsh vision was not reactionary but visionary. His carceral utopia of discipline and redemption in reciprocal reinforcement, freed from its premodern and economically grounded past, was already on its way.

Bates even started sounding different on Alcatraz. Once a critic of its lack of rehabilitative functions, he now argued that even with the strictest "discipline" in the federal system, Warden Johnston ensured "that no brutality or inhumanity shall be practiced."[150] Bates's change of mind pleased Cummings, who, now retired, was defending the prison against media depictions of torture and mistreatment, and criticisms from his successor, Attorney General Frank Murphy. Cummings vented: abolishing this "symbol of the triumph of law and order" would be a "tragedy."[151] Bates shared Cummings's distaste for the "selfish and ill-timed" press reports and agreed that the institution was "humanely and efficiently administered" and its inmate treatment gave no "cause for concern."[152]

Whereas in the early 1930s Cummings and Bates represented distinct strains of New Deal penology, their carceral liberalism now converged on Alcatraz. While Bates defended rehabilitation for serving discipline, Cummings defended his unforgiving prison on reformist grounds. Cummings's 1939 defense of Alcatraz turned on the dyad of control and humanity—mirrored in his depiction of Bates as a "career penologist of long experience ... both a scholar and a realist." Cummings stressed Alcatraz's decency: Its prisoners enjoyed designated time to "talk freely" and smoke cigarettes. They could choose between "light" or "heavy" portions of the "good and wholesome" mess hall offerings, although they had to finish their plates unless sick. And despite its housing the 300 of the most seemingly dangerous inmates out of 17,000 federal prisoners—despite a founding purpose of unremittingly detaining the irredeemable—"even some of those in Alcatraz may sometime reform," Cummings conceded. Consulting with Bates, he had transferred some prisoners from Alcatraz to other prisons. In other words, security and redemption were like yin and yang, each containing a seed of the other.[153]

In response to his piece, Cummings received reassurance that Alcatraz would survive its public relations stumble and would serve "an essential public need through the years."[154] One letter hailed Alcatraz's "stringent discipline without brutality," which secured "humane treatment for the other nine tenths of society." For the sake of "honest men crushed ... by inexorable circumstances," America should "stiffen her back against the brigand and racketeer in high places as well as low" and "let hardened criminals have the hard rock."[155] Bates applauded the diplomatic tone of Cummings's article, which he guessed was "a little more dignified than you would have liked it to be."[156] Roosevelt responded with encouragement that "no one is in in a better position to explain the purpose" than its architect Cummings, but stayed neutral on the controversy between his attorneys general.[157] Despite internal disagreements in the war-on-crime coalition, the island prison was secure in the New Deal state. It would stay open until 1963.

But carceral liberalism was not mere synthesis of discipline and reform—it contained one more paradox, a critique of itself, a radical dissent that legitimated the whole. The minority report lived in Howard Gill, author of volume 5 of the *Survey of Release Procedures,* published in 1940. Gill, once a superintendent at Norfolk Prison Colony in Massachusetts, issued a scathing indictment of prison growth. Gill lamented the increasing reliance on prisons. The public were told "that only with high walls, steel bars, and cage-like cells were criminals kept from breaking forth to murder, rob and rape law-abiding citizens," but prison construction "created a vicious circle." The system fueled "as much desperation and degradation as it has sought to restrain." Incarceration had become blunt and indiscriminate, sometimes allowing "the most dangerous criminals" more "freedom" than lesser offenders. Prison design harmed prisoners and poisoned their will. Subjecting virtually all prisoners to "interior cell blocks, originally designed as punishment cells" was in fact "unnecessary, expensive, and detrimental to health and morale."[158]

Interestingly, volume 5 included the most radical indictment of carceral systems, focused as it was on prisons themselves. And yet the radicalism of its critique barely extended to the problem of race, which would come to define the penitentiary in future years. Here and there Gill mentioned segregation and racial discrimination, but only in several passing mentions, such as noting that Texas prisons "usually separated" the races, as did Mississippi's. Gill also gestured toward the strange racial practices of carceral discipline—but with very little commentary. He noted the curiosity that in Missouri's "prison farms . . . a dozen white inmates act as unarmed guard-foremen over negro crews working in the fields."[159] In this respect Gill embodied the colorblind conceit of carceral liberalism. As he leveled the most adamant criticism of any of the volumes, he spent little time on the long-term racial consequences of the system that the national government was building in cooperation with the Jim Crow South and the discriminatory North.

Nevertheless, volume 5 dissented from the dominant ethos of prison discipline, articulated by Bates and Cummings in defending Alcatraz. In prisoners "the maintenance of discipline" remained "only skin-deep while underneath there smolder the fires of revolt, kept hot by the demands of those in authority." Prison order relied on a myriad of "rules and regulations, not only for inmates but for guards and officers alike"—rules enforcing good manners, banning unpatriotic behavior, and much else. Unwritten rules were potentially tyrannical. The relationship between officer and prisoner resembled that between India's higher castes and "untouchables."[160]

But Gill's outlook was fatalistic. The need to shield society "from the depredations of the abnormal, sub-normal, or vicious criminal" made prisons necessary, however evil. This short-term pragmatism accompanied a long-term pessimism; searching the American history of incarceration for "rehabilitation, moral, physical, intellectual or industrial, does not incline one to an optimistic conclusion."[161] Volume 5 marked the radical boundary of carceral liberalism, simultaneously building and lamenting the instruments of repression.

NEW DEAL PENOLOGY did not fail to limit incarceration despite itself, but instead drove a mutually symbiotic relationship between punishment and rehabilitation. With the profitable industrial prison fading into the past, reformers reconciled different correctional priorities, managing short-term and long-term challenges to political order. Roosevelt and Bates translated the northeastern penological traditions they occupied to confront the structural and ideological challenges to national legitimacy. This meant recognizing federalism—encouraging and learning from both incarceration and release at the state level. Ideologically it meant the construction of a new program, carceral liberalism, an ecumenical temperament that accommodated different penological approaches, embracing both the doctrine of discipline and the promise of redemption.

Purging private profit made discipline itself a public good. Freed of nineteenth-century sensibilities of austerity, the modern system served a distinctively twentieth-century liberalism. Focusing on discipline itself meant that parole and prison sentences were mutually constitutive. Prison labor now served public order, outside and inside prison walls. As the domestic state grew, so did its needs, and prisoners could fulfill them. In 1938 prisoners' work provided many goods—cotton duck, canvas, shoes, brushes, clothing, metal transfer cases, metal specialties, brooms, castings, wooden furniture, and rubber deck. Other prisoners labored in laundry services, reforestation, road construction, building construction, farming, dairy, canning, printing, and mattress and pillow making.[162]

Inside the prisons, modern liberalism finally normalized the Foucauldian model of discipline for its own sake. Corrections and the welfare system could become intertwined. Prisoners would be instructed in liberal values. In New York's Wallkill State Prison, criminological classes invited prisoners to ask holistic questions about political economy, such as "Why do we have depressions?" and "[What is] the place of government in solving social and economic problems"?[163] Future public education would become expedient conduits to the carceral state. In the meantime, the Survey of Release Procedures pondered the transition made by inmates and whether an "intermediate" institution between "the state training school and the state penitentiary" could serve socialization.[164]

Even though the New Dealers might have not predicted it, their penal state had an ominous racial trajectory.[165] To be sure, paternalistic authorities at the WPA considered prison educational activities "for the benefit of Negroes."[166] And in the 1930s the NAACP struggled somewhat successfully at the local level to desegregate northern detention centers. At the time, the full racism of modern incarceration was not as clear as it would become. Scholars have indeed found racial disparities becoming more conspicuous with the rise of mass incarceration in the late twentieth century. And although sociologist Christopher Mueller argues that the enduring shift occurred alongside trends of Black northward migration before the 1950s, Mueller also shows that in state prison populations, at least, the short-term trend moved toward less racial disparity in both the North and South in the 1930s.[167] Over the same decade, however, the New Deal war on crime accommodated subtle changes that could have contributed to the long term trajectory: while state prison populations told one story, the federal incarcerated population became less white throughout the 1930s, from 75 percent in 1932 to 69 percent in 1940 and 66 percent in 1946 (see Figure 8.5).[168] In state institutions, growing disproportionately in the South, white prisoners in 1937 served an average of 16.4 months compared to 19.5 months for nonwhites. Although for auto thefts whites served more time and sentences for robbery were identical, nonwhites served considerably longer sentences for murder, manslaughter, forgery, and rape.[169] Ultimately, the longer-term emphasis on rehabilitation, welfare, and state use for prison labor hardly constrained the carceral state's social disparities any more than its social control.

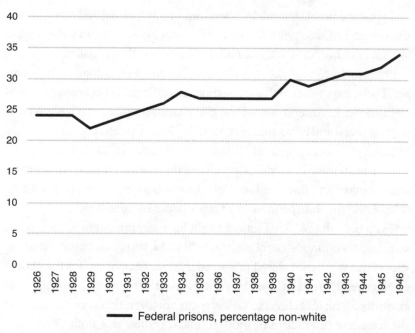

Figure 8.5   Racial disparity in federal prisons, 1926–1946. Data source: *Historical Corrections Statistics in the United States*, Table 3-32, 66.

The New Dealers were not neutral or agnostic on imprisonment—they were ambivalent, meaning they had distinct tendencies toward both strengthening and lessening America's reliance on prisons. This ambivalence brought together the unforgiving isolation of Alcatraz, the Survey of Release Procedure's intellectual ambitions of defending parole, the New Deal's material expansion of carceral systems, and the diversity of ideas in such carceral liberals as Roosevelt, Cummings, Bates, and Gill. The ambivalence of carceral liberalism, along with its respect for federalism, fueled the surge of all systems of correctional supervision at all levels of government through the 1930s and ultimately laid the foundations for America's modern carceral capacity.

CHAPTER 9

PREVENTION, REPRESSION, AND NEW DEAL CRIMINOLOGY

Within the more progressive expressions of liberalism, the operative tension appears in the word *prevention*. The word captures both the nurturing assurances of the welfare state and the dystopian prospect of preemptive discipline. Through prevention modern liberalism offers a healthier, kinder society with fewer pathologies that require coercive correction. At the same time its promise to root out social ills before they metastasize invites relentless policing and dreams of the panopticon.

Attorney General Homer Cummings brought this tension deep into the conceptualization of his national war on crime. At his December 1934 National Crime Conference he and others emphasized "crime prevention."[1] Cummings was referring to prevention mainly as an alternative to repression—namely, a focus on juvenile welfare to reduce the need for policing and incarceration. But sometimes prevention had a more inclusive connotation. For Roosevelt, prevention and enforcement were linked, as were welfare and repression. "Repression," a word the war-on-crime coalition used frequently, generally carried a neutral connotation—to repress or forcibly subdue lawlessness was necessary but not sufficient for law and order. At the conference the president promised to go beyond "mere repression" and work to unite "every crime-preventing, law-enforcing agency of every branch of Government." Targeting the "lawless and the criminal elements" was a "component part" of the greater "objective" of promoting a "healthy national life"—a project that included "feeding and clothing the destitute."[2] The conference's emphasis on prevention was both reaction and provocation, responding to organized crime and soliciting a new federal science of law and order. It prioritized a new federal role in shaping criminology as an intellectual and practical undertaking. To spearhead the national crime prevention agenda Cummings tapped Justin Miller, dean of Duke Law School, as head of his Attorney General's Advisory Committee on Crime.

Scholars have peripherally addressed the New Deal Justice Department's self-conscious place in the history of criminology and in particular its transformative fixation on crime prevention.[3] Claire Potter identifies Justin Miller as an authentic liberal, whose contradictory embrace of both "decentralized community work" and "a strong state" lost out to the coherent policing vision of J. Edgar Hoover.[4] On the other hand, in contextualizing Hoover's efforts to get Miller fired, Kathleen Frydl notes that Hoover was institutionally jealous of Miller's support for Senator Copeland's nationalized police force.[5] In general terms the literature typically casts New Deal criminology in opposition to the repressive state.[6] Some authors stress the 1930s liberals' differences from Progressive Era reformers, who prioritized the practitioner art of policing over social welfare. Others compare the New Deal's humane criminological clarity to the later-twentieth-century reliance on coercion.[7]

As for crime prevention itself, historians typically locate it as a Progressive Era project of juvenile welfare mostly operating at the local level.[8] Khalid Gibran Muhammad has highlighted this period's "crime prevention" as a reformist approach to immigrant youth mostly foreclosed to Black Americans.[9] Beyond its occasional monographic appearances, the term is elusive, lacking a settled meaning in the longer sweep. New York's Society for the Prevention of Crime, founded in 1878, recommended "swift and certain enforcement" in a streamlined legal system, concerning itself with public opinion, firearms, gambling, and corruption.[10] After the social worker aspect proliferated among northern progressives, the term gained academic purchase in the interwar period, usually connoting juvenile behavior,[11] with prevention as an alternative to repression.[12] Often hygiene organizations, tied to reformatories, pursued alternatives to punishment.[13] Into the early 1930s many crime prevention outfits focused on criminal tendencies in youth.[14] Behavioral clinics and special programs oriented toward crime prevention existed in Berkeley, Colorado, Chicago, Detroit, Minneapolis, Cincinnati, and Pittsburgh.[15] These were all local undertakings. An exception among institutions was the Labor Department's Children's Bureau—founded by social workers including Lillian Wald and Florence Kelley and formalized by Congress in 1912—which stood alone among federal agencies in its interest in juvenile justice, guiding the creation of new standards for juvenile courts in 1923.[16]

Despite lacking much of a national center, crime prevention united practitioners with academics across the country by the time the New Deal began. Berkeley's August Vollmer personified this duality. He criticized police departments for neglecting "crime prevention as a distinct function,"[17] praised the New York Police Department's Crime Prevention Bureau, and championed a national unit of the sort Cummings also advocated.[18] Vollmer so prioritized these ideas that in 1933 he attributed Nazi Germany's militant policing partly to the nation's deficiency in crime prevention.[19] At Harvard Law, Sheldon and Eleanor Glueck saw widespread social dysfunction requiring a multilayered constellation of social and institutional remedies, yet their research had pessimistic implications. In 1930 the Gluecks published a study that questioned the efficacy of the Massachusetts Reformatory, and undertook a more comprehensive Harvard Crime Survey.[20] Their 1933 study of a thousand delinquent boys identified key themes—native-born sons of foreign parents, low educational achievement, inferior intelligence, bad educational equipment, and bad economic conditions, nine-tenths of the troubled kids hailing from "broken homes."[21] More so than Vollmer's approach, their criminology often lent itself to emphasizing incarceration. Sheldon Glueck taught at Harvard's Institute of Criminal Law, which organized a curriculum for correctional administrators.

This institutional, social, and intellectual history of crime prevention received new national attention under Cummings and Miller, who sought to leverage the idea toward political and cultural goals. In the short-term

Miller hoped to create a federal crime prevention bureau or at least a "clearing house of information" about the social causes of crime.[22] The constraints of federalism only raised the stakes of intellectual leadership, and crime prevention became the criminological language the Justice Department appropriated to legitimate itself while welcoming the criminological progressives into the war-on-crime coalition. In that sense Roosevelt's goal of "expert service" to coordinate the power of "home, school, church, community and other social agencies" was not so humble.[23] It was in the area of crime prevention that the criminologists and the federal government most clearly delved into the world of policing gender. Family relations mediated the relationship between society, both its triumphant structure and its many fallen pathologies, and the blank-slate child. These relations would turn importantly on the proper guidance of father and mother. Crime prevention also offered a conduit for the more "feminine" side of the social state's intersection with policing after the end of the Progressive Era and Alcohol Prohibition. Miller, along with the other New Dealers, accepted the importance of state coercion. But in a broader context Miller hoped that "a more wholesome background of public opinion" was moving beyond "repressive phases of crime control" to embrace a "well-rounded program."[24] And yet federal crime prevention struggled to become more than a discursive exercise. As Prison Bureau chief Sanford Bates was paraphrased saying in 1937, "It is one thing to admit the importance of crime prevention, but a far more difficult thing to do something about it."[25]

Nevertheless, even with the failure of crime prevention or a permanent bureau to materialize, something striking arises about the aspirations of New Deal criminology. Its abortive ambitions reveal an underappreciated theoretical trajectory toward which the modern liberal state has pushed policy even where it has fallen short in practice. While the coalitional objects of New Deal crime prevention complemented the repressive state, the more idealistic formulations were in the abstract even more accommodating of carceral repression. The radicalization of crime prevention meant a broad appreciation of societal conditions, which implicated the bulk of state activity at the very time it was greatly expanding. The greater the emphasis on welfare, the greater the ambitions for surveillance and correction. And so, in the New Deal imagination, prevention went from complementing repression to accommodating repression, from accommodating repression to imagining new forms of repression yet to exist. And by the late 1930s Miller's crime prevention vision proved too ecumenical and ambitious for its own good—fully embracing the very repression that prevention had first sought to make obsolete. The criminology that survived the decade, overtaken by pragmatic approaches, was therefore hardly the most unforgiving version under consideration.

COMPLEMENTING REPRESSION

In the twilight of 1934 Justin Miller enthusiastically took the lead in New Deal criminology. It would be the great fulfillment of an illustrious academic life. Miller had law degrees from the University of Montana and Stanford and practiced on behalf of the California State Commission on Immigration and Housing before returning to academia. He was a law professor at the University of Oregon, the University of California, and the University of Southern California before becoming dean of the Duke University Law School, a post he maintained while starting his work for Cummings.[26] Not wanting to lose momentum after the 1934 national crime conference, Miller wrote to Cummings on Christmas Eve, urging a meeting as soon as possible.[27] On January 4, 1935, Miller reiterated the "importance of *continuity* in advertising," and did not want the "favorable impression to die out," since the crime conference had been "universally recognized as having been highly successful."[28]

Miller's focus on "advertising" revealed his self-conscious understanding of the relationship between perception and reality, ideas and institutions. The Advisory Committee on Crime had both cultural and institutional goals, which Miller recognized as coming together through his intellectual guidance. Miller envisaged a permanent Bureau of Crime Prevention to educate law administrators and conduct research into the causes of crime and ways to prevent it, for both adults and children.[29] In May the Advisory Committee declared its informational and institutional aims—federal "leadership" on crime prevention and building a new "permanent structure."[30] Contenders for the permanent institution's name included the "Federal Crime Institute," the "Federal Institute of Criminal Justice," and the "National Crime Institute."[31] But for the rest of the decade "crime prevention" proved the most enduring organizing idea.

The goal of marking the New Deal state as intellectual leader of criminology drove an ecumenical formulation of crime prevention's meaning—stretched leftward to include welfare and rightward to include enforcement. From the beginning, an ecumenical definition served the practical purpose of welcoming criminological institutions and community groups into the war-on-crime coalition. Funding came through the Works Progress Administration.[32] Miller's committee included Judge Scott M. Loftin, Assistant Attorney General Keenan, J. Edgar Hoover, and Bureau of Prisons head Sanford Bates.[33] Early plans included training for federal investigators, parole, probation and parole officials, and prosecutors; more scientific research "under laboratory conditions"; and stronger official ties with academia.[34] Miller's ideas included the creation of a chair of criminology in the Library of Congress, promotion of radio technology, better harmonization of state and federal laws, and collaboration with the US Chamber of Commerce.[35]

New Deal crime prevention consistently strived for academic corroboration in pursuit of both rigor and legitimacy.[36] Recognizing the need to professionalize criminal justice officials, Miller's team considered that the Bureau of Education could handle training schools.[37] But they were confident formal academia needed more engagement.[38] The incapacity of Hoover's agency, now called the Federal Bureau of Investigation (FBI), to meet demand for training highlighted the need for university involvement. Northwestern University specialized in criminological training and published the *Journal of Criminal Law and Criminology,* and Harvard and the University of California hosted serious criminological study.[39] The Crime Prevention Bureau, it was thought, could help design classes and course curricula.[40] Miller networked with those aspiring to bridge competing criminological schools. R. C. Sheldon from the Big Brother and Big Sister Foundation proposed a "Crime Prevention Institute" to include such luminaries as Miller, Hoover, Bates, Miriam Van Waters, and August Vollmer, but also intellectual competitors Sheldon Glueck and Edwin Sutherland.[41] R. C. Sheldon even claimed that Glueck signed on as president, which Glueck denied consenting to.[42]

Crime prevention allowed productive coordination with localities. Cummings approved the inclusion of US Conference of Mayors representative Daniel Hoan, Milwaukee's socialist mayor, who offered assistance on behalf of the major cities.[43] Miller's team respected how seriously Hoan took crime prevention.[44] Miller also approved of New York governor Herbert Lehman's "very active" work for "crime reform programs," and considered giving more substantial assistance.[45] Miller had an ally in California's Earl Warren, a Republican with "sound judgment and long experience" on crime prevention.[46]

Even in its most narrow connotations, Miller's crime prevention would complement rather than replace state coercion. Miller sought to transcend the popular "hunting down and killing outlaws" and "severe programs of repression" and lamented public ignorance about parole, probation, and prevention.[47] And yet he thought that Congress not only undervalued "educational and preventive work" but also neglected reforms for "effective prosecution."[48] Miller maintained that "preventive and curative measures" could get deserved attention without depriving "proper emphasis to a rigorous program of detention, apprehension, prosecution and punishment."[49] He valued enforcement, not only by the Justice Department but through Treasury's taxation power, the Post Office's criminal pursuits, and the Labor Department's Children's Bureau.[50] This integration of approaches reached across the government. A November 1935 press release from the Women's Division of the Democratic National Committee featured comments by Attorney General Special Assistant Stella Akin, addressing crime prevention and praising both Cummings and the new FBI training school.[51]

Although the relationship between Miller and J. Edgar Hoover harbored jealousies and animosities, in terms of state building, a constructive—not irreconcilable—tension existed between Miller's prevention and Hoover's repression. Miller's main criticism of Hoover's ilk was that they lacked curiosity about the holistic nature of crime control, partly attributable to structural factors. The FBI's mobility precluded active engagement in crime prevention. Miller admired Hoover's "good work," but resented when he left "his own field" to criticize others. Miller along with Sanford Bates disagreed with Hoover's wholesale attack on probation and parole. While he called Hoover's plan for training and professionalization "very good," Miller wanted to do more than the publicly demanded enforcement strategies.[52] He lamented Hoover's "lack of knowledge" not only about programs of education and social work but about "judges, prosecutors, probation officers, parole officers, prison administrations [and] jail administrators."[53]

Concerned with public relations, Miller disliked the media's depiction of a divergence between him and the FBI. He claimed to dislike the press's sometimes "vicious antagonism against Mr. Hoover."[54] Hoover encouraged consultations with Miller to understand crime prevention.[55] Miller reciprocated the recognition of expertise. Willing to share criticisms of Hoover with Cummings, Miller nevertheless protested when a reporter spun an encounter to depict a conflict between their visions.[56] He denied his reported complicity in the Probation Association's open criticism of Hoover, and reminded Cummings that he had "highly" commended the FBI's work.[57] Responding to rumors that the Justice Department planned to rid of Hoover, Miller expressed dismay at the press's depiction of "a divided house."[58]

The meaning of crime prevention sometimes complemented enforcement and sometimes it outright included it. The ambiguities of meaning and branding carried over to questions of what a permanent institution would do. Miller asked Cummings whether the Crime Prevention Bureau should undertake "crime prevention and criminal law administration generally" or only serve as an advisory board with a humbler charge.[59] The capacious visions became apparent in the legal constraints that precluded a unilateral bureaucratic creation. Instrumentally, prevention was distinct from enforcement—which carried jurisdictional implications. Assistant Solicitor General Angus MacLean advised Cummings that he had great leeway in creating bureaus for the "detection and prosecution of crimes"—the Bureau of Investigation had arisen this way—but not the "prevention of crimes." He suggested getting explicit authorization, which they proceeded to attempt.[60] Two versions of joint resolutions arose, and MacLean recommended the more open-ended one.[61] Miller undertook a public relations effort to downplay the Justice Department's ambitions.

It was a delicate issue, as the press prematurely reported that Cummings had already created the bureau.[62] Cummings and Miller remained committed to the intellectual value of their plans. Cummings saw a federal bureau as an opportunity to "justify" his Crime Conference and Advisory Committee's recommendations, and to "round out our structure" of their outreach. He meanwhile considered alternative bureaucracies, like a Bureau of Criminal Administrative Training and Information.[63]

Even if a permanent bureau would prove elusive, the Advisory Committee itself temporarily functioned like a "clearing-house of information." In the summer of 1936 the Advisory Committee mailed about 1,800 requests for information about crime prevention to every conceivably relevant source—state attorneys general and district attorneys, civic organizations and community chests, religious and anti-vice organizations, newspapers and libraries, chapters of the Boy Scouts and the Young Women's Christian Association. Miller pursued Cummings's interest in "all government agencies whose functions might be construed as crime preventive"—state and local children's bureaus and police units, newly created federal welfare agencies, the Rural Research Unit of the Works Progress Administration, the Federal Housing Administration, and the Civilian Conservation Corps.[64] Through such prolific solicitation, Miller sought recognition from academia, private institutions, and state and local governments, while legitimating crime prevention itself as an idea. Miller repeatedly lauded Cummings for inspiring dialogue and he boasted of having "stimulate[d] interest in crime prevention throughout the United States."[65] Crime prevention conferences indeed proliferated nationwide.[66]

The production of crime prevention knowledge would require a broad, inductive search for what the term could mean and therefore how to pursue such knowledge. Unlike the Wickersham Commission, this project unfolded with authentic curiosity about what many sources of insight might bring. While Miller relayed Cummings's hope of "securing the cooperation" of government agencies, to others Miller passed along Cummings's wish to "secure information" on "instructional and research work" implicating "Crime Prevention, Police Science and Criminal Law Administration generally." Miller recognized the academic character of his undertaking, identifying the relevancy of "law, political science, sociology, psychiatry, and several of the other medical and biological sciences, as well as physics and chemistry."[67]

A deluge of responses rewarded the solicitation effort. Juvenile aid bureaus, police training schools, child protective programs, youth work programs, and Big Brother and Big Sister groups sent material. Miller's team, effectively administered by Helen Fuller, an official transferred from the public lands division, surveyed crime prevention strategies, researching "all forms of recreational, vocational and other activities designed to discover and eliminate the cause of crime."[68] They collected surveys of juvenile delinquency, scoured sociological studies, and assembled bibliographies of many hundreds of entries.[69]

ACCOMMODATING REPRESSION

Working through the correspondence, Miller's team contemplated the boundaries of crime prevention. Miller's capacious and slippery understanding of crime prevention coexisted with repression in two distinct ways—both in recognizing the importance of policing as a component of the overall struggle against crime, and in the recognition of repression as a component of the welfare emphasis on juvenile and social factors. Although the institutional needs of the war-on-crime coalition drove a formula of prevention that complemented repression, it was the foundational progressive focus that always held the potential for a true fusion in meaning. By homing in on youth, crime prevention potentially homed in on everything. Childhood implicated the family, and indeed all the background societal conditions thought to encourage or discourage criminality. The progressive rather than the conservative connotations of prevention went beyond complementing repression to accommodating it.

An April subcommittee report suggested a range of activities, many of them geared toward producing more crime conferences, working toward institutional permanence, and maintaining public relations to encourage widespread approval of it all. One sub-item out of many was a charge to furnish "leadership in crime prevention" with a specific goal of "discovering the underlying factors in the delinquency of children."[70]

Even this seemingly specific focus implicated all the societal conditions thought to encourage or discourage criminality. At a time when New Dealers imagined an expansive state role in nurturing society, the comprehensiveness of definitions took on importance. The Advisory Committee sifted through newspaper editorials that blamed crime on an apathetic or immoral population, poor education, and "society" itself.[71]

The more the Advisory Committee focused on preemption, especially among juvenile delinquents, the broader became its concern with the greater public welfare. Miller found encouragement in his posture that the wider its plan of attack, the better. R. K. Atkinson of the New York Police Department's Crime Prevention Bureau had "only one suggestion" but it was more easily said than done. He believed "any plan on crime prevention must be a broadly conceived community approach" that mobilized both "social and recreational forces."[72] E. L. Johnstone of the National Conference of Juvenile Agencies said a "national policy" alone could produce a "unified attack" necessary for crime prevention.[73]

Societal ills often pointed to economic conditions, which implicated all organs of the welfare state. Law enforcers eagerly explained the crime problem in economic terms. Estimates characteristically put the lawbreaking cost at $120 per capita.[74] First Lady Eleanor Roosevelt also stressed the economic costs, which she figured were "three times the annual cost of the Federal Government" in her 1935 speech identifying lawbreaking as arising from social conditions.[75] The Advisory Committee maintained a traditional focus on prevention among juveniles, but even this definition became unmanageably extensive, implicating the whole infrastructure of state power. Cummings and Miller pondered the "Social Aspects of Crime Prevention"[76] and their interlocutor Wilhelm Keuhme of the Labor Alliance believed that aside from the few born "with a warped mind," most criminals were economically desperate and that changing "economic conditions" could "rid the country of crime." Bogdan Lukamski of the Social Welfare Protective Committee urged censorship against romantic portrayals of crime and federal command of the school system and media, with authority consolidated under the governors and federal government to pursue rich and poor lawbreakers equally. Cummings took seriously the social equality angle, passing along the words of Don Castle, former San Quentin inmate whose pamphlet

"I Go to Prison" emphasized systemic corruption, estimating that 75 percent of inmates were on the "side of right and justice," even as "the big shots, and the politicians, lawyers and judges who protect and direct them" evaded justice.[77]

Social welfare became the key to harmonizing the juvenile wayward-ness to the greater puzzle of political economy. Chicago economist Paul Douglas, whose partisan loyalties shifted out of disappointment with Democrats' milquetoast devotion to labor, nevertheless summarized the New Deal approach in a pamphlet published while he served on the NRA's Consumer Advisory Board. The Depression destabilized life for children. Douglas concluded that "happy" people with "expansive and rounded personalities" needed to "feel relatively secure," which required feeling "the everlasting arms or . . . perhaps even better still, the feeling that their family will be protected economically."[78] Douglas represented the trending understanding of social welfare as a key strategy against law-breaking. But problematic family life brought attention back to adult wrongdoing and the traditionally punitive state. When it came to family, liberals and Hoover overlapped in their worldviews. "Crime begins at home," Hoover told an audience, lamenting that "we are doing nothing— to protect that home." He averred that those under voting age accounted for 20 percent of crimes. Parents' lax discipline explained how children could commit nearly a thousand murders and tens of thousands of bur-glaries and larcenies annually.[79]

Raising the stakes was the fear that above a certain age people were beyond hope. The Big Brother and Big Sister Federation's Herbert Wil-liams, for example, considered sexual deviancy an environmental im-purity toward which youth were naturally hostile. A boy who is ex-posed to "companions engaging in sex perversions is at first horrified and then gradually develops matter of fact attitudes toward the prac-tice and later begins to indulge in it." Emphasizing the rehabilitative po-tential of youth implied older children were a lost cause. Most "con-firmed criminals" were "incurable," according to a "composite picture" of criminality created by Kansas City police, finding those under sev-enteen more salvageable.[80]

The synergy between welfare and repression came into clear focus with eugenics. As determinist eugenics was giving way to environmentalism, all youth became legible risks. This trend did reinforce one fixation on rigid biological categorization—that of gender. A midwestern survey by Williams indicated that boys prone to delinquency ranged from "feeble-minded to near genius," although he recognized differences between the genders. Troubled girls were "more interested in sex" and more "over-developed physically" than their male counterparts, who were in turn "more resistant to authority."[81] Miller's own views marked the era in which eugenic science was casting off racial determinism in favor of environmentalist explanations. Miller's 1930 article "Does Prolific Breeding Cause Crime?" saw birth control as a preventive strike against abortion and the "closely related offense . . . of child murder."[82] Sterilization remained relevant—thirty states had some sterilization law, seventeen of them for convicted criminals.[83] Miller was a charter member of an organization favoring "sterilization of the unfit." Its representative told Miller he believed "sterilization of the feebleminded and mentally diseased" would sharply diminish American and international criminality, and identified promising experiments at San Quentin prison. While "some question" might exist as to sterilizing "criminals under compulsion," the "voluntary" sterilization of inmates had no informed opposition except in the Catholic Church.[84] But Miller's eugenic thinking was evolving. He offered criticism to Marion Norton, whose manuscript "The Biological Aspects of Crime" contained crude errors that appeared to betray imbalanced and antiquated racial views. Norton conceded the correction: the manuscript claimed eight times "more male Negro murderers" but should read "Negroes murdered." The original draft wrongly described an open immigration policy before World War I, when in fact "certain classes of defectives" were excluded. (Norton did not acknowledge East Asian exclusion.) Norton believed that numerous factors drove crime but "a fanatical environmentalism" distracted people from "man's inherent quality."[85]

Eugenics was no panacea, just an important tool among many. Sheldon Glueck regarded crime prevention as including "*any* technique which seems reasonable in the light of known facts and the suggestions of various authorities in the fields of criminology, mental hygiene, social work."[86] At the 1935 annual meeting of the Big Brother and Big Sister Federation, Glueck outlined his vision—national, scientific, holistic, and eugenic—stressing economic justice and calling for a Federal Crime Prevention Bureau. He advocated a "voluntary sterilization law" for every jurisdiction. Glueck's approach, like Miller's, was environmentalist. He explained that a "substantial percentage" of criminals had "mentally defective" or "diseased" family members, and had suffered "erratic"—either "too lax or unduly repressive"—discipline as children. Poverty and criminality both became "tribal traditions" in families. The anti-crime cause required a "systematic, continuous attack on all fronts of biological pathology." The school, the community, the home, the welfare office, municipalities, and all social institutions must wage preventive war on such dysfunction. The federal government had to expand to secure economic justice, help the underprivileged, and build a crime prevention bureau to serve as a "clearing-house and service-station" for local efforts.[87]

Miller's broad vision exposed internal tensions in its social consciousness and economic justification, and threatened to subsume crime control's most repressive instruments. For Miller, liberalism could and should embrace both social activism and federal police power. While most prevention discourse focused on "the work of juvenile courts and other children's agencies," Miller stressed the "need for research work in connection with major crimes committed by adults" and used the analogy of "disease prevention."[88]

But not all activists and reformers agreed with Miller's broad formulation. ACLU director Roger Baldwin, who himself had been an activist reformer of juvenile justice, forcefully rebuked Miller's outreach. He insisted his organization had "not much to offer" for the study. The ACLU, to the contrary, focused on "crime by those who are supposed to uphold law and order." Reining in lawless enforcement better served the ACLU's "conception of crime prevention." Miller attempted to reconcile Baldwin's response to his own philosophy, conceding that "official lawlessness" complicated efforts for police "reorganization" and insisting the ACLU's mission was, despite Baldwin's protests, "definitely crime preventive."[89] Miller's progressive criminological esthetic could not win over everyone on the left, some of whom detected danger in his societal ambitions.

Ironically, a voluminous understanding of crime prevention, arising from a concern about youth, threatened to displace its earlier emphasis on discrete juvenile programs. Miller's broad approach indeed repelled some youth leaders. Lester F. Scott of the Campfire Girls insisted the organization did not "claim to *prevent crime*," doubting that many of its members were "potential criminals." Girl Scouts national director Josephine Schain apologetically told Miller she could not help. Miller tried to persuade Brackin Kirkland of Boys Club, over his protestations, that "your work fits in very nice with the Attorney General's larger program of crime prevention and control."[90] By seeking to examine all social conditions that led the young astray, crime prevention was becoming deracinated from its original focus on youth.

VISUALIZING REPRESSION

In the late 1930s, crime prevention leadership moved from the Justice Department to the Treasury.[91] The 1935 Social Security Act authorized Roosevelt to form the Interdepartmental Committee to Coordinate Health and Welfare Activities, chaired by Assistant Secretary of the Treasury Josephine Roche, who had served as Denver's first full-time woman police officer.[92] Among its units was a Technical Committee on Probation, Parole, and Crime Prevention—as it was finally named. This Technical Committee convened members from across the welfare state— Frank Bane of the Social Security Board, Commissioner of Education John Studebaker, Mary Hayes of the National Youth Administration, Irma Ringe from the WPA, the Children Bureau's Katherine Lenroot, and CCC director Robert Fechner. Its war-on-crime brass included Gustav Peck from the Prison Industries Reorganization Administration, Robert Beattie from the Census Bureau's Administration of Criminal Statistics, Attorney General Special Assistant Brian McMahon, Wayne Morse from the Attorney General's Survey of Release Procedures, Federal Parole System supervisor Richard Chappell, and F. Lovell Bixby from the Bureau of Prisons.[93]

Initially Justin Miller dominated the Technical Committee, bringing with him Helen Fuller, who had de facto run the information clearinghouse. By October 1936 Fuller was working with Miller almost every day.[94] Under their leadership at the Technical Committee, "crime prevention" seemed at least as nebulous and unmanageable as at Justice. Miller, serving as chair, opened the first meeting pontificating on everything from the CCC's employment of young men to interdiction of marijuana. In his theoretical, even ponderous, discussion Miller even lamented the connotative limitations of the term "prevention": he wanted a positive term, analogous to "public order" or "public health"—phrases that stressed the maintenance of the desirable, not the *prevention* of the undesirable. He urged three avenues of action—a new federal department, more coordination, and, vaguely, more attention to neglected factors in public order. The meeting aired pleas for more coordination among agencies and across states, particularly in the South, and more openness toward rehabilitation. Disagreements arose as to whether rehabilitation was underappreciated or unrealistically prioritized as a panacea. Participants complained about CCC's shortsighted exclusion of parolees and probationers. But Ringe argued that viewing WPA recreation and art programs as crime prevention dangerously underestimated the crime problem.[95]

If anyone shared Miller's holistic appreciation of "crime prevention," it was Helen Fuller.[96] Fuller's listing of crime prevention activities included preventive police work, training, juvenile courts, coordinating councils, community councils, recreational and leisure programs including the Works Progress Administration, the Public Works Administration, the National Youth Administration, the Boy Scouts, crime commissions, religious activities, Education, Health, Demonstration Projects, and research.[97] Fuller understood crime prevention as surpassing questions of juvenile well-being, since adult students needed guidance too.[98] In 1938 she worked closely with *Building America,* a publication sponsored by the Society for Curriculum Study to produce a series of pro–New Deal features. She portrayed the predicament of crime prevention strategically. She arranged to get photographs from the FBI for the editor and worked to "simplify" the outline to the special edition on crime. She recommended a contextual story of what causes crime and how to control it, and suggested that the editor contact the Crime Prevention Association of Philadelphia, whose new publication *Crime Prevention Pays* articulated her general take. *Building America* echoed Cumming's description of crime as a misfortune preindustrial America had largely avoided.[99]

In the Technical Committee meetings, the need for ever more information gathering became a main theme. The Census Bureau had researched the administration of criminal justice, and now further research could track cases from arrest through trial. The Bureau of Prisons had studied penal treatment. What was needed now was a wider examination into programs' efficacy. The Office of Education studied city behavior clinics, college and community crime prevention programs, statistics for day-schools and the disabled, and adult prisoners. What was needed now was further evaluation of crime prevention school projects. The WPA had studied after-treatment adjustment and causes of delinquency. What was needed now was an enlargement of these studies.[100]

In late 1937 the meetings became markedly bolder in emphasizing both discipline and welfare. In October the Technical Committee considered a new Department of Welfare to house various crime prevention functions.[101] The committee's theoretical and welfare emphasis radicalized the notion of crime prevention—homing in on the root social conditions of criminality. This societal consciousness only further accommodated the repressive state. An early document laid out a typology of criminality—dangerous, violent, habitual (like forgers and perjurers), vice criminals, and juvenile—as well as means of prevention: noncarceral treatment, rehabilitation, repression, and even preemptive strategies toward criminality. One disadvantage with repression articulated in committee discussion was indeed its constrained scope. The FBI had brought repression "to a point of perfection never before known in this country, or, perhaps, in the world." But crime control was encumbered by its impotence against the not-yet-guilty. Americans would willingly "apply the most harsh, arbitrary and repressive measures to one who has violated the social code" but not "apply any sort of supervision, discipline, or 'regimentation' to a person who has not committed a crime." And yet "in every community, large numbers of persons [were] more or less inadequate. [Their] lives must be more or less supervised, controlled and directed, by procedures similar to . . . probation."[102]

In addition to pondering preemptive probation of the innocent, and lamenting the infeasibility of universal surveillance of vulnerable communities, the Technical Committee became increasingly drawn to connections between welfare and punishment. The more they considered welfare and healthcare as important to prevention, the more their investigations had to grapple with prisons, where "practically all" Justice Department health and welfare functions took place.[103] Academic literature had meanwhile reinforced this connection.[104] Involuntary psychiatric commitment had long fused crime prevention to detention.[105] Some indeed argued that criminal correctional systems, in their rehabilitative function, qualified as part of prevention.[106] Prison officials including Sanford Bates had always been some of the most supportive of crime prevention.[107]

More generally, the Roosevelt administration undertook a unity of welfare and correction while accommodating the many tensions between the two. The Justice Department quantitatively expanded the carceral state and advanced new rationales for correction with Alcatraz. Justin Miller had worked with Cummings and the WPA to understand and advocate parole and probation through its Survey of Release Procedures.[108] Roosevelt's Prison Industries Reorganization Administration (PIRA) had worked to transition state prison labor away from private profit. Interviews with these projects integrating reform and discipline encouraged the committee's understanding of correctional systems as sites of "public health." Its studies examined institutions of "hospitalization, education, vocational guidance and social welfare."[109]

Unifying welfare and incarceration resonated across the New Deal state but also provoked bureaucratic jealousies. In 1938 PIRA's Gustav Peck became a dissenting voice within the Technical Committee, especially after Miller stepped away as chair. Kathleen Lowrie became the acting chair, and a subset of the committee was entrusted to finalize its report, which fell largely on Helen Fuller.[110] In February Peck protested that these women had not consulted him in preparation of the final report, "apparently written without the knowledge" of his own organization's work on political economy. For two and a half years his agency had undertaken surveys of the kind suggested in the report, and this "obvious omission, albeit unintentional," revealed a "woeful lack of knowledge." He ominously said it would be "extremely unfortunate" for the report to be distributed on behalf of the committee when "only two or three people" actually produced it. Lowrie and Fuller mulled over how to neutralize Peck's "threatening" attitude. He was offered to draft an addendum letter.[111]

The Technical Committee's radicalism became an obstacle to its success. On the one hand, broadening the crime prevention definition and most of its reform ambitions served New Deal criminological discourse. Crime prevention was now "the all-embracing field of activity which includes theoretically all phases of crime control as well as the positive services which prevent even the initial occurrences of delinquency or crime." Including all anti-crime repression in its definition, the report yet purported to push against the "primitive thinking" that saw "killing the offender, outlawing him, or placing him in a dungeon" as the primary or sole mechanism of crime prevention. The report assessed the crime preventive activities, direct and indirect, in agencies ranging from the Social Security Board and the Farm Security Administration to the National Youth Administration and the WPA. An "adequate attack . . . on the problem of crime prevention" would require a programmatic shift in governing approach, a consideration of "the provision for economic security and personnel security."[112] The CCC hired a million young men in 1936, which was seen as keeping them from committing crimes. The FSA's rural committee was "indirectly engaged" with the problem, and the Social Security Board was perceived to be keeping people secure. Educating children had a "relation to the total problem of social welfare." The Office of Education needed a crime prevention division, the Children's Bureau should expand its Delinquency Bureau, and "school and college activities [should be] directed toward crime prevention." The WPA needed to attend more to troubled youth. A new "interdepartmental council" could help mitigate redundancy. Each department's crime control bureau needed "continuous development." A "progressive attitude" would permeate the institutional trajectory.[113] This broad vision of crime prevention vision did not provoke resistance within the administration.

On the other hand, Cummings disliked the report's most daring substantive reform proposal. The committee suggested a new Bureau of Prisons, Probation, and Parole to make rehabilitation and punishment into equal priorities. This Bureau could conceivably remain in the Department of Justice, but the committee controversially proposed a better fit in a new Department of Welfare.[114] Cummings considered this idea unrealistic and dangerous. Although he "some time ago . . . recommended the establishment of a Crime Prevention Unit in the Department of Justice," he insisted to Roche that Justice maintain penal and correctional operations, which were "not strictly a welfare activity in the usual meaning of that term."[115] Cummings's more strident criticism five days later warned against institutional reorganization "merely for the intellectual satisfaction," and called it "from almost every standpoint . . . unwise" to meddle with the well-working system. Detection, investigation, and apprehension were all functions of the Justice Department, with the FBI playing a special role. And indeed, the harmonization of crime suppression, treatment, and rehabilitation worked best under one bureaucracy. But whereas the Technical Committee wanted the coercive repression of incarceration run by welfare bureaucrats, Cummings wanted the welfare aspects of prevention run by his department that specialized in coercion. Subsuming criminal justice into the welfare bureaucracy, lumping prisoners in with the "unfortunate [would be] unfair to the latter," and evoked memories of "days when the insane were placed in jails and the poor in workhouses." In this age of war-on-crime federalism Cummings could appeal to the wisdom of the states: Model progressive jurisdictions like New York separated criminals from the needy through their departments of health, mental hygiene, social welfare, and corrections. California's Department of Welfare was distinct from its Department of Penology. Connecticut's Commissioner of Welfare did not meddle with the board of directors' management of corrections.[116]

The Technical Committee report won approval from various bureaucracies, but never produced a crime prevention bureau—much less a Department of Welfare housing America's prisoners.[117] Cummings eventually agreed to forward the report to Roosevelt but included his reservations.[118] In 1940 Hatton Sumners from the Interstate Commission on Crime asked Roche for cooperation from the Interdepartmental Committee to better understand crime prevention and cooperation. But Roche was at a loss of how to respond, since Roosevelt never indicated whether to distribute the report.[119] In the end the grand vision of national crime prevention had become too radical, too preventive, too repressive— and died in committee.

NEW DEALERS DID NOT SO MUCH debate the expansiveness of crime prevention as accept its nebulous breadth until the institutional implications appeared impractical, even dangerous, to Cummings. Generally, Miller was representative in seeing crime as a problem of social dysfunction warranting broad socioeconomic reform. This vision bridged the theorists to the practitioners, the local to the national, and accommodated the diverse war-on-crime coalition. Definitional malleability gave crime prevention its currency throughout the 1930s, fueling both intellectual exploration and the search for institutional permanence. But although the conceptual capaciousness fostered broad appeal, it also proved delicate. The seemingly narrow focus on juveniles was already unworkably expansive, and the radicalization of the idea drove its redefinition—first from a competitive alternative to repression to a complement to repression, then from a description that included repression to a vision for expanding repression. At its theoretical apogee, crime prevention surpassed the liberalism of the New Deal war on crime and achieved an almost utopian, totalitarian character. Miller's team envisioned not only a fusion of welfare and punishment, but a humanitarian police state that could include and transcend the known methods of discipline with the dream of preventing crime, even from the innocent.

The rise and fall of New Deal crime prevention have broad implications for liberal criminology. Historians recognize the punitive and prohibitionist edge of Progressive Era reform, the 1930s expansion of the FBI and criminal code, the postwar foundations of mass incarceration. To make sense of the New Deal's place there are two common and conflicting interpretations. One is a tale of New Deal formalism and centralism blunting the aspirational welfare approaches of progressive social workers. The other is the tale of a reformist path not taken, a vision more humane than Progressive Era social control, tragically swallowed by the security and carceral states of the mid-twentieth century.

The temptation to find a historical fork in the road, where welfare progressivism lost out to an unforgiving carceral repression, must yield to a more discomforting possibility. In disentangling aspirations from acquiescence, it is fruitful to look more carefully at how the New Deal drove both carceral expansion and criminological ideas too idealistic to materialize. Every version of New Deal crime prevention fully valued repression in concert with reform, and to the extent reformist ideas proved too theoretical or impractical, the untaken path was one toward both more welfare idealism and more illiberal repression.

Even though New Deal criminology failed in its concrete institutional goals and utopian aspirations, it successfully integrated social and state institutions behind a synthesis both pragmatic and aspirational, where practitioners of state violence and reformist dreamers all had their place. They would contest in the future, but for the time being they brought new legitimacy to the overarching agenda of law and order—a vision that promised both discipline and welfare and built a new liberalism defined by its commitment to social and national security.

PART V

THE LIBERAL SECURITY STATE,

1935–1945

Shortly before the 1938 midterm elections, Roosevelt gave a radio address urging voters to ratify the New Deal's reformation of liberalism. This liberalism was a practical governing program, a synthesis of democratic liberty and state-guaranteed security. Roosevelt's speech carried the familiar themes he brought to office in 1933, but now he could point to several years of experimentation. More explicitly than before, Roosevelt situated his program against the deformities of totalitarianism, unmoored populism, and the conservatism of the Republican Party. While people abroad suffered "the flares of militarism and conquest, terrorism and intolerance," Roosevelt's liberalism prioritized the "security of every individual." It was "tolerant enough to inspire an essential unity among its citizens" and "militant enough to maintain liberty against social oppression at home and against military aggression abroad." While "Fascism and Communism—and old-line Tory Republicanism" did not threaten America directly, they could chip away at its democratic foundations. The "New Deal" affirmed "democracy, humanity" and "civil liberties"—advanced by Democrats at all levels of government. Roosevelt endorsed for reelection Senator Robert Wagner, a champion of "constructive statecraft and steadfast devotion to the common man and the cause of civil liberties," and Michigan governor Frank Murphy, who "avoided bloodshed" by refusing to violently suppress a General Motors workers' strike. Roosevelt also backed the reelection of New York governor Herbert Lehman, whom he applauded specifically for his innovative use of "law enforcement."[1]

By the late 1930s Roosevelt's liberalism emphasized the emancipatory role of government "security"—against antidemocratic ideologies, against economic injustice and partisan obstruction, and against crime. Histories have recognized the importance of security to the state Roosevelt built, but have rarely juggled the criminological element with the welfare and warfare elements.[2] The late 1930s stress on security is somewhat cordoned off from the early 1930s and later twentieth-century wars on crime. Criminologist Jonathan Simon has identified three principles of governance—liberty, security, and community—that reinforce and undercut one another in complex ways, and whose balancing in the New Deal gave way to a more Hobbesian carceral equilibrium in the late twentieth-century war on crime. Yet crime policy was central in the construction of the New Deal liberal security state—advanced on the distinctive premise that liberty, security and community were more mutually reinforcing than adversarial.[3]

Accounts have traditionally described Rooseveltian liberalism as a historical construction rather than a reductively definable philosophy, a program shaped by the governing experimentation and strategic realism necessitated to ameliorate the Depression and mobilize for war. Historians have convincingly described World War II's transformative impact on liberalism and the security state. Wartime liberalism appeared even more pragmatic than earlier varieties, more accommodating of industrial capitalism, global power, national security, and national enforcement of civil rights.[4] But if policy conditions acclimated liberalism to bureaucratic administration, executive planning, coercive nationalism, and state power, then crime and punishment are curious factors to overlook. A sensitivity to this history must accommodate a cohesive account of crime fighting, national security, and liberalism as a state-building program.

In fact, it was New Deal experimentation with fighting crime that provided the bridge between the welfare state and the security state. Anti-crime innovations became a persuasive model for a new equilibrium between expansive national and local power, a balance between state violence and political legitimacy.[5] Explanations of the rise of the modern security state in the last years before Pearl Harbor should account for the institutional and ideological transformations driven by criminal enforcement.

Recognizing that the New Deal war on crime did not stop in the mid-1930s, but instead continued, complicates teleological accounts of war preparation.[6] Instead of looking backward at the 1930s security and surveillance state through the retrospective lens of Cold War America, we should consider the peacetime consolidation of coercive infrastructure as a contingent, essentially political development. In addition to the state building outlined in the previous chapters, several factors contributed to this infrastructure. First, the perceived successes of the war on crime consummated a new politics and indeed political economy of law and order—a reorientation at all levels of government, from the federal to the local, toward a legibly progressive outlook that saw economic injustice and crime as twin threats to domestic security. This new liberalism simultaneously achieved a bipartisan consensus while serving the partisan rhetoric and understandings of left-liberal Democratic politics. Second, the FBI integrated domestic policing and political surveillance, a recasting of liberalism as the muscular protection of American values. Finally, the institutional and ideological transformation was perfected in the last three years before Pearl Harbor, reinforced by innovations in federalism and with the New Deal's critics on both left and right assimilated into a patriotic security-state liberalism. By 1941 the war on crime legitimated an immense and intricate enforcement and intelligence leviathan, boasting both unprecedented power and a deference to law and liberty, which World War II would test and solidify rather than create.

Throughout these developments, security-state liberalism championed enormous state power and proclaimed respect for civil liberties—at least against the foils of American criminals, homegrown vigilantes, domestic reactionaries, and lawless foreign despotisms. Crucial to this process was the normalization of a "progressive" war on crime and a redefinition of terms. The administration's complex relationship to the very concept of *repression,* as transfigured through New Deal criminology, maintains its relevance. Memories of the lawless repression of World War I and the Red Scare haunted both radicals and moderates within the New Deal coalition. The progressive wing of New Deal criminology aimed to transcend "mere repression" in cutting off criminality at the source—identifying and addressing the socioeconomic causes of social dysfunction. But it also mostly embraced the state's violent power to subdue criminals. By the end of the 1930s, anticipating another national emergency, many on the radical edges of the New Deal coalition came to fear lawless repression more than the coercive state. By the eve of war all registers of the crime-fighting state had prepared liberalism for its greatest modern challenge. As it turns out, after generations of legitimacy crises in the face of diffuse and divisive manifestations of lawlessness, government instability had given way to a liberal security state that could pass the test of world war and define postwar America. New Deal economics, the new Democratic Party, the new liberalism, and a national defense posture cooperated in making this security state—and the war on crime had brought them together.

CHAPTER 10

THE NEW POLITICAL ECONOMY

OF LAW AND ORDER

While endorsing his New York gubernatorial successor, Herbert Lehman, for reelection, President Roosevelt underlined their shared commitment to war-on-crime liberalism. Indeed, the president devoted most of his Lehman endorsement on November 4, 1938, to crime policies, as though they best captured the New Deal spirit Roosevelt wanted to affirm. The president stressed three components of the new law-and-order ethos—jurisdictional harmony across town and country, enforcement's egalitarian ends, and the mutual protection that democracy and a lawful security state afforded each other. "No national administration" could be "enduringly effective" if "cut from the people by state and local political machinery," said Roosevelt as he doted on New York's small rural communities alongside its "huge city of seven million people, and many other cities, great and small." Americans everywhere should acknowledge "the need of active law enforcement," which must be balanced in liberal means and ends: "Equal protection of the law" meant "human rights as well as property rights" and "prosecution in high financial places as well as in low places." Roosevelt urged "more active law enforcement" against "lords of the underworld, but also against the lords of the over world." In addition to prosecuting criminals, government must attend to the "evil social conditions which breed crime. . . . Good government can prevent a thousand crimes for every one it punishes." Furthermore, law and order in the narrow sense would ensure it in the broader sense: hearty policing infrastructure undergirded the political system. While the struggle for "social justice and economic democracy has not the allure of a criminal jury trial; it is a long, weary, uphill struggle." To secure both "good government and American democracy," Roosevelt urged a vote for Lehman—who had embraced "every progressive Federal measure" against lawlessness—along with other politicians "known for their experience and their liberalism."[1]

Boasting the democratic state's egalitarian vigilance against lawlessness was now good politics—indeed, for both parties—despite falling crime rates. Having peaked in the early 1930s, homicides declined every year in the second half of the decade, from just over eight killings out of every 100,000 people down to just over six in 1940.[2] Even still, in these years before World War II preparation, the security state was fortifying against a retreating enemy. A new and permanent war against crime, even falling crime, helped shape the modern state. Not for the last time, politicians competitively cheered policing and incarceration. As Roosevelt's more controversial policies irritated even some of his allies, the new crime consensus eclipsed electoral politics. While radicals still questioned the New Deal's coercive planning, they warmed to its war on reactionary lawlessness.

Late-1930s liberalism found a new relationship with crime and punishment that became recognizable for generations. "Liberalism" long referred to a temper, if not a wholesale philosophy, a civic predilection toward individualism, universalism, prudential limits on state power, the rule of law, material progress, urban modernity, class harmony, and democratic freedom. Amid rising capitalism, liberalism prioritized economics and its political relevance, sometimes called political economy. But on law and order, crime and punishment, liberalism was unstable. Institutional and cultural limits on power froze the capacity of state mobilization, even as defending social order and private property motivated state activism. Transformations of the liberal order often pivoted around the paradoxes of enforcement that vexed all generations of liberals. From the Gilded Age on, the law-and-order state's legitimacy faltered on class lines, stumbled in its major role in urban governance, and divided the parties against each other and within. It is well known that the New Deal re-created political economy across class, urbanity, and partisanship.[3] Taken as a whole, twentieth-century liberalism reconciled nineteenth-century, progressive, and social-democratic approaches to welcome workers into a growing middle class as the model socioeconomic register of political life; integrated the peculiar policy aims of city life with the nation's imagined community and planned suburbs; and cast the Democratic Party with the starring role in setting the agenda while enlisting the Republican Party as a sometimes recalcitrant supporting actor. Yet in these three regards—class mediation, city governance, the bipartisan collaboration—an undervalued achievement was the constructive organizing against lawlessness, the central policy question that had undercut legitimacy since Reconstruction. The New Deal finally delivered a new political economy of law and order fitting of a modern liberal state.

THE CLASSES OF CRIME

From the 1870s through the 1920s, lawlessness accentuated the class divide. The progressives hoped imposing order could bring peace between rich and poor, whose myopic class interests had unleashed anarchy. Unifying capital and labor against the common enemy of disorder proved difficult. For a liberal state in which law was prized, the outsider would be the lawbreaker. But defining *lawbreaker* further divided the classes. The engines of state power alienated the different classes in different ways. Gilded Age police sometimes won over rich Americans while siding with workers in specific contexts. The police fell short of the professionalization that middle-class reformers championed. Such divisions peaked during Prohibition, sometimes described as an effort to "make the world safe for hypocrisy."[4] Liberalism is no stranger to internal tensions, but it can only sustain so much hypocrisy.

The New Deal's egalitarian language of law and order triumphed in unifying the press, politicians, criminologists, and even labor radicals. A liberal conception of criminality thrived on a maximized definition of the law-abiding and unapologetic vigilance against illegality. Of course, in theory and especially practice, classist understandings persisted.[5] Despite disparities between theory and practice, a conception of criminality that could unite the classes was authentic to the New Deal's economic zeitgeist. Liberals had to believe that they valued equality under the law. The Great Depression reminded Americans that criminals could come from anywhere, including the privileged classes.

The press reinforced this perception. In 1932 the *Atlanta Daily World* reported a numbers racket trial of 110 "from all walks of life"—including "college students, barbers, bootleggers, street women, business women, professional gamblers, two deacons from local churches, housewives, hustlers, porters, and society women."[6] The next October the *New York Times* reported "prominent Brooklyn residents" counting among the seventy-three indicted for a laundry racket.[7] In the sensationalized early-1930s banditry wave, white middle-class predation inspired middle-class panic. Whereas progressives saw bourgeois America as the bulwark against greedy and needy lawlessness, the new law-and-order consensus promised to protect the middle class from malefactors among their own ranks. State bar associations and Cummings railed against the "lawyer criminal," a species the *ABA Journal* demanded to "exterminate."[8] The war-on-crime coalition knew that progressive professionalization had not made people lawful. Only a vigilance across all politics and culture could do that.

Through redefining the criminal in subversion of class lines, New Deal policies promised salvation from socioeconomic conflict. In the early summer of 1934, as anxieties about racketeering and kidnapping persisted, Roosevelt pledged justice would reach the predatory rich. While signing legislation to empower Hoover's Division of Investigation, the president promised, in addition to "gangster extermination," a "broader program designed to curb the evil-doer of whatever class."[9] The Wagner Act's passage brought credibility to the left-wing edge of Roosevelt's populist rhetoric, which sharpened at the end of his first term. The president's resonant 1936 convention speech pitted the "despotism" and "economic slavery" of "economic royalists" against the Constitution's lawful order, which stood against both "mob rule and the over-privileged alike."[10]

Out of the 1930s came the highly powerful trope of "white-collar" crime. Criminologist Edwin Sutherland typically gets credit for coining the term in 1939 and launching its sociological theorization taken up by social scientists and popular intellectuals.[11] But in fact, such terminology was floating around already. In 1933 a concerned citizen wrote to New Deal criminologist Raymond Moley, skeptical that Roosevelt would rein in "white collar rackets," using the term much as Sutherland later did.[12] Sutherland claimed to challenge common assumptions that crime had a "high incidence in the lower class and a low incidence in the upper class," yet in 1939 Sutherland's theorization was following a socioeconomic attitude already resonant in Democratic politics, labor agitation, and the popular press. Indeed, as he himself stressed, "practically everyone now agrees" that the "robber barons" were "white-collar criminals."[13] While organized labor had long grappled with violent strikebreaking, Sutherland's "white collar" criminology, scholars note, underscored a more subtle illegality—crimes of "financial gain" and "nonviolence," "systemic" offenses involving the "breach of trust, and diffuse victimization." He emphasized the economic cost as far greater than that of street crime. Sutherland nevertheless intended to harmonize white collar-crime with broader scientific understandings. By defining white-collar crime as "committed by a person of respectability and high social status in the course of his occupation," Sutherland searched for factors beyond psychology and biology.[14]

Sutherland's egalitarian criminology, informed by economics and sociology, conceived of justice in both securitarian and liberal terms. The threat came from everywhere: "criminality" appeared in "land offices, railways, insurance, munitions, banking, public utilities, stock exchanges, the oil industry, real estate, reorganization committees, receiverships, bankruptcies, and politics." Society was impoverished by misrepresentations, manipulations, briberies, embezzlements, and tax violations. The remedy, presumably, was an admittedly imperfect criminal state, whose laws and administration "the upper class has greater influence in moulding . . . to its interests than does the lower class." Sutherland accepted that state power was discernible under a class analysis that considered not only income and wealth, but something less quantifiable, although he did not elaborate. But while government was itself riddled with white-collar criminals, in the hierarchy of wrongdoing he agreed with John Flynn that "The

average politician is the merest amateur in the gentle art of graft, compared with his brother in the field of business."[15]

Far from lighting a path away from state repression, Sutherland embraced a maximalist definition of criminality—including accessories, fugitives from punishment, and subjects disciplined outside the narrow
criminal justice system. Among white-collar crimes he included the
"illegal sale of alcohol and narcotics, abortion," and "illegal" medical
"services to underworld criminals." He condemned the "quacks, ambu-
lance chasers, bucket-shop operators, dead-beats, and fly-by-night swin-
dlers" and as many as "two thirds of the surgeons in New York City"
who illegally "split fees." Sutherland's determination to conceptualize
white-collar offenses as analogous to other criminality evinced war-on-
crime liberalism, which opportunistically fluctuated between formalism
and conventionalism to define the lawbreaking enemy. Sutherland built
his category around legal positivism: white-collar crime counted as crime
at least "because it is in violation of the criminal law." Yet alongside this
legal positivism, Sutherland employed folksy common sense to broaden
his category of the damned: "convictability rather than actual conviction
should be the criterion of criminality."[16]

While the literature underscores Sutherland's sociological triumph
over the multidisciplinary Gluecks, Sutherland's white-collar formulation
in fact served the impersonal, rationalizing, and even economizing pursuit of lawbreaking.[17] He sought a unified "hypothesis that will explain
both white-collar criminality and lower class criminality" and suspected
all of it was a "learned" process of "differential association." When the
"rules of the game" incentivized antisocial behavior, lawbreaking would
result.[18] Over time, Sutherland's theorization complemented the modern
criminal state's merciless pursuits—unrelenting punitiveness that fell disproportionately on the poor, people of color, and marginalized communities, but which would willingly make an example out of someone from
the respectable classes.

For middle-class and working-class Americans to believe in the new
class-blind vision of law and order that Sutherland helped to legitimate,
they would want to see some proof of concept. The 1930s offered some
evidence of the theory in practice. High-profile prosecutions targeted
finance men who had over-leveraged securities and ripped off investors.

In 1932 Wilbur B. Foshay received a sentence of fifteen years in federal prison, later reduced by Roosevelt, for defrauding investors of the Public Utilities Consolidated Corporation.[19] The New Dealers made their own example of Howard Colwell Hopson. Hopson's AG&E system had comprised twenty-four subholding companies and 166 operating companies. After its stock crashed, the Senate Committee on Banking and Currency launched the Pecora investigation and in 1933 called Hopson to testify. In 1935 the New York Public Service investigated him while Hugo Black spearheaded a congressional inquiry, courtesy of the 1935 Public Utility Holding Company Act that empowered the Securities and Exchange Commission to regulate and dismantle public utility holding companies. A federal grand jury subpoenaed Hopson in April 1940. In May he was indicted on mail fraud, conspiracy, and illegal profits. In January 1941 a judge sentenced him to five years for each count and he went to federal prison until 1944.[20]

While white-collar crimes especially rankled the white-collar law-abiding, the egalitarian law-and-order promise also enticed workers by policing those close to their own intra-class conflicts. Laborers and police had an ambivalent relationship since the Pullman Strike. Police departments provided upward working-class mobility and even situational allies against federal enforcers; but also tolerated and sometimes joined anti-union violence.[21] The state's uncertain relationship with vigilantes marred all levels of government. Injunctions, criminalization, and regulation historically ensnared workers, from regressive enforcement of the Sherman Act through the syndicalism laws, and many activists were initially skeptical that the New Deal would break with the past. They typically viewed lawless anti-worker violence as a telling breach in the liberal promise of law and order—but they split on whether the breach damned the irredeemable state as capital's reliable ally or provided an opening for reform.

Perhaps because the state so typically protected the bosses, even small gestures toward labor encouraged hope. Labor's developing expectations for law enforcement became apparent in the American Civil Liberties

Union's evolving posture toward liberalism. Having largely approached free speech as a surrogate for the rights of labor agitation, the ACLU increasingly saw due process as a corollary of workers' and minorities' civil rights. As late as the early 1930s this posture adopted a largely anti-government cast. In California's 1934 general strike, the state ACLU regarded the police and vigilantes as allied enemies. Vagrancy charges and exorbitant bail kept seventeen strike sympathizers in jail for over a month. Despite distrusting state power, California's ACLU leaders nevertheless petitioned for redress up the scales of government. Fancying themselves as heirs of Jefferson's struggle against the Tories, they appealed to Republican governor Frank Merriam's "oath to defend" the federal and state constitutions to stop the district attorney and protect the "victims of this lawlessness." To federal authorities they warned that these "flagrant violations of the law" were dragging the state outside "its rightful place in the Union."[22] For the ACLU, vigilantism threatened both civil rights and labor rights, apparent in the high-profile "beating and tarring and feathering of two in Santa Rosa."[23]

But amidst these labor struggles, the popular war on crime complicated the ACLU's posture. The organization saw police and vigilante lawlessness as expressions of class warfare, and so was ambivalent toward the feasibility of government remedies while recognizing the prophylactic value of due process rights. Although ACLU activists sought Merriam's intervention against local police brutality, they remained skeptical of state centralization. In 1934 they opposed Raymond Cato's proposal for a state police force.[24] Members were frustrated that Merriam's Conference on Crime Prevention gave little opportunity to air "civil liberty issues."[25] By the late 1930s the ACLU expressly prioritized due process rights concerning search and seizure and trial by jury.[26]

Particularly after the Wagner Act, labor activists increasingly saw the federal government as a potential ally, at least compared to local and state police with cozier ties to vigilantes. Local police were an especially intractable adversary, increasingly integrating the war on crime with national security but with extraconstitutional activities that defied jurisdictional clarity. Los Angeles police chief James E. Davis, having headed the vice squad during Prohibition, had launched a "Red Squad" to ferret out suspected communists, and won reformist accolades for prolifically firing police for misconduct. Now Davis relied on quasi-vigilante groups operating within their own jurisdictional twilight zone. In 1936 Davis deployed a hundred men to California's border to stop indigent nonresidents from entering. The ACLU complained to the Interstate Commerce Commission that these men were committing extralegal violence. But under the state action doctrine, Davis's shock troops were not clearly actionable public agents. Federal officials could not intervene without evidence that the border enforcers performed "under State authority or direction."[27] ACLU activists derided the notion that Davis's anti-vagrancy forces did not qualify as state action, given their apparent support "by the City Council, by the Mayor, by the City Attorney and by the Board of Police Commissioners."[28] The federal impotence could inspire at least two pessimistic conclusions—that reform could brighten the line between vigilante and state and render Davis's men an even more untouchable rogue menace; or that it was futile as ever to seek government solutions to government-backed class warfare.

But ACLU activists kept attempting to liberalize the security state. Across the nation, they supported efforts at the New York Constitutional Convention to stop the training and organization of private militaries. The national organization saw violent vigilantes, increasingly differentiated from the state apparatus, as a persistent threat that made an expansive federal power against private lawlessness more attractive. Much as the NAACP's Walter White hoped to direct the Lindbergh anti-kidnapping law against interstate lynchings, the ACLU hoped that expanded federal policing could protect workers' civil rights. The 1936 kidnapping of white labor lawyer Henry Paull in Michigan prompted the National ACLU board to help the Justice Department prepare its prosecution.[29] The organization maintained focus on local state violence, linked the "incredible police brutality" in the 1937 Ponce Massacre in Puerto Rico to "gross violations of civil rights," and hoped for redress from Roosevelt and Interior Secretary Ickes.[30] The ACLU nevertheless still feared misdirected federal power, demanded civilian control over the military, and especially worried that civilians would become prosecuted by military courts.[31] One notably welcome national development, occasioned by the Wagner Act, was the La Follette Committee. In the late 1930s up to the eve of war, the Committee uncovered egregious uses of industrial spies and violence by Pinkertons, the William J. Burns International Detective Agency, and other private actors. Chaired by progressive Republican Robert M. La Follette, the committee did not result in very far-reaching legal reforms, but it marked an encouraging retreat from the federal-vigilante associations of the World War I era.[32]

By the end of the 1930s, Democratic rhetoric, academic criminology, and labor agitation indulged the promise of class-blind law and order. This promise would always have a mixed record in practice. As with race, law-and-order policy would never truly target people equally across class or race. But the ideal that no one was above the law would be central to modernizing political economy and legitimating the liberal state.

THE CITIES OF CRIME

American liberalism, capitalism, and democracy came of age in the city. At nearly every rite of passage, the city struggled with the policy problem of lawlessness. Nationwide, Gilded Age crackdowns, progressive purity policing, and Prohibition aimed to legitimate lawful order in its urban cauldrons. Even before the New Deal, the criminology of practitioners and academics began weaving the cities together. Despite formal differences in segregation law, northern and southern policing shared a resemblance in racial discipline. From East Coast to West Coast, in Jacob Riis's New York and August Vollmer's Berkeley, departments underwent familiar patterns of professionalization. But in the 1930s the city challenge brought forth more sustainable responses on the scale of national liberalism. Local policing finally shared a common language with the national state. A new culture of law and order tied federal politics to neighborhood practice, advancing national imaginations that prized local policing for decades to come.[33]

War-on-crime liberalism triumphed in the interwar generation when Americans became majority urban. Rural and small-town criminality dominated headlines and captivated criminologists in the early 1930s, but by decade's end crime would become widely seen as a city problem. The trope of urban crime thrived in the 1930s, 1940s, and beyond, shaping class and party politics. The trope always relied on a selective reading of empirical evidence. Considering violent crime, statistical trends differed in the cities and countryside in ways that defied oversimplification. FBI statistics for 1937 suggested more than three times the rape and murder rates in rural areas, but higher larceny and auto theft rates in cities. Statistics from 1940, on the other hand, generally suggested more per capita crime in bigger cities than smaller ones.[34] Nevertheless, a selective reading of crime, typically associated with the urban poor and people of color, served the new political economy that promised to balance welfare and repression, freedom and security. Attention to addressing root causes could reform an outdated capitalism even as police proliferated to keep its symptoms in check. Read more broadly, city criminality implicated the politicians, lawyers, and business classes that New Deal criminology promised not to overlook. As with business regulation, city police could alleviate the pathologies of capitalist modernity.

Thus did war-on-crime liberalism promise liberation from America's rural past, but with some humility. Pragmatic and measured law enforcement could mitigate if not abolish the paradoxes of anarchy and despotism. In a break from the deliverance offered by the progressives, New Dealers would reconfigure the paradoxes aware they could not be eradicated. Discussing the regulation of urban life, Donald Stone of the Public Administration Service conceded that "conscientious and diligent" people could not "pass a day in a large city without breaking one or more laws," yet most such laws were "necessary; to erase them from the statute books would result in utter public confusion." These laws carried the anachronistic burden of "an enforcement procedure carved out of a rural and lawless society by our medieval ancestors," back when crimes were fewer and less complicated.[35] But the liberals did not promise to abolish anachronism.

As popular culture and politics reached new levels of nationalization, the lawlessness question invited new relationships across states, cities, and the nation. Constitutional federalism meant subsidiarity between federal and state power, but the cities always presented a jurisdictional quandary, as city loyalties sometimes gravitated toward those interests of the nation—or global networks—and sometimes more toward the states. Material federal support of local police, bypassing the states, had origins with the 1919 Dyer Act, but achieved a much greater scale under the 1930s FBI.[36] More generally, urban policing confounded the symbiotic development of federalism and liberalism. The pathologies of industrialization, namely the "labor question," had marred the cities, but the war on crime presented new challenges for urban authorities seeking to cast their own remedies as less parochial than those of state authorities.

California, a hotbed of both progressivism and burgeoning conservative recalcitrance, contributed importantly in the simultaneous defining of law-and-order liberalism for the nation and cities. The Los Angeles police department embodied interwar political tensions. In the early 1920s August Vollmer had briefly served as police chief, instituting some enduring reforms. In the 1930s police chief James E. Davis personified the city's law-and-order politics and marked the complexities of a coalition that included anti-Davis activists as well as Vollmer, a loyal New Dealer with a distinct civil libertarian streak. Davis's reactionary violence against labor activists and deployment of vigilantes against vagrants helped push the ACLU into the arms of the New Deal Justice Department; he was also the voice that wooed America to fall in love with his city's quest for law and order. Despite Davis's reliance on legally dubious shock troops, he advertised Vollmer's dear cause of professionalism to the wider culture. Debuting in 1933, *Calling All Cars,* hosted by Davis, became the first successful radio show about city policing, and would eventually spawn an entire genre of programming. *Calling All Cars* made middle-class, mostly white Americans understand the commonality of the city experience as a struggle between modernizing civility and every type of criminal, with the honest policeman securing the boundary.

The show left lasting legacies. One was the identification of Los Angeles with the modern problem of law and order, the site of this American challenge writ large. After a century of culturally important crime fiction, it was significant that the technological police drama finally flourished in 1930s Los Angeles. As its successor show *Dragnet* later explicated, Los Angeles was "the city of crime," and *Calling All Cars* successfully highlighted Los Angeles as a place both exceptional and distinctively American, its pathologies and triumphs both peculiar and representative. All cities, after all, were cities of crime, but the City of Angels was first among equals. *Calling All Cars* pioneered new associations between criminality and a sprawling urban landscape that soon characterized film noir and immortalized Hollywood's role in defining the city, America, and the modern world for one another. Initially broadcast in California, Nevada, and Arizona, by the late 1930s it was syndicated on the East Coast. With syndication the historical imagination would henceforth drive eastward, a reversal of the pioneer narrative that relied concretely on technical modernization. Los Angeles, more than the great cities of the Northeast, or even the Midwest and South, was a civilization constructed around the automobile. What would transpire was the midcentury fascination with the car chase, the new venue in which cops and crooks raced amidst middle-class commuters innocently caught in the middle. The show was sponsored by Rio Grande Oil Company, a fitting moniker for a geographical and cultural touchpoint imbuing the urbanization of the nature's future with the nineteenth-century frontier spirit. Through programming like *Calling All Cars,* Los Angeles would come to represent the country as much as New York.

The show helped redefine the criminal archetype, often carved out from the socioeconomic middle along with his victims, and nurtured sympathy for the local beat cop. Its stories offered free national advertising to enforcement technologies like modus operandi and fingerprinting. Scholars have examined the show's legitimation of large municipal police departments, "precisely the type most castigated for their brutality," depicting a professionalism that eschewed the third degree.[37] In contrast, as the show portrayed, it was the criminals who engaged in heartless torture. Crucially, the show not only whitewashed city policing, but cast crime in a new light—cruel, unrelenting, a threat to all classes coming from every direction. The show played on the ironic transformation of the new crime, which turned the sympathetic bootleggers, patronized by middle-class transgressors in the 1920s, into hardened villains in the 1930s. Whereas alcohol had once defined interwar criminality, the real crime was in offending good old American decency. In one early episode a bandit brags of the drink he shares with his partner: "This is real whiskey. I wouldn't wash my feet in that stuff I peddle." As if to further distinguish the brutal crimes of the Depression era from the more benign illegalities under Prohibition, the naïve sidekick confides that he "don't like the idea of a stickup job. . . . I always run my business respectable. I've been an honest bootlegger and I don't like the idea of breaking the law that way."[38]

<hr />

Meanwhile, even as Northern California was losing its dominance in defining the state for the nation, its greatest city followed America's hegemonic policing trends. Despite tensions with Democrat August Vollmer's progressivism across the Bay, San Francisco maintained the inertia of professionalization. Grappling with urban nuisances helped to construct the state's new liberalism. Over the 1930s its investigatory and arrest processes became standardized, its paperwork routinized, its uniforms regularized. In San Francisco's central-eastern District 9, police orders frequently reminded patrolmen of novel standards. An order in February 1936 reminded police to make their reports at the station, which should consist of two single-spaced pages and include "time, location, first and last name in full and middle initials, addresses, and phone numbers, both home and business, of all principals and witnesses, besides giving all material facts connected therewith."[39] This fixation on paperwork regularity mirrored federal developments even absent direct coordination.

Disciplining police was an explicit strategy in disciplining the city. Responding to "complaints . . . about the conduct" of his men, District 9 captain Arthur Christiansen related unprofessional conduct to a lackadaisical posture toward social disorder. He decried officers for being "indifferent about enforcing the vagrancy, traffic and begging laws" and addressing traffic accidents. These disciplinary shortcomings plagued the chain of command. "Officers drinking intoxicating liquor and consorting with women while on duty" revealed "a lack of supervision by their platoon superiors."[40] Police tolerating or "themselves indiscriminately" committing traffic violations eroded their respect among subordinates.[41] Unprofessional and noticeably "insolent" police also alienated the respectable public, who complained "about the discourteous manner members of this Company treat people."[42] The Chief's Office blamed such misbehavior for undercutting the egalitarian promises of policing, and lamented the alleged "discourtesy displayed" by police "toward newspaper-men."[43]

Professionalism served political neutrality, a delicate priority of liberalism. San Francisco's 1934 waterfront strike raised the stakes. The captain instructed police to refrain from backing either "side of the controversy" except to enforce the law "regardless of . . . personal feelings or prejudices."[44] This meant avoiding "Unnecessary roughness, abusive or offensive language towards strikers or any other person."[45] Police who failed to stop violence were reprimanded.[46] Police chief William Quinn reassured Upton Sinclair campaign officials that they would suffer no interference, that his police would only "make arrests and raids . . . where we are positive that organizations have been formed for the purpose of overthrowing the United States government."[47] To be sure, this formal neutrality remained structurally anti-labor. The need to protect private property trumped any "sentiments or feelings . . . as to the right or wrong of the employers of strikers."[48] At the same time warnings not to "take sides in labor trouble" captured a distinct 1930s ethos of avoiding the appearance of bias.[49] Certainly it was a far cry from Gilded Age patronage politics. In the 1934 general election, San Francisco police were barred from actively engaging "City and county politics, relative to the election or appointment of public officials." Such participation was insubordinate and "subversive of the best interest of the merit system."[50] The next year police received reminders to stay neutral in a special election.[51] In 1936 they were urged to crack down on those "giving away or furnishing any alcoholic beverages to any person in this City" during the polls.[52]

Outside of dramatic strikes and elections, the San Francisco police prioritized social order, increasingly burdensome traffic, and vice. They enforced regulations on gathering junk—one person per vehicle and no "unlicensed junk gatherers."[53] They investigated illegal ads on automobiles. Modernity's bustle brought problems like noise complaints, ballplayers disrupting traffic, unlicensed kite-flyers tangling up electrical wires,[54] and dangerous juvenile antics derailing streetcars.[55] Police routed out unlicensed sheet music dealers,[56] flower peddlers,[57] fortunetellers,[58] and corsage sellers.[59] They enforced dancehall ordinances honed by location and time.[60] Fraud and counterfeiting were endemic.[61] City police became soldiers in the "nation wide drive" toward "stamping out the narcotic evil" across America." Police were "to be vigilant in picking up all known addicts and peddlers of narcotics." Narcotic sales were "closely associated" with "the criminal element," and those charged with drug violations had their fingerprints taken.[62]

In practice enforcing social order was not neutral across class or race. On paper the police protected and served people from all walks of life, and sometimes victims represented vulnerable communities. They attempted to protect Jews being defrauded with fake subscriptions to the *Jewish Examiner.*[63] But in practice enforcement of class-blind law drew lines to privilege the respectable. The captain repeatedly warned of "degenerates" seen around "the parks, squares, and schools."[64] In July 1936 the chief emphasized that "women and children" in these parks and playgrounds "are being annoyed by degenerates."[65] One 1934 order commanded the arrest of "every beggar" on the street, whether peddling pencils, gum, or "outright begging," along with "every narcotic fiend."[66] Another order established a "vigorous campaign with a view of arresting all known beggars, vagrants, drug addicts and other undesirables." Police were deployed to "parks, playgrounds and isolated parts of this district; where degenerates may hangout." Addicts were seen as inclined toward other crimes. Yet police orders sometimes recognized economic hardship. "Many honest men are temporarily out of employment," one clarified, ". . . through no fault of their own, which does not constitute vagrancy. Under these circumstances they must not be molested."[67] Another directed officers to guard the property of those arrested for drunkenness.[68] Police had to navigate an implicit distinction between respectable and lowly beggars and addicts.

The wars on vice were conspicuously inequitable across race and gender. Vice policing often targeted gambling, particularly "Chinese gambling."[69] Police associated Chinese neighborhoods with "illegal punch boards, and slot machines."[70] Police received orders to monitor Chinese shrimp camps[71] and in 1936 "to visit [certain Chinese gambling] premises at least once every two hours until further orders."[72] Outside of references to Chinese gambling, explicit racialized language appeared rarely in District 9's Police Captain Orders—with some jarring exceptions. In March 1934 the captain boasted "with satisfaction" that two officers had arrested "Pearl Wilson, a negress prostitute" and urged "every member of this company to arrest on sight every negress prostitute." It was necessary to make the district uncomfortable for these sex workers, "a very vicious criminal element and a cause of unlimited trouble." Any officer who "fails to prevent any negress prostitute operating on his beat will be severely disciplined."[73]

Vice policing was time consuming and significant to legitimating governance. Historian Anne Gray Fischer shows how after reaching the nadir of legitimacy during Prohibition, "police leaders and their political allies recognized that sexual policing" allowed "urban police forces to achieve a stunning transformation in the eyes of white Americans from corrupt goons to urban saviors."[74] In this transformative period, a narrative of woman victimhood gave way to themes of woman criminality, expressed in highly racialized and gendered ways. The victim-criminal dichotomy for urban women not only brought legitimacy to city policing, as Fischer persuasively illustrates, but served the state generally in its most pronounced sites of policymaking. Most American women, even Black women, would not endure the level of state violence that cities like San Francisco unleashed on suspected sex workers. In the long term, urban liberalism sought a hardened differentiation between those protected and served and those isolated and subdued. If in practice equality was a mirage, even in theory the criminalized would be classified outside the polite liberal order.

In the development of securitarian liberalism, the tensions and solidarity among cities, states, and the nation were perhaps clearest in the president's home state.[75] New York and its municipal namesake boasted competing Progressive Era legacies and thus competing claims to the liberal future. The statewide New York Society for the Prevention of Crime long targeted the city as the cauldron of criminality and corruption—and in eyeing both New York City and Albany, it attacked the corrupting influence of politics in urban culture and the state at large. In the 1930s the Society pursued a broad crusade against vice, gambling, and all lawbreaking, aiming to restrict movies and objectionable films, particularly for youth, and create state departments of police. It championed legislation supported by the Legion of Decency and the Archdiocese of New York and favored criminal procedure reform.[76] Other organizations focused even more on the city. The Citizens Committee on the Control of Crime (CCCC) had officials assigned to each borough. They favored "strengthening of law enforcement" through "critical study by a non-political body." Bringing together attorneys, bankers, and business executives, with Harry F. Guggenheim as their chairman, they credited themselves as "neither a group of vigilantes nor of reformers."[77] The organization straddled the political divide, as right-wing Charles Lindbergh cheered their efforts against "conditions of crime and corruption in New York City," which he called "one of America's most fundamental problems" when he gave them $250.[78] The group enjoyed support from the Chamber of Commerce and the Merchant Association of New York.[79]

Different approaches to crime within city and state jurisdictions often replicated partisan divisions. New York Republicans had more influence on the city war on crime and Democrats competed with them from Albany—a rough reversal of the partisan-jurisdictional correlations that defined the nineteenth century. In 1935 Governor Lehman called a special court session to investigate vice, racketeering, and organized crime in New York City. He sought the appointment of an attorney like George Z. Medalie, Thomas D. Thacher, or Charles H. Tuttle to become a prosecutor—and considered Republican Charles Evans Hughes Jr. as well. He ignored recommendations to tap partisan adversary Thomas E. Dewey, despite Dewey's high-celebrated success as US Attorney in prosecuting gangster Waxey Gordon, sentenced to ten years on tax evasion.[80] These real partisan tensions could obscure the degree of convergence, even alongside competition, over combating lawlessness. In 1935 Lehman made Dewey a special prosecutor, and they shared credit for New York's war on crime. Lehman thanked the CCCC for the "great value to the city and state in the maintenance of law and order," and touted Dewey's anti-racketeering efforts.[81] Dewey, something of a carceral liberal himself, supported a bill to keep juveniles out of adult jails, with the support of the Prison Association of New York.[82]

In jurisdictional terms, New York crime policy was a microcosm of the New Deal aim to reconcile federal and state power. But within the state, unlike at the national level, railing against jurisdictional twilight zones benefited Republicans. Dewey favored the "long-range" study of crime "by experts" and in 1937 condemned a "labyrinth of procedure and overlapping jurisdictions, which would almost seem to have been specially designed for the comfort of criminals." He found agreement with Republican mayor Fiorello La Guardia, who wanted to centralize the state's criminal jurisdiction and abolish redundant county courts. The mayor and Dewey appeared before city leaders to raise money for the Guggenheim Committee's anti-crime campaign. Dewey warned that the struggle between organized crime and society was "reaching a crisis" amidst the public's "amazing indifference." The mayor noted that New York City had "five counties within a city" and wanted trial venues determined by institutional specialization rather than proximity to the offense.[83]

THE POLITICS OF CRIME

Along with hosting the new dynamic between state and city, New York demonstrated that the burgeoning law-and-order consensus buttressed an ecumenical and nonpartisan liberalism, including in its aspirations for class. The Republican LaGuardia, much like the Democrats, sought to turn the war on crime from liability into an asset by smoothing over the labor question. "No greater mistake can be made by organized labor," he warned, "than to assume the attitude that weeding out or selecting any crook from its midst is unfriendly to labor."[84] New York's vanguard role in law-and-order politics was spotlighted by its White House connections. As governor, Roosevelt gained executive experience combatting crime, and his successor proudly carried this legacy forward. Herbert Lehman was Roosevelt's lieutenant governor during the late 1920s prison strikes. Lehman advocated a comprehensive crime-prevention strategy, reform of prisoner treatment, and rehabilitation and parole, and advised Roosevelt on appointments for New York's Prison Commission and Legal Commission in 1930.[85] As president, Roosevelt touted New York's war on crime for its progressive approach. Both men pursued broad coalitions around an activist social welfare agenda balanced by a flexible liberalism.

New York thus captured the New Deal's dual branding of liberalism as a Democratic Party triumph and a neutral bipartisan cause. After Lehman became governor, the New York Society for the Prevention of Crime's president saw him as an important ally.[86] On Lehman's left, social worker Lillian Wald corresponded with the governor in affectionate solidarity, as he shared the proceedings from Cummings's 1934 crime conference.[87] The next year Lehman trumpeted a program with partisan and cross-partisan resonance. He publicized the successes of Dewey, his right-hand man.[88] Mirroring Cummings's conference, Lehman hosted an inclusive event, "Crime, the Criminal and Society."[89] It showcased a diversity of reform proposals, from Lehman's universal fingerprinting idea to Republican former US attorney George Medalie's proposal for appointed attorneys general.[90]

Linking New York to the nation, the bipartisan consensus became apparent in the posture of anti–New Deal conservatives—from the American Bar Association to disillusioned progressives and Democrats who ultimately joined the Old Right. Raymond Moley, speaking at Lehman's 1935 crime conference, hailed the state as a "bright spot," and outlined a middle ground between the legacy of draconian Baumes Laws and the "equally irrational school of thought" that understood criminality in purely psychiatric or social terms without "moral condemnation."[91] Economic policy was starting to divide Moley and the president, but Moley continued to espouse law-and-order pragmatism. Moley championed the familiar panoply of training, specialization, centralization, FBI modeling, probation and parole improvements, and professionalization, and discounted promises of a criminological panacea. Decrying single-minded utopianism was characteristic of the New Dealers' self-conscious differentiation from fringe ideologues and extremisms of left and right. Those peddling a cure-all had "rushed in with remedies for crime, rushed in with remedies for the depression" and the "remedies were the same":

> If he believes in Communism, the removal of Capitalism will do the trick. If he is a single-taxer, the removal of the landlord will do it. If he wants complete freedom to make unlimited profits, the destruction of the New Deal will do it. If he hates prohibition, the Twenty-first amendment will do it. For a while people were dragooned into supporting prohibition because, forsooth, drink caused crime. Then later we were dragooned into the opposition, because, forsooth, prohibition caused crime.

Moley's rejection of panaceas also implicated talk about lawless politicians. "If our particular obsession is political corruption," Moley noted the supposed surefire solution of the ballot box. He found this unconvincing.[92]

Despite its limitations, Moley still valued electoral politics. Although in 1935 Moley was defending liberal pragmatism against fanatical utopianism, he was drifting from the president in emphasis. By the next year, as Lehman and Roosevelt won reelection with anti-crime platforms, Moley supported Republican presidential hopeful Alf Landon. Moley's defection starkly illustrated how the war-on-crime coalition transcended the New Deal coalition. Moley—the Columbia law professor and Empire State's prolific Democratic speechwriter, the Brain Trust architect who appropriated the term "the Forgotten Man" on behalf of the welfare state, the pioneering criminologist who under Cummings oversaw the New Deal's first major crime survey—had soured on Roosevelt's constitutional experimentation. But throughout 1936 and the rest of the decade, Moley maintained pride for the administration's crime initiatives.[93] Moley hailed Cummings in May for his "courageous backing of Hoover" against his detractors and for championing FBI professionalization.[94] In June he told Cummings that shielding "the Federal instrumentalities for criminal justice against politics and inefficiency" was among "the high spots of this Administration." Cummings had heroically and "intelligently interpreted the work" of "two national leaders," Hoover and Prison Bureau director Sanford Bates.[95] In his 1939 book Moley took credit for the administration retaining Hoover and expanding his power.[96]

By November 1936 the bipartisan success of Roosevelt and Cummings's coalition—a prospect unthinkable during Prohibition's destabilizing transpartisan divides—meant that those who supported war-on-crime liberalism could base their party support on other issues. Governor Lehman echoed Roosevelt's multipronged embrace of prevention and repression. In 1936 he won reelection, receiving popular recognition for prioritizing crime. The *Times* celebrated Lehman's "war on crime" and his sixty-point law-and-order program.[97] Editorial cartoons championed his crime bills as much-needed common sense against the lawbreaking endemic across the classes (see Figure 10.1). The New York State Sheriffs Association sought Lehman as a convention participant and the New

Figure 10.1 "Lehman Anti-Crime Bills," drawing by Rollin Kirby, 1936. Herbert Lehman Papers, Box 1403, Rare Book & Manuscript Library, Columbia University in the City of New York. By permission of the Estate of Rollin Kirby Post.

York State Police Conference asked him to address its banquet.[98] Lehman began 1937 urging the state legislature to adopt what remained of his previous year's sixty-point anti-crime program. He championed a bureau of crime prevention, a state department of justice modeled after the federal Justice Department, a division of state police and central bureau of criminal investigation, an in-service training program for police, optional consolidation of local police units, nonpersonal service of subpoena for evasive witnesses, a rule allowing trial judges to review evidence and advise the jury, gubernatorial clemency advice from judges, a felony murder law, women on juries, and a "farm colony or work camp" for the "detention of alcoholics and vagrants."[99]

Like Roosevelt and Cummings, Lehman embraced a liberalism that admired the traditional institutions of state repression as well as promises of restraint. Like J. Edgar Hoover, Lehman respected the American Legion, ensuring that New York rolled out the red carpet for its presence. The Legion's Matthew Troy thanked him for a welcoming "Shrine of Americanism."[100] Law enforcement agencies respected Lehman. National organizations like the American Prison Association, the leading association of prison administrators, solicited his participation at luncheons and events.[101] In 1938 the New York State Association of Chiefs of Police offered to adjust the schedule of their annual convention to feature him as a speaker.[102] Civil libertarian groups also respected Lehman. An ACLU event celebrating the 150th anniversary of the Bill of Rights requested his presence in both his "official capacity" and in recognition of his "valiant defense and championship of civil liberties."[103]

Unburdened by national considerations, Lehman enjoyed more political flexibility than Roosevelt. Lehman's willingness to identify areas for bureaucratic improvement could provoke concern on the left. Leo Allen, head of the National Social Service Division, worried that his talk before the New York State Association of Public Welfare Officials was too hostile to the welfare state. In criticizing selfish officials within the "relief machinery," Lehman had aided detractors pushing for obstructive investigations and had elicited "doubts in the minds of organized labor, the unemployed and progressive social workers."[104] Yet in some respects, the governor's vision was arguably too progressive for the soft nationalism of war-on-crime federalism. While Lehman cheerfully agreed with Cummings on the national priority of surveying parole across the country, his proud reformism clashed with an optimistic approach to interstate compacts.[105] The interstate crime conference run by Richard Hartshorne particularly struggled to get New York's full participation. The governor believed the antiquated parole and probation policies of many states remained unworthy of New York's full reciprocity. Investigating the question for Lehman, Joseph Moore reported that "Missouri itself has no parole system which can be properly called as such."[106] Lehman affirmed that New York could not join a "blanket compact with any states with whose parole and probation methods and policies we are not familiar."[107]

Perhaps because he did not need southern support and faced fewer executive power limits than Roosevelt, Lehman also venerated civil rights and constitutional limits more than national New Deal Democrats. His 1938 talk before the ABA reflected both tendencies. Black American R. B. DeFrantz thanked him for a speech that stressed "exact equality for all groups in our complex population."[108] Gloria French agreed with his dissent from Roosevelt's Supreme Court plan, suggesting it was a "hardly perceptible" transition toward "dictatorship and the shadow of Communism which are creeping over our land."[109] Paul Shea praised him as a "constitutional democrat" who should be president.[110] Many others, including Republicans, praised the well-publicized speech.[111]

Despite nuanced differences among Lehman, his fellow travelers and opponents, New York's 1938 gubernatorial race confirmed the new unifying consensus around law and order. Dewey, now challenging Lehman, pledged to continue the "State war" against crime and in support of housing and labor. "The restoration of public confidence in the law and in its officers is a task of the first importance to the community," he announced. "The era of cynical contempt of the law is at an end."[112] Dewey's campaign threatened Democratic state rule like nothing since the early 1920s. With some labor support, the Republican had defeated Tammany associate Harold B. Hastings for district attorney. Dewey hoped to surpass his popularity in New York County. In an election between two crime warriors, he needed something else on which to win. A *New York Herald Tribune* writer wondered whether Dewey could "develop anything beyond the crime-and-politics issue to appeal to the average voter?" Despite recent differences over court-packing, Roosevelt urged the public to support Lehman, namely for his anti-crime credentials, applauding the incumbent for eagerly enlisting "law enforcement, young and vigorous prosecutors, irrespective of politics."[113] By a margin of 1.26 percent, Lehman won the challenge against his own partner against crime. On law and order perhaps the outcome hardly mattered. Although accusations of lawlessness continued in partisan messaging, a vote for either candidate meant approval of New York's bipartisan merging of repression and prevention against crime.[114]

In 1939 both parties competed over amplifying and reforming law and order. Partisan tensions, compounded by jealousies between cities, fueled scandalous accusations of lawlessness in New York's Society for the

Prevention of Crime.[115] Backed by Dewey, New York Republicans proposed expanding search and seizure powers and an extended statute of limitations for conspiracy charges. While excluding warrantless wiretap intelligence, the legislation would allow other fruits of warrantless searches to be admissible. The bill would prohibit telephone or telegraph companies from divulging message contents, but would provide for the notification of the district attorney in the event of apparent criminal activity. Democrats' competing proposal would make the carrying of a loaded revolver a felony and increase the conspiracy statute of limitation to five years.[116] That year Dewey earned a Cardinal Newman Award for his criminal justice triumphs.[117]

The bipartisan politics of law and order would come to define America from the 1940s onward. In July 1940 the New York State Association of Chiefs of Police applauded Lehman's address.[118] After winning the governorship in 1942, Republican Thomas Dewey would inherit and escalate the war on crime he had helped the Democrats wage.

NEW DEAL LIBERALISM promised to address America's problems with attention to both the particular and the general. By reviving work programs to the poor, social security to the middle class, or stability to finance, it would serve all classes of Americans. By managing the awkward transformations of the modernizing urban landscape, it would benefit the whole nation. By updating the Democratic Party's ethos, Roosevelt's liberals would enjoy outsize influence in redefining liberalism in nonpartisan terms, a project in which Republicans became begrudging but active junior partners. In all these facets, the New Deal revamped the political economy of the United States. In the reconciliation of working- and middle-class aspirations, the updating of the city's bourgeois liberal temper, and the affirmation of a new politics that served both parties but especially Democrats, law and order played an underappreciated but major role of mediation.

Into the late 1930s, as a hot war in Europe and Asia raged, American liberalism thrived on being simultaneously distinctive and ecumenical. In the longer term the paradoxical exceptionalism and universalism would dominate world affairs—propelled with a violent energy inversely proportional to the outward illiberalism of regimes and doctrines against which New Deal America would define itself in the 1940s. At home, the liberal state had its dress rehearsal of mobilization by practicing on the domestic lawless. The spirit of this mobilization was tailored to replace progressivism for the middle class—but it promised room for rich and poor as well. It was the recognizable program of the cities—but also the country and suburbs. It was the mission of the Democrats—and good Republicans too. Before shaping the globe, this description of liberalism as the province of particular identities and also the property of America itself animated the law-and-order state. In the war on crime, as with other wars, hot and cold, real and analogical, the liberal state would finally secure American values against the lawlessness of both anarchy and despotism.

CHAPTER 11

ANALOGUES OF WAR

On September 19, 1938, as Hitler eyed the Sudetenland, J. Edgar Hoover marshalled forces against a threat at home. Although "presumably at peace," America was already in a "domestic war" pitting "the forces of law and order against a subversive enemy"—crime. Hoover summoned the American Legion, the civic veterans group founded in 1919, to join the "orderly forces of Government." He estimated that 4.6 million criminals, an "army of lawlessness," the "Huns and Vandals of the modern [day]," were inflicting a "record of carnage that could scarcely be equaled by the invasion . . . by a foreign foe." Institutional failures aided these common lawbreakers bringing "suffering and death into the homes of all classes of our citizens." Public corruption, "demoralized law enforcement agencies," and "venal politics" now clasped the "blood-caked hand of crime." The United States moreover faced ideological threats—communism and fascism—"the antithesis of American belief in liberty and democracy." Hoover called for a "crusade" defending "true Americanism."[1]

This speech, "Soldiers in Peacetime," captured not only Hoover's posture toward crime and subversion but also the moment's uneasy mix of war fatigue and war preparation. Because his audience recalled the "horrors" of battle, Hoover trusted they knew how to "campaign for peace, without undermining our National Defense."[2] This paradoxical pacifist militarism defined interwar America, with implications beyond what Hoover probably meant. The country was shell-shocked from two decades of turmoil—the Red Scare, repression of immigrants and dissidents, race riots, civil wars over liquor and crime, emergency New Deal regulation, popular upheavals and assassination attempts, extremist temptations and apprehensions about liberal capitalism. These anxieties were "rooted in the Great War," a phrase Hoover used to describe the American Legion, but the words also generally captured the era. These war troubles were directed inward. Yet by the late 1930s, dissension was yielding to consensus. Even ACLU founder Roger Baldwin, unimpressed by the New Deal and dreading war and repression, finally warmed up to Roosevelt's liberalism at the very moment when such threats became most palpable.

For two decades, conscientious objectors, social workers, and labor agitators demanded de-escalation while militarists worked to arm the state. In the last anxious years of peace, Roosevelt faced the challenge of recruiting radical antifascists to his left and militant patriots to his right into a new security-state coalition. By 1941 Roosevelt and his Republican detractors, left-wing activists, and J. Edgar Hoover—adversaries since World War I—united behind a new kind of security state in behalf of the 120 million "true" Americans who opposed communism, fascism, class war, and criminality. The new unity was more inclusive yet more vigilant than ever before. More Americans than ever could share a new uncompromising solidarity against lawless and foreign threats to the liberal order. This solidarity, ideologically and institutionally forged in the New Deal crime consensus, drove the effective transformation of the war-on-crime coalition into a security-state coalition, and guided Americans as they confronted the Axis Powers.[3]

SECURING NEW DEAL AMERICA

Dissent from liberal complacency with repression had rarely focused on crime. The New York ACLU appreciated crime warrior Herbert Lehman as a civil liberties guardian, while ACLU executive director Roger Baldwin uncomfortably watched the national scene. Baldwin co-founded the ACLU after submitting himself to incarceration for dodging Wilson's draft. No fan of censorship, Baldwin uneasily related with the radical left's illiberal currents. He valued Marxist class analysis and defended communists' rights, but he never joined the Communist Party. Communists criticized his support of "free speech for Nazis," and saw his group as "ivory tower liberals expressing the ideas of a decrepit and bankrupt middle-class liberalism." But he recognized this opposition as "honest. Communists make no pretense of supporting free speech on principle."[4] Baldwin nevertheless criticized leftists who only supported "Liberty for Our Side," and his respect for civil liberties eventually warmed him to the very bourgeois liberalism he originally protested.[5]

Baldwin worried that reformist attempts to save capitalism from itself would reinforce corporate power. He expressed early skepticism that the New Deal would actually protect labor. He suspected that "despite himself" Roosevelt would become "bound by the enormous power of property interest" and that his "weight" would ultimately bring "monopoly capital to an even stronger position." In 1934 Baldwin saw economic similarities between the New Deal and fascist Germany and Italy, even if the analogy was "not by any means complete."[6] He agreed with Clarence Darrow's thorough critique of the National Recovery Administration as corporatist.[7]

Baldwin's labor emphasis ironically muted his critique of the New Deal's domestic repression.[8] He regarded the New Deal's unfortunate mainstream resonance as mitigating its repressive capacity. The New Deal would not become truly fascist so long as it lacked a "substantial opposition to suppress." What remained was a threat to political extremists— syndicalism laws and property interests seeking to outlaw the fringe movements threatening the status quo.[9] But Baldwin was not especially concerned about regular criminal defendants. The ACLU involved itself in high-profile disputes like the Scottsboro cases.[10] And in March 1936 Baldwin rebuked Justin Miller's crime prevention outreach, defining the ACLU's priority as crimes committed by law enforcement.[11] And yet a few months later Baldwin expressed confidence that "the rights of defendants" were neither "a political issue," nor any longer "seriously under attack."[12]

While Baldwin saw crime and punishment as deeply intertwined with labor, his main concern was complacency toward the growing state on questions of labor and peace. In 1935 he pondered a "general strike" to prevent another war. "War in the Pacific looms," he warned, "with the United States playing the role of aggressor."[13] He thought that "only the most naïve liberal," hoping to preserve "law and order" and stem "violence against scabs," would "resort to the ultimate power of the State." Myopic liberals ignored the "lawlessness of the troops." Roosevelt's government allowed "unchecked" militarism and rewarded foreign and domestic ambitions with "the greatest peace-time war machine in our history."[14] Baldwin would only come to accept the New Deal security state after it promised to avoid the chaotic repression that ensnared him in World War I.

The New Dealers' support for the FBI encapsulated liberal acquiescence in state coercion. Cummings's war on crime amplified the FBI, which in turn embraced professionalism, scientific forensics, and war-on-crime federalism. While the New Deal activated this institutional transformation, the FBI protected the New Deal state, both narrowly and broadly understood. Roosevelt welcomed Hoover's Bureau powers in securing his own vision in both partisan and general terms. As the war-on-crime consensus shaped the contours of political engagement, the New Deal's domestic power drew skepticism from both left and right. Critics feared that the administration would trample constitutional liberties whether to protect the economic elite or to pursue radical change. These criticisms became marginalized by the logic of electoral politics, the moderating appeal of Roosevelt's program among extremist alternatives, and the security state itself. Directing surveillance against the New Deal's political enemies turned the FBI into the enforcement arm of Roosevelt's agenda. Securing New Deal America in turn redefined and liberalized the security state.

Roosevelt used Hoover's Bureau against the liberal state's opponents, both extremists and routine partisans. Taking office amid lawlessness, Roosevelt prioritized the security of both his presidency and the nation. He saw the political value of surveillance. In 1935 he asked the Justice Department to "find out who is paying for" a pamphlet accusing him of creating "a socialist regime."[15] The FBI scrutinized anti–New Deal activists in the Protestant Civic Welfare Organization and advocates of Roosevelt's impeachment.[16] The Bureau reported on Robert Edward Edmondson, an economist accusing the administration of involvement in a conspiracy among foreigners, communists, and Jews.[17] In October 1935 Hoover warned that veterans evacuated from the Florida Keys after a deadly Labor Day hurricane "might undertake some act of physical violence upon the president."[18] For their part anti–New Dealers feared "interference from Washington."[19] Roosevelt saw the security of his own presidency as carrying stakes for democratic freedom itself, a concern reinforced by Smedley Butler's warning of a possible fascist coup. In August 1936 FDR asked Hoover to develop a "broad picture" of the extremist threat.[20] Hoover suggested revitalizing his Bureau's controversial General Intelligence function, exploiting a loophole that allowed surveillance at the State Department's behest.[21] In September Hoover acted on Roosevelt's request, five days before Hoover informed Cummings.[22] Roosevelt and Hoover now had a relationship independent of the attorney general. Roosevelt later asked Hoover if criminal libel could be used against *Liberation Magazine* for its harsh criticism of the president.[23]

Although FBI spying persisted across administrations, it is a mistake to deemphasize Roosevelt. Hoover's Bureau pursued crime fighting and surveillance largely according to the administration's policy priorities. Moreover, the New Dealers spied on critics through methods besides the FBI.[24] In 1935, facing political and judicial obstacles to New Deal regulation, Roosevelt enlisted Senator Hugo Black to subpoena opponents of a proposal to give the Securities and Exchange Commission antimonopoly powers. Under Black the US Senate Special Committee to Investigate Lobbying Activities subpoenaed telegrams and tax information going back to 1925, before journalists, the FCC, and Congress reined in the Committee. Although its mission creep provoked ACLU opposition, many progressive New Dealers defended the Committee.[25]

The administration also scrutinized left-wing threats to the New Deal state. Labor activism strengthened liberalism within the ideological incubation of welfare institutions, but radicalism threatened stability. J. Edgar Hoover worried about a WPA strike in October 1936.[26] He worried about communistic tendencies in the American Youth Congress.[27] In July 1937 he reported on the threat of a Workers' Alliance plan to sponsor a WPA hunger march. The march, financed by the Communist Party, was planned as a "pilgrimage for peace and security." But such protests among WPA workers threatened the New Deal order.[28]

Meanwhile, the ACLU increasingly saw vigilantes not as the security state's shock troops but as a lawless menace. As vigilante violence became formalized, the organization sought relief from higher levels of government. In the "Westwood vigilante case" they hoped federal action would prove the lesser evil against a "mob of company union men apparently in cooperation with . . . 'law enforcement'" that displaced 500 people from their homes at night. The ACLU was undergoing both radicalization and a shifting posture toward the national state. Its activists were still skeptical of fingerprinting and worried about war repression. In March 1938 ACLU officials strongly opposed H.R. 9605, an industrial mobilization bill, which "under the guise of taking the profits out of war, would, in such an event, plunge the country into a dictatorship from which it might not escape without strife and bloodshed." They did not trust the president "to fix prices on everything, including wages, to seize and control any property, to license all industry and register those employed in it, to conscript every person between the ages of twenty-one to thirty-one, to regulate the order of filling contracts of any kind, and to expend the income of this country as he sees fit." But while they still feared economic planning under militarism, they increasingly valued "law and order" as a beacon for federal help.[29] The National ACLU decried "unauthorized military organizations" using "private military and political uniforms" to intimidate people.[30] The ACLU also considered litigation to challenge California policies against vagrant migration.[31]

While the ideological contours of security-state liberalism developed, so too did the foundations of security-state federalism. Institutional ties among federal, state, and local authorities blurred the line between national security and crime fighting. The FBI's activities had not slowed since its celebrated adventures in 1933 and 1934. In early 1935 the FBI reported thirty-nine fugitives located and apprehended, the "highest figure recorded . . . in a considerable period of time."[32] Between 1934 and

1940, the FBI helped solve 797 bank robberies.[33] Year by year, Attorney General Cummings negotiated to expand the bureaucracy.[34] Embarrassing press reports that he threatened to quit over FBI budget cuts pressured the administration to heed his plan for growth.[35] Cummings envisaged an inflated role for Hoover's Bureau, advocating to add "prevention" to its function in the "detection and prosecution of crimes."[36] This rapid domestic aggrandizement elicited concern and admiration. At stake were jealousies in the Treasury, whose Secret Service protected the president. In 1935 the FBI worried that Morgenthau was "somewhat annoyed and irritated" by its responsibilities to protect the Capitol.[37] But others pushed for greater FBI powers. In May 1936 Senator Arthur Vandenburg argued that the FBI should have more independent aviation capacity to "make the 'G Men' even more formidable than they are today."[38]

All the while, the FBI nurtured networks with local enforcers. Beginning in 1935 its training academy forged well-appreciated ties to police nationwide.[39] Hoover thought the academy so impressive that it demonstrated the extraneousness of a national police force.[40] Roosevelt was applauded as an ally of local policing.[41] Sharing forensic intelligence transformed the traditionally local street-level pursuits into a modernized, preemptive, national undertaking.

For security-state federalism, the most important technological ingredient was fingerprinting collaboration, which inspired new policy ideas across agencies. Fingerprints from the War Department's enlistment records aided hundreds of local criminal justice efforts.[42] A 1937 reorganization bill allowed the removal of fingerprint classifiers from civil service competition.[43] J. Edgar Hoover pondered the use of fingerprinting for non-criminal purposes.[44] One big plan stalled because of practical limits rather than civil liberties implications.[45] When August Vollmer requested Roosevelt's endorsement of universal fingerprinting in Berkeley, Cummings warned that the bureaucracy could not keep up with the potential national interest.[46] To be sure, fingerprinting was politically charged: Roosevelt delayed a fingerprinting mandate for CCC workers until after the 1936 election.[47] But Roosevelt and his cabinet supplied their prints to the FBI to encourage public support.[48] The New Deal state proved useful. The WPA collected workers' fingerprints and local officers collected those of transients, revealing thousands of fugitives. In

1939 Hoover imagined a future when Americans clamored for universal fingerprinting. Far from being a "violation of civil liberties," it was "liberty-insurance."[49]

In ideological and institutional terms, the FBI's analogues of war converged with the New Deal's. The war on crime was both a metaphor and not a metaphor.[50] Cummings's war was the corollary to Roosevelt's mobilization against economic hardship. Into the late 1930s Roosevelt labored to make an ideologically compelling rhetorical case for "security" in respect to foreign threats.[51] But the war on crime had already been compelling rhetoric for years. In April 1937 Hoover touted law enforcement's "patriotic duty toward the welfare of America" and condemned the "dishonorable guns of the underworld" whose "crime army . . . marshals its forces" of "more than 4,300,000 criminals"—an approximation he often revisited with slight variation. The struggle required all available resources. While he aimed for "re-establishment of the tradition" that looked down on crime's "vermin-like aspects," Hoover's criticism of modernist experimentation echoed Roosevelt's criticism of Prohibition. Hoover also agreed with the New Dealers that repression alone was insufficient. Hoover wanted a criminological curriculum in "every college in America." Law enforcement needed higher recruiting standards. The "parasites" of "municipal corruption" needed rooting out. A critic of gratuitous experimentation, Hoover nevertheless condemned "reactionary" urban "officials" who thwarted "forward-looking" visions of law enforcement.[52] Later that month Hoover told journalists that the "forward-looking newspaperman" must expose "municipal corruption."[53] Elsewhere Hoover stressed the "definite relationship" between battling lawlessness and protecting the economy, the deep connection between "national and local business security."[54] Hoover's subordinate Lee R. Pennington echoed his boss. In January 1938, he hailed federal-local cooperation against "the ravages of the lawless," which cried for resistance from "all the 40,000 law enforcement agencies."[55] Like Roosevelt and Hoover, Pennington emphasized "scientific crime detection" and education. He boasted that 85 percent of FBI special agents now had legal training.[56] The FBI's analogues of war, much like the New Deal's, brought all policy mobilization under the umbrella of good governance.[57]

In the liberal security state dominated by the Justice Department, the Treasury also understood the connection between crime and security. In

1937 the Treasury Committee on smuggling kept abreast of the wiretapping bill.[58] It maintained awareness of reorganization plans and proposals to consolidate agents into central regional buildings. In Boston, Newark, and Louisville, most agents were stationed in the Post Office. Elsewhere they rented space or were spread across buildings. The late-1930s Treasury also felt the strain on global crises. Chinese imports declined after Japan's 1937 invasion and anxieties about Hitler became impossible to ignore. The Treasury agents gave increasing attention to the military. In September 1939 Roosevelt's declaration of a Limited Emergency drew the Treasury Committee's attention to the FBI and Neutrality violations. They concluded that enforcement of neutrality and anti-smuggling efforts would complement each other.[59]

By the late 1930s, liberalism and the security state were coming to a mutual understanding. Liberals embraced the multijurisdictional war on crime and an empowered FBI to defend the New Deal state from unrest, extremism, and fascism. Local police supported by the FBI appreciated Roosevelt, and so did J. Edgar Hoover. In 1937 Roosevelt congratulated him for twenty years of service, to which Hoover responded that "Words are inadequate to express my appreciation." He vowed "to endeavor to merit that confidence and faith."[60] Although Hoover did not espouse left-liberalism, his commitment to defending Roosevelt's government, including in its partisan strength, made him a major asset to New Deal liberalism.

Germany's ambitions meanwhile heightened fears of world war. Its 1938 unification with Austria and the Treaty of Munich did not quench Hitler's thirst for long. In 1939 the war's European theater would start in earnest. Securing New Deal America would take on a new meaning and within its earned place in Roosevelt's circle of confidence, the FBI would come to defend liberalism more broadly—the creed of the republic itself.

THE TWO-FRONT WAR

From 1939 through 1941 the objective and subjective conditions coalesced for a new kind of security state—modernized, stable, and liberal. The infrastructure of war-on-crime federalism blossomed into security-state federalism, as Hoover's Bureau served as dispatch for the nation's military and police.[61] Criminal law weaponized against the subversive continued to build the domestic state. The war-on-crime consensus gestated into a security consensus as the specters of totalitarian ideology and global calamity activated war preparation. Wielding the most awesome powers, Roosevelt brought previously conflicting voices into his state-building mission.[62] The ACLU's criticisms softened and Republicans began to trust Roosevelt even with powers they found constitutionally suspect. Political factions in opposition since World War I converged in previously unthinkable ways into a synthesis of radicalism, progressivism, and conservatism. As liberals embraced the security state, the security state took on a more liberal cast. From the right and left, critics warning of New Deal threats to liberty helped liberalize the security state, which they increasingly hoped would guard the democratic order. This ideological and institutional coalescence prepared the security state for the war and the years beyond.

In the institutionally pivotal year of 1939, the new attorney general, Frank Murphy, would prove as revolutionary as Cummings. Murphy took office in January with a civil libertarian reputation, having refused, as Michigan's governor, to call troops out to suppress the United Auto Workers.[63] Hoover appreciated his plans to "rebuild the Nation's law office" and to purge political influence from promotions.[64] But Murphy did much more. He officiated the criminological state's marriage to national defense, and by elevating Hoover's Bureau as leader of both national intelligence and domestic policing, Murphy prepared the security state for its next national crisis. Intelligence leadership previously fell to an informal committee run by representatives from State, Treasury, War, Justice, Navy, and the Post Office. But Murphy reasoned in June that with its massive data resources, technical laboratory, and identification division, the FBI should co-direct national intelligence with the Military Intelligence Division and the Office of Naval Intelligence (ONI).[65] Roosevelt issued the order.[66] These three bodies would coordinate all intelligence of espionage, counter-espionage, and sabotage—a rebalancing of power that subordinated the secretary of the Treasury and the Postmaster.[67] The newly constrained secretary of state would continue intelligence gathering but had to appraise the big three of its operations.[68] Although at year's end the administration restricted these officials' access to census files, they were invited to make specific requests for census information.[69]

The foreign-policy implications of the FBI's new role unfolded soon enough, but the domestic impact was immediate. After an August non-aggression pact between Europe's two totalitarian giants, Nazi Germany followed by the Soviet Union invaded Poland in September. After the Nazi invasion, Murphy suggested that state and local law enforcement share in defense intelligence gathering.[70] Roosevelt empowered Murphy to instruct the FBI to take charge of investigations of espionage, sabotage, and violations of neutrality on a "comprehensive and national basis." Murphy then asked "all police officers, sheriffs, and all other law enforcement officers" that they provide "to the nearest" FBI representative any relevant "information obtained," including regarding "subversive activities."[71]

The FBI's intensifying intimacy with local police facilitated this transition. Police now became the eyes and ears of a national bureaucracy that was only fully authorized to investigate crimes five years before. Having solved 154 out of 156 kidnapping cases since 1932, Hoover applauded the FBI's new capacity to scan files of eleven million fingerprints in three minutes.[72] By late 1939 goals included the comprehensive fingerprinting of aliens and passport applicants.[73] The Wisconsin Chief of Police Association praised J. Edgar Hoover and Murphy, the FBI and its crime laboratory, fingerprinting database, information clearing house, and statistical records.[74] Security-state federalism served local authorities. The FBI furnished fingerprints and forensic assistance and helped detect recidivistic convicts.[75] Police appreciated the integration of the wars against crime and subversion. In 1940 the Pacific Coast International Association of Law Enforcement gathering in Mexico resolved to defend the FBI against "subversive forces in this country."[76]

The liberal security state drove an ideological split in both the right and left. In targeting the right, Roosevelt now fixated on opponents of democracy more than New Deal critics. Antifascist vigilance had for years encouraged left-leaning activists. In 1936 the National Blue Shirts of America, claiming 38,000 members, had supported Roosevelt busting up pro-Nazi meetings.[77] In the following years the emphasis on right-wing extremism intensified. National-security concerns animated FBI investigations of alleged German-American Bund Groups suspected of wanting a coup, pro-fascist Silver Shirts, and espionage in Navy yards.[78] Hoover monitored possible Nazi fifth-columnists in New York City[79] and investigated anti-Semitic activities, including a circular warning that Roosevelt hoped to "make the world safe for communistic jewry [*sic*]."[80]

Anticommunism itself divided the right. Communism within and outside the United States vexed J. Edgar Hoover.[81] But compared to more reactionary anticommunists, Hoover's posture jibed with Roosevelt's. As with McCarthyism years later, the more virulent anticommunists legitimated the liberals' more moderate anticommunism. The House Un-American Activities Committee, under conservative Texas Democrat Martin Dies, was the most convincing of foils. The Committee harassed unions and saw New Deal liberalism itself as potentially subversive.[82] It accused the New Deal of privileging communists, and the FBI investigated its allegations that the Federal Writers Project restricted employment to Workers' Alliance members.[83] In attempting to pit Hoover against Roosevelt, Dies irritated both. Some on the right feared that even Hoover did not appreciate Dies's warnings. Roosevelt worried that Dies would obstruct FBI investigations.[84]

The liberal security state also drove a wedge in the left. The ACLU distinguished the New Deal's responsible anticommunism and its illiberal counterparts, condemning in June 1939 the reckless "anti-democratic propaganda . . . aimed allegedly at Communism and in part against Jews," but "in fact directed against progressive movements, the New Deal, and the C.I.O."[85] While patriotic leftists preferred the FBI over Dies, and patriotic conservatives supported the New Deal state against the Nazi threat, Roosevelt sought to clarify the line between protecting New Deal partisanship and protecting the United States. In August 1939, prompted by scandal of WPA employees lobbying in the 1938 election, the president signed into law the Hatch Act, which restricted lobbying by federal employees.

In addition to communists, fascists, and criminals, vigilantes became an important enemy of both Roosevelt and Hoover. Peaceful activists found encouragement in this stance. In blunt contrast to World War I's disgraces, anti-vigilantism rounded out the liberal security state. Long opposed to mob violence, the ACLU national leadership prepared in October 1939 to ask Murphy and Hoover for "clarification" of the Justice Department's "position" on vigilantes who "intended to cooperate with the Department."[86] That same month, Hoover railed against criminals' "onslaughts," the "devious machinations" of those with "enemy modes of thought and action," and "subversion in all its forms." But while cautioning against the "lecherous barnacles of venal politics," Hoover also warned against a "witch hunt." "Bands of vigilantes" were "un-American, unpatriotic, and subversive." The security state must be lawful, rational, and tempered to defend the "law-abiding nation."[87]

The liberal security state promised unprecedented pluralism alongside vigilance against the truly un-American. Peaceful radicals enjoyed new protection under this umbrella, and in turn they were beckoned to join democracy's violent struggle against authoritarianism. In early 1939 Baldwin recognized his movement had become less radical but now "democracy [was] on the defensive" and had replaced socialism as the relevant bulwark against fascism's urgent onslaught.[88] The immediate threats were fascists, vigilantes, and indeed communists, not anti–New Deal conservatives and labor agitators. Baldwin's concern with communists sharpened with Stalin and Hitler's cooperative pact. The radical left could cheer the liberal state's crackdowns on Nazi sympathizers, future Cold Warriors could applaud its muscular anticommunism, and those scarred by Red Scare trauma found hope in its rule of law.[89]

A common interpretation that Roosevelt's government moved rightward in these moments does not easily explain Baldwin's gravitation toward the administration on the eve of war. His second thoughts came about because of the Justice Department more than the welfare state. Toward the end of Cummings's tenure, Baldwin lamented that Justice Department corruption investigations into Puerto Rico had trouble overcoming the governor's obstruction.[90] ACLU activists had hopes for Frank Murphy's new Civil Liberties Unit, which beginning in 1939 amplified criminal enforcement to defend workers. The ACLU lauded the "new machinery for the protection of labor's rights through the National Labor Relations Act" and similar legislation in several states. A liberalization of "labor injunction laws" had meanwhile brought a "sharp drop in strikes," which meant "fewer violations of civil rights."[91] While

Baldwin once championed agitation against the state, he now welcomed the state's conciliatory reforms.[92] The ACLU's newfound comfort with the liberal state coincided with its alienation from other radicals, exacerbated further by divisions over the Nazi–Soviet pact.[93] Meanwhile, the FBI stepped up its vigilance against disloyalty. After the German invasion of Poland, Hoover widened the Detention Index to include citizens and foreigners whose "presence at liberty . . . in time of war or national emergency would be dangerous to the public peace."[94] Far from marking a shift toward conservatism, the security state's antifascist vigilance along with its new prioritization of labor rights signaled a distinctive liberalism.

Murphy spent his last months as attorney general lobbying for an FBI capable of waging a two-front war—against criminals and against enemies of the state. In September 1939 he requested an additional 150 FBI personnel.[95] Its new national defense duties included major investigations and protection of industrial plants. Murphy could point to plant protection in elaborating on the FBI's expanding needs. In 1939, manufacturing infrastructure endured 10,800 explosions and 23,700 fires.[96] Murphy did not want defense burdens to drain its crime-fighting resources. Anticipating the next fiscal year, from mid-1940 to mid-1941, Murphy saw only $7.444 million allocated for the FBI. This might suffice for peacetime but now the FBI needed another $1,531,315 and 144 investigative special agents,400 additional agents for emergency defense work, and a reserve item budget of $500,000 instead of $200,000. Murphy estimated that manpower shortages left a third of the investigative work undone.[97] Indeed, the FBI's defense burdens had grown. When Roosevelt took office, the FBI handled about thirty-five national defense cases annually. This figure climbed to 250 for fiscal year 1938, 1,651 for 1939, 16,000 for 1940 and 68,000 in 1941.[98]

Murphy's vision of a two-front war would fully integrate the metaphorical and nonmetaphorical dimensions of the security state.

THE NEW LIBERAL MOBILIZATION

Pacifist militarism, interwar America's defining paradox, crested in the two years before Pearl Harbor. Having long feared war, liberal officials became sanguine toward mobilization. In December 1939, Herbert

Lehman averred that "adequate preparedness is not an incentive to war as some would have us believe." Lehman agreed with George Washington that "during peace is the time to prepare against war."[99] The next month Frank Murphy became an associate justice on the US Supreme Court. His replacement for attorney general, Robert Jackson, continued his predecessor's transformation of the war on crime into defense systems. In 1940 and 1941 the architects of security-state liberalism decisively triumphed over those, left and right, who worried the state would smother constitutional liberties.

Institutional consolidation continued despite some grumblings. Jackson's Justice Department inherited immigration enforcement, a contentious issue since the 1920s, from the Department of Labor. Labor Secretary Frances Perkins expressed mild concerns that the usurpation would tarnish "one of the humanitarian functions of the government." Then she dissented forthrightly. Opposed to a formal state of emergency after Hitler's invasion of Poland, Perkins warned against the "greater infringement on civil rights and personal freedom." She decried the increasingly exclusionary immigration policy and resisted J. Edgar Hoover's pressure to fingerprint foreigners to estimate their numbers. But State and Justice pushed for the reorganization, which Roosevelt implemented in May 1940. Thousands of immigration officials moved to the Justice Department.[100]

The administration meanwhile laid the groundwork for mass detention. Congress passed the Alien Registration Act, requiring all foreign nationals to register with the federal government. The Alien Registration Unit, Postal Service, and FBI built a detailed database, eventually comprising five million files. Hoover compiled a list of both aliens and citizens subject to arrest in the case of war. The Special Defense Unit had its own enemies list. The Custodial Detention Index, with thousands of names, was mostly completed in 1940.[101]

The year 1940 was vital for the liberal security state. In 1940 Congress increased penalties for peacetime Espionage Act violations and the FBI enjoyed its greatest expansion in hiring and qualitative investigatory powers.[102] It was also an election year, and many voters were anxious about entering the war. In this atmosphere there was significant concern for dissenters' civil liberties.[103] Surveillance soon targeted critics of war mobilization. The FBI started a defense plant informant program that would last nearly twenty years.[104] Roosevelt lifted restrictions on FBI wiretapping in May. The same month, after Roosevelt's sweeping address on national security provoked a slew of dissenting telegrams, the president asked Hoover to examine them and note "the names and addresses of the senders."[105] Hoover sought evidence of more than mere disagreement.[106] A New York City teachers' union telegram criticizing Roosevelt's armament plans traveled up the chain to Hoover.[107] In June Democratic congressman John Lesinski asked the FBI to investigate someone overheard suggesting that the Germans were better prepared than America.[108] The Bureau crosschecked telegrams and letters with names tracing to Hoover's earliest days in antisubversion, even consulting names from World War I and the Red Scare.[109] Once again a Democratic administration's Justice Department was scrutinizing suspected Kaiser sympathizers and evaders of Wilson's draft—this time, two decades after the fact. Hoover kept Roosevelt abreast of these dissenting voices.[110]

These investigations seldom produced naked repression, partly because the administration saw some political value in restraint and nuance. The FBI mediated an agreement between the ACLU and Dies. He would stop harassing the organization, which in turn purged communists.[111] The New Dealers and Dies meanwhile began converging on foreign threats. Dies wanted tightened borders and deportations to counter Nazis and communists entering from Mexico. On June 10 Roosevelt concurred that communist, fascist, and Nazi activities "should not be under-estimated," but renounced repression and antidemocratic measures, at least in name. He had faith in the intelligence triad of the FBI, War Department, and Navy Department.[112] And yet vigilance against disloyalty still inspired dissent. The ACLU criticized Roosevelt for wiretapping "subversive activities."[113] For Baldwin, "surrender of our liberties in an emergency" still posed the true threat. We "would need no Hitler then to conquer us. Totalitarianism would have conquered us from within."[114]

Mobilizing for a two-front war became even more compelling after the Nazi invasion of Paris in June 1940.[115] The administration became increasingly vigilant, as Robert Jackson entertained a seven-point program including a loyalty pledge to remove communists from government.[116] The heightened resolve against subversion coincided with celebrations of security-state federalism. The International Association of Chiefs of Police praised Hoover.[117] Pennington warned an American Legion audience in July that every "good citizen must . . . guard against all subversion" including "Communism, Fascism, Naziism." The United States had room for "only one 'ism'—Americanism."[118] In August, the interstate commission on crime convened a conference of governors and state attorneys general. US Solicitor General Francis Biddle declared that alien control, espionage, sabotage, and subversion would "test our . . . Americanism" and affirmed that "Common defense" relied on the "normal channels of local, state and national law enforcement."[119] America's future lay in the interaction among its different institutions. Stressing collaboration over confrontation, Dies urged more coordination between the State Department, Justice, and his own committee. He thought poor communication interfered with fifth-column surveillance.[120]

All the while the security state's defenders boasted its modern respect for civil liberties. Dissent sometimes restrained the administration, halting Jackson's plan to expand wiretapping.[121] More important, the government took credit defending the rule of law. National security required "the greatest possible public confidence" in law enforcement, as Pennington put it.[122] Officials stressed lawfulness and legitimacy. In March, R. B. Jordan condemned anti-Hoover agitation as "designed to undermine public confidence" and praised the FBI National Police Academy as "the greatest single guarantee that law enforcement will protect civil liberties." Only "untrained and unprofessional law enforcement officers" threatened rights. The FBI's uniform crime reporting, clearing house of data, and technical lab ensured justice over reckless local vagaries.[123] In late June Edwin M. Watson depicted the FBI as the principal guardian of freedoms even as war loomed. Given "the task of preserving and defending democratic institutions" against corruption and subversion while "scrupulously protecting the civil liberties of law abiding citizens," America was lucky to have J. Edgar Hoover.[124] Roosevelt urged vigilance against the enemy and misdirected domestic panic. He hailed cooperation from the states "to strengthen our lines of defense" and federal and state legislative efforts against "subversive activities, . . . seditious acts, [and] those things which slow up or break down our common defense program." The "common defense" should utilize "the normal channels of local, State and national law enforcement." Calling the "untrained policeman . . . as ineffective as the untrained soldier," Roosevelt hoped that state officials would resist "the prejudice and emotional haste which characterized much of similar legislation during the last world war."[125]

War mobilization meanwhile shaped the NAACP's struggle against anti-Black lawlessness, even as war threatened to overshadow their efforts. In early 1938 NAACP officials worried that ongoing deliberation over naval legislation would upstage the anti-lynching campaign. But they saw an opening to analogize foreign and domestic threats to democracy. Walter White applauded Roosevelt for his "courage in speaking out . . . against the oppression of the Jewish population in Europe" and warned that Black Americans would feel "no protection" if anti-lynching legislation faltered. The failure to combat white supremacist terror would embolden efforts to "propagandize among Negroes."[126] After Murphy took over, the Justice Department was beginning to investigate police brutality, but still found lynching to be a private crime unactionable under the state action doctrine.[127] As war talk dominated, the NAACP argued that a new law was more needed than ever. Recalling the Black soldiers lynched after World War I, the NAACP warned that "to preserve democracy" abroad, America "must wipe out undemocratic practices [like] lynching" within.[128]

A marked decline in lynching, even despite the lack of a new federal law, was dividing activists. In 1940 the Southern Women for the Prevention of Lynching celebrated the first supposedly lynching-free year. The NAACP replied that lynching had gone underground, noting three whites who died that year.[129] Although 1939 had seen few incidents, Walter White argued that historically "lynching varies in an inverse ratio to the intensity of the campaign against it." "Democracy itself" was at stake, and if he "were a communist, a Nazi," or a Fascist "and wanted to destroy or weaken American Democracy, I would work unceasingly" against "anti-lynching legislation." Presciently predicting wartime civil rights rhetoric, White argued that in "a second world war," Black Americans would again "be called upon . . . to die for Democracy." Although the most recent publicized lynching victims were not Black, White argued that lynching lawlessness transcended race. In a desperate hope to unite the spirit of reunion with the promise of Reconstruction, he observed that the celebrated author of *The Life of Robert E. Lee* favored the federal anti-lynching bill.[130]

The Justice Department would do more to challenge anti-Black lawlessness in the next several years. For now its civil liberties posture on labor and vigilantism was causing real ambivalence in the ACLU. In October Baldwin worried about both lawless vigilantes and state power. Whether targeting Jehovah's witnesses, communists, or German-American Bundists, "widespread intolerance" imperiled "political democracy itself." Baldwin identified an "unprecedented strain on peace-time democracy" and feared "lawless action by mobs, aroused by citizens and local officials."[131] As for the Justice Department, its enormous powers were real. Robert Jackson could prosecute seditionists, mandate obedience in the Armed Forces, and enforce America's first peacetime conscription law, signed by Roosevelt in September. The administration was investigating conscientious objectors and registering Americans with international political connections through the Alien Registration Law. These developments would spell trouble under an attorney general "unsympathetic with civil liberty." A cruel Justice Department could "stifle criticism and dissent." But Baldwin trusted "Jackson, whose liberalism is outspoken" and whose powers were "unlikely to be abused." Baldwin's optimism harbored one major caveat: war could change everything.[132]

Even aside from war, by the early 1940s the ACLU's conceptualization of civil liberties had transformed. Historian Laura Weinrib shows how its approach morphed from a right of agitation to a value-neutral check on state power.[133] The ACLU started as more anti-state and partisan toward labor interests and became more pro-state and moderate on class struggle. New Deal labor policies help explain the change, as did the judicial efficacy of generically libertarian arguments, for which the ACLU increasingly cooperated with the anti–New Deal right. The ACLU's First Amendment understanding became more anti-state in its definition of freedom at the moment it became more pro-state in its expectations for redress.

Complementing the irony Weinrib identifies is the paradoxical transformation of the state itself. Government under the New Deal developed from something more conservative and associational to something more expansive and yet emancipatory.[134] Within the national executive, legislative, and judicial apparatuses, the deliberation over rights actually reinforced the sociological premises of pre–Progressive Era liberalism. Federal expansion, within the FBI no less than in the welfare state, redefined liberalism so as to simultaneously repudiate and reaffirm the nineteenth-century's transactional individualism. On the one hand, the state would become empowered to advance the general welfare—deeming as anachronistic the *answers* offered by nineteenth-century liberalism. On the other hand, central-state empowerment gave new credibility and purchase to the *questions* classical liberalism posed about government and individuals. The liberal security state more explicitly recognized a relevant dialectic between the individual and the collective, and thus civil rights and civil liberties became disassociated from questions of competing interests within the class and social order and moved toward the question of individual flourishing. Both parties to this question would have a shared stake in the world created by the New Deal state. While in measurable terms Roosevelt's government was more activist than progressive predecessors, and while some left-wing sympathizers embraced state power like never before, together they vindicated a vision of the modern liberal individual that Gilded Age politics and law could less convincingly affirm. Just as social welfare would be individualized as social insurance, the modern liberal state would secure negative rights along with positive rights, civil liberties along with social entitlements. The New Deal and war-on-crime coalition's promise had been to make the relationship between government and citizen less of a zero-sum game.

The liberal security state's bipartisan resonance also liberalized the Republican opposition. On his right flank, Roosevelt was accustomed to accusations that he trampled constitutional rights. But in the election season Republicans conceded the remarkable premises of Roosevelt's security state. Presidential candidate Wendell Willkie accused the New Deal of conflating its partisan agenda with American interests. But the Willkie campaign accepted some core assumptions about social welfare, even calling relief a "matter of justice" and accusing his opponents of treating it as a mere prophylactic to discourage "revolution."[135] Raymond Moley and Republican gubernatorial candidate Thomas Dewey collaborated on a speech that blamed Roosevelt for inefficient war preparation— criticizing both an "astronomical sum voted for national defense," and the "[in]sufficient naval, air or military force to meet a menace on both seaboards"—not a difference of principle with the administration but a criticism of management. Republicans urged more cooperation with Mexico and Canada, decried the earlier appeasement of Hitler and urged that tax increases rather than debt fund military expansion. They advocated criminal pursuit of regulatory violators for the sake of security: America needed a "simple mobilizing organization like the war industries board" with "price control over everything."[136] Despite their quibbles, Moley and his Republican colleagues conceded the need for a security state integrated with welfare and crime control, one far removed from the political economy or upside-down federalism of the Republican 1920s.

After his second reelection in 1940, Roosevelt could more comfortably enjoy bipartisan support. Herbert Lehman was "very happy," notwithstanding his unease with court-packing. The election on the brink of war soldered the fusion of New Deal liberalism with Americanism. The nation had a "duty to unite all of our forces, all of our energies, all our deepest loyalties, behind our President in defense of America."[137] Alf Landon, who lost to Roosevelt in 1936, now conceded "that relief can be more honestly and efficiently administered by a federal agency than a local one." Landon worried that the atmosphere might devolve into mob rule and Roosevelt's breathtaking powers would "fall into the hands of a Hitler." Landon thought Roosevelt acknowledged the awesomeness of his powers, which "cannot be trusted" except to "a people's government."[138] A few months later Landon clarified his fear that fascism "would come from" the New Dealers' "enemies . . . through their heirs, successors and assigns."[139] Republican Hill Blackett mused that anti-Roosevelt activism had to focus on the "long-time issue" of constitutional government.[140] Even Republicans were grateful Roosevelt held power, constitutional or not, for the terrible danger of the security state was that it might one day cease to be liberal.

Roosevelt began his third term, in 1941, as he did his first: pressured to leverage emergency powers to address a national crisis. A district judge in Texas, noting Hitler's rampage abroad and Charles Lindbergh's antiwar extremism at home, urged Roosevelt to "take over" and "declare martial law, if necessary." Roosevelt should also aim leftward and put strikers "in a concentration camp" if it came to it.[141] Although the liberals running the military would not embrace such proposals, they appreciated the urgency. Secretary of War Henry Stimson called strikes more "harmful in their total effect than actual physical sabotage." The Military Intelligence Division and ONI wanted to stop strikes "without detriment to the legitimate bargaining functions of labor," and petitioned for greater FBI powers to stop them.[142] Roosevelt generally believed that "Communists and other subversive elements" justified an expansion of FBI's authority over "subversive control of labor."[143] J. Edgar Hoover suggested that subversive speech be suppressed.[144] And indeed, the FBI soon inherited the Treasury's task of checking the loyalty of employees within defense organizations.[145] In February 1941 Roosevelt asked Jackson about offering FBI facilities to the Coordinator of Commercial and Cultural Relations between the American Republics to cooperate in "eliminating totalitarian agents" within the organization.[146] In June Roosevelt deployed troops to break a strike in Los Angeles. Federal marshals raided the Social Workers Party headquarters in Minneapolis.[147]

Law enforcement came under tighter federal influence. In February Pennington reminded local police of their access to FBI's lab facilities, but they should report defense cases rather than investigating themselves.[148] A unanimous resolution from the National Police Academy Associates pledged fealty to Roosevelt "as far as National Policy is concerned" and "cooperation to the Federal Bureau of Investigation in coordinating the forces of Law Enforcement in the work of National Defense."[149] Roosevelt in turn valued the group's "devotion to the Nation's welfare."[150] Every week FBI representatives attended conferences with military and Treasury leaders.[151] By October 1941 security and law enforcement officials had attended over 500 regional conferences. On the eve of US entry into the international conflict, the legal community continued to cheer the war on crime. The Vermont Bar Association president hailed the Bureau "for the absence of the gangster, for the absence of the kidnaper and for the security of our homes." The FBI had "restored this country at one time to a basis of law and order in a period when lawlessness was the rule rather than the exception."[152]

The New Deal judiciary was meanwhile preparing to accommodate the security state's concentrated authority. Robert Jackson retired as attorney general in August 1941 and joined his predecessor Frank Murphy on the Supreme Court. Two liberal security-state attorneys general now sat on the Court along with Hugo Black, Roosevelt's surveillance man from the Senate, and four other Roosevelt appointees. Court-packing had proven unnecessary to produce an almost entirely Rooseveltian Court. As Francis Biddle took over as attorney general, new constitutional interpretations lay in wait to support his machinery's expanding power. On some issues, at least, centralization tipped toward civil liberties. State and federal centralization finally resolved the legal question of California's exclusionary violence toward interstate migrants. Whereas Los Angeles police chief Davis's border vigilantes were deemed nonstate actors that federal law could not constrain, California had since formalized its rule against indigent migration. In November of 1941 the Supreme Court struck down California's law, a major watershed in the consolidation of jurisdiction over interstate movement, an open question since the late nineteenth century.[153] But in the next few years the Supreme Court's affirmation of federal jurisdiction westward would have much more ominous implications for human rights.

AS THE SECURITY STATE UNDERTOOK final war preparation, both the labor left and enthusiasts for a new Red Scare found common ground. Baldwin, that tireless critic of bourgeois liberalism, a pacifist imprisoned during Wilson's war, had evolved in his appreciation. He saw that the New Deal's "controlled capitalism marks an advance," and celebrated free speech, labor gains, and a decline in lynchings.[154] While they denied class analysis, liberals were valuable protectors of the persecuted, the ones who "form the bridge across the chasm" "between the established order" and social reform. The liberals were the translators, ready to "interpret the new to the old." And they cherished civil liberties, which were becoming redefined. "Of all the objectives which most readily unite the liberals," Baldwin wrote, "the fight for civil liberties takes first place." Moreover, just as the left needed liberals, the need was mutual. The New Deal was the domestic version of the popular front against fascism and depended on "labor and the Left" for its "fighting power."[155] Baldwin now even understood the liberals' "prejudice against Communists," which was "not unreasonable" even if sometimes unfair. He hoped that if reasonable radicals joined with the liberal security state, there would be less dissent to suppress. Voluntary "national unity" rather than "enforced conformity" could mean "an emergency without repression."[156] Perhaps even a wartime security state could withstand the temptation to destroy civil liberties, Baldwin seemed to suggest for the first time.

And so Baldwin, unimpressed by the early New Deal and relatively unconcerned about criminal due process, finally became comfortable with Roosevelt's liberalism at the moment when war and repression of dissent, his two greatest fears, became most likely. Murphy, Jackson, and even J. Edgar Hoover as much as Roosevelt himself had won Baldwin over with their promises to suppress reactionary lawlessness, and left-wing patriotism had in turn helped liberalize the security state. The FBI would eagerly conquer the lawlessness within the very infrastructure of repression. Lee Pennington distinguished the new security state from the ways of old, when "public hysteria" doomed "many lawabiding citizens" with suspicious names and accents to "Concentration camps."[157] Baldwin agreed with the new FBI attitude.

In June Hitler betrayed Stalin, invading the Soviet Union, and their falling out drove some communist fellow travelers back into the liberal security-state coalition. Red-baiters and socialist fellow travelers could unite against lawlessness, in the name of American values. The FBI and local police, modernized by the war on crime and entrusted to secure New Deal America from its partisan and illiberal enemies, would uphold law and liberty in its next crusade. The responsible left and right, Democrats and Republicans, all foes of totalitarianism and vigilantism, believed in Roosevelt to lead the way. Shed of their Progressive Era contradictions and their interwar anxieties of pacifist militarism, the ecumenical liberals of 1941 were finally ready for the more orderly repression war would bring.

For two decades, Baldwin had anxiously awaited another international war. Even as the Justice Department's gestures toward civil liberties encouraged him, he still feared a wartime police state. After Japan's December 7 attack on Pearl Harbor the security-state coalition swelled. Isolationists to Roosevelt's right joined the military and his left flank enlisted in his national liberalism. Baldwin now equivocated on the very meaning of pacifism. As he told the War Resisters League, he opposed "*participation* in all wars," but that did not mean neutrality. Pacifists could champion the Union in the Civil War. Gandhi backed the British in World War I.[158] Won over by the liberal security state's vigilance against domestic lawlessness, Baldwin now awaited its ultimate test with an open mind.

CHAPTER 12

TRIAL BY FIRE

After Pearl Harbor, the Tennessee Valley Authority (TVA) became a testing ground for liberal commitments to rehabilitation and law and order. The pressures of war encouraged more leeway in hiring convicts and more nuanced consideration of the time lapsed since conviction, offenses without moral turpitude, and the jurisdictional idiosyncrasies in categorizing felonies and misdemeanors. What began as an issue of wartime expediency reinforced what one TVA official considered a "general sociological principle" in line with the guidance of J. V. Bennett, director of the Bureau of Prisons.[1]

The wartime TVA fully encapsulated the intersection of social welfare, law-and-order liberalism, and national defense. War turned its Public Safety Service (PSS) forces into a national defense unit and accelerated professionalization. Deliberation on subsidizing replacement uniforms focused on disparities with private war industrial practices. TVA security officials undertook broader training, including skills in self-defense, firearms, swimming, driving, legal knowledge, typewriting, police experience, traffic control and fire experience, and public relations. Trainees required at least an eighth-grade education.[2] The Army required each PSS member to become part of the military police's civilian auxiliary, sub-ject to the Articles of War—which posed complications for New Deal labor policy since these were among the nation's first unionized police forces. The PSS's military importance became clear when eight German saboteurs arrived intending to attack TVA installations. The TVA po-lice guarded energy lines that powered the Aluminum Company of America, a prime target for sabotage. During the war they coordinated with "the Army, the Federal Power Commission, the Federal Bureau of Investigation, and the U.S. Coast Guard." They helped the FBI locate a fugitive of eleven years and assisted in pursuing black market gasoline peddlers. As threats to military-industrial facilities waned, so too did the PSS's military importance. Nevertheless, by April 1944 Colonel Stacy Knopf could declare that "perhaps 90%" of TVA's "work is directly or indirectly devoted to the war effort. It is primarily a war agency." By late 1944 there were about 400 TVA guards.[3]

As it turned out, war spawned a permanent security state—one that increasingly touted inclusiveness, the public welfare, and law and order—that helped navigate the modernization of liberalism. For this symbiotic development two conditions had to hold. First was institutional ground-work. The Justice Department and FBI laid this groundwork, inte-grating and updating national defense and local policing to ensure sus-tainable operation. Second was the political factor. Permanence would require what Woodrow Wilson's security state lacked: broad consensus across partisan, regional, class, and bureaucratic lines. It had to be prag-matic for the conservatives and progressive enough for the New Deal's left wing, balancing vigilance toward illiberal outsiders with tolerance toward the edges of allowable opinion. Political illegitimacy brought down Re-construction, the Red Scare, and Prohibition. The war-on-crime coalition had secured this legitimacy in time for war.

Historians have well explained how war ratified, moderated, and mod-ernized New Deal liberalism. The war brought lasting momentum to state capacity and planning; it tempered the most anticapitalist impulses of the New Deal through the expediencies of the military-industrial com-plex; it breathed new life into the politics of civil rights and inclusion that the domestic New Deal had advanced less decisively. An overlooked parallel and related trajectory marked law enforcement and criminal justice—liberals would henceforth tout the potential for law enforcement in helping to build an America of community, freedom, equality, and security. War indeed clarified what New Deal crime policies achieved. By 1941 Roosevelt's coalition had met the institutional and ideological conditions—honing the instruments of repression and refining their relationship to politics, building consensus for a liberalized security state. In the twilight of US entry into World War II, war-on-crime liberalism had become security-state liberalism, war-on-crime federalism had gestated into security-state federalism. World War II tested and proved this refinement and transformation, which could boast allegiance from right to left and East to West.

Histories of the dyadic wartime foundations of the welfare state and security state often skip over the crime-fighting state. Stories of both institutions and ideas largely acknowledge the permanent security state arising from the war but not the antecedent role of 1930s criminal justice. Economic historians recognize wartime government expansion whose quantitative changes dwarfed New Deal experimentation.[4] But the literature on state capacity has not always grappled with the cultural dimensions. Fables of liberalism have stressed the ideological development without generally integrating criminal justice. Alan Brinkley noted the intertwined arcs of liberalism and government growth, including their relation to repression, without much focus on crime and punishment.[5] More recent research on government growth and legitimacy gestures toward state repression without situating it at the center of liberalism.[6]

In fact, the war on crime, the security state, and the revolution in liberalism converged in the governing experiments that accompanied and survived the war. The qualitative and cultural changes facilitating the state's structural development invite a closer look at the role of New Deal criminal justice powers in the wartime state's metamorphic relation to liberalism. The practical needs of wartime security depended on enforcement infrastructure that Roosevelt had rescued from its precarious fate following the Prohibition decade. His team perfected this machinery, transformed federalism, and redefined liberalism in time for war. Former attorney general Frank Murphy's vision of an FBI suited for a two-front war against criminals and enemies of the state now faced its trial by fire. The regime's capacity to prosecute criminals and accused traitors, maintain martial law in Hawaii and concentration camps for mainland Japanese Americans and Alaska's Aleuts, relied on the New Deal stabilization of the infrastructure of state violence.[7] On the political side, liberalism had become acclimated to the capacity of repression, and so the security state could survive the war despite such infamies as internment. With its unprecedented scope and polite restraint, its terror and proceduralism, the security state's wartime resilience boded well for the future of American power. In both institutional and ideological terms, World War II proved that the New Deal war on crime had legitimated national enforcement authority.

SECURITY-STATE FEDERALISM AT WAR

At the center of the security state's wartime successes was the transformed Federal Bureau of Investigation. After an uncertain 1920s the Bureau spent the 1930s proving itself. It had proven flexible enough to combat gangsters, useful to local police and surveillance, a hospitable complement to New Deal criminology, and a potential ally to labor and civil rights. The institutional timing was crucial. Peacetime nurturing of relations with local police produced an infrastructure ready for wartime activation. It is doubtful such immediate mobilization would be possible without the groundwork laid under Cummings, Murphy, and Jackson.[8]

The wartime FBI was a powerhouse of international, national, and local reach. By December 1941, the Bureau claimed fifty-five field offices in all forty-eight states.[9] Inflated from eight years of war against crime, overseeing police intelligence, and achieving peer status alongside the Office of Naval Intelligence and Military Intelligence Division, the FBI also ran intelligence for the whole western hemisphere. On June 20, 1940, Roosevelt informally requested that the FBI manage surveillance in the Americas. A year and a half later, about two weeks after Pearl Harbor, the new attorney general, Francis Biddle, undertook to formalize the arrangement.[10] On December 23, 1941, Biddle authorized an FBI Special Intelligence Service. All departments and agencies received orders to "clear directly" any surveillance of the western hemisphere with the Bureau. Biddle's confidential directive applied to Mexico, Central America,

South America, the Caribbean, and Canada. One week later Roosevelt directed the State Department, Justice Department, Military Intelligence Division, and the Office of Naval Intelligence to work out the specifics and avoid redundancy. Roosevelt allowed for foreign collaboration but feared the public backlash should the agencies fall outside domestic control. The president even asked Biddle whether the State, War, and Navy Departments would allow foreign government intelligence to fall under the Bureau's "direct control and supervision."[11] The trusted FBI became deployed into international affairs of ambiguous jurisdiction. After a civilian seaman attached to an Army vessel docked in the harbor of Oran—angry for being disallowed from inviting a French civilian onboard for lunch—stabbed a night watchman with a butcher knife, it was FBI officials who secured the assailant's sentence upon return to a federal penitentiary.[12]

As the FBI saw matters, the national security state was hard to disentangle from crime control. In January 1942 J. Edgar Hoover released a comprehensive directive on the national security role of domestic police. The FBI was now "the agency designated by the President of the United States to coordinate police activity in our National Defense effort." Its familiar criminal justice responsibilities combined with important duties in the war against the Axis. In an echo of the last decade's priorities, the wartime FBI served as the progressive clearing house of information, the investigatory leader, and the authority on enforcement techniques, training, technical analysis, uniform crime reporting, spies, saboteurs, fifth-columnists, enemy agents, and propagandists. The FBI collaborated with European allies, visiting England to study air raid efficacy. While London's police personnel jumped from 20,000 at peacetime to 35,000 at war, American police also multiplied. The FBI touted its comprehensive training program, some fifty-four civilian defense courses. It recommended educational initiatives on everything from arrest techniques to fingerprints, crime prevention to air raid precautions. The Internal Security Squad of police departments could cooperate with the FBI to ferret out spies and saboteurs. The Bureau affirmed that in wartime "investigations and all other work," caution would ensure "proper, legal and ethical conduct of investigations, thereby maintaining the civil rights of all."[13] Even in the stress of total war, indeed thriving on it, the wartime FBI would secure liberalism.

Far from being distracted by war, the FBI could now achieve its 1930s aspirations toward local crime. As much of the world burned, American streets became laboratories in local–federal cooperation. The federal government even boosted its support for local vice policing.[14] Coordinating against pedestrian lawbreaking served a sustainable defense infrastructure. The FBI valued neighborhood-level support and touted the smallest triumphs over criminality even as pilots endured apocalyptic clashes on the islands of Japan. FBI leaders took pride in local impact, hailing a National Police Academy graduate for catching an arsonist in Michigan.[15] Its lab experts and expert testimony proved especially helpful in hit and run offenses from North and South Carolina to beyond.[16] Fiber evidence secured convictions of reckless drivers.[17] An accused murderer confessed when confronted with blood stains, soil samples, and FBI lab results.[18] Forensic evidence extracted an admission to a gruesome attack on a twelve-year-old girl.[19] The FBI lab helped solve a prison murder case in Memphis, Tennessee.[20] Investigations of minor crimes revealed larger offenses: a drunken driving case in May 1943 discovered an escaped convicted murderer.[21]

Fingerprint intelligence proved especially fruitful. Routinized memos reporting successful investigations repeated the same line about the "value of fingerprinting in identifying victims in traffic accidents"—once in sloppy reference to an airplane crash.[22] Fingerprints identified repeat offenders. One man arrested in Indiana as a vagrant, sentenced for grand larceny, paroled in 1941 and sentenced to another five years, had been arrested in 1915 and 1919.[23] A fingerprint on a Lugar pistol helped convict a murderer in Georgia.[24] And the fingerprints regime extended abroad. J. Edgar Hoover claimed international success as evidenced in an arrest by "Metropolitan Police of Scotland Yard."[25] In 1943 the FBI found fingerprint matches in 64.68 percent of its cases, and by 1944 boasted a repository with 78,916,494 prints, nearly one hundred times as many as two decades earlier.[26] Sometimes fingerprints brought closure, such as when the Alabama Highway Patrol identified a deceased soldier.[27] (See Figure 12.1.)

Figure 12.1 Fingerprinting at the US Army in World War II. Federal Bureau of Investigation/Wikimedia Commons.

New Deal gun control faced its most convincing trial in wartime. Cummings had stressed firearms as a national dilemma. Firearms databases to address everyday crimes became a convincing legacy, and firearms forensics proved effective. Such tracking finally solved a case that eluded officials for two years in Alton, Illinois.[28] Firearms tracing helped catch a man who escaped from a prison camp in Bassett, Virginia, and undertook a lethal interstate crime spree.[29] Ballistic examinations helped secure life imprisonment for a convicted killer in Akron, Ohio.[30] With firearms forensics security-state federalism of course reinforced local prejudices. FBI firearms evidence helped ensure an electric chair sentence and life imprisonment for "two negro boys" who robbed a business in November 1942 in Columbus, Ohio, resulting in a death.[31]

The interstate logic of the war on crime continued to drive federal enforcement. The FBI maintained its first major enforcement purpose going back a generation: Mann Act investigations against human trafficking. New legislation extended its authority in January 1941 and in fiscal year 1943 the FBI took credit for 751 convictions.[32] Armed with the White Slave Traffic Act, the FBI captured Ellen Lucille Moore, "notorious madam of Fargo, North Dakota," also known as "Big Lou." The security state tracked Big Lou as she went to Minneapolis attempting to procure sex workers for her home in Fargo.[33] Federal officials pursued interstate violations of lottery regulations, busting four rival lottery syndicates that distributed millions of tickets.[34] An FBI Field Division, using the Federal Extortion statute and forensic methods on a threatening letter, nabbed a man who, desperate for money to pay for trade school, threatened to kill singer Bing Crosby.[35]

The FBI also led efforts against crimes specific to war obstruction. Investigators and enforcers targeted fraud, sabotage, espionage, subversion, and treason. The FBI had followed bankruptcy racketeering—financial crimes and frauds—even before the war. Pursuing those accused of financially exploiting the war effort complemented the New Deal efforts against white collar crime. The FBI investigated a woman in Buffalo, New York, dressed as a nurse soliciting money on behalf of the administration to fund furloughs of men stationed abroad.[36] FBI agents sent men to prison for dodging military service. They investigated Arturo Bernardo Vela in Texas, a notary public, for charging people to administer oaths and gouging Mexican registrants to fill out Selective Service forms. The FBI laboratory uncovered a fraudulent use of a typewriter by George Ross of Washington, Virginia, who faked his age to avoid conscription. His wife, a Selective Service board member, now faced punishment. Walter Alvin Johnson of Laredo, Texas, was investigated for ingesting pills procured from a doctor in Mexico to raise his blood pressure and avoid the draft.[37]

Coordinating with other agencies, the FBI enforced American patriotism, barring known criminals from sensitive or esteemed wartime positions. The Civil Service Commission sent the FBI the fingerprints of an applicant for a position as steward's storekeeper with the War Department. The person had been arrested for larceny in Jacksonville in 1917. A fugitive from Miami, he served three years for embezzlement, had forgeries in 1927 in Texas and Louisiana, was arrested in 1937 and 1940 for drunkenness and in 1942 for "disloyalty in the Naval forces."[38] Another applicant lost an Air Corps position after his fingerprints surfaced in a past embezzlement.[39] Fingerprints also caught escaped war prisoners.[40]

The Bureau also pursued more nefarious obstructionists—spies and saboteurs. On the eve of war, the federal conviction of Michael William Etzel in Baltimore, for damage to aircraft, became the first FBI sabotage investigation to detect a motive "clearly to prevent the United States from furnishing aid to countries who are at war with Germany." This twenty-two-year-old blamed the German government for the war but did not want to see the German people suffer. He received a fifteen-year sentence in November 1941.[41] In 1942 the Justice Department took over administration of the Foreign Agents Registration Act, a 1938 law that originally mandated State Department registration by those engaged in a "political or quasi-political capacity" with foreign institutions. The Registration Act caught a man of Austrian descent serving as a Japanese agent.[42] Sometimes those with German American Bund connections were caught propagandizing on behalf of the Nazis.[43] One man was caught sharing US Army Ordnance Depot blueprints, plans, and data with foreigners.[44] John da Silva Purvis, born in Portugal and intermittently living in the United States since 1920, conspired to violate the espionage act and communicate with German intelligence, sharing maps of New York City. He received a ten-year sentence.[45]

Some transgressions blurred the line between obstruction and idiosyncratic criminality. The FBI often suspected arson to be sabotage. A Forest Service investigation of a fire in Mississippi's DeSoto National Forest resulted in suspended jail time and probation for a twenty-three-year-old and an eighteen-year-old.[46] The 1940 Federal Train Wreck statute sometimes ensnared saboteurs with sundry motives of reckless frivolity rather than fascist sympathy. This distinction did not spare James Howard, a Black seventeen-year-old, from a sentence of more than three years for obstructing a railway to see if the Missouri Pacific Railroad would jump off its tracks.[47] Everyday suspects sometimes blamed Nazis for their offenses, with mixed success. After claiming a Nazi sympathizer hired him to place rocks and detonators along the Florida East Coast Railway, a man finally confessed to having no accomplices and faced four years in a federal penitentiary.[48]

A fuzzy line distinguished radical protest from obstruction. The FBI worried about the peace movement of Ethiopia for its "anti-white attitude and pro-Japanese sympathy" and "plan for the resettlement of negroes in Africa modeled upon the program of the Universal Negro Improvement Association." Asians allegedly appeared in Chicago meetings, encouraging Blacks to return to Africa.[49] The FBI feared the Pacific Movement of the Eastern World, "another Negro organization" founded through the auspices of Naka Nakane, a Japan sympathizer who modeled operations after the Universal Negro Improvement Association. Calling themselves a Back to Africa movement, they allegedly pushed war resistance. The FBI investigated such efforts in St. Louis, Kansas City, Cincinnati, Philadelphia, and New York City.[50]

Treason is the traditional paragon of national security and criminal law intersecting. The Constitution explicitly mentions it along with few other crimes. Under Roosevelt the modern security state succeeded in the first treason conviction since George Washington. The German-American Max Stephan, born in Besigheim in 1892, injured during World War I in which he served his homeland as a censor, resigned as a police officer and moved to Quebec in 1928. After he and his wife's restaurant ran afoul of Canadian liquor law, he moved to Detroit in 1933. The couple made false statements regarding their US residency and became American citizens in 1935. During World War II he helped Hans Peter Krug, a German POW in Canada, who escaped and through a series of acquaintances met Stephan in Detroit. They celebrated Krug's birthday with beer and German food, after which the young airman took the bus to Chicago, then Columbus, New York, Philadelphia, Harrisburg, Cincinnati, Louisville, Memphis, Dallas, and San Antonio. Suspicious of Krug, the hotel keeper at San Antonio called the FBI.[51]

Through its network of agents and coordinated intelligence with Canada, the FBI constructed a detailed account of how Krug moved through a Toronto welfare office and entered the country. The administration investigated Krug, Stephan, Stephan's wife for "un-American statements," and his friend Theodor Donay, who authored an anti-Semitic variation of "Silent Night, Holy Night." The FBI documentation showcases a dramatic interaction between criminal law and national security, even in a humorous instance where Krug told interrogators his pants were a "military secret." When asked if the distinction "between pants and un-derwear ... constitutes a military secret," Krug responded, "of course. ... You can't walk down the street in your underwear." Stephan, Krug, and his American collaborators all faced wartime justice. Donay was sen-tenced to prison for six and a half years. Stephan himself was convicted and sentenced to death.[52] In the first federal treason conviction since the 1790s, Roosevelt showed leniency but not as much as George Wash-ington, who pardoned a Whiskey Rebel. Roosevelt commuted Stephan's sentence to life in prison. It was a *liberal* security state.

WAR LIBERALISM

But *how* liberal was the security state? Remarkably liberal, according to the ACLU's Roger Baldwin. Within two years of war, he concluded that the "prophets who foretold the collapse of democratic liberties ... have been confounded by the extraordinary record of war-time freedom." Fed-eral censorship of speech and print were "administered with an easy hand," imprisoning only eighty-three people for their utterances.[53] White supremacist violence persisted, but Baldwin invoked Roosevelt's language defending civil liberties, aspiring to a "world which squares with the Four Freedoms, the Atlantic Charter, and the other democratic ideals." Baldwin's optimism withstood the worst wartime injustices. Japanese internment was "the greatest blot" on a "record of general sanity and tolerance."[54] Baldwin thought it "plain to reasonable people" that the president's evacuation orders "went far beyond military necessity," and the subordination of whole areas "under the army's control" lacked "pre-cedent in law and policy." Even here, Baldwin searched for the bright side, celebrating challenges in the judiciary.[55]

Even putting internment aside for the moment, Baldwin perhaps ex-aggerated the state's "easy hand." Measured by capacity, war liberalism built the largest engine of repression in US history.[56] Besides the intern-ment of US citizens of Japanese descent, the government used its FBI Custodial Detention list to detain 5,100 Japanese nationals, 3,250 German nationals, and 650 Italian nationals, most of whom posed no threat. More than half were released by the middle of 1943, and still hundreds more were released by the end of the year. The administration also restricted the movement of 890,000 "enemy aliens," clearing the bulk of them, and 600,000 Italian nationals, before the end of 1942. Among the detained German nationals were Jews who had fled the Nazis.[57] Sanguine postwar assessments moreover downplayed the severity of the war's dozens of espionage and sedition prosecutions.[58] The war occasioned constant strikebreaking and the compelled service of over ten million conscripts, two awesome uses of state power to curtail civil liberties that Baldwin found objectionable in World War I.[59] The effective enforcement of martial law in Hawaii would have been unworkable in past eras.

Wartime political economy also relied on crackdowns. In 1938 ACLU activists had opposed an industrial mobilization bill, fearing that wartime planning would give Roosevelt dictatorial control over the economy. The War Department too anticipated that war would drive economic regimentation.[60] Wartime economic policy—in a war effort that consumed 40 percent of GDP—indeed built repressive capacity. But ironically, the unprecedented economic regimentation spawned repressive measures that were often more diffuse than autocratic. Enforcing economic rules indeed leveraged social pressure and policing at all levels, as price controls drove rationing to its high point in US history.[61]

In January 1942 the Emergency Price Control Act established four enforcement mechanisms—injunctions, license suspensions, treble damages, and criminal proceedings in federal court. Starting in September 1943, the Office of Price Administration had a dedicated Enforcement Department, whose thousands of investigators and hundreds of attorneys accounted for 11.6 percent of the total budget for the Office of Price Administration (OPA) by 1945.[62] Rationing spawned new black markets. Money counterfeiting plummeted as ration currency counterfeiting became the more lucrative crime. The ubiquity of violations helped most offenders escape criminal penalty. A 1943 investigation found 57 percent of businesses to be in violation.[63] Of the 333,151 cases the OPA investigated in 1943, only an estimated 9,260 yielded criminal prosecutions, although prosecutions sometimes commenced under other statutes like the Second War Powers Act or, occasionally, local government, particularly in New York City—the municipal exemplar of security-state federalism. Officials did not generally regard price control offenses as "criminal," a distinction some analysts attribute to classism.[64] But some contemporary criminologists dissented. Writing in the early 1950s, Marshall Clinard argued that even violations outside criminal statutes were "sociologically [legible] as a 'crime,'" and found wartime enforcement against black markets helped legitimize Sutherland's formulation of "white-collar" crime.[65] In the longer term, wartime regulation, rampant lawbreaking, and selective enforcement made possible a labyrinthine leviathan with arbitrary power.

War liberalism went beyond questions of state capacity and individual rights. In constructing a legitimating ethos around the garrison state, perception mattered as much as reality, and lawful order as much as abstract justice. Broad public support made the war a more palatable, predictable regime than what Baldwin remembered from Wilson's war and Palmer's raids. Repressing lawlessness became the main defense against accusations of repression. By conquering lawlessness within the infrastructure of repression, American leaders expressed their commitment to law and liberty, to Roosevelt's Four Freedoms, and pursued repression in service of democracy. In his last State of the Union address, Roosevelt touted the United States as an international model for having overcome its original sin of anarchy. Roosevelt quoted historian Albert Hart: the American Revolution "left behind . . . 'an eddy of lawlessness and disregard of human life.'" For many years, Roosevelt elaborated, separatist movements and insurrections threatened the national cohesion necessary to tackle this lawlessness. But now the United States was truly united, dedicated to liberalism and law, devoted to the global pursuit where "humanly possible" of "the fulfillment of the principles of the Atlantic Charter."[66] The selective affirmation of universalism, stability and legitimacy, the triumph of a polite regimentation over vigilante collaboration, made the security state liberal.

This aspirational universalism made expressions of racism and bigotry all the more conspicuous.[67] It was also politically salient, as Roosevelt's coalition was moving from the South to the urban North.[68] The wartime Justice Department amplified its civil rights protections of Black Americans. The FBI conducted more investigations of lynchings and police brutality, and federal officials found ways to treat lynchings conducted with law enforcers' cooperation as instances of state deprivation of constitutional rights. In 1941 under Biddle the Civil Liberties Unit became rebranded as the Civil Rights Section (CRS), and stepped up criminal investigations and enforcement. With its Thirteenth Amendment cases, the Justice Department's CRS found its most potent weapon to defend Black Americans. Peonage and involuntary servitude were not merely extreme violations of labor rights; they were the private affront to Reconstruction most legible even under Constitutional interpretations of the state action doctrine that foreclosed punishing most other private depredations. In 1943 the CRS won a conviction in a slavery case.[69]

But the New Deal's contradictory management of racial issues, mediated through war-on-crime federalism, often stumbled. As Black Americans joined the struggle against the Nazis, the paradoxes of Jim Crow America became all the more jarring. Black soldiers faced discrimination and violence. Racists beat a Black army nurse for violating the color line on a Montgomery bus.[70] The 1943 race riot in Detroit exemplified a peak in the breakdown of law, and a crucial watershed in the racialized violence of the twentieth century. Whereas Black self-defense was a prominent feature of the 1919 riots, the 1943 bloodshed even more resembled the instances of Black Rebellion that would proliferate in the late 1960s and punctuate the late twentieth and early twenty-first century. At the same time, the white mob participation recalled the riots and pogroms of the Progressive Era and early interwar period. In Detroit, where thirty-four people died, the volatility that conflicting racial goals brought to the New Deal coalition hinted at an ominous future. Few other instances as effectively belied the pretense of domestic wartime tranquility. Roosevelt invoked the 1807 Insurrection Act and it took 6,000 federal troops and nearly 1,900 arrests to bring law and order to Detroit. Both participants and bystanders were swept up, and among those who faced charges, 970 were Black and 212 white. A massive show of force at all levels of state power helped contain the most explosive contradictions of law-and-order liberalism from producing a comparable eruption for another generation.[71]

Throughout the war, racism posed challenges for liberalism as well as federalism. Policing the Zoot Suit rioters in Los Angeles tested the security state's institutional and ideological composition. The Mexican Americans wearing Zoot suits, distinguished by large jackets with padded shoulders, evoked the jazz stylings of Black America. Their flagrant attire flouted the fabric allotments of wartime rationing.[72] In 1942 tensions rose as police targeted hundreds of young Americans for their clothing. After a jury convicted a dozen Zoot suit wearers of murder in 1943, hundreds of soldiers and sailors from across the country rampaged through Mexican American neighborhoods, brutalizing people in the offending garb.

Structural tensions outlined the relationship between institutions and ideology. Juxtaposed with lofty wartime promises, the affronted sailors appeared an anachronism. They were vigilantes, policing not just racial order but the New Deal's wartime commitments to austerity. The mostly white sailors returning to California were violently defending whiteness and masculinity, but also the Democratic regime's progressive political economy. Local police largely aided the white sailors—a spontaneous convergence in vigilante violence from both local and federal agents on the public payroll.[73] But an official rebuke from Washington was louder than any comparable anti-vigilante statement from World War I. The Army and Navy cooperated with city authorities to contain the violence.[74] The racialized January 1943 murder trials of Hispanic teenagers frustrated the administration, which hoped its Good Neighbor Policy and wartime diplomacy might smooth relations with Mexico and Latin America. War-on-crime federalism had helped direct the racial politics in the South toward a contradictory New Deal consensus, but in the West the New Deal enforcement state had less credibility among the opposing forces. The aspirationally colorblind Roosevelt administration lamented the racist motivation but doubted it was actionable. Eleanor Roosevelt more forthrightly blamed the violence on "the attitude toward Mexicans in California and the States along the border."[75] The *Los Angeles Times* responded that the violence found provocation in "the weird costumes worn by the gangsters, who have included many [anti-white] racists," and accused the First Lady's racial emphasis of having an "amazing similarity to the Communist party line."[76]

The FBI meanwhile struggled to frame its mission as one of blind justice and even racial neutrality. The Bureau outwardly expressed universalism that marked a break from World War I. Despite his own conservative and racist views, Hoover wanted to avoid perceptions of ideological bias. It was an especially sensitive matter now that the United States found itself allied with the communist Soviet Union. One anonymous document, presumably by Hoover or a top official, disputed accusations that the Bureau cared more about the radical left than the fascist threat, noting that no communists endured sabotage convictions since July 1939. The document claimed that communist rather than fascist loyalty drew attention because Martin Dies provided lists of suspects.[77] Surely not all anticommunist vigilance came from Hoover. When the FBI, strained for resources, tried to scale back its scrutiny of employees at the Office for Emergency Management, it was Roosevelt who insisted they maintain forty investigations per week.[78]

In war Hoover decried the enemy within while cautioning against destructive racist excess. The FBI responded to racial unrest with its "Survey of Racial Conditions" and conspiratorial claims that Black journalists and activists had Axis and communist sympathies.[79] Yet Hoover detested the "Munich-minded men" who had to be "forever quarantined." He touted "free speech" as the "incomparable fruit of democracy," while admitting he preferred repressing "a few Quislings and potential Fifth Columnists" over putting "millions in a state of unendurable slavery," but his condemnation of Nazi sympathizers had a corollary—American universalism, which precluded naked bigotry. A "horde" of Americans adopted "the deadly infection of anti-Semitism." Their "Axis line" and propaganda "exceeded the lies of a Goebbels." Patriotic immigrants, on the other hand, strengthened America, which "became great because it fused into one great melting pot the best of old world culture, seasoned by the conditions of a young and vigorous Nation." The "children of parents born abroad" gave "structural and virile strength" to the country, and only "a few of them lack the qualities essential in a real American." It was therefore the duty of "every red-blooded American . . . to protect and aid the foreign-born whose character of Americanism puts to shame many of our native citizens."[80]

This universalism, however selective in practice, required the suppression of vigilantism. The scourge of "lawlessness" included those who illegally attacked foreigners. Because "oppression of sincere liberty-loving aliens is one sure way to develop a Fifth Column," Americans "must be vigilant, but not vigilantes."[81] Hoover's opposition to vigilantism extended to conscription enforcement. The American Legion assisted the government in bringing in 15,000 alien enemies and in pursuing draft dodgers, but unlike the American Protective League's sloppy collaboration with the Wilson administration, which had temporarily detained approximately 100,000 "slackers," collaboration was now lawful and effective, yielding 7,000 convictions but more important 135,000 enlistees.[82]

This effort against vigilante lawlessness meant protecting the antiwar movement, whose much smaller numbers compared to the Great War made it easier to approach as a marginal threat. As in World War I, the repression often came from state governments and vigilantes, but this time the federal posture had changed. Even before the war, the dynamic was perhaps clearest in the persecution of Jehovah's Witnesses. They were subject to deportations, beatings by mobs, arrests, tarring and feathering, and even castration. There were 2,000 expulsions in forty-eight states, and children were thrown out of schools. But the federal security state eventually came to their aid, and threatened local officials with prosecution under federal statutes.[83]

Wartime marginalization of the FBI's critics further normalized its vast power. High-profile calls to scrutinize the Bureau met opposition. George W. Norris of Nebraska, chief architect of the Tennessee Valley Authority, incurred harsh criticism for advocating investigations of the FBI back in 1940. "I hope you were misquoted," E. C. Arnold wrote to him. Only "the criminal" and the corrupt should fear the FBI.[84] As a harbinger of a political sea change, Norris lost his seat in the 1942 election season.

The most striking sign of the times was Roger Baldwin's qualified support of the wartime regime and FBI. Baldwin sat on a manuscript complaining that the FBI had grown ten times beyond its World War I appropriations and repressed "subversive opinions." Baldwin described Hoover as essentially having "the mentality of the average professional patriot, modified in recent years by professions of liberalism." Baldwin worried that fascists endured less scrutiny than communists, that the Dies Committee influenced the FBI, military intelligence, secret service and anticommunism, formulating an attack on the "liberalism of the New Deal itself."[85] But he withheld publication, seeing Hoover as the lesser evil compared to Dies. A meeting with Hoover convinced Baldwin that the Bureau chief "largely changed his views on the dangers from labor and the left. He is violently anti-Dies and all the witch-hunting for reds." Meanwhile, Attorney General Biddle and the FBI's wartime record demonstrated a "scrupulous adherence to legal methods, and no trespass beyond the legitimate field of investigation." There were a "few exceptions," only "to be expected in so large an organization," with all its "transgressions . . . apparently disciplined."[86] In his assessments of the security state, Baldwin was beginning to see democratic freedom as the norm and lawlessness as the exception.

As for the "exceptions" Baldwin had in mind, an important general point is warranted. The most aggressive exercises of domestic power usually arrived at the intersection of presidential power with the criminological state, the subordination of the rule of law to the democratically elected executive. The complexity of the liberal security state emerged in the FBI's record and reputation, and in the very fact that the war's notorious abuses came less from mobs, or the Justice Department or even the military, but from the presidency. In substance, the least liberal, least democratic expressions of the security state arose from the most liberal and most democratic parts in form. Three examples illuminate this paradox—the Nazi saboteur trials, martial law in Hawaii, and, the program that most troubled Baldwin, Japanese internment.[87]

At its apex the security state blended civil and military authority, transgressing the traditional limits of both. Its liberalism was a function of its own graces. Among the most radical expressions of the new regime's power was the Nazi saboteur case. The FBI confronted the eight infamous saboteurs and hoped to obtain cooperation and a guilty plea from one in exchange for Roosevelt's pardon. Instead, Roosevelt ordered that they all face a military tribunal, the first on American soil since the conviction of Lincoln's assassins, freed from the procedural protections afforded by court martial. With Biddle's assistance Roosevelt circumvented the need to formally suspend habeas corpus, and then circumvented the traditional military role under the Articles of War to review the trial record, adopting that authority all for himself.[88] Although there arose institutional jealousies—for example, slighted Secret Service agents who had tracked the spies only to see the FBI claim the credit—Roosevelt's effective subordination and micromanagement of both civilian and military legal authority peaked, within the continental United States, with the Nazi saboteur cases.[89]

Militarization was fullest in the West, the frontier from whose horizon the Japanese war planes had attacked. Alcatraz, a civilian facility adopted from the military, once again became a venue of national security strategizing. Transferred from the Navy to the Justice Department, the prison island was considered as a site for the military's antiaircraft guns.[90] Farther west, in the territory of Hawaii, national fears about the large Japanese American plurality culminated in a form of repression in ways both more inclusive and more complete than anything on the mainland. The federal government had prepared more than a decade for extreme measures against the specter of Japanese disruption. The Hawaii Sugar Planters Association had networked with the ONI, the Military Information Division, and the FBI since the 1920s to track the Japanese American population of Hawaii.[91] Fears about sabotage prompted President Roosevelt in 1936 to request the creation of a list of suspected Japanese on Oahu, "who would be the first to be placed in a *concentration camp* in the event of trouble."[92] One year before Pearl Harbor, as the FBI ramped up security-state federalism on the continent, the Bureau urged the Honolulu Police Department to build its own espionage unit. But detention policies would not suffice. There were too many Japanese Hawaiians to intern them all—37 percent of the civilian population by 1941. To manage Japanese Hawaiians required something more and martial law schemes circulated since the 1920s.[93]

The martial law and military occupation of Hawaii marked the war's purest expression of New Deal law enforcement power, administered under Harold Ickes's Department of Interior with his initial full support.

Within hours of Pearl Harbor, territorial governor Joseph Poindexter proclaimed martial law. Lieutenant General Walter C. Short established an even more extreme military law, subsuming civilian life under his own territorial rule and immense discretion. Although fewer than 1,500 were interned, the custodial detention index immediately triggered arrests. The FBI directed the roundup with military help. The Honolulu police's espionage unit helped arrest Japanese Hawaiians on custodial detention lists—including Shinto and Buddhist clergy, Japanese language school teachers, and community leaders.[94] Beyond those detained, almost all inhabitants underwent greater control than most mainland Americans. Military law turned the territory into an open-air prison, suspending virtually the entire Bill of Rights for almost everyone.[95] Military "general orders" policed society. Civilian police sometimes clashed with military authorities but generally enforced military dictates.[96] Other local officials welcomed the state of affairs, which afforded new opportunities for governance. Honolulu police chief William Gabrielson only wished his mentor August Vollmer could see martial law's benefits—all the equipment Gabrielson requested, "no delays, no fuss with attorneys, no jury trials"—and said the war should inform how the "normal, peacetime organization of a police department must be reorganized."[97]

POLICING AT THE HORIZON OF DEMOCRACY

Within the continental United States, the most pronounced intersection of civilian power, military power, and criminal law also occurred in the West—in the program of Japanese American evacuation, relocation, and internment. Roosevelt's internment policy required the smooth coordination of many levers of state power. The army seized and detained inmates in "assembly centers." From there they went to one of ten camps run by the War Relocation Authority (WRA), a new civilian agency.[98] The Works Projects Administration, previously involved in building and renovating jails and prisons, helped run the assembly and relocation centers for over half of 1942.[99] Roosevelt's Executive Order 9066 and General John Dewitt's Public Proclamation No. 3 became enforceable through criminal penalties. Concerning the designated military zones, congressional legislation on March 21, 1942, made it a misdemeanor offense, punishable by a year in prison and $5,000 fine, to knowingly defy "an Executive order of the President, by the Secretary of War, or by any military commander designated by the Secretary of War."[100] Local police, including all the way in New York, helped with the arrests.[101] Internment was thus an extension of federal criminal power, enforced concurrently across jurisdictions and agencies, as well as an assertion of ultimate law enforcement authority over the western states.

Internment's innovations in criminal law produced the wartime apotheosis of security-state federalism. Internment meant securing law and order, including the building of internal systems within the policed boundaries of the camps. The federal government daily policed the population in the most intimate ways. A June 1942 police report for Tulare Assembly Center documented a water fight in the shower and spitting out the window as examples of "disorderly conduct."[102] Offenses ranged from public intoxication—a young man caught "drinking 'sake'"—to alleged political disloyalty.[103] While internment enhanced national criminal jurisdiction in the West, it required national and state officials to share enforcement duties. At Tule Lake Segregation Center, the maximum-security facility that held about 16,000 of those deemed most unruly, officials contemplated both the jurisdictional novelties and the mission to keep order. A memorandum noted that the federal government had "not accepted exclusive federal jurisdiction over the land" and so "criminal jurisdiction of the State of California prevails." The state district attorney would cooperate with federal officials, serving both federal and state government.[104] Officials saw themselves as guardians of order, checking a "disorderly group" pushing around other inmates.[105]

Policing the camps was a high-water mark of both the refinement and tensions of security-state liberalism. Camp personnel echoed this ethos—in their breadth of duties and the emphasis on order, training, and community engagement. Within a relocation center, patrolmen were hired for surveillance, "the protection of property and persons, enforcement of laws and ordinances" and "traffic control." High school graduates with police training and law enforcement experience, or who undertook college coursework on policing, could apply to be personnel.[106] A standard Army Relocation Authority job description for a patrolman emphasized "the protection of life" and "property" as well as "law and order." Patrolmen would monitor those "known to be disloyal" and those "whose loyalty to this country is doubted." They would guard against "sabotage" and "riot" and would ideally have experience in law enforcement.[107] Such personnel reported to the internal security officer, who would need even more experience and law enforcement training.[108] At the top stood the chief of internal security, ultimately responsible for "enforcement of all rules and regulations relating to the management of peace and order within the boundaries of the area occupied by the segregation center," as well as maintaining the "operation of an intelligence program" to guard against "subversive activities."[109] Tule Lake chief of internal security Willard E. Schmidt personified securitarian liberalism, advocating that administrative police use shotguns, which "would only result in a slight casualty case and in only a few exceptional cases . . . death," compared to the more lethal .45 pistols.[110]

Officials also sought discipline for their security force. When five fathers intended to be let out with their sons on Boys Day were collectively punished for the transgressions of one, WRA director Dillon Myer reprimanded the officers. The "police force" should not "act as judge" but only as "arresting officer, making investigations, providing information . . . serving as witness." This collective punishment was "not the kind of justice that we in WRA believe in."[111] Over in Arizona, Fred Graves said the police officer at the Gila River Project should "always be courteous. Always control your temper. Always offer assistance to residents in need of your official aid. Always be firm but not officious. Always remember the dignity of your position. Always show respect for your superior officer. Always carry out your assignments without argument. Always enforce the law without fear or favor." Although officers were "granted authority to make arrests where a violation of the law occurs in [their] presence" they lacked "authority to take a person into custody on hearsay information."[112] In 1945 Schmidt was laying out plans for more training, a new contraband room and squad room, a new lecture room and jail, and the deputization of more personnel.[113]

Policing the interned community meant a new balance between pluralistic accommodation and racial repression. Buddhist priests were valued as a source of stability who appealed to the population's spirituality.[114]

Security officials worked with Japanese American "evacuee leaders for the maintenance of law and order."[115] But although Japanese American community leaders assisted with security, the racial hierarchy ensured that white officers were more trusted. The chief of internal security at the Granada Project in Amache, Colorado, awaited having "my Caucasian Police-men at full strength so we can take over when the Army decides to move out."[116]

Internal security meant stamping out subversion through the strategic use of force. One effective means against dissent was the threat of harsher repression. At Tule Lake, a man named Shimizu and seventeen others found themselves detained in the stockade for political reasons. In February 1944 Shimizu assured the WRA that if it asked "for our assurance that we do not meddle in politics again, we will, in every [respect], cooperate."[117] They were released upon pledging their "desire . . . [to] see the normalcy re-established in this Tule Lake Center and ever-lasting peace preserved by the spirit of cooperation and better understanding between the Administration and the Colony."[118] The next month the coordinating committee happily reported that the "condition of the center has improved" but "complete normalcy is still far away."[119] Maintaining the correct political ethos at the camps balanced negotiation and repression.

The jurisdictional and political paradoxes of internment reached not only into the camps but up to the presidency. Roosevelt and his team were the face of internment as much as of the peacetime New Deal.[120] Roosevelt made his most infamous decision after years of pondering restrictions on Japanese American liberties. In 1936 he floated the idea of internment in Hawaii, before his secretaries of the army and navy convinced him that their general detention list would suffice. Roosevelt hardened on Japan after Hitler's invasion of Poland and he saw Japanese Americans as proxies for Japan's empire. An FBI report in November 1940 that rebutted the military's pessimism about Japanese Hawaiian loyalty failed to move him.[121] The Federal Communications Commission found no basis for accusations of signaling to Japan and an Office of Naval Intelligence investigation in autumn 1941 found both Issei and Nisei to be loyal.[122] Attorney General Biddle hoped to avoid mass internment and labored in December 1941 to surgically implement detentions.[123] But the administration adopted the mass evacuation policy after a few more months of deliberation. General John DeWitt, whom Biddle described as tending toward "the views of the last man to whom he talked," turned in favor of internment at a crucial moment, persuaded partly by a commission chaired by Supreme Court Justice Owen J. Roberts. On February 17 Biddle caved to DeWitt, rejecting Biddle's assistant James H. Rowe and Alien Enemy Control Unit director Edward J. Ennis's pleas against evacuation orders.[124] DeWitt's "Final Recommendation" branded the Japanese an "enemy race" and "military necessity" became the rationale in the *Final Report, Japanese Evacuation from the West Coast*.[125]

The administration defended its policy as a liberal alternative to something more repressive. It is true that state and federal officials, many opinion leaders, and many Americans harbored extreme anti-Japanese sentiments, especially after Pearl Harbor. But Biddle later disclosed that as late as March 1942 a secret report found that on the West Coast "outside of Southern California, less than one half of those interviewed favored internment of Japanese aliens, and only 14 percent the internment of citizens of Japanese ancestry."[126] Within a year many Americans would express more extreme animosities than those of the administration. By December 1942, after internment was well underway, almost half of Americans opposed returning Japanese Americans to the coast even after the war.[127] By then Roosevelt could point to more extremist sentiments when defending his position as moderation. The Dies Committee decried the "government's alleged coddling of the Japanese in the camps," as Roger Baldwin observed, which made actual policy seem comparatively humane.[128]

In professing to occupy the higher ground, the administration embraced distinctively colorblind and polite language.[129] So outwardly racist and uncompromising were some voices, the administration could adopt rhetorical dedication to safety and humanity. Dillon Myer rejected the term "concentration camp" and postured against urges of unabashed racism.[130] In November 1943 Myer rebutted the American Legion's Japanese Exclusion League, which opposed Japanese American resettlement in the West. He appealed to the Legion's shared devotion to "uphold and defend the Constitution of the United States of America." The WRA could effectively determine loyalty, Myer insisted, as he defended Roosevelt's belief that Americanism was a "matter of the mind and heart," and "is not, and never was, a matter of race or ancestry." Although he knew that "a great many people" felt "that all persons of Japanese ancestry should be confined under heavy guard for the duration of the war," Myer considered "such a proposal fundamentally un-American" and "contrary to the constitution." He believed America's interest, consistent with "democratic faith," required "opportunities for all its citizens without regard for race and ancestry."[131] But even in hoping to provide a humane and assimilationist alternative, the WRA's New Dealers trampled rights and humiliated the victims of internment in their systematic scrutiny to root out disloyalty.[132]

Insofar as Roosevelt deserves credit for any restraint the program had, he also deserves blame for its final indecency. In one of his few relevant public statements, Roosevelt situated himself between extremes, defending gradual releases and noting that "a great many lawyers" found "that under the Constitution they can't be kept locked up in concentration camps."[133] All that said, Roosevelt's own legal experts approved the supposedly moderate internment policy as implemented. Biddle commissioned a report on its constitutionality from New Deal lawyers Benjamin Cohen, an architect of the court-packing scheme, Oscar Cox, and Joseph Rauh, whose memo affirmed the "fact" that the "Japanese who are American citizens cannot readily be identified and distinguished from" the disloyal.[134] Even if many voices demanded a more uncompromising policy, Roosevelt and his legal team's posturing exposed the authoritarian potential of the new liberalism.

Aside from the predictable attitudes of Dies, the American Legion, and Baldwin, idiosyncratic disagreements signaled the potential for realignment within security-state liberalism, and its limitations despite internal dissent. Baldwin opposed the program, but in the vital early moments the ACLU was reluctant to involve itself in legal challenges.[135] Many leftwing and civil rights groups failed to acknowledge the full racism or injustice of Roosevelt's order, although NAACP officials did voice concerns about the mistreatment of evacuees.[136] Most newspapers endorsed internment, but Old Right opponents of the New Deal counted among the most vocal critics. R. C. Hoiles at the *Orange County Register* wrote, "Few, if any, people ever believed that evacuation of the Japanese was constitutional. It was a result of emotion and fright."[137] While the American Communist Party extended its support for war to strong endorsement for internment, J. Edgar Hoover was opposed, and tried numerous times to moderate the administration's policy.[138] When asked his opinion, August Vollmer cited his "unbounded faith in J. Edgar Hoover," and said he "would unhesitatingly approve the release of evacuees" whom Hoover thought "worthy to be released." The majority "of the native-born persons of Japanese parentage are undoubtedly good citizens and will not give the government any trouble if released," Vollmer continued.[139] Compared to some of the most reliably liberal New Dealers, the Old Right detractors, the old-guard progressive Vollmer, and even Hoover represented a more traditional attitude, skeptical of scaling up federal power. Yet Hoover still enforced the policy and Vollmer still counted himself a Democrat dedicated to wartime security. Support for the security-state did not cleanly track support for its notorious excesses. Internment was not a deal breaker. Reasonable liberals disagreed. Such pluralism could obscure a multitude of repressions.

The minds associated with Roosevelt's constitutional legacy mostly capitulated to internment, as reflected by the Supreme Court's three major relevant decisions. In 1943 the Court unanimously affirmed the curfew order in *Hirabayashi v. United States*. Justice Frank Murphy concurred while condemning racist policy in the abstract.[140] The next year the Court affirmed the Executive Order 9066 by a 6–3 majority.[141] Having failed to pack the Court, Roosevelt still dominated its bench with appointees, most of whom again upheld his policy preferences. Yet the *Korematsu* decision notably divided his appointees. His former attorneys general Murphy and Jackson, who greatly expanded the FBI, joined the lone conservative Owen Roberts in dissent, but Roosevelt's other six men on the bench ratified internment. Roosevelt's former surveillance man in the Senate, Hugo Black, penned the notorious decision, joined by Roosevelt appointees and celebrated liberals Harlan Stone, Felix Frankfurter, Stanley Reed, William Douglas, and Wiley B. Rutledge. Then, in *Ex parte Endo*, the Court unanimously condemned the continuing detention of an American deemed loyal—a narrow repudiation late in the war.[142]

The legal defenses of internment, far from being an aberration, bridged the New Deal and its war on crime to the principles of postwar legal liberalism. Columbia Law's Herbert Wechsler, co-author of *Criminal Law and Its Administration* in 1940, was invited into the Justice Department's Criminal Division the same year to help reform federal criminal law. He became assistant attorney general in charge of the Department's War Division, which oversaw questions of internment, foreign agent registration, martial law, and military bombing intelligence. Wechsler was key in crafting the administration's response to the challenges of internment policy in *Korematsu* and *Ex parte Endo*. While downplaying the DeWitt Report's claims of Japanese American espionage, the Wechsler defense embraced the report's emphasis on the failures of assimilation, and defended the military's actions as reasonable given what was known. Wechsler's challenge employed a "draconian standing doctrine" to undercut Fred Korematsu's standing, a common argumentative technique in New Deal jurisprudence. Wechsler's arguments found their way into Justice Black's decision. After World War II, Wechsler became the main author of the American Law Institute's Model Penal Code. His stress on the authority of the federal government to make such decisions, reaching its peak with internment, helped shape liberal jurisprudence for generations, despite the horrors most liberals would come to express about internment itself.[143]

Japanese internment pushed the security-state consensus to its limits and revealed how far the most respectable champions of New Deal liberalism would countenance oppression before walking it back. Japanese internment was the bleak exception that proved the rule. Not mainly as Roger Baldwin meant it—as an exceptional overreaction contrasted with an otherwise restrained civil liberties record—but in a more fundamental and troublesome sense. Internment was the most radical expression of the securitarian margins of the new liberalism, the defining demonstration of its contours of power and underlying ethos, an instance not of the state's failure to live up to its values but a disturbing revelation of what liberal rule really meant. Many Americans had feared the "radical moment" of the 1933 National Industrial Recovery Act, seeing it as experimentation with borderline fascistic economic planning, marking the mobilizing potential and terrible power of Roosevelt's hybrid system of democracy and oligarchy; and many had denounced the 1937 court-packing scheme as another presidential flirtation at the precipice of where constitutionalism eclipsed into autocracy—but Japanese internment revealed something yet more discomforting.[144] It revealed that New Deal liberalism was just flexible enough, just fearful enough, to confine a whole racial group to concentration camps based purely on national origin, so long as there existed some semblance of legal authority a shade or two more formalistic and humane than the doctrines that legitimated naked totalitarianism.

In its formalism, modernity, and rejection of the antiquated forms of ad hoc repression, internment affirmed the institutional and ideological strength of the liberal security state. It was an illiberal program that helped in the pragmatic construction of the new liberal ethos, at least in its constitutional theory and proceduralism. It was not vigilantism, even though it was not justice. It mobilized security-state federalism in unprecedented ways. It tested the workability of federal jurisdiction in the West. Even its repudiation further legitimated the mechanisms on which it relied. After the government's embarrassing retreat from the policy, the infrastructure remained, the machinery had been perfected, and now those who had divided like polite gentlemen on internment could again come together in good standing and build the liberal state.

IN AFFIRMING FEDERAL AUTHORITY and capturing the American imagination, the liberal security state emerged victorious from the crucible of war mobilization. Frank Murphy successfully equipped the FBI to confront both common crime and the wartime enemy. The Bureau's cooperation with local police and sheriffs against security threats both large and small demonstrated the war on crime's continuing relevance to a modern, bureaucratic infrastructure of coercion. Roosevelt's mastery over law enforcement now extended to Tule Lake and Hawaii, and the continental security state won the approval of labor radicals previously fearful of both federal and local police. By war's end, politics no longer centered on progressivism, that trans-partisan middle-class reformism that fashioned associational America in the early twentieth century. Crime policies, the security state, and wartime mobilization forever altered the political landscape. Roger Baldwin looked back on 1944 as a year when the "remarkable war record of maintaining freedom of public debate and minority rights" continued "with even less interference" by either "public or private agencies." And even as Japanese internment was winding down, the Supreme Court began a new chapter of protecting Black American civil rights.[145] Hope for redemption lay in the increasingly dominant central state.

Roosevelt reclaimed and refined liberalism through the ordeals of Depression and armed conflict, an undertaking that transformed the nation itself. The war brought New Deal planning, the security state, and criminalization into their clearest combinations. The new ethos gripped both parties. In an October 1943 *Look* interview, Wendell Willkie expressed hope that the Republican Party would reclaim liberalism as electoral strategy. The Democrats professed a "monopoly of liberalism," but were ruled by two illiberal forces, big-city political machines and the "southern Democrats" who ran "the South's political machinery by denying the vote to a majority of its citizens, white and colored." Willkie conceded that his own party had become corrupted and "forgot its own great liberal traditions," and so it needed a "victory *within itself*," in which the "progressive and courageous members . . . must now re-establish its great liberal traditions" and "carry them forward to solve the problems of a new world." The Republicans had to become "*the great American liberal party.*"[146] In 1944 Roosevelt himself applauded Americans for having in "the last three elections . . . transcended party affiliation," clamoring for "leadership . . . to advance the lot of the average citizen." He said Americans would seek "that same kind of liberalism to build our safer economy for the future."[147] Over time both parties would compete to represent economic opportunity, civil rights and justice, a rejection of machine corruption.

In November 1944, more Americans voted for Roosevelt than Republican Thomas Dewey, who had both climbed to national politics as governors famous for combating New York's criminals. The political future belonged to the crime warriors, to politicians like Roosevelt and Dewey. And Earl Warren. Serving as California's attorney general and governor, the liberal Republican Warren championed progressive crime policies, centralization, and Japanese internment. In hearings in March 1942 Warren called the threat too urgent for civil procedure, arguing that the absence of Japanese American sabotage and espionage only proved they were quietly preparing a nefarious attack.[148] In 1944 Warren gave a keynote address to Republicans boasting the "spirit of youth" and the "energetic West."[149] Warren indeed represented the West, along with the future of bipartisan politics. He had overseen California's Japanese American evacuations, the program that convincingly brought national criminal and military jurisdiction to the West. Years later as chief justice of the US Supreme Court he would finally protect substantive liberalism in the South and in America's courtrooms. From wartime internment to civil rights, Warren played leading roles in the closing chapters of the nation's long story of law and legitimacy since 1865—the quest for enforcement authority that culminated in the mutually constitutive forces of modern liberalism and modern security.

War, Cold War, and the struggle against segregation tested the liberal state. But it was the New Deal war on crime that refined and prepared the liberal state for its great trial. In World War II the enforcement state could finally answer three big questions. One had lingered since Roosevelt's election: Would the New Deal's legitimation of enforcement authority withstand the test of a major national crisis? The Great Depression did not alone answer this question. True legitimation of the national state meant societal consent toward its instruments of coercion. The liberalism that arose in the 1930s, before shaping the rest of the twentieth century, had to prove itself adept at waging a multifront war.

The second question traced back to World War I, after which the security state collapsed and withered. Yes, World War II could mobilize American institutions, but would they ratchet back to triviality after peace? World War II was different from World War I in large part because the New Deal was different from peacetime Wilsonian progressivism. Every year under Roosevelt the state's coercive edge was sharpened. Every year its support grew. The war-on-crime coalition made the security state coalition of World War II not just possible but enduring. The institutions and relations built in the 1930s would survive where those built in the 1910s had not. Roosevelt and his attorneys general adopted an interwar chaos of authority, exacerbated by the Red Scare, Prohibition, the Great Depression, kidnappers, and gangsters, and retooled the machinery of repression to be robust enough, refined enough, and just liberal enough to withstand the pressures of World War II without collapsing into the anarchy that followed World War I.

The third question had deep roots in the nineteenth century. What would be the role of the national government after the Civil War? The racial and regional divisions in particular threatened to undercut the legitimacy of even a workable domestic central state. War and conquest could mobilize Americans but they also provoked backlash. World War II tested the New Deal realignment that had been facilitated through war-on-crime federalism. An elastically defined but aspirational liberalism now united the previously oppositional forces in American society—one whose own contradictions would prove manageable for at least the first chapters of the Cold War. This American creed was tested in the war on crime and withstood greater challenges at war, but after 1945 a larger coalition than ever could embrace it. The government that policed the world in the name of democracy was now fit to police the streets of America, in times of peace no less than times of war.

A look to the 1940s and beyond invites attention to the seeming paradox of liberal acquiescence in the security state—its national secrets, its military-industrial complex, its unlimited surveillance, war without end, deadly police raids, and mass incarceration. But if this is a paradox, it is one that originated with modern liberalism itself, from the very first moments of its creation. To gain political support for modern government with all its promises and power, the New Dealers needed to conquer the phantoms of lawlessness. In doing so, they built a regime that unified law enforcers and academics, sheriffs and federal spies, radicals and conservatives, white supremacists and racial liberals, and that could even establish martial law and concentration camps without losing all legitimacy in the eyes of champions for civil liberties and civil rights. It was not *despite* or *during* but instead *through* that process—the New Deal's adoption of the war on crime and construction of the modern security state—that American liberalism and law and order as we know them were born.

EPILOGUE

The liberal state Roosevelt built blossomed beyond his death. For some time after, the New Deal coalition, the war-on-crime coalition, and the security-state coalition would also endure. Looking back, we can understand much of the tumultuous story of political legitimacy and stability as a tale of these different coalitions struggling to maintain the simultaneous dominance they achieved in the 1930s and 1940s.

Roosevelt's death in April 1945 made Harry S. Truman president. On questions of political economy, crime, and the security state, Truman governed as a New Deal liberal. There was no retrenchment after World War II comparable to that in the 1920s. In 1947 Truman signed the National Security Act, codifying the architecture for the postwar imperial presidency and intelligence empire, and authenticating the bond between American liberalism and the security state. The Act consecrated the ad hoc surveillance precedents of World War II and kept domestic authority in the FBI. As scholars have shown, Truman also targeted lawlessness as a threat to civil rights in ways that ultimately served the modernization of the carceral state.[1]

In 1950 Attorney General William E. Powers, carrying Cummings's legacy forward, hosted a national conference on crime. Truman's address consonantly struck familiar chords, expressly integrating the many themes his predecessor had spent twelve years bringing together. The recent rise in crime was an "inevitable" result of the last war and alongside "vice and greed" it afflicted "rural areas" and "cities" nationwide. Truman's liberal approach would stress interjurisdictional cooperation to make "law enforcement better and more effective." But it would also prioritize "prevention": "education, religion, and home training, family and child guidance, and wholesome recreation." It would stress human welfare, "wipe out our slums, improve the health of our citizens, and eliminate the inequalities of opportunity which embitter men and women and turn them toward lawlessness." To avoid becoming a "totalitarian government which does not believe in rights for anybody except the state," America must affirm Biblical values. It also needed equality under the law and civil liberties: police themselves must obey the law even as "mob violence" also threatened "the right to a fair trial, the right to vote, and the right to exercise freedom of speech, assembly, and petition."[2]

Roosevelt had built this unified strategy against lawlessness and for liberalism and security, and Truman integrated it with the Cold War. This law and order program remained fairly stable across major factions and parties even through the 1950s, when the liberal security state navigated its trials like civil rights and McCarthyism by further reinforcing the center and marginalizing the fringes as lawless and un-American. In the 1960s, however, political legitimacy began seriously to fray. The overlapping coalitions that built the New Deal state were collapsing. War-on-crime federalism could no longer manage the opposing aspirations of Black Americans and white racial conservatives. Postwar liberals tried to maintain Roosevelt's ecumenical vision but it collapsed under too many fractures.

In the ferment of 1968 these fractures became overwhelming.[3] Martin Luther King Jr. and Robert F. Kennedy exposed tensions in liberalism, national security, and civil rights, before being gunned down. Launched in response to the earlier Watts Riots, the Kerner Commission's conclusions outlined an answer to racially charged lawlessness that was at once humane and determined, but what materialized was Lyndon Johnson's war on crime. In June 1968 Johnson signed into law the Omnibus Crime Control and Safe Streets Act, establishing block grants and marking a new era of war-on-crime federalism that would persist beyond the cooperative federalism of his welfare state. Black city rebellions exploded into a new crescendo that would persist into the next decade.[4] The lawlessness of police brutality and machine politics marred the 1968 Democratic National Convention in Chicago. In *Terry v. Ohio*, Supreme Court Justice Earl Warren, joined by Hugo Black and Thurgood Marshall, affirmed the right of police to stop and frisk suspects, even when it was acknowledged that the practice reinforced structural racial disparities.[5] In the presidential election Democrat Hubert Humphrey, stubbornly devoted to the Vietnam War, and unreconstructed segregationist George Wallace, revealed the fatal fissures in Roosevelt and Truman's party. Wallace meant something more racially and politically sectarian than the New Dealers did when he demanded "law and order," and Richard Nixon, having appropriated the term for the modern American right, won the presidency. He inherited the war on crime and the security state from Johnson, who told him that he would come to rely on and trust J. Edgar Hoover.[6]

"Law and order" had a less ecumenical and liberatory meaning now, but the war-on-crime coalition still had triumphs ahead. Through the 1970s it was the New Deal and security state coalitions that suffered. Deindustrialization and privatization ended the era of Roosevelt's political economy. Watergate, the Vietnam War, and surveillance scandals discredited the liberal security state. But in the late twentieth century the bipartisan war on crime was resurrected, this time skewed toward repression over prevention, prisons and police over rehabilitation. Mass incarceration and the modern war on drugs united Republicans and Democrats from Ronald Reagan to Bill Clinton, Strom Thurmond to Joe Biden. Crime fighting became one of the most reliable state-building avenues through the 1990s until its excesses drew increasing demands for reform and leniency. The cooperative federalism of New Deal and Great Society political economy had withered, but war-on-crime federalism remained.[7]

In the twenty-first century we seem to be witnessing something like the crises of legitimacy that Roosevelt inherited. The bipartisan security-state coalition was revitalized after 9/11 through the war on terror, but its own overreach, especially the Iraq war, helped produce broad cynicism about American power. The management of the 2008 financial crises spawned widespread cynicism about US political economy and its elites. The politics of law and order have become scrambled. In the 2020s the American right has called for the abolition of the FBI whereas the left has maintained more distrust for immigration enforcement and the local police. Yet reverberations of both the progressive and the repressive elements of war-on-crime liberalism are still detectable. There is still some interest for sentencing and drug law reform in both parties. After decades of falling crime, a recent uptick in crime has revitalized some energy for liberal law-and-order politics. It seems unlikely, however, that America's multigenerational legitimacy crisis will be as adeptly managed as happened through the convergence of structural, political, and contingent factors that built New Deal law and order.

In asking how to restore trust in America's institutions, it must first be recognized how that trust was built in the first place. The New Deal brought about an exceptional era for American government, not just in political economy but in political stability. Contemporary Americans grapple toward reclaiming a modern government unusual in the sweep of American history, dependent on law and order in both their broad and narrow senses. They mostly see liberalism and law and order as arising from the fog of World War II and the early Cold War. This fog obscures how lawless post–Civil War America was through seven decades when regional hatreds, racial pogroms, corruption, and suspicion marred every governing institution. The New Deal's enforcers needed a deference from society and the states that would be more reliable than in the past. Earlier occasions of transformative national mobilization arose from exigencies and usually wars. But federal law-enforcement power receded after Reconstruction and after World War I. Prohibition, the most ambitious peacetime enforcement experiment, only clarified the constitutional and ideological crises.

The New Dealers overcame previous barriers to nurture unprecedented consensus around crime, which finally legitimated national enforcement authority. Politically speaking, the achievement bridged the parties, while bringing labor, the white South, and Black Americans behind institutions they long had cause to distrust. Culturally speaking, the agenda achieved pathbreaking collaboration and consensus among criminologists, legal minds, and enforcers. In structural terms, this achievement reconciled previously competing federal agencies and the national and state authorities. The restructured federalism enabled not only crime fighting but the New Deal state itself.

This new form of government, continually reliant on its enforcement authority, defined American politics at the center of the twentieth century—with its most celebrated triumphs characterizing the years between 1933 and 1968. These decades were the peak of modern liberalism and of deference to law and order. In both the mechanics and the ideological resonances, the 1930s war on crime stabilized the instruments of repression, which converged into a security state that survived World War II without collapsing into chaos. Over time, the new regime facilitated multipronged militancy against domestic crime but also enforced civil rights, overtook the states as the primary collector of tax revenue, constructed a growing regulatory apparatus, and cultivated the largest permanent overseas presence of all the world's nations.

New Deal liberalism and the modernizing security state reinforced one another in their genesis and development. The liberalism aided in political legitimation, promising protection that was at once more inclusionary and yet uncompromising toward outsiders, with conceptions of lawlessness both more egalitarian yet accommodating of traditional social, economic, and political power. In revolutionizing law enforcement and national power, the New Dealers transformed liberalism. Roosevelt intended to do so through the welfare state, but experimentation with enforcement similarly shaped his pragmatic, national liberalism, in both its legal and its social theory. Through combating criminality, liberalism resolved its interwar contradictions in favor of vigilance against lawlessness and subversion.

Every flavor of liberalism before had entertained an unstable balance of realism and idealism. The Reconstructionists recognized freedom was impossible without equality but overestimated their vision's purchase among white Americans. The classical liberals cast themselves as realists on the limits of power but were taken by idealism about industrialization. The progressives recognized the costs of inequity but idealized the redemptive power of the state. The New Deal liberals grasped these failures of past liberalisms and embraced the difficult, even cruel consequences of power. But they were complacent about the permanence of their own settlement and its long-term costs.

Although the New Deal liberals' fusionism of repression and restraint dissolved earlier paradoxes, points of agreement could not forever captivate as many factions as Roosevelt had. The New Deal coalition is long gone.[8] But the war-on-crime coalition has reappeared, time and again, into this century, building a broad consensus to expand incarceration and militarize policing at every scale. How long that coalition can live past its broader liberal context in which it gestated, or whether law and order can be rebuilt as a political and not just a narrow enforcement project, we have yet to see. Revisiting the contradictory conditions in which it first happened might inform the next generation to address the social and cultural dilemmas of their own time.

ABBREVIATIONS AND INITIALIZATIONS
USED IN NOTES

Abbreviations referring to source collections generally correspond to manuscript collections listed below, unless specified as published or online. Some initials and abbreviations appearing in the notes do not have a corresponding entry here, because the author transcribed them from the individual documents and sometimes their precise meaning is not clear.

AAF	Alcatraz Administrative Files
ACLUNC	American Civil Liberties Union of Northern California records, 1900–2000 (bulk 1934–2000)
AGAC	Attorney General's Advisory Committee on Crime
AGAC GC	Attorney General's Advisory Committee on Crime, General Correspondence
AGAC SF	Attorney General's Advisory Committee on Crime Records, Subject Files
AGSRP	Records of the Attorney General's Survey of Release Procedures
APPUCSB	American Presidency Project, University of California, Santa Barbara (online)
AVP	August Vollmer Papers
AWN	Wardens' Notebook Pages, Alcatraz
BOPAF	Records of the Bureau of Prisons, Administrative Files
BPD	Berkeley, California, Police Department Records

CaptO#	Captain's Order Number
CR73:78	*Congressional Record, Proceedings and Debates of the Second Sessions of the 73rd Congress of the United States,* vol. 78 (1934) (published)
DCBC	Department of Commerce Bureau of the Census
DEASF	Drug Enforcement Administration Subject Files, 1916–1970
DOJ	Department of Justice
DOJA	Department of Justice Abstracts
ERP	Eleanor Roosevelt Papers
FBI	Federal Bureau of Investigation
FDRGP	Franklin D. Roosevelt Governorship Papers
FDR Letters	*F.D.R.: His Personal Letters, 1928–1945* (published)
FFMP	Frank F. Merriam Papers
GC	General Correspondence
HAP	Harry Anslinger Papers
HCDOJ	Speeches of Attorney General Homer Stille Cummings, Justice Department website (online)
HHSF	Herbert Hoover Subject Files
HLP	Herbert Lehman Papers
HMP	Henry Morgenthau Papers
ILP	Ivy Lee Papers
JAERR	Japanese American Evacuation and Resettlement Records, 1930–1974
JFP	Jerome Frank Papers
LDWP	Lillian D. Wald Papers
LFCR	Legal File: Cases Rejected (online NAACP collection)
LFCS	Legal File: Cases Supported (online NAACP collection)
LND	The Living New Deal (online)
LPP	Lee Pennington Papers
MFTAG	Memorandum for the Attorney General
MWDP	Mary W. Dewson Papers
NAACPHV	NAACP Papers, Library of Congress, History Vault (online)
NBC	National Broadcasting Company

NCB	ACLU, Northern California Branch, 1900–1978
OF10	Official Files 10, Department of Justice
OF10b	Official Files 10b, Department of Justice, FBI Records
OF21	Official Files 21, Department of Treasury
OF117	Official Files 117, Crime
OF431	Official Files 431, Narcotics
OFD	Osmond Fraenkel Diaries
OWWP	Orlando Winfield Wilson Papers
PAGCC	*Proceedings of the Attorney General's Conference on Crime* (published)
PETSG	Papers of Eleanor T. and Sheldon Glueck, 1911–1972
PHSC	Papers of Homer S. Cummings
PICCHWA	President's Interdepartmental Committee to Coordinate Health and Welfare Activities
PIRA	Prison Industries Reorganization Administration
RBP	Roger Baldwin Papers
RMP	Raymond Moley Papers
ROLEC	Records of the Office of the Assistant Secretary for the Enforcement and Operations, Records of the Office of Law Enforcement Coordination
RSPC	Records for the Society for the Prevention of Crime
SF	Subject File(s)
SFPD9	San Francisco Police Department Records, Police District No. 9
SFPDRSFPL	San Francisco Public Library, San Francisco Police Department Records
SPHC	*Selected Papers of Homer Cummings* (published)
SRP	*Attorney General's Survey of Release Procedures* (published)
TVAGM	Tennessee Valley Authority Papers, General Manager's Office
TVAPC	Tennessee Valley Authority Papers, Personnel Correspondence Files
WPA	Works Progress Administration
WESP	Willard E. Schmidt Papers

NOTES

INTRODUCTION

1. Address, Brooklyn, NY, 30 October 1936, APPUCSB.

2. The phrase "war on crime" adeptly captured the 1930s effort—its battles, strategies, tactics, fronts, public relations, and ideological and material mobilization.

3. Herbert Corey, *Farewell, Mr. Gangster: America's War on Crime* (New York: D. Appleton–Century Co., 1936), 6, 7, 3; a "flattered" J. Edgar Hoover wrote Corey's foreword (v).

4. See Roger M. Smith, *Liberalism and Constitutional Law* (Cambridge, MA: Harvard University Press, 1990 [1985]).

5. Ira Katznelson, *Fear Itself: The New Deal and the Origins of Our Time* (New York: W. W. Norton, 2013) 234–238.

6. See Andrew Preston, *The Invention of National Security* (Cambridge, MA: Harvard University Press, 2024).

7. Anti-crime reforms were indicative of New Deal responses to "the impotence of local governments," writes William E. Leuchtenburg, *Franklin D. Roosevelt and the New Deal, 1932–1940* (New York: Harper and Row, 1963), 334.

8. Mary M. Stolberg, "Policing the Twilight Zone: Federalizing Crime Fighting during the New Deal," *Journal of Policy History* 7, no. 4 (1995): 394.

9. Claire Bond Potter, *War on Crime: Bandits, G-Men, and the Politics of Mass Culture* (New Brunswick, NJ: Rutgers University Press, 1998).

10. Kenneth O'Reilly, "A New Deal for the FBI: The Roosevelt Administration, Crime Control, and National Security," *Journal of American History* 69, no. 3 (December 1982): 640; Athan Theoharis, *The FBI and American Democracy: A Brief Critical History* (Lawrence: University Press of Kansas, 2004), 38; Rhodri Jeffreys-Jones, *The FBI: A History* (New Haven, CT: Yale University Press, 2007).

11. In the "law-and-order decade," the New Deal drove "significant expansion of the federal role in criminal justice and police reform." Samuel Walker, *A*

Critical History of Police Reform: The Emergence of Professionalism (Lexington, MA: Lexington Books, 1977), 131, 139. Beverly Gage's book suggests both tensions and affinities between the FBI and New Deal. Gage, *G-Man: J. Edgar Hoover and the Making of the American Century* (New York: Penguin Random House, 2022).

12. Matthew G. T. Denney, "'To Wage a War': Crime, Race, and State Making in the Age of FDR," *Studies in American Political Development* 35, no. 1 (2021): 16–56.

13. Emily M. Brooks, *Gotham's War within a War: Policing and the Birth of Law-and-Order Liberalism in World War II-Era New York City* (Chapel Hill: University of North Carolina Press, 2023), 174.

14. Kathleen J. Frydl, "Kidnapping and State Development in the United States," *Studies in American Political Development* 20 (Spring 2006): 26.

15. See Laura Kalman, *The Strange Career of Legal Liberalism* (New Haven: Yale University Press, 1998); Jessica Wang, "Imagining the Administrative State: Legal Pragmatism, Securities Regulation, and New Deal Liberalism," *Journal of Policy History* 17, no. 3 (2005); Morton Horwitz, *The Transformation of American Law, 1870–1960: The Crisis of Legal Orthodoxy* (Oxford: Oxford University Press, 1992); Anne Kornhauser, *Debating the American State: Liberal Anxieties and the New Leviathan, 1930–1970* (Philadelphia: University of Pennsylvania Press, 2015). For a view that is contrary to "conventional" New Deal accounts of the end of progressive moralism, see Michael Willrich, "Criminal Justice in the United States," in *The Cambridge History of Law in America*, vol. 3: *The Twentieth Century and After (1920–)*, ed. Michael Grossberg and Christopher Tomlins (Cambridge: Cambridge University Press, 2008), 209–211; see also his claim that there is a "belligerent coexistence" between "crime control and socialization," in Willrich, *City of Courts: Socializing Justice in Progressive Era Chicago* (Cambridge: Cambridge University Press, 2003), 310.

16. Lawrence M. Friedman, *Crime and Punishment in American History* (New York: Basic Books, 1993); Khalil Gibran Muhammad, *The Condemnation of Blackness: Race, Crime, and the Making of Modern Urban America* (Cambridge, MA: Harvard University Press, 2010), esp. chap. 3; Samuel Walker, *A Critical History of Police Reform: The Emergence of Professionalism* (Lexington, MA: Lexington Books, 1977); Joseph Gerald Wood, "The Progressives and the Police: Urban Reform and the Professionalization of the Los Angeles Police" (PhD diss., UCLA, 1973); Janis Appier, *Women: The Sexual Politics of Law Enforcement and the LAPD* (Philadelphia: Temple University Press, 1998); David J. Rothman, *Conscience and Convenience: The Asylum and Its Alternatives in Progressive America* (Boston: Little, Brown, 1980); Rebecca M.

McLennan, *The Crisis of Imprisonment: Protest, Politics, and the Making of the American Penal State, 1776–1941* (New York: Cambridge University Press, 2008); Alfred W. McCoy, *Policing America's Empire: The United States, the Philippines, and the Rise of the Surveillance State* (Madison: University of Wisconsin Press, 2009; Lisa McGirr, *The War on Alcohol: Prohibition and the Rise of the American State* (New York: W. W. Norton, 2015), 218, 221; James T. Sparrow, *Warfare State: World War II Americans and the Age of Big Government* (New York: Oxford University Press, 2013), 50.

17. Jonathan Simon, *Governing through Crime: How the War on Crime Transformed American Democracy and Created a Culture of Fear* (Oxford: Oxford University Press, 2009); Elizabeth Hinton, *From the War on Poverty to the War on Crime: The Making of Mass Incarceration in America* (Cambridge, MA: Harvard University Press, 2016); Naomi Murakawa, *The First Civil Right: How Liberals Built Prison America* (Oxford: Oxford University Press, 2014). Also see Christopher Lowen Agee, *The Streets of San Francisco: Policing and the Creation of a Cosmopolitan Liberal Politics, 1950–1972* (Chicago: University of Chicago Press, 2014); Max Felker-Kantor, "Liberal Law-and-Order: The Politics of Police Reform in Los Angeles," *Journal of Urban History* 46, no. 5 (2020): 1026–1049.

18. Gage, *G-Man,* brings the criminal-justice and surveillance stories together. See also Katznelson, *Fear Itself,* 158, 324–334; O'Reilly, "A New Deal for the FBI," 640.

19. Margot Canaday, *Straight State* (Princeton, NJ: Princeton University Press, 2011), 5.

20. Potter, *War on Crime,* 200.

21. Benno Netelenbos notes the Weberian "interrelation between objective and subjective meanings" and distinguishes between a sociology tradition that stresses subjective belief and another that highlights "socially institution-alised expectations about the legitimacy of political power." Netelenbos, *Political Legitimacy beyond Weber: An Analytical Framework* (London: Palgrave-Macmillan, 2016), 2, 13.

22. Even with different theories of "legitimacy," social scientists have sought quantitative measures. Eric W. Schoon suggests that "[an] appropriate unit of analysis for research on legitimacy is a *dyad* (i.e., two nodes and a tie), consisting of an *object* of legitimacy (the thing being evaluated), an *audience* (the source of evaluation), and a *relationship* that connects the two." Schoon's review essay synthesizes and reconciles studies that measure "moral legiti-macy," "pragmatic legitimacy," and "empirical legitimacy." Schoon, "Opera-tionalizing Legitimacy," *American Sociological Review* 87, no. 3 (2022): 479,

484. Historians might best approach legitimacy through broad qualitative assessment, not normative evaluation. Although positive legitimacy suggests stability, which has normative implications, philosophy could judge these different patterns of governance across different criteria.

23. Frydl, "Kidnapping and State Development," 18.

24. Arthur M. Schlesinger Jr., writing about Roosevelt's first hundred days, identified the New Dealers in the president's inner circle as socioeconomically and geographically diverse but "predominantly middle class," mostly college-educated, and experienced in city government. They were "generalists" and "represented divergent and often clashing philosophies"—from "laissez-faire liberalism" and the "agrarian tradition" to "trust-busting liberalism" and "Theodore Roosevelt–Herbert Croly Progressivism." A broader definition could include activists and thinkers in solidarity with Roosevelt. See Schlesinger, *The Age of Roosevelt: The Coming of the New Deal, 1933–1935* (Boston: Houghton Mifflin, 1958), 18–19. According to James S. Olson, ed., *Historical Dictionary of the New Deal: From Inauguration to Preparation for War* (Westport: Greenwood Press, 1985), 369, historians including Schlesinger distilled the term "New Deal" to mean Roosevelt's "political and economic policies," which had "come to symbolize Roosevelt's political philosophy as well as the role of the Democratic party and the federal government in dealing with the Great Depression." Olson traces the term to Stuart Chase, an economist with Georgist and Fabian influences whose 1932 book foreshadowed Roosevelt's program. Chase's book did not discuss crime much but lamented the graft that protected "speakeasies" and suggested that reforming Prohibition could help reduce racketeering. Chase, *A New Deal* (New York: Macmillan, 1932), 14, 36.

25. Historians emphasize the interplay between values and practical politics. See Lizabeth Cohen, *Making a New Deal: Industrial Workers in Chicago, 1919–1939* (Cambridge: Cambridge University Press, 1990), 8; Alan Brinkley, *The End of Reform: New Deal Liberalism in Recession and War* (New York: Vintage Books, 1996 [1995]); David M. Kennedy, *Freedom from Fear: The American People in Depression and War, 1929–1945* (New York: Oxford University Press, 1999). Ira Katznelson's periodization includes the entire Roosevelt–Truman agenda, including Jim Crow complacency and national security. Katznelson, *Fear Itself*, 158.

26. On Roosevelt's popularization of an American liberal creed, see Helen Rosenblatt, *The Lost History of Liberalism: From Ancient Rome to the Twenty-First Century* (Princeton, NJ: Princeton University Press, 2018), 361–363. Pushing against dialectical tales of liberalism versus conservatism, Brian Balogh concedes that the 1930s and 1940s are the "toughest case" for his own

state-building narrative approach that stresses associational collaboration. See Balogh, *The Associational State: American Governance in the Twentieth Century* (Philadelphia: University of Pennsylvania Press, 140.

27.   William J. Novak argues that pre–New Deal social-democratic state building has been obscured by the "myth of the New Deal State." Novack, *New Democracy: The Creation of the Modern American State* (Cambridge, MA: Harvard University Press, 2022), 263.

28.   John Rawls emphasizes "public reason" advancing liberal democracy's "higher law," especially during the Revolution, Reconstruction, and the New Deal. Rawls, *Political Liberalism* (New York: Columbia University Press, 1993), 333–334.

29.   In the 1930s, perhaps progressivism pivoted from its bipartisan association with expertise toward a more impatient egalitarian liberalism.

30.   The New Dealers' liberalism sought "only to change institutions" and abandoned the Progressives' "Emersonian hope of reforming man." Leuchtenburg, *Franklin D. Roosevelt and the New Deal*, vii.

31.   On the midcentury New Deal order, see Jefferson Cowie, *The Great Exception: The New Deal and the Limits of American Politics* (Princeton, NJ: Princeton University Press, 2016).

32.   See Elizabeth Hinton and DeAnza Cook, "The Mass Criminalization of Black Americans: A Historical Overview," *Annual Review of Criminology* 4 (2001): 261–286.

33.   Trevor George Gardner, "Immigrant Sanctuary as the 'Old Normal': A Brief History of Police Federalism," *Columbia Law Review* 119, no. 1 (January 2019): 9.

34.   Jonathan Obert, *The Six-Shooter State: Public and Private Violence in American Politics* (Cambridge: Cambridge University Press, 2018), 7.

35.   Daniel C. Richman, "The Past, Present, and Future of Violent Crime Federalism," *Crime and Justice* 34 (2006): 377–439.

36.   Daniel C. Richman and Sarah Seo, "How Federalism Built the FBI, Sustained Local Police, and Left Out the States," *Stanford Journal of Civil Rights and Civil Liberties* 17 (2022).

37.   See James T. Patterson, *The New Deal and the States: Federalism in Transition* (Princeton, NJ: Princeton University Press, 2015 [1969]).

38.   Christopher Capozzola highlights the dichotomy in World War I. Capozzola, *Uncle Sam Wants You: World War I and the Making of the Modern American Citizen* (Oxford: Oxford University Press, 2010), 15.

PART I. THE LIMITS OF LIBERAL MOBILIZATION, 1865–1932

1. Beverly Gage, *G-Man: J. Edgar Hoover and the Making of the American Century* (New York: Penguin Random House, 2022), 148.

2. On Prohibition and police legitimacy, see Anne Gray Fischer, *The Streets Belong to Us: Sex, Race and Police Power from Segregation to Gentrification* (Chapel Hill: University of North Carolina Press, 2022).

3. Progressive Era historiography long emphasized social control; see Robert H. Wiebe, *Search for Order* (New York: Hill and Wang, 1966). Richard White urges historians to revisit Gilded Age corruption; see White, *The Republic for Which It Stands: The United States during Reconstruction and the Gilded Age, 1865–1896* (New York: Oxford University Press, 2017), 2. Laura F. Edwards frames the legal history of Reconstruction as the nationalization of liberal rights in *A Legal History of the Civil War and Reconstruction: A Nation of Rights* (New York: Cambridge University Press, 2015).

1. "THE MOST LAWLESS NATION"

1. Kerry R. Oman, "The Beginning of the End: The Indian Peace Commission of 1867–1868," *Great Plains Quarterly* 22, no. 1 (2002): 35–51.

2. "Lawless Negroes," *New York Times*, 4 January 1869; "Lawless Italians," *New York Times*, 12 August 1889.

3. "Lawless Strikers," *New York Times*, 28 May 1883; "Lawless Gamblers," *New York Times*, 21 April 1883; "Lawless Coal Miners," *New York Times*, 21 March 1883; "Lawless Chinese," *New York Times*, 31 July 1885.

4. "Lawless Kentucky," *New York Times*, 6 September 1874; "Lawless Texas," *Los Angeles Times*, 20 December 1889.

5. "Lawless Law," *New York Times*, 10 January, 1886; "Censured by Lawless Senate," *New York Times*, 21 January 1892.

6. In *American Homicide* (Cambridge, MA: Belknap Press of Harvard University Press, 2009), Randolph Roth tracks interracial violence during the beginning of Reconstruction (343); after Reconstruction, homicides fell in much of the nation (411). Dramatic change came in the Southwest at the turn of the century (387). In Los Angeles County, homicides plummeted from 198 per 100,000 adults per year in the late 1860s and early 1870s down to 23 per 100,000 in the 1880s and 1890s (403). Roth correlates lower homicide rates with trust in government.

7. Gary Gerstle categorizes most pre–New Deal federal authority powers as examples of "exemption," "surrogacy," or "privatization." Gerstle, *Liberty and*

Coercion: The Paradox of American Government from the Founding to the Present (Princeton University Press, 2015), 89–124.

8.   See Allen Steinberg, *The Transformation of Criminal Justice, Philadelphia, 1800–1880* (Chapel Hill: University of North Carolina Press, 1989), 196–223.

9.   "In the aftermath of abolition, as under slavery," writes Eric Foner, "planters complained of widespread theft by blacks." Foner, *Reconstruction: America's Unfinished Revolution, 1863–1877* (New York: Harper, 2002 [1989]), 202. On Southern perceptions of Black criminality, see Leon F. Litwack, *Been in the Storm So Long* (New York: Vintage, 1980), 267–272.

10.   Mississippi Black Codes (1865), in *American Constitutionalism*, vol. 2, *Rights and Liberties*, ed. Howard Gillman, Mark A. Graber, and Keith E. Whittington (Oxford: Oxford University Press, 2020).

11.   1866 Civil Rights Act, 14 Stat. 27–30.

12.   US Constitution, Amendment 14.

13.   Chad Alan Goldberg, *Citizens and Paupers: Relief, Rights, and Race, from the Freedmen's Bureau to Workfare* (Chicago: University of Chicago Press, 2007), chap. 2.

14.   Theda Skocpol, *Protecting Soldiers and Mothers: The Political Origins of Social Policy in the United States* (Cambridge, MA: Harvard University Press, 1992), chap. 2.

15.   Joan M. Jensen, *Army Surveillance in America, 1775–1980* (New Haven, CT: Yale University Press, 1991), 41.

16.   Ulysses S. Grant, Proclamation 199, 3 May 1871, APPUCSB.

17.   Allen W. Trelease, *White Terror: The Ku Klux Klan Conspiracy and Southern Reconstruction* (Baton Rouge: Louisiana State University Press, 1971).

18.   See William F. Duker, *A Constitutional History of Habeas Corpus* (New York: Praeger, 1980); William Wiecek, "The Great Writ and Reconstruction: The Habeas Corpus Act of 1867," *Journal of Southern History* 36, no. 4 (1970): 530–548.

19.   At least forty-one Black sheriffs served throughout the South. Eric Foner, *Freedom's Lawmakers: A Directory of Black Officeholders during Reconstruction*, rev. ed. (Baton Rouge: Louisiana State University Press, 1996 [1993]), xvii, xxvii.

20.   New Orleans's Black police representation partly traced back to Black participation in the War of 1812. See Dennis C. Rousey, "Black Policemen in New Orleans during Reconstruction," *The Historian* 49, no. 2 (February 1987): 223–243.

21.   Jonathan Obert, *The Six-Shooter State: Public and Private Violence in American Politics* (Cambridge: Cambridge University Press, 2018), 57–59.

22. Nicholas Lemann, *Redemption: The Last Battle of the Civil War* (New York: Farrar, Straus and Giroux, 2006), 184.

23. Rebecca M. McLennan, *The Crisis of Imprisonment: Protest, Politics, and the Making of the American Penal State, 1776–1941* (New York: Cambridge University Press, 2008).

24. Foner, *Reconstruction*, 530–531.

25. Chief Justice Taney warned that Black citizenship rights could lead to the right to bear arms. *Dred Scott v. Sandford*, 60 U. S. 393, 450. See Saul Cornell and Justin Florence, "The Right to Bear Arms in the Era of the Fourteenth Amendment: Gun Rights or Gun Regulation?," *Santa Clara Law Review* 50, no. 4 (2010): 1043–1071.

26. *United States v. Cruikshank*, 92 U.S. 542 (1876).

27. Obert, *The Six-Shooter State*, 249.

28. Gregory P. Downs, *After Appomattox: Military Occupation and the Ends of War* (Cambridge, MA: Harvard University Press, 2015).

29. *Civil Rights Cases*, 109 U.S. 3 (1883).

30. Edward L. Ayers, *The Promise of the New South: Life after Reconstruction* (Oxford: Oxford University Press, 2007 [1992]), 155.

31. Whites enjoyed "virtual immunity" when "accused of crimes against black men and women." Leon F. Litwack, *Trouble in Mind: Black Southerners in the Age of Jim Crow* (New York: Vintage, 1998), 253.

32. "He Talks about the 'Rustlers,'" *Chicago Daily Tribune*, 18 April 1892; "Lawless Indians," *Chicago Daily Tribune*, 25 December 1887.

33. Mitchel P. Roth, *Crime and Punishment: A History of the Criminal Justice System* (Belmont, CA: Wadsworth, 2005), 172.

34. Contrast Roth, *American Homicide*, and Mathieu Couttenier, Pauline Grosjean, and Marc Sangnier, "The Wild West IS Wild: The Homicide Resource Curse," *Journal of the European Economic Association* 15, no. 3 (1 July 2017): 558–585, with Terry L. Anderson and Peter J. Hill, *The Not So Wild, Wild West: Property Rights on the Frontier* (Stanford, CA: Stanford Economics and Finance, 2004).

35. Richard Maxwell Brown, "Western Violence: Structure, Values, Myth," *Western Historical Quarterly* 24, no. 1 (1993): 4–20.

36. At century's end, Butch Cassidy and others worked with private business interests; in the twentieth century the phenomenon receded. Obert, *The Six-Shooter State*, 222–224.

37. Randy McFerrin and Douglas Wills, "High Noon on the Western Range: A Property Rights Analysis of the Johnson County War," *Journal of Economic History* 67, no. 1 (2007): 69–92.

38. Laurence Armand French, *Policing American Indians: A Unique Chapter in American Jurisprudence* (Boca Raton, LA: Taylor and Francis), 49–54; Andrew R. Graybill, *Policing the Great Plains: Rangers, Mounties, and the North American Frontier, 1875–1910* (Lincoln: University of Nebraska Press, 2007); Pekka Hämäläinen, *Indigenous Continent: The Epic Contest for North America* (New York: Liverlight, 2022), 458.

39. Paul T. Lockman Jr., "The Black Regulars: Buffalo Soldiers during the Indian War Era as Crime Fighters and Peacekeepers on the Western Frontier, 1866–1892," *Social Science Journal* 41, no. 4 (2004): 675–681.

40. Nudie E. Williams, "Bass Reeves: Lawman in the Western Ozarks," *Negro History Bulletin* 42, no. 2 (1979): 37–39.

41. See Franz Oppenheimer, *The State: Its History and Development Viewed Sociologically* (New York: Vanguard Press, 1914); Arthur A. Ekirch, *The Civilian and the Military* (New York: Oxford University Press, 1956).

42. Roth, *American Homicide,* relates national unification to reduced homicide in Italy and fewer arrests in Germany (298). On police centralization in the United States compared to civil-law countries, see Cliff Roberson and Dilip K. Das, *An Introduction to Comparative Legal Models of Criminal Justice* (Boca Raton, LA: Taylor and Francis, 2016), chap. 3. On class resistance, see Steve Fraser, *The Age of Acquiescence: The Life and Death of American Resistance to Organized Wealth and Power* (New York: Little, Brown, 2015), pt. 1.

43. Hidetaka Hirota, *Expelling the Poor: Atlantic Seaboard States and the Nineteenth-Century Origins of American Immigration Policy* (New York: Oxford University Press, 2016).

44. Edward K. Spann, *The New Metropolis: New York City, 1840–1857* (New York: Columbia University Press, 1983).

45. On bourgeois liberalism being shaped by fear of disorder, see Sven Beckert, *The Monied Metropolis: New York City and the Consolidation of the American Bourgeoisie, 1850–1896* (Cambridge: Cambridge University Press, 2001).

46. Terry Golway, *Machine Made: Tammany Hall and the Creation of Modern American Politics* (New York: W. W. Norton, 2014), 95, 115.

47. Herbert Spencer thought lenient penalties would discipline "civilized" citizens, whereas the "less civilized" required "inflictions of bodily pain and

death." He criticized "suffering and demoralization needlessly caused by our severe laws in the last century" and pondered the "legitimate extent" necessary to "coerce the criminal." Authority came from the rights of individual victims, past and potential, to restitution and isolation from criminals: "Equity requires that the restraint of the criminal shall be as great as is needful for the safety of society; but not greater." Spencer, "Anglo-American Philosophies of Penal Law," *Journal of the American Institute of Criminal Law and Criminology* 1 (1910): 862, 863, 870.

48. On Republican liberal ideology, see Heather Cox Richardson, *West from Appomattox: The Reconstruction of America after the Civil War* (New Haven, CT: Yale University Press, 2007).

49. On contractual conceptions, see Amy Dru Stanley, *From Bondage to Contract: Wage Labor, Marriage, and the Market in the Age of Slave Emancipation* (Cambridge: Cambridge University Press, 1998). Also see Barbara Young Welke, *Law and the Borders of Belonging in the Long-Nineteenth-Century United States* (Cambridge: Cambridge University Press, 2010). Nancy Cohen argues that liberals entertained robust government but when frustrated retreated to laissez-faire absolutism. Cohen, *The Reconstruction of American Liberalism, 1865–1914* (Chapel Hill: University of North Carolina Press, 2002). Cohen defines liberalism as a commitment to freedom, tolerance, self-rule, the rule of law, and justice (6).

50. On nineteenth-century policing and liberalism, see Adam Malka, *The Men of Mobtown: Policing Baltimore in the Age of Slavery and Emancipation* (Chapel Hill: University of North Carolina Press, 2018).

51. "They were in many ways the standing armies that the founding fathers feared," writes Sam Mitrani (*The Rise of the Chicago Police Department: Class and Conflict, 1850–1894* [Urbana: University of Illinois Press, 2013], 2–3, 4).

52. William Graham Sumner and Albert Galloway Keller, *The Forgotten Man* (New Haven, CT: Yale University Press, 1918).

53. Jensen, *Army Surveillance in America,* attributes *Posse Comitatus* legislation not to Reconstruction but to Northern attention to "labor and management" (29–32).

54. Robert Justin Goldstein, *Political Repression in Modern America from 1870 to 1976* (Urbana: University of Illinois Press, 2001), 23, 41.

55. See Beverly Gage, "Why Violence Matters: Radicalism, Politics, and Class War in the Gilded Age and Progressive Era," *Journal for the Study of Radicalism* 1, no. 1 (2007): 99–109.

56. Goldstein, *Political Repression,* 15, 50–53.

57. Goldstein, *Political Repression*, 45, 59.

58. Wiliam H. Carwardine, *The Pullman Strike* (Chicago: Charles H. Kerr, 1973 [1894]), introduction by Virgil J. Vogel, xxi.

59. Cohen, *Reconstruction of American Liberalism*, 194.

60. Goldstein, *Political Repression*, 45, 59.

61. Nick Salvatore, *Eugene V. Debs: Citizen and Socialist* (Urbana: University of Illinois Press, 1982), 114.

62. Salvatore, *Eugene V. Debs*, 131.

63. Robert L. Stern, "The Commerce Clause and the National Economy, 1933–1946," *Harvard Law Review* 59, no. 5 (May 1946): 647.

64. See William E. Forbath, *Law and the Shaping of the American Labor Movement* (Cambridge, MA: Harvard University Press, 1991). On the 1920s, see Christopher L. Tomlins, *The State and the Unions: Labor Relations, Law, and the Organized Labor Movement in America, 1880–1960* (Cambridge: Cambridge University Press, 1985), 60–95.

65. Regarding Jane Addams "and the Victorians," Michael McGerr writes that "the working class and the upper class" were "threatening because of their economic power, their alien cultures, and their mutual hostility." McGerr, *A Fierce Discontent: The Rise and Fall of the Progressive Movement in America, 1870–1920* (New York: Free Press, 2003), 54.

66. On progressive reformism filling vacuums of institutional failure, see Daniel T. Rodgers, "In Search of Progressivism," *Reviews in American History* 10, no. 4 (1982): 113–132.

67. On intellectual resonances between capital and individualism predating material interest, see Cohen, *Reconstruction of American Liberalism*, 226–233.

68. Carl Smith, *Urban Disorder and the Shape of Belief: The Great Chicago Fire, the Haymarket Bomb, and the Model Town of Pullman* (Chicago: University of Chicago Press, 1994); T. J. Jackson Lears, *No Place of Grace: Antimodernism and the Transformation of American Culture, 1880–1920* (Chicago: University of Chicago Press, 1994 [1981]); Charles R. McCann Jr., *Order and Control in American Socio-Economic Thought: Social Scientists and Progressive-Era Reform* (London: Routledge, 2012).

69. Charles Postel, *The Populist Vision* (Oxford: Oxford University Press, 2007).

70. Karl Jacoby, *Crimes against Nature: Squatters, Poachers, Thieves, and the Hidden History of American Conservation* (Berkeley: University of California Press, 2003).

71. Skocpol, *Protecting Soldiers and Mothers.*

72. See Daniel S. Nagin, "Deterrence in the Twenty-First Century," *Crime and Justice* 42, no. 1 (2013): 199–263.

73. Thomas G. Blomberg and Karol Lucken, *American Penology: A History of Control* (New Brunswick, NJ: Transaction, 2010), 74–75.

74. "The just society was one in which social relations of all kinds were cooperative rather than antagonistic in nature," but this "only existed in reformers' ethical imagination," writes Rebecca M. McLennan, *The Crisis of Imprisonment,* 378.

75. On policing's search for the "state's capacity to solve problems" in the Progressive Era, see Johann Koehler and Tony Cheng, "Settling Institutional Uncertainty: Policing Chicago and New York, 1877–1923," *Criminology* 61, no. 3 (2023): 1–28.

76. Riis to Moss, 13 April 1901, RSPC, box 1.

77. Roth, *Crime and Punishment,* 173–174; Report and Proceedings of the Senate Committee Appointed to Investigate the Police Department of the City of New York, 1905.

78. Herbert Croly, *The Promise of American Life* (New York: Macmillan, 1909). See William E. Leuchtenburg's introduction to Theodore Roosevelt, *The New Nationalism* (Englewood Cliffs, NJ: Prentice-Hall, 1961).

79. Gene E. Carte and Elaine H. Carte, *Police Reform in the United States: The Era of August Vollmer, 1905–1932* (Berkeley: University of California Press, 1975); Willard M. Oliver, *August Vollmer: The Father of American Policing* (Durham, NC: Carolina Academic Press, 2017); Sarah A. Seo, *Policing the Open Road: How Cars Transformed American Freedom* (Cambridge, MA: Harvard University Press, 2019), 64–112.

80. Vollmer proudly noted that since 1900, priorities had shifted "from brawn to brain, illiteracy to scientific training. "Police Progress in Practice and Principles," 28 June 1930, BPD, box 48: Speeches, etc.

81. Lombroso's eugenics combined hereditary and environmental factors. See Marvin E. Wolfgang, "Pioneers in Criminology: Cesare Lombroso (1835–1909)," *Journal of Criminal Law, Criminology, and Police Science* 52, no. 4 (1961): 361–391.

82. Thomas G. Blomberg and Karol Lucken, *American Penology: A History of Control* (New Brunswick, NJ: Transaction, 2010), 68–69. See also Khalil Gibran Muhammad, *The Condemnation of Blackness: Race, Crime, and the Making of Modern Urban America* (Cambridge, MA: Harvard University Press, 2010); and Kali N. Gross, *Colored Amazons: Crime, Violence, and Black*

Women in the City of Brotherly Love, 1880–1910 (Durham, NC: Duke University Press, 2006).

83. McCann, *Order and Control,* 22; Kunal M. Parker, *Making Foreigners: Immigration and Citizenship Law in America, 1600–2000* (New York: Cambridge University Press, 2015).

84. Gwendolyn Mink, *Old Labor and New Immigrants in American Political Development: Union, Party and State, 1875–1920* (Ithaca, NY: Cornell University Press, 1990).

85. Litwack, *Trouble in Mind,* 306.

86. Ida B. Wells, *Southern Horrors: Lynch Law in All Its Phases* (New York: New York Age Print, 1892).

87. Ann V. Collins, *All Hell Broke Loose: American Race Riots from the Progressive Era through World War II* (Santa Barbara: Praeger, 2012), xvi, 19–22, 53.

88. Litwack, *Trouble in Mind,* 256. On convict leasing, see David M. Oshinsky, *Worse than Slavery: Parchman Farm and the Ordeal of Jim Crow Justice* (New York: Free Press, 1997).

89. *Plessy v. Ferguson,* 163 U.S. 537 (1896). Unlike the *Lochner*-era cases, *Plessy* affirmed state government police power over private property rights. Progressives' "legal realism" arguably contrasted with *Plessy*'s anachronistic reasoning. Some historians see segregation harmonizing with progressive modernity; see Maureen A. Flanagan, *America Reformed: Progressives and Progressivism, 1890s–1920s* (New York: Oxford University Press, 2007), 120–121.

90. McGerr, *A Fierce Discontent,* 193–195.

91. Ayers, *The Promise of the New South,* 154.

92. Muhammad, *Condemnation of Blackness,* 72–85, 13, 27, inter alia.

93. Goldstein, *Political Repression,* 63–67.

94. Goldstein, *Political Repression,* 89–90, 90, 97–98.

95. Daniel C. Richman and Sarah Seo, "How Federalism Built the FBI, Sustained Local Police, and Left Out the States," *Stanford Journal of Civil Rights and Civil Liberties* 17 (2022): 429.

96. Theresa Kaminski, "'The Sex Side of Life': Mary Ware Dennett's Pioneering Battle for Birth Control and Sex Education," *The Historian* 61, no. 1 (1998): 152–153.

97. On the Mann Act and "the Progressive Era's faith that thorough investigation could lead to solutions for any social ill," see Jessica R. Pliley, *Policing*

Sexuality: The Mann Act and the Making of the FBI (Cambridge, MA: Harvard University Press, 2014), 3.

98. Robert L. Stern, "The Commerce Clause and the National Economy, 1933–1946," *Harvard Law Review* 59, no. 5 (May 1946): 650.

99. Pliley, *Policing Sexuality,* 51, 110.

100. Richman and Seo, "How Federalism Built the FBI," 436.

101. Athan Theoharis, *The FBI and American Democracy: A Brief Critical History* (Lawrence: University Press of Kansas, 2004), 15–16.

102. Daniel C. Richman, "The Past, Present, and Future of Violent Crime Federalism," *Crime and Justice* 34 (2006): 377–439.

103. *Lochner v. New York*, 198 U.S. 45 (1905).

104. Katherine Unterman, *Uncle Sam's Policemen: The Pursuit of Fugitives across Borders* (Cambridge, MA: Harvard University Press, 2015).

105. Theodore Roosevelt's Fourth Annual Message, 6 December 1904, APPUCSB.

106. Alfred McCoy, *Policing America's Empire: The United States, the Philippines, and the Rise of the Surveillance State* (Madison: University of Wisconsin Press, 2009).

107. Julian Go, "The Imperial Origins of American Policing: Militarization and Imperial Feedback in the Early 20th Century," *American Journal of Sociology* 125, no. 5 (March 1, 2020).

108. Paul Kramer, *The Blood of Government: Race, Empire, the United States, and the Philippines* (Chapel Hill: University of North Carolina Press, 2006); Mae M. Ngai, *Impossible Subjects: Illegal Aliens and the Making of Modern America* (Princeton, NJ: Princeton University Press, 2014).

109. This "enduring American state-building problem of inadequate political and economic integration . . . persisted until the New Deal restructuring of the political economy," writes Richard Franklin Bensel, *Yankee Leviathan: The Origins of Central State Authority in America, 1859–1877* (New York: Cambridge University Press, 1990), 433.

110. Gerstle, *Liberty and Coercion,* 128.

2. "ANARCHY OR DESPOTISM"

1. "House, 176 to 55, Overrides Veto of War Prohibition," *New York Times,* 28 October 1919.

2. "Dry Enforcement Law Enacted by False Pretenses, Elihu Root Says," *San Francisco Chronicle,* 7 November 1919.

3.   *Jacob Ruppert v. Caffey,* 251 U. S. 264, 307 (1920).

4.   William E. Leuchtenburg, "The New Deal and the Analogue of War," in *Change and Continuity in Twentieth-Century America,* ed. John Braeman, Robert H. Bremner, and Everett Walters (Columbus: Ohio State University Press, 1964), 81-143.

5.   Randolph Bourne, *The State* (Tucson, AZ: See Sharp Press, 1998). Government power is more than "the size or duration of its institutions," writes Christopher Capozzola, *Uncle Sam Wants You: World War I and the Making of the Modern American Citizen* (Oxford: Oxford University Press, 2010), 12-13.

6.   The war was "the extraordinary culmination of the progressive movement" and its "best opportunity," and also "the death knell for the progressive movement," writes Michael McGerr, *A Fierce Discontent: The Rise and Fall of the Progressive Movement in America, 1870-1920* (New York: Free Press, 2003), 280-281.

7.   Harry N. Scheiber, *The Wilson Administration and Civil Liberties, 1917-1921* (Ithaca, NY: Cornell University Press, 1960).

8.   Robert Justin Goldstein, *Political Repression in Modern America from 1870 to 1976* (Urbana: University of Illinois Press, 2001), 100-101.

9.   Goldstein, *Political Repression,* 113, 115; 249 U.S. 211 (1919).

10.   Laura Weinrib, *The Taming of Free Speech: America's Civil Liberties Compromise* (Cambridge, MA: Harvard University Press, 2016), 105.

11.   Goldstein, *Political Repression,* 128.

12.   Goldstein, *Political Repression,* 129.

13.   See Joan M. Jensen, *Army Surveillance in America, 1775-1980* (New Haven, CT: Yale University Press, 1991), 141-144. On vigilantism, see Capozzola, *Uncle Sam Wants You,* 52, inter alia.

14.   Goldstein, *Political Repression,* 112.

15.   Report of the Board of Governors of the National Bureau of Criminal Identification, RMP, box 214.

16.   Burns's Letter to Police Chiefs, 12 November 1921, RMP, box 214.

17.   John M. Barry, *The Great Influenza: The Story of the Deadliest Pandemic in History* (New York: Penguin, 2004).

18.   Goldstein, *Political Repression,* 145-146. Also see Ahmed White, *Under the Iron Heel: The Wobblies and the Capitalist War on Radical Workers* (Berkeley: University of California Press, 2022).

19.   See David Kennedy, *Over Here: The First World War and American Society* (Oxford: Oxford University Press, 1982); Daniel T. Rodgers, *Atlantic Crossings:*

Social Politics in a Progressive Age (Cambridge, MA: Harvard University Press, 1998).

20. Goldstein, *Political Repression*, 155, 159.

21. Weinrib, *Taming of Free Speech*, 116

22. Goldstein, *Political Repression*, 145–146.

23. See Lisa McGirr, "The Passion of Sacco and Vanzetti: A Global History," *Journal of American History* 93, no. 4 (2007).

24. Goldstein, *Political Repression*, 183

25. Ann V. Collins, *All Hell Broke Loose: American Race Riots from the Progressive Era through World War II* (Santa Barbara: Praeger, 2012), 71.

26. "For Action on Race Riot Peril," *New York Times*, 5 October 1919.

27. Alfred L. Brophy, *Reconstructing the Dreamland: The Tulsa Riot of 1921; Race, Reparations, and Reconciliation* (Oxford: Oxford University Press, 2002), 27.

28. Collins, *All Hell Broke Loose*, 16, 65.

29. Brophy, *Reconstructing the Dreamland*, 63.

30. David Taft Terry, *The Struggle and the Urban South: Confronting Jim Crow in Baltimore before the Movement* (Athens: University of Georgia Press, 2019).

31. Silvan Niedermeier, *The Color of the Third Degree: Racism, Police Torture, and Civil Rights in the American South, 1930–1955*, trans. Paul Cohen (Chapel Hill: University of North Carolina Press, 2019).

32. 262 U.S. 390 (1923). Social reform idealism against liberal individualism contributed to the postbellum conservative backlash, observes McGerr in *A Fierce Discontent*, chap. 9. Michael Willrich locates the "first war on crime" in Prohibition Era Chicago, the "tide of American progressivism" having fallen after World War I. See Willrich, *City of Courts: Socializing Justice in Progressive Era Chicago* (Cambridge: Cambridge University Press, 2003), 281.

33. Trevor George Gardner, "Immigrant Sanctuary as the 'Old Normal': A Brief History of Police Federalism," *Columbia Law Review* 119, no. 1 (January 2019): 34.

34. John Allen Krout, *The Origins of Prohibition* (New York: Knopf, 1925), 297.

35. See Daniel Okrent, *Last Call: The Rise and Fall of Prohibition* (New York: Simon and Schuster, 2010), 42.

36. McGerr, *A Fierce Discontent*, 83.

37. Lisa M. F. Andersen, *The Politics of Prohibition: American Governance and the Prohibition Party, 1869–1933* (Cambridge: Cambridge University Press, 2013), 63, 283.

38. Jack S. Blocker Jr., *Retreat from Reform: The Prohibition Movement in the United States, 1890–1913* (Westport, CT: Greenwood Press, 1976), 10–15.

39. Jimmie Lewis Franklin, *Born Sober: Prohibition in Oklahoma, 1907–1959* (Norman: University of Oklahoma Press, 1971).

40. Andersen, *The Politics of Prohibition*, 227.

41. On progressives and Prohibition, see Lisa McGirr, *The War on Alcohol: Prohibition and the Rise of the American State* (New York: W. W. Norton, 2015), 25.

42. Marc Mappen, *Prohibition Gangsters: The Rise and Fall of a Bad Generation* (New Brunswick, NJ: Rutgers University Press, 2013).

43. Weinrib, *Taming of Free Speech*, 163

44. On automobiles, policing, and federalism, see Sarah A. Seo, *Policing the Open Road: How Cars Transformed American Freedom* (Harvard University Press, 2019).

45. McGirr, *The War on Alcohol*, 31–37.

46. Daniel C. Richman and Sarah Seo, "How Federalism Built the FBI, Sustained Local Police, and Left Out the States," *Stanford Journal of Civil Rights and Civil Liberties* 17 (2022): 443.

47. David E. Kyvig, *Repealing National Prohibition* (Kent, OH: Kent State University Press, 2000), 108.

48. US Constitution, Amendment 18. The Sheppard-Towner Act of 1921, another concurrent jurisdiction experiment, produced maternal and child aid distribution with less pronounced chaos than Prohibition. See Theda Skocpol, *Protecting Soldiers and Mothers: The Political Origins of Social Policy in the United States* (Cambridge, MA: Harvard University Press, 1992), chap. 9.

49. During Prohibition, writes Trevor George Gardner, federal investment "exceeded that of any prior criminal enforcement initiative, yet never translated into an effective national enforcement regime." Gardner, "Immigrant Sanctuary," 37.

50. Robert Post, "Federalism, Positive Law, and the Emergence of the American Administrative State: Prohibition in the Taft Court Era," *William and Mary Law Review* 48, no. 1 (2006): 27.

51. Gardner, "Immigrant Sanctuary," 37, 44–45.

52. Michael A. Lerner, *Dry Manhattan: Prohibition in New York City* (Cambridge, MA: Harvard University Press, 2007), 73, 76.

53. Kyvig, *Repealing National Prohibition*, 108.

54. Additional Memorandum on the Subject of Proposed Federal Amendment, 2 August 1933, RMP, box 214.

55. Memorandum in Support of Proposed Amendment to the United States Constitution Giving Congress Concurrent Jurisdiction with the States over Certain Crimes, 1 August 1933, RMP box 214.

56. Chamber of Commerce . . . on the Subject of National Police Bureau, 24 September 1925, RMP, box 214.

57. Memorandum on Federal Police Reorganization, RMP, box 214.

58. Hoover to Vollmer, 13 April 1926; Hoover to Vollmer 4 March 1927; Hoover to Vollmer, 19 March 1932—all BPD, box 14: FBI.

59. Uthai Vincent Wilcox, "The American Policeman," *Welfare Magazine,* March 1928, 289.

60. Superintendent's Report, November 1920, RSPC, box 10: Annual Report 1920.

61. Post, "Federalism, Positive Law," 17–21; on interesting divides over wiretapping, see 27.

62. Lerner, *Dry Manhattan,* 65.

63. "Ohio 'Drys' Demand a National Drive against Gov. Cox," *New York Times,* 16 July 1920.

64. "Prohibition Issue Dead, Cox Repeats," *New York Times,* 14 September 1920.

65. Text of John W. Davis's Address Accepting Presidential Nomination, *New York Times,* 12 August 1924.

66. See McGirr, *The War on Alcohol,* chaps. 4 and 5.

67. *Literary Digest,* 13 September 1924, 32; "The Most Lawless Nation," *Washington Post,* 24 April 1929.

68. "U.S. Most Lawless Nation through Dry Law, Judge Asserts," *Washington Post,* 8 April 1926.

69. Irving Fisher, *Prohibition at Its Worst* (New York: Macmillan, 1926), 229–230, 238.

70. Mabel Walker Willebrandt, *The Inside of Prohibition* (Indianapolis: Bobbs-Merrill, 1929), 123, inter alia.

71. 1928 Democratic Party Platform, 26 June 1928, APPUCSB.

72. "Prohibition Evils," *Irish Times,* 29 October 1928. On the 1928 realignment, see McGirr, *The War on Alcohol,* chap. 6.

73. Roosevelt to Betts, 21 December 1928, in *F.D.R.: His Personal Letters, 1928–1945,* ed. Elliott Roosevelt (New York: Duell, Sloan and Pearce, 1950), 20 (hereafter cited as *FDR Letters*).

74. Roosevelt to Howe, 3 October 1929, *FDR Letters,* 75.

75. Roosevelt to Bowie, 9 October 1930, *FDR Letters,* 146.

76. Roosevelt to Lewisohn, 4 February 1930, *FDR Letters,* 106–107.

77. To Vollmer, 19 July 1926, RMP, box 24, folder 30.

78. Miller to Moley, 18 October 1928, RMP, box 37.

79. Also see Raymond Moley, *Tribunes of the People: The Past and Future of the New York Magistrates' Courts* (New Haven, CT: Yale University Press, 1932).

80. Moley, "The Initiation of Criminal Prosecution by Indictment or Information," RMP, box 204.

81. FDR to Moley, 24 February 1930, RMP, box 198.

82. Sutherland to Moley, 1 December 1928, RMP, box 206.

83. Moley, "Memorandum on an Institute of Criminology," RMP, box 206.

84. Roosevelt to Gannettt, 4 January 1930, *FDR Letters,* 99–100.

85. For Release in Morning Newspapers of Monday, 27 January 1930, RMP, box 198.

86. Roosevelt to Owen, 28 January 1929, *FDR Letters,* 25.

87. David M. Kennedy, *Freedom from Fear: The American People in Depression and War, 1929–1945* (New York: Oxford University Press, 1999), 60.

88. Roosevelt to Bonbright, 11 March 1930, *FDR Letters,* 109.

89. Howe to Roosevelt, 23 May 1930, *FDR Letters,* 126.

90. Roosevelt to Bonbright, 11 March 1930, *FDR Letters,* 109–111.

91. Roosevelt to Guffey, 26 June 1930, *FDR Letters,* 134.

92. Lerner, *Dry Manhattan,* 295.

93. "Crime War Everyone's," *New York Times,* 26 November 1930.

94. Daniel C. Richman, "The Past, Present, and Future of Violent Crime Federalism," *Crime and Justice* 34 (2006): 385.

95. Homer Cummings and Carl McFarland, *Federal Justice: Chapters in the History of Justice and the Federal Executive* (New York: Macmillan, 1937), 478.

96. "New War on Crime Revealed," *Los Angeles Times,* 23 August 1931.

97. Address of William D. Mitchell, "Abdication by States of Powers under the Constitution," HHSF, box 46, folder: Justice 1932–1933.

98. Roosevelt to Howe, 21 May 1929, *FDR Letters,* 61.

99. "Reports of the Wickersham Commission," *Journal of Criminal Law and Criminology* 22, no. 4 (November 1931), 613.

100. Britt to Wickersham, in "Enforcement of the Prohibition Laws: Official Records of the National Commission on Law Observance and Enforcement," 71st Congress, 3rd Session, Senate Document 307, 1:110. Also see McGirr, *The War on Alcohol*, 220–229.

101. National Commission on Law Observance and Enforcement, Report on Police, Washington DC, 26 June 1931, 14:1, 45.

102. "Police Forces Denounced in Wickersham Report," *Washington Times*, 2 August 1931, 1; "Our Crime Problem, Crime and the State Police," *New York Times*, 2 August 1931.

103. Relman Morin, "A Police Chief Lasts Eighteen Months: Why No One Sticks in This Position," *Los Angeles Times*, 9 August 1931, K5.

104. "Wickersham Board on Police Editorial," *Los Angeles Times*, 4 August 1931, A4.

105. Evine to Vollmer, 9 October 1931, AVP, box 14: U.S. National Commission on Law Observance and Enforcement.

106. "Police Chiefs Take Issue," *New York Times*, 2 August 1931, 19.

107. Baldwin to Moley, 15 August 1931, RMP, box 3.

108. Moley to Baldwin, 23 September 1931, RMP, box 3.

109. "Memorandum for Mr. Rosenman," 7 August 1931, *FDR Letters*, 209.

110. Kyvig, *Repealing National Prohibition*, 115.

111. Lerner, *Dry Manhattan*, 298–299.

112. Mappen, *Prohibition Gangsters*, 119.

113. Kathleen J. Frydl, "Kidnapping and State Development in the United States," *Studies in American Political Development* 20 (Spring 2006): 20–24

114. "Hoover's Order Spurs Hunt for Baby's Killers," *Chicago Daily Tribune*, 14 May 1932.

115. Public No. 189, 47 Stat. 326, chap. 271.

116. Howell to Roosevelt, 2 December 1931, *FDR Letters*, 229–232.

117. Wald, "To the Editors of the Outlook," 28 April 1932, LDWP, microfilm, reel 26.

118. "Address Accepting the Presidential Nomination at the Democratic National Convention in Chicago," 2 July 1932, APPUCSB.

119. "Here's Hoover's Dry Law Stand," *New York Times*, 12 August 1932.

120. See Fred Siegel, "The New Left, the New Right, and the New Deal," in *The Liberal Persuasion: Arthur Schlesinger, Jr., and the Challenge of the American*

Past, ed. John Patrick Diggins (Princeton, NJ: Princeton University Press, 2017), 152.

121. Kyvig, *Repealing National Prohibition,* 116–136, 161.

122. Goldstein, *Political Repression,* 202–203.

123. Francisco E. Balderrama and Raymond Rodríguez, *Decade of Betrayal: Mexican Repatriation in the 1930s* (Albuquerque: University of New Mexico Press, 2006).

124. "Bonus Groups Favor Repeal in 'Platform,'" *Washington Post,* 20 June 1932.

125. Goldstein, *Political Repression,* 197.

126. "Finds Radicals and Criminals in Bonus Army," *Chicago Daily Tribune,* 12 September 1932.

127. "Eviction of Bonus Army from Capital Rescinded," *LA Times,* 23 July 1932.

128. See Donald J. Lisio, "A Blunder Becomes Catastrophe: Hoover, the Legion, and the Bonus Army," *Wisconsin Magazine of History* 51, no. 1 (Autumn 1967); Statement on the Justice Department Investigation of the Bonus Army, 10 September 1932, APPUCSB.

129. "Hoover at Madison Assails Roosevelt," *New York Times,* 6 November 1932.

130. Summary of Editorial Content on President, 14 November 1932, HHSF, box 40, folder: Election Result (1932).

PART II. PERFECTING THE MACHINERY, 1933–1934

1. "Assassin Shoots 5 Times," *New York Times,* 16 February 1933. Eric Rauchway, in *Winter War: Hoover, Roosevelt, and the First Clash over the New Deal* (New York: Basic Books, 2018), emphasizes the assassination attempt in the high-stakes lame-duck period.

2. Roosevelt took office as "kidnapping stories thronged front pages across the country" and faced "the Great Crime Wave of 1933–1934." Bryan Burrough, *Public Enemies: America's Greatest Crime Wave and the Birth of the FBI, 1933–1934* (New York: Penguin Press, 2004), 14, 16.

3. On Roosevelt's "radical moment" in navigating American liberalism in an extremist climate, yielding the abortive and collectivist NIRA, see Ira Katznelson, *Fear Itself: The New Deal and the Origins of Our Time* (New York: W. W. Norton, 2013), 234–238.

3. "THE BASIC IDEA OF DEMOCRACY"

1. "Critic Issues an Appeal to See This Film," *Chicago Daily Tribune*, 31 March 1933.

2. Hoover to Attorney General, 23 February 1933, PHSC, box 114, folder: Herbert Hoover.

3. Justice Research and Statistics Association, *Crime and Justice Atlas 2000*, U.S. Department of Justice, 38. FBI statistics found non-negligent homicides rising during January to June 1933, reaching 3.3 out of 100,000 population, compared to 2.8 out of 100,000 from January to June 1931. Contrast *Uniform Crime Reports* 4, no. 2 (July 1933), table 1, to *Uniform Crime Reports* 2, no. 7 (July 1931), "Percentage Table of Part I Offenses," 5.

4. "Slayings in Nation Up 100% since 1900," *New York Times*, 27 April 1934.

5. "Moley Confers with President on Crime Wave," *China Press*, 4 August 1933.

6. "Zangara Given Death Penalty by Miami Judge," *Chicago Daily Tribune*, 11 March 1933.

7. Getchell to Roosevelt, 13 July 1933, OF117.

8. Upshaw to Roosevelt, 28 August 1933, OF117.

9. "Wets Fear Crime Wave Following Repeal of Eighteenth Amendment," *Washington Post*, 1 March 1933.

10. Athan Theoharis, *The FBI and American Democracy: A Brief Critical History* (Lawrence: University Press of Kansas, 2004), 40–41.

11. Memo for Mr. Stanley, 1 August 1933, PHSC, box 114, folder: J. Edgar Hoover.

12. Curt Gentry, *J. Edgar Hoover: The Man and the Secrets* (New York: W. W. Norton, 2001), 153; "Walsh Will Enforce Dry Law So Long as It Lasts, He Says," *New York Times*, 2 March 1933; "Walsh Was Noted for Fearlessness," *New York Times*, 3 March 1933; Mary M. Stolberg, "Policing the Twilight Zone: Federalizing Crime Fighting during the New Deal," *Journal of Policy History* 7, no. 4 (1995): 401.

13. "Cummings Sees the Law as a Living Thing," *New York Times*, 3 September 1933.

14. Homer Cummings and Carl McFarland, *Federal Justice: Chapters in the History of Justice and the Federal Executive* (New York: Macmillan, 1937).

15. Speech by Cummings, Bridgeport, Connecticut, 15 April 1933, OF10, box 1.

16. Broadcast over the Network of NBC, 24 April 1933, OF10, box 1.

17. Attorney General to President, 1 February 1934, OF10, box 2.

18. Speech by Cummings, 15 April 1933, OF10, box 1.

19. Franklin D. Roosevelt, Inaugural Address, 4 March 1933, APPUCSB.

20. Attorney General, 1 June 1933, OF10, box 1.

21. Executive Assistant to the Attorney General, 19 April 1934, OF10, box 2.

22. Attorney General, 17 September 1934, OF10, box 2; Attorney General, 11 November 1933, OF10, box 2. The administration wound down the Hoover-era policy of Mexican "repatriation." See Fernando Saúl and Alanís Enciso, *They Should Stay There: The Story of Mexican Migration and Repatriation during the Great Depression* (Chapel Hill: University of North Carolina Press, 2017).

23. Wendy L. Wall identifies a new mid-1930s national consensus in *Inventing the "American Way": The Politics of Consensus from the New Deal to the Civil Rights Movement* (Oxford: Oxford University Press, 2008). Historians have long engaged labor's premature optimism given Roosevelt's "balanced" approach to economic classes. William E. Leuchtenburg, *Franklin Roosevelt and the New Deal, 1932–1940* (New York: Harper and Row, 1963).

24. "Intermediary Plan Decried by Pastor," *New York Times*, 7 March 1932; "Detroit Priest Calls the Death Challenge to Wipe Out Gangster," *New York Times*, 13 May 1932.

25. Attorney General, 29 March 1933, OF10, box 1.

26. Getchell to President, 13 July 1933, OF117, box 1.

27. Dear Sir (Attorney General), 12 September 1933, OF117, box 1.

28. To Howe, 4 August 1933, OF117, box 1.

29. Jones to Roosevelt, 25 July 1933, OF117, box 1.

30. Miller, Charles A., 30 August 1933, OF10, box 1.

31. Clark to Howe, 26 May 1933, OF117, box 1.

32. Joseph A. Nelson, OF10, box 2, folder: DOJA, January–April 1934.

33. Dixon, Walter L., 23 May 1934, OF10, box 2.

34. Refer to Department of Justice, 4 May 1933, OF10, box 1.

35. MFTAG, 21 November 1933, OF10, box 1.

36. Letter to James A. Moss, 14 August 1933, APPUCSB.

37. Quotation in Tim Weiner, *Enemies: A History of the FBI* (New York: Random House, 2012), 69.

38. Cummings, "Predatory Crime," National Broadcasting Company, 11 September 1933.

39. Joseph B. Keenan, "Federal War on Crime," *New York Times,* 6 August 1933, E4.

40. Moss to Howe, 29 December 1933, OF117, box 1.

41. Stanley, Hon. William, 9 August 1934, OF10, box 2.

42. Eric Rauchway, *Winter War: Hoover, Roosevelt, and the First Clash over the New Deal* (New York: Basic Books, 2018), 3.

43. Racketeering, U.S. Bureau of Investigation, 22 May 1933, RMP, box 214.

44. Nugent to Moley, 21 August 1933, RMP, box 212.

45. Estes to Moley, 11 August 1933, RMP, box 211.

46. Dixon to Moley, 5 August 1933, RMP, box 211.

47. Dealey to Moley, 5 July 1933, RMP, box 211.

48. Doyle to Moley, 16 August 1933, RMP, box 211.

49. Assistant to Francis V. Costello, 15 August 1933, RMP, box 211.

50. Roberts to Moley, 23 August 1933, RMP, box 212.

51. Johnson to Moley, 5 August 1933, RMP, box 212.

52. J. Randolph Mann, RMP, box 212.

53. Clark to Hoover, 7 August 1933; Hoover to Clark, 16 August 1933; both RMP, box 211.

54. James E. Ryan, 3 August 1933, Indiana, RMP, box 212.

55. Hawkins to Moley, 6 August 1933, RMP, box 212.

56. Carter to Moley, 10 August 1933, RMP, box 211.

57. Gage to Moley, 15 August 1933, RMP, box 212.

58. Hampton to Moley, 8 August 1933, RMP, box 212.

59. Endicott to Moley, 2 August 1933, Iowa, RMP, box 211.

60. Nix to Park, 28 July 1933, RMP, box 212.

61. Chicago Law and Order League, 21 September 1921, RMP, box 211.

62. Galway to Roosevelt, 4 August 1933, RMP, box 212.

63. Ouzts to Moley, 2 August 1933, RMP, box 212.

64. Fillbrandt to Moley, 8 August 1933, RMP, box 211.

65. Stafford to Moley, 8 August 1933, RMP, box 212.

66. Douglass to Moley, 7 August 1933, RMP, box 211.

67. Chadbourn to Moley, 20 August 1933, RMP, box 211.

68. Royer to Moley, 2 August 1933, RMP, box 212.

69. Wampler to Moley 3 August 1933, RMP, box 212.

70. Farnsworth to Moley, 7 August 1933, RMP, box 211.

71. Castlebury to Moley, 14 August 1933, RMP, box 211.

72. Quaytman to Moley, 9 August 1933, RMP, box 212.

73. Clark to Roosevelt, 6 August 1933, RMP, box 211.

74. Favis To Moley, 25 August 1933, RMP, box 211.

75. Fulton to Moley, 3 August 1933, RMP, box 211.

76. McGrady to Moley, RMP, box 211.

77. Lillard to Moley, 9 August 1933, RMP, box 212.

78. Roberts to Moley, 3 August 1933, RMP, box 212.

79. Winn to Moley, RMP, box 212.

80. Hoover to Clark, 16 August 1933, RMP, box 211.

81. Freese to Moley, 2 August 1933, RMP, box 211.

82. Jones to Moley, 9 August 1933, RMP, box 212.

83. Dusey to Moley, 11 August 1933, RMP, box 211.

84. Fox to Moley, 8 August 1933, RMP, box 211.

85. Jenkins to Moley, 21 August 1933, RMP, box 212.

86. Lentzen to Moley, 3 August 1933, RMP, box 212.

87. Suggestions of Earl Warren, 18 August 1933, RMP, box 214.

88. Ellis to Moley, 16 August 1933, RMP, box 211.

89. National Police Bureau, Confidential, RMP, box 212.

90. Cummings, "Modern Tendencies and the Law," Address to ABA, 31 August 1933, HCDOJ.

91. See Charles Bright, *The Powers That Punish: Prison and Politics in the Era of the "Big House," 1920–1955* (Ann Arbor: University of Michigan Press, 1996).

92. Office memorandum to Keenan, 1 August 1933, in Carl Brent Swisher, ed., *Selected Papers of Homer Cummings, Attorney General of the United States, 1933–1939* (New York: Charles Scribner's Sons, 1939) (hereafter cited as *SPHC*), 29.

93. Memorandum from Bates, 8 August 1933, in *SPHC*, 30.

94. Letter to Dern, 14 October 1933, in *SPHC*, 30.

95. "An Island Prison," *Washington Post,* 15 October 1933, 6.

96. Beverly Gage, *G-Man: J. Edgar Hoover and the Making of the American Century* (New York: Penguin Random House, 2022), 148.

97. Gage, *G-Man,* 153–154.

98. Hoover to Cummings, 16 August 1933, PHSC, box 114, folder: J. Edgar Hoover.

99. Matthew Denney emphasizes the break between Cummings's New Deal "holistic vision" and the war on crime that later came. Matthew G. T. Denney, "'To Wage a War': Crime, Race, and State Making in the Age of FDR," *Studies in American Political Development* 35, no. 1 (2021): 13.

100. Hughes approved an aluminum company deal that Cummings opposed on antitrust grounds. Cummings to House, 8 February 1933, PHSC, box 114, folder: Misc., House.

101. Murphy to Cummings, 2 April 1934, PHSC, box 135.

102. Cummings, "Our Widening Life," address delivered at Oglethorpe University, Georgia, 27 May 1934, https://www.justice.gov/ag/speeches -attorney-general-homer-stille-cummings.

103. "A Twelve Point Program," Address Delivered before . . . Daughters of the American Revolution, 19 April 1934, PHSC, box 213.

104. Cummings to Mr. President, 21 July 1933; "New Deal's Results," 18 July 1933, *Pittsburgh Press,* OF10, box 1.

105. Keenan to Howe, 1 August 1933, OF10, box 1.

106. Cummings to President, 7 November 1934, OF10, box 2.

107. Speech by Cummings, 15 April 1933, OF10, box 1.

108. Cummings to President, 4 May 1933, OF10, box 1.

109. Cummings to Mr. President, 29 May 1933, OF10, box 1.

110. Attorney General to President, 10 March 1934, OF10, box 2.

111. Attorney General, 28 July 1933, OF10, box 1.

112. Peter H. Irons, *The New Deal Lawyers* (Princeton, NJ: Princeton University Press, 1982).

113. Quotation in Claire Bond Potter, *War on Crime: Bandits, G-Men, and the Politics of Mass Culture* (New Brunswick, NJ: Rutgers University Press, 1998), 122.

114. Cummings, "The Campaign against Crime," 22 November 1933, HCDOJ; Cummings, "Progress toward a Modern Administration of Criminal Justice in the United States," 27 April 1936, in *SPHC*, 45–48.

115. Memorandum for Tugwell, 20 April 1933, OF10, box 1.

116. Attorney General, 7 September 1933, OF10, box 1.

117. Attorney General Cummings, 4 April 1933, OF10, box 1.

118. Acting Attorney General to President, 26 October 1933, OF10, box 1.

119. Attorney General to Howe, 25 May 1934, OF10, box 2.

120. Attorney General, 11 September 1933, OF10, box 1.

121. Director of the Budget, Attorney General, State, Secretary, 28 May 1934, OF10, box 2.

122. Secretary of Labor, 18 June 1934, OF10, box 2.

123. Cummings to President, 17 November 1933, OF10, box 1.

124. Secretary of Agriculture, 17 October 1933, OF10, box 1.

125. Federal Emergency Relief Administrator Hopkins, 11 November 1933, OF10, box 1.

126. Opinion of the Attorney General, 13 April 1934, OF10, box 2.

127. Exec. Order . . . Jurisdiction to the Attorney General for Determination, OF10, box 2.

128. Referred to the Attorney General, 15 November 1934, OF10, box 2.

129. Attorney General, 23 August 1933, OF10, box 1.

130. Cummings to President, 9 October 1933 OF10, box 1.

131. Broadcast over the Network of NBC, 24 April 1933, OF10, box 1.

4. "FEDERAL BULLETS"

1.   Lawrence M. Friedman, *Crime and Punishment in American History* (New York: Basic Books, 1993), 271, stresses 1934's importance. Matthew G. T. Denney, "'To Wage a War': Crime, Race, and State Making in the Age of FDR," *Studies in American Political Development* 35, no. 1 (2021): 39, sees the war on crime peaking in 1934, with a ratchet effect. Michael Willrich credits the 1934 statutes together with the 1937 Marihuana Tax Act for expanding federal "criminal jurisdiction . . . and especially the Bureau of Investigation." Willrich, "Criminal Justice in the United States," in *The Cambridge History of Law in America*, vol. 3: *The Twentieth Century and After (1920–)*, ed. Michael Grossberg and Christopher Tomlins (Cambridge: Cambridge University Press, 2008), 210–211. Bryan Burrough accentuates the early 1930s in *Public Enemies: America's Greatest Crime Wave and the Birth of the FBI, 1933–1934* (New York: Penguin, 2004). The early 1930s cultural resonance and state building are the focus of Clare Potter's *War on Crime: Bandits, G-Men, and the Politics of Mass*

Culture (New Brunswick, NJ: Rutgers University Press, 1998). David E. Ruth, *Inventing the Public Enemy: The Gangster in American Culture, 1918–1934* (Chicago: Chicago University Press, 1996), 8, minimizes the New Deal's impact. Others distinguish the early 1930s FBI war on crime from later 1930s national security questions. See Athan Theoharis, *The FBI and American Democracy: A Brief Critical History* (Lawrence: University Press of Kansas, 2004); and Kenneth O'Reilly, "A New Deal for the FBI: The Roosevelt Administration, Crime Control, and National Security," *Journal of American History* 69, no. 3 (December 1982): 638–658.

2. *Congressional Record, Proceedings and Debates of the Second Sessions of the 73rd Congress of the United States*, vol. 78 (1934) (hereafter cited as CR73:78), 10–11. On Prohibition repeal as a repudiation of one of the very "powerful political lobbies," see David M. Kennedy, *Freedom from Fear: The American People in Depression and War, 1929–1945* (New York: Oxford University Press, 1999), 139. Lisa McGirr, *The War on Alcohol: Prohibition and the Rise of the American State* (New York: W. W. Norton, 2015), shows how Prohibition both expanded federal power and mobilized the backlash that redirected its 1930s ideological trajectory.

3. Annual Message to Congress, 3 January 1934, APPUCSB.

4. National Radio Forum, 10 January 1934, *SPHC*, 11–12.

5. "Slayings in Nation Up 100% since 1900," *New York Times*, 27 April 1934.

6. CR73:78, pt. 1, 120.

7. Public No. 62, 48 Stat. 152.

8. See Daniel C. Richman, "The Changing Boundaries between Federal and Local Law Enforcement," *Criminal Justice* 2 (2000): 81–82, 87.

9. "A Twelve Point Program," 19 April 1934, PHSC, box 213.

10. Cummings to Ashurst, 15 March 1934, CR73:78, pt. 3, 2947.

11. CR73:78, pt. 8, 8129; on S. 2842, allowing spousal testimony, see CR73:78, pt. 3, 2947; Moley, "To the President," 15 May 1934, OF10, box 2.

12. CR73:78, pt. 7, 6854.

13. CR73:78, pt. 1, 450.

14. CR73:78, pt. 8, 8043, 8148, 8653.

15. CR73:78, pt. 6, 5737–5738; CR73:78, pt. 4, 3732.

16. CR73:78, pt. 6, 5738.

17. CR73:78, pt. 6, 5735.

18. CR73:78, pt. 5, 5082.

19. CR73:78, pt. 6, 5859.

20. S. 822, CR73:78, pt. 7, 7255.

21. For final House deliberations on S. 2252, "A bill amending the Lindbergh Act," see CR73:78, pt. 8, 8127–8218. On S. 2845 see CR73:78, pt.7, 6981.

22. See Joseph B. Keenan, "Bills Drafted by Department of Justice in Aid of Law Enforcement," *ABA Journal* 20, no. 4 (April 1934): 306.

23. Memorandum for the President from Stephen Early, 17 May 1934, OF10, box 2.

24. Statement on Signing Crime Bill, 18 May 1934, APPUCSB.

25. Bell, Memorandum for the President, 19 November 1934, OF10, box 2.

26. CR73:78, pt. 10, 10590.

27. CR73:78, pt. 10, 10865.

28. Beverly Gage, *G-Man: J. Edgar Hoover and the Making of the American Century* (New York: Penguin Random House, 2022), 156–157, 171.

29. "A Twelve Point Program," in *SPHC*, 24, 25–26.

30. Shepherd to Hall, 2 June 1933, OF117, box 1.

31. Carol Skalnik Leff and Mark H. Leff, "The Politics of Ineffectiveness: Federal Firearms Legislation, 1919–38," *Annals of the American Academy of Political and Social Science*, vol. 455, *Gun Control* (May 1981), 53–54.

32. CR73:78, pt. 1, 456.

33. CR73:78, pt. 10, 11400.

34. CR73:78, pt. 11, 12400.

35. CR73:78, pt. 7, 6855.

36. Carl Bakal, *The Right to Bear Arms* (New York: McGraw-Hill Book Co., 1966), 166–177, stresses missed opportunity rather than accomplishment.

37. "Moley Detached for Crime Survey," *New York Times,* 3 August 1933. On the internal politics behind the transfer, see Julius W. Pratt, "The Ordeal of Cordell Hull," *Review of Politics* 28, no. 1 (1966): 76–98.

38. Moley, "To the President, First of Three Sections of a Report," 15 May 1934, OF10, box 2.

39. "First Section Draft," RMP, box 214.

40. The First of Three Sections of a Report . . . , 15 May 1934, RMP, box 214.

41. Wildman to Morgenthau, 30 August 1934, OF21, box 20, folder: Treasury— Alcohol Tax Unit, 1934–1935.

42. Attorney General, 5 March 1934, OF10, box 2.

43. Minutes of the Meeting, 11 September 1934, ROLEC, box 1.

44. Minutes of the Meeting, 30 October 1934, ROLEC, box 1.

45. Minutes of the Meeting, 9 October 1934, ROLEC, box 1; Minutes of the Meeting, 11 September 1934, ROLEC, box 1.

46. Memorandum for Morgenthau, 18 September 1934, ROLEC, box 1; Minutes of the Meeting, 11 September 1934, ROLEC, box 1.

47. Coast Guard Headquarters, 12 December 1934, 20 December 1934, ROLEC, box 1.

48. Exec. Assistant to Attorney General to Howe, 21 April 1934, OF10, box 2.

49. Howe to Attorney General, 2 May 1934, OF10, box 2; Director of Bureau of Budget to Sec. of State, 26 April 1934, OF10, box 2.

50. Dedication of the Building for the Department of Justice, Washington, D.C., October 25th 1934 Program, President, Chief Justice, OF10, box 2.

51. Dedication of the New Building for the Department of Justice, 10 May 1934, PHSC, box 218; Albert W. Fox, "Dedication of New Home of Department of Justice," *American Bar Association Journal* (November 1934).

52. Roosevelt to Attorney General, 10 May 1934, PHSC, box 218.

53. Justice Department, 26 September 1934 (1 October 1934), OF10, box 2.

54. Attorney General, 21 March 1934, OF10, box 2.

55. Attorney General, 20 July 1934, OF10, box 2.

56. Stephens, Harold M., 6 August 1934, OF10, box 2.

57. Cummings to President, 21 July 1934, OF10, box 1.

58. MFTAG, 6 September 1934, OF10, box 2.

59. Attorney General, 14 September 1934, OF10, box 2.

60. Baldwin thought that "Roosevelt, despite himself, is bound by the enormous power of property interest" and might ultimately bring "monopoly capital to an even stronger position." Baldwin to Winston, 6 November 1934, RBP, box 10, folder 9.

61. Confidential MFTAG, 11 September 1934, OF10, box 2.

62. CR73:78: 7–23.

63. Kenneth O'Reilly, "The Roosevelt Administration and Black America," *Phylon* 48, no. 1 (1987): 14.

64. Alan Brinkley found that the New Deal's consolidation and redefinition of liberalism often overlooked "issues of race, ethnicity, family, gender, and

personal behavior—in part because they feared the cultural and political battles such issues had produced in the 1920s." Brinkley, *The End of Reform: New Deal Liberalism in Recession and War* (New York: Vintage Books, 1996 [1995]), 9. In *Racial Realignment: The Transformation of American Liberalism, 1932–1965* (Princeton, NJ: Princeton University Press, 2016), Eric Schickler stresses labor history in Black receptivity to the New Deal and liberalism's shift toward civil rights.

65. Address by Cummings, 30 October 1934, HCDOJ.

66. Tennessee and Mississippi Sheriffs and Peace Officers Association, 8 November 1934, OF10, box 2.

67. *New York Times*, 11 December 1934.

68. Hebron, James M., 20 August 1934, OF10, box 2; Early to McIntyre (telegram), 13 September 1934, OF10, box 2.

69. Kannee to White House, 22 September 1934, OF10, box 2; Cummings, Homer, 25 September 1934, OF10, box 2.

70. Address to Conference on Crime, 10 December 1934, APPUCSB.

71. Address by Glueck, 11 December 1934, *PAGCC*.

72. Hoover, "Detection and Apprehension," 11 December 1934, *PAGCC*.

73. Fulton Oursler, "Opportunities of the Press in War against Crime," 11 December 1934, *PAGCC*.

74. Sanford Bates, "Protection as a Penal Policy," 12 December 1934, *PAGCC*.

75. Address by Anslinger, 13 December 1934, *PAGCC*.

76. Address by Cummings, 10 December 1934, *PAGCC*.

77. Address by Glueck, 11 December 1934, *PAGCC*.

78. Scott M. Lofflin, "Opening Remarks," 12 December 1934, *PAGCC*.

79. William Draper Lewis, "Restating Criminal Law and Improving Criminal Procedure," 13 December 1934, *PAGCC*.

80. Gordon Dean, 11 December 1934, *PAGCC*.

81. Address by Anslinger, December 13, 1934, *PAGCC*.

82. Joseph B. Keenan, "The Federal Government and the Crime Problem," 12 December 1934, *PAGCC*.

83. Earl Warren, "Organizing the Community to Combat Crime," 12 December 1934, *PAGCC*.

84. Address by Gilbert Bettman, 11 December 1934, *PAGCC*.

85. J. C. B. Ehringhaus, "The State's Crime Problem," 12 December 1934, *PAGCC*.

86. "Mob Violence Hit in Program," *Chicago Defender,* 29 December 1934.

87. "The Crime Conference," *Chicago Defender,* 22 December 1934.

88. Laura Weinrib, *The Taming of Free Speech: America's Civil Liberties Compromise* (Cambridge, MA: Harvard University Press, 2016), 199.

89. Earl W. Evans, "Crime, the Community and the Lawyer," 12 December 1934, *PAGCC.*

90. H. V. Kaltenborn, "Radio and Crime," 11 December 1934, *PAGCC.*

91. Address by Grove Patterson, 11 December 1934; address by Stanley Walker, 11 December 1934—both *PAGCC.*

92. Charles W. Hoffman, "Cincinnati Juvenile Court," 11 December 1934, *PAGCC.*

93. Katharine F. Lenroot, "Old and New Methods of Dealing with Vagrants and the Delinquents," 13 December 1934, *PAGCC.*

94. Address by Anslinger, 13 December 1934, *PAGCC.*

95. Sanford Bates, "Protection as a Penal Policy," 12 December 1934, *PAGCC.*

96. James A. Johnston, "The Function of the Modern Prison," *PAGCC.*

97. Hoover, "Detection and Apprehension," *PAGCC.*

98. Hoover, "Detection and Apprehension," *PAGCC.*

99. Public No. 291, 48 Stat. 881.

100. *Uniform Crime Reports* 3, no. 4 (January 1933): 4; *Uniform Crime Reports* 4, no. 4 (January 1934): 4; *Uniform Crime Reports* 5, no. 4 (January 1935): 4.

101. Roosevelt, *Public Papers of the Presidents of the United States, F.D. Roosevelt, 1934,* 3:242–243.

PART III. THE WAR ON CRIME CONSTITUTION, 1933–1941

1. Norbert C. Brockman, "The History of the American Bar Association: A Bibliographic Essay," *American Journal of Legal History* 6, no. 3 (July 1962): 269–285.

2. Scholars contest the plan's effect on Supreme Court voting. See Daniel E. Ho and Kevin M. Quinn, "Did a Switch in Time Save Nine?," *Journal of Legal Analysis* 2, no. 1 (Spring 2010): 69–113.

3. William J. Donovan, "An Independent Supreme Court and the Protection of Minority Rights," *American Bar Association Journal* 23, no. 4 (1937): 254–296.

4. *Strauder v. West Virginia,* 100 U.S. 303 (1880); *Bush v. Kentucky,* 107 U.S. 110 (1883); *Powell v. Alabama,* 287 U.S. 45; *Brown v. Mississippi,* 297 U.S. 278;

Wong Wing v. United States, 163 U.S. 228; *Meyer v. Nebraska,* 262 U.S. 390 (1923); *Bartels v. Iowa,* 262 U.S. 404 (1923); *Pierce v. Society of Sisters,* 268 U.S. 510 (1925); *Whitney v. California,* 274 U.S. 357 (1927); *Stromberg v. California,* 283 U.S. 359 (1931); *De Jonge v. State of Oregon,* 299 U.S. 353 (1937).

5.   See, for example, William E. Forbath, "The New Deal Constitution in Exile," *Duke Law Journal* 51, no. 1 (2001): 165–222.

5. THE ANTI-CRIME CONSENSUS IN LEGAL THOUGHT

1.   Memorandum Approving a Bill for Judicial Reform, 26 August 1937, APPUCSB.

2.   Moley, "What Is Constitutional Government?," 6 April 1937, RMP, box 238.

3.   Moley to Van Nuys, 26 July 1937, RMP, box 90.

4.   To Joseph C. O'Mahoney, 26 July 1937, RMP, box 90.

5.   Johnson to Moley, 13 March 1937, RMP, box 90.

6.   Cummings, "Modernizing Federal Procedure," *ABA Journal* 24, no. 8 (August 1938): 626.

7.   Jackson questioned the "economic value of our formulae of 'due process of law' or of 'freedom of contract' to the 12,000,000 American families whose average income in the prosperous year of 1929 was under $1,500.00." Robert J. Jackson, "The Bar and the New Deal," *ABA Journal* 21, no. 2 (February 1935).

8.   See Peter H. Irons, *The New Deal Lawyers* (Princeton, NJ: Princeton University Press, 1982). Daniel J. Hulsebosch focuses on economics in "The New Deal Court: Emergence of a New Reason," *Columbia Law Review* 90, no. 7 (November 1990): 1973–2016. Bruce Ackerman harmonizes political culture and constitutional history in *We the People: Transformations* (Cambridge, MA: Harvard University Press, 1998), 312–382.

9.   *Moore v. Dempsey,* 261 U.S. 86 (1923). Michael J. Klarman argues that *Moore* was the first of four interwar cases in which "the constitutional law of state criminal procedure was born." Klarman, "The Racial Origins of Modern Criminal Procedure," *Michigan Law Review* 99, no. 1 (October 2000): 48. Also see Megan Ming Francis, *Civil Rights and the Making of the American State* (New York: Cambridge University Press, 2014), 127–129.

10.   *Powell v. Alabama,* 287 U. S. 60, 76.

11.   Extending the due process clause to Bill of Rights protections reverberated in future cases. See Samuel Hendel, *Charles Evans Hughes and the Supreme Court* (New York: King's Crown Press, Columbia University, 1951), 96–97.

12.   Robert E. Ireton recognized *Powell* as balancing federalism with procedural "due process": "The borderland of federal and state authority" must be studied with "a sense of delicacy and a faculty of keen discernment." Ireton, "Due Process in Criminal Trials," *United States Law Review* 67 (1933): 89.

13.   The "Lochner era" began in 1905 when the Supreme Court overturned New York labor regulation on Fourteenth Amendment "due process" grounds. According to traditional narratives, the Court's conservatives stifled economic regulation until the court-packing scheme intimidated them into upholding New Deal legislation. For critical accounts, see G. Edward White, *The Constitution and the New Deal* (Cambridge, MA: Harvard University Press, 2000); Duncan Kennedy, *The Rise and Fall of Classical Legal Thought* (Washington, DC: Beard Books, 2006 [1975]); Barry Cushman, *Rethinking the New Deal Court: The Structure of a Constitutional Revolution* (New York: Oxford University Press, 1998); Howard Gillman, *The Constitution Besieged: The Rise and Demise of Lochner Era Police Powers Jurisprudence* (Durham, NC: Duke University Press, 1993); Morton Horwitz, *The Transformation of American Law, 1870–1960: The Crisis of Legal Orthodoxy* (Oxford: Oxford University Press, 1992); and David Bernstein, *Rehabilitating Lochner: Defending Individual Rights against Progressive Reform* (Chicago: University of Chicago Press, 2011). On the Warren Court's political impact on such narratives, see Laura Kalman, *The Strange Career of Legal Liberalism* (New Haven, CT: Yale University Press, 1998).

   Discourse on "substantive due process" has often conflated the issues of federal authority over state policies and whether economic regulation violates due process. Nuanced opinions on economic policy, criminal procedure, and federalism defy the typical Lochner story ending in 1937. Sutherland supported federal intervention against states for both "substantive due process" and procedural protections. Butler opposed federal securing of state defendants' rights but scrutinized federal and state regulation. And in 1923 Butler and Van Devanter joined McReynolds in *Meyer v. Nebraska,* upholding the Fourteenth Amendment right to teach German. Sutherland (and Holmes) dissented. 262 U.S. 390 (1923). Yet in 1931 all the Court's conservatives dissented from a decision that struck down Minnesota's laws restraining anti-Semitic and hateful speech. See *Near v. Minnesota,* 283 U.S. 697 (1931). Legal thinkers could, moreover, support judicial review of state but not federal legislation.

14.   Roger M. Smith, *Liberalism and Constitutional Law* (Cambridge, MA: Harvard University Press, 1990 [1985]), 67, traces interpretive due process disagreements "to the basic tension between the empiricist and rationalistic natural law theories that were combined in early liberalism and American constitutional thought."

15. Postwar legal literature grappled with politicized distinctions. See Virginia Wood, *Due Process of Law, 1932–1949: The Supreme Court's Use of a Constitutional Tool* (Baton Rouge: Louisiana State University Press, 1951).

16. A 1938 Census Bureau survey found that about one-fifth of defendants went to trial. Judicial Criminal Statistics, U.S. Dept. of Commerce, 1938, 8, DCBC, box 48.

17. Attorney General, 27 March 1933, OF10, box 1; William Draper Lewis, 11 April 1934, OF10, box 2.

18. George Z. Medalie, "Making Criminal Prosecution More Effective," *ABA Journal* 21, no. 8 (August 1935): 504–505.

19. "Seek Facts on Criminal Law from the Bar," *ABA Journal* 20, no. 1 (January 1934); George T. McDermott, "The Work of the American Law Institute," *ABA Journal* 21, no. 9 (September 1935).

20. William Shafroth, "The Bar Reports on Some Phases of Criminal Law," *ABA Journal* 20, no. 8 (August 1934).

21. "Fifty-Seventh Annual Meeting Deals with Important Problems," *ABA Journal* 20, no. 10 (October 1934): 651–652.

22. Newman F. Baker and Earl H. DeLong, "The Prosecuting Attorney: Powers and Duties in Criminal Prosecution," *American Institute of Criminal Law and Criminology* 24 (1933): 1025. One prosecutor called the defendant a "human gorilla," "a slobbering wild boar," and a "mad dog." See Baker, "Prosecuting Attorney: Legal Aspects of the Office," *Journal of Criminal Law and Criminology* 26, no. 5 (1936): 661.

23. Cummings, "Immediate Problems for the Bar," *ABA Journal* 20, no. 4 (April 1934): 213.

24. "A Twelve Point Program," 19 April 1934, PHSC, box 213.

25. "Attorney General Recommends Bills Relating to Criminal Law," *ABA Journal* 20, no. 5 (April 1934).

26. "Resolutions Adopted by the Crime Conference," *ABA Journal* 21, no. 1 (January 1935).

27. Cummings to Howe, 26 April 1934, OF10, box 2.

28. Joseph P. Chamberlain, "Department of Current Legislation," *ABA Journal* 19, no. 3 (March 1933).

29. Philip Kates, "A New Deal for Justice," *ABA Journal* 20, no. 3 (March 1934).

30. "Criminal Procedure and Rule-Making Authority," *Journal of the American Judicature Society* 18 (1935): 187.

31. Justin Miller, "Lawyers and the Administration of Criminal Justice," *ABA Journal* 20, no. 2 (February 1934).

32. Cummings, "Immediate Problems for the Bar," 212–213.

33. "Address of Attorney General Cummings to Judicial Conference, Fourth Circuit," *ABA Journal* 21, no. 7 (July 1935): 403.

34. "A Twelve Point Program," 19 April 1934, PHSC, box 213.

35. Cummings, "The Lawyer Criminal," *ABA Journal* 20, no. 2 (February 1934): 82.

36. Cummings, "Progress toward a Modern Administration of Criminal Justice in the United States," *ABA Journal* 22, no. 5 (May 1936): 345.

37. Pierre Crabités, "Why American Criminal Justice Is a Failure," *ABA Journal* 23, no. 9 (September 1937): 700–702.

38. "Fifty-Seventh Annual Meeting Deals with Important Problems," 652.

39. Address of Chief Justice Hughes, *ABA Journal* 19, no. 6 (June 1933).

40. Clarence E. Martin, "The Growing Impotency of the States," *ABA Journal* 19, no. 9 (October 1933): 548.

41. To Roosevelt, 5 August 1935, OF10, box 2.

42. Cummings to President, 23 December 1935, OF10, box 3.

43. State courts, for example, considered federal trends when ruling on their own state constitutions' right to waive a jury trial. See Erwin N. Griswold, "The Historical Development of Waiver of Jury Trial in Criminal Cases," *Virginia Law Review* 20, no. 6 (1933–1934): 655–669.

44. Edward D. Ransom, "Criminal Law and Procedure—Appeal by State—Constitutionality of Statutes—Due Process of Law," *Michigan Law Review* 37, no. 1 (November 1938): 103–113.

45. Wm. Brunyate, "The American Draft Code of Criminal Procedure, 1930," *Law Quarterly Review* 49, no. 2 (April 1933): 192–214.

46. J. A. C. Grant, "The Bill of Rights and Criminal Law Enforcement," *Annals of the American Academy of Political and Social Science* 175, "The Shadow of War" (September 1934): 213.

47. Ernest C. Carman, "A Plea for Withdrawal of Constitutional Privilege from the Criminal," *Minnesota Law Review* 22 (1938): 209–210.

48. Cummings, "Extending the Rule-Making Power to Federal Criminal Procedure," *Journal of the American Judicature Society* 22, no. 4 (1938): 151–153.

49. Cummings, "Modern Tendencies and the Law," *ABA Journal* 19, no. 10 (October 1933).

50. "Progress toward a Modern Administration of Criminal Justice in the United States," 27 April 1936, *SPHC*, 45–48.

51. *Lochner* was as much about "police power" as "due process," observes G. Edward White, *Constitution and the New Deal*, 265.

52. Raymond Moley, "To the President, First of Three Sections of a Report . . . ," 15 May 1934, OF10, box 2.

53. Gordon Dean, "Interstate Compacts for Crime Control," *ABA Journal* 21, no. 2 (February 1935): 89.

54. MFTAG, 5 July 1935, OF10, box 3. Laski wrote two *Guardian* columns in June 1935 on American constitutionalism and Supreme Court obstruction of the "positive State." The second focused more on federalism and the clumsy amendment process, and urged Roosevelt to "remake the American Constitution upon a model to which the document of 1787 will bear no substantial resemblance," which would likely have grabbed Roosevelt's attention. Harold J. Laski, "Dilemma of Government," *Manchester Guardian*, 17 June 1935; Laski, "States Rights and Nation's Needs," *Manchester Guardian*, 18 June 1935.

55. Federalism was conspicuously transformed through compacts. See David Riesman, review of *The Rise of a New Federalism* by Jane Perry Clark, *Harvard Law Review* 52 (1938): 175.

56. "Progress toward a Modern Administration of Criminal Justice," 27 April 1936, *SPHC*, 45–48. Despite much agreement, Cummings stressed disagreement: historical distrust of federal power—from the Virginia and Kentucky Resolutions, the Nullification crisis, and Reconstruction—exposed the breach between federal and state. Man's "insatiable desire for certainty" made compromise difficult, but the Constitution furnished an "organic process of government," a "process of adaptation and growth," and not a "legalistic vacuum." Cummings disbelieved any "absolute theory of one and only one rational construction of the Constitution." Cummings, "The American Constitutional Method," *ABA Journal* 22, no. 1 (January 1936). Maria Ponomarenko underlines incomplete oversight of states concerning antitrust, the FBI, prison administration, and police brutality, and casts Justice as somewhat at the "periphery of the New Deal state." Ponomarenko, "The Department of Justice and the Limits of the New Deal State, 1933–1945" (diss., Stanford University, 2010), 10.

57. *Congressional Record, Proceedings and Debates of the Second Sessions of the 73rd Congress of the United States,* vol. 78 (1934), 6854.

58. Cummings, "Immediate Problems for the Bar," 212; Kathleen J. Frydl, "Kidnapping and State Development in the United States," *Studies in American*

Political Development 20 (Spring 2006): 39–41; Joseph B. Keenan, "The Federal Government and the Crime Problem," 12 December 1934, *PAGCC*.

59. Vollmer to Aguero, 15 February 1935, AVP, box 44.

60. Vollmer to Hoover, 2 March 1935, AVP, box 44.

61. Vollmer to Niles, 11 June 1934, AVP, box 43.

62. Vollmer to Nusbaum, 17 November 1933, AVP, box 42.

63. Wilson to Vollmer, 5 September 1934, OWWP, box 1: "Letters Written by Wilson, 1928–1938."

64. Clarence E. Martin, "Shall We Abolish Our Republican Form of Government?," *ABA Journal* 19, no. 8 (August 1933): 435.

65. Martin, "The Growing Impotency," 552.

66. John Dickinson, "Crime and the Constitution," *ABA Journal* 21, no. 11 (November 1935): 739–743.

67. John J. Parker, "Is the Constitution Passing?," *ABA Journal* 19, no. 9 (September 1933): 570–575.

68. Peter Molyneaux, "Texas Governor to War on Crime," *New York Times*, 20 January 1935, E7.

69. The Attorney General, 5 June 1934, OF10, box 2: DOJA May–June 1934.

70. "Interstate Crime Commission Makes Recommendations," *ABA Journal* 22, no. 1 (January 1936).

71. John Edgar Hoover, "Work of the Division of Investigation, United States Department of Justice," *Tennessee Law Review* 13 (1935): 149, 150.

72. Justin Miller, "The Attorney General's Program for Crime Control," *ABA Journal* 21, no. 8 (August 1935).

73. Dean, "Interstate Compacts for Crime Control," 89–90.

74. "Massachusetts Police," *New York Times*, 14 March 1934, 18.

75. "State Bar Activity in Fields of Criminal Law and Judicial Selection," *ABA Journal* 21, no. 2 (February 1935).

76. Paul Musgrave, "Bringing the State Police In: The Diffusion of U.S. Statewide Policing Agencies, 1905–1941," *Studies in American Political Development* 34 (April 2020): 3–5.

77. Gerard N. Magliocca, "Huey P. Long and the Guarantee Clause," *Tulane Law Review* 83 (2008): 1.

78. James M. Kieran, "Lehman Maps Out State Crime War," *New York Times,* 6 October 1935, 68.

79. Attorney General, 4 November 1935, OF10, box 3, folder: Sep–Dec 1935, Abstracts.

80. W. A. Warn, "Lehman Opens Way for War on Crime," *New York Times,* 12 January 1936, E12.

81. Russell Owen, "Dewey Seeks Allies for a War on Crime," *New York Times,* 7 July 1935, E10; Lehman to Guggenheim, 15 June 1937, ILP, box 56, folder 8.

82. William A. Beasly, "California Unifies Enforcement Agencies to Fight Crime," *ABA Journal* 20, no. 12 (December 1934): 757.

83. Record 29, 16 October 1933, SFPDRSFPL.

84. "I agree with you that the states ought to support the Interstate Commission on Crime," Vollmer wrote to Clarence Beck at the Topeka Attorney General's Office, "but it is possible that the Governor of this state may think differently." Vollmer to Beck, 19 March 1936, AVP, box 44.

85. Frank F. Merriam, Proclamation, 5 July 1934, FFMP, carton 1: Proclamations, 1934–36; An Act to Prevent the Entry into California of Paupers . . . , FFMP, carton 1: Misc. to Be Sorted–2.

86. Vollmer estimated that 90 percent of police were unqualified, wasting 80 percent of tax dollars, and Merriam claimed that only a "stronger, more determined, more intelligent [police] organization" could combat organized crime. "Educated Policemen Demanded," *Los Angeles Times,* 22 March 1935; Vollmer to Charles H. Bock, 27 May 1935, AVP, box 44.

87. Vollmer to Merriam, 6 January 1936, AVP, box 44; Merriam to Vollmer, 10 January 1936, AVP, box 22; Vollmer to Merriam, 20 January 1936, AVP, box 44.

88. Vollmer to Merriam, 3 February 1936, AVP, box 44.

89. Merriam to Vollmer, 14 February 1936, AVP, box 22.

90. Merriam to Vollmer, 21 February 1936, AVP, box 22.

91. Megladdery to Vollmer, 17 May 1937, AVP 22; Vollmer to Merriam, 5 May 1937, AVP, box 45.

92. Vollmer to Harshorne, 2 December 1938, AVP, box 45.

93. Earl Warren, "A State Department of Justice," *ABA Journal* 21, no. 8 (August 1935): 495.

94. Attorney General, 11 February 1935, OF10, box 4.

95. Attorney General, 17 June 1935, OF10, box 3.

96. 294 U.S. 317 (1935); 295 U.S. 330 (1935); 295 U.S. 495 (1935); 297 U.S. 1 (1936). Very few "split decisions" undercut specifically New Deal programs. See Clarence J. Shearn Jr., "Split Decisions in the Supreme Court in Invalidating Federal and State Enactments and Attempted Exercises of Power, 1933–1937," *ABA Journal* 23, no. 5 (May 1937): 329–330. Osmond K. Fraenkel identified the post-*Schechter* era as the "twilight of states' rights." Fraenkel, "Constitutional Issues in the Supreme Court 1936 Term," *University of Pennsylvania Law Review* 86 (1937–1938), 38–76.

97. Frederick H. Stichfield, "The Supreme Court Issue," *ABA Journal* 23, no. 4 (April 1937).

98. *Strauder v. West Virginia,* 100 U.S. 303 (1880); *Bush v. Kentucky,* 107 U.S. 110 (1883); *Powell v. Alabama,* 287 U.S. 45; *Brown v. Mississippi,* 297 U.S. 278; *Wong Wing v. United States,* 163 U.S. 228; *Meyer v. Nebraska,* 262 U.S. 390 (1923); *Bartels v. Iowa,* 262 U.S. 404 (1923); *Pierce v. Society of Sisters,* 268 U.S. 510 (1925); *Whitney v. California,* 274 U.S. 357 (1927); *Stromberg v. California,* 283 U.S. 359 (1931); *De Jonge v. State of Oregon,* 299 U.S. 353 (1937).

99. "Memorandum Approving a Bill for Judicial Reform," 26 August 1937, APPUCSB.

100. Edward T. Folliard, "U.S., Local Officers Wipe Out Jealousies," *Washington Post,* 17 October 1937, B5.

101. "A 'New Deal' against Crime," *Washington Post,* 17 October 1937, 1.

102. *Palko v. Connecticut,* 302 U. S. 319 (1937).

103. "Crime and Criminal Practices," Senate Report 1189, 9 August 1937, 2.

104. "Crime and Criminal Practices," 5–7, 12, 14.

105. Allen to Peters, 28 July 1936; Libbey to Clapp, 2 October 1939; Morgan to Kline (Cross Index Sheet), 31 August 1936; Karr to Bradnet, 22 August 1936— all TVAGM, box 419, folder: Guards, Guides, Policemen, Detectives.

106. Allen to Watnchi, 24 August 1936 (Cross Index); Allen to Peters, 1 September 1936 (Cross Index)—both TVAGM, box 419, folder: Guards, Guides, Policemen, Detectives.

107. McMurchy to Allen, 7 December 1936, TVAGM, box 419, folder: Guards, Guides, Policemen, Detectives.

108. Analysis of Duties, TVAPC, box 39: Development of Police Rating System.

109. Hoisington to Glass, 7 April 1937, TVAPC, box 39.

110. Hoisington to Members of the Public Safety Service, 17 June 1937, TVAPC, box 39.

111. Edward S. Corwin summarized the New Deal attitude: "As the practical grounds for assertion by the National Government of its powers over interstate business operations have expanded, the theoretical basis in constitutional law and theory for such assertion has deteriorated; and for this somewhat paradoxical situation the Supreme Court is to an important extent responsible." Corwin, *The Commerce Power versus States Rights* (Gloucester, MA: Peter Smith 1962 [1936]), 5.

112. J. Edgar Hoover, *Journal of Criminal Law and Criminology* (July–August 1933), 475.

113. Attorney General to President, 6 February 1935, OF10, box 2.

114. Miller, "The Attorney General's Program for Crime Control."

115. Public No. 334, 49 Stat. 863; Public No. 339, 49 Stat. 867; Public No. 340, 49 Stat. 867.

116. Roosevelt to Cummings, 23 December 1936; Attorney General to President, 14 December 1936—both OF10, box 3.

117. "Courts may not inquire into the motives of Congress in exercising its powers; they will not undertake, by collateral inquiry as to the measure of the regulatory effect of a tax, to ascribe to Congress an attempt, under the guise of taxation, to exercise another power denied by the Federal Constitution." *Sonzinsky v. United States*, 300 U.S. 506, 507 (1937).

118. Richard J. Bonnie and Charles H. Whitebread explain the political shift in *The Marihuana Conviction: A History of Marijuana Prohibition in the United States* (Charlottesville, VA: University of Virginia Press, 1974), 154, concerning "federal responsibility." The "Supreme Court posed the only restraint," and a weak one. Both the Marihuana Tax Act of 1937 and the Firearms Act of 1934 have drawn Fifth Amendment self-incrimination criticism. In *Leary v. United States* the Fifth Circuit Court rejected the Fifth Amendment argument, after which the Supreme Court unanimously overturned the statute. See "The Marijuana Tax and the Privilege against Self-Incrimination," *University of Pennsylvania Law Review* 117, no. 3 (1969); *Leary v. United States*. 395 U.S. 6 (1969).

119. Frank R. Strong, "Cooperative Federalism," *Iowa Law Review* 23 (1938): 459.

120. Sam B. Warner, "Uniform Pistol Act," *American Institute of Criminal Law and Criminology* 29 (1938): 529.

121. "Firearms and the Crime Problem," 5 October 1937, SPHC, 83–84, 89.

122. Dickinson, "Crime and the Constitution," 739.

123. Miller to Farland, 28 February 1936; Farland to Miller, 27 February 1936—both in AGAC GC, box 2, folder: Crime Prevention.

124. Attorney General to President, 14 December 1936, OF10, box 3.

125. Department of Justice for Release, 4 May 1937, OF10, box 4.

126. Public No. 785, 52 Stat. 1250.

127. Carl Bakal, *The Right to Bear Arms* (New York: McGraw-Hill, 1966), 179.

128. See "The Emergence of a Nationalized Bill of Rights: Due Process and a 'Higher Law' of Liberty," *Brooklyn Law Review* 490 (1938).

129. Cummings, "Modernizing Federal Procedure."

130. There were 56,332 US district court cases on July 1, 1936. Of these, 10,993 were criminal. There were 51,629 total cases on June 30, 1937. Of these, 11,011 were criminal. A Table Showing Total Number of Cases Pending in the United States District Courts, PHSC, box 69, folder 4. Statement on S3233.

131. Criminal Rule Making, Statement and Recommendations of Honorable Homer Cummings, Annual Report of the Attorney General for the Fiscal Year 1938, PHSC, box 114: Misc.

132. Cummings to Roosevelt, 14 and 17 December, 1938, PHSC, box 69.

133. Attorney General to President, 17 April 1938, OF10, box 4.

134. Cummings to Cotter, 17 December 1938, PHSC, box 71.

135. Frank Hogan to Cummings, 24 November 1938, PHSC, box 71.

136. He put it, "You have carried your Department through a difficult period . . . suggesting legislation. . . . As a result the homes of America are safer . . . [,] interstate crime has been checked . . . [,] great strides have been made in improving judicial procedure." Roosevelt to Cummings, 31 December 1938, OF10, box 5.

137. For Immediate Release, 15 November 1938, OF10, box 5.

138. *United States v. Miller,* 307 U.S. 174 (1939); 390 U.S. 85 (1968).

139. "Constitutional Limitations on Firearms Regulation," *Duke Law Journal* 18, no. 4 (1969): 773–801.

140. President Wickersham's Address, *ABA Journal* 21, no. 6 (June 1935): 342–344.

141. Wyzanski to Cummings, 29 September 1938, PHSC, box 69, folder 1.

142. McFarland, "Administrative Law—Its Symptoms and Diagnosis," 25 May 1939, PHSC, box 69, folder 1.

143. Pendleton Howard, "American Criminal Justice and the Rules of the Game," *ABA Journal* 24, no. 5 (May 1938).

144. Fraenkel, "Constitutional Issues."

145. William A. Dunn, "Our Dangerous Criminal Procedure," *Journal of Criminal Law and Criminology* 30, no. 6 (1940): 894.

146. See Joseph Postell, "The Anti-New Deal Progressive: Roscoe Pound's Alternative Administrative State," *Review of Politics* 74, no. 1 (Winter 2012): 53–85.

147. Roscoe Pound, "Legal Interrogation of Persons Accused or Suspected of Crime," *American Institute of Criminal Law and Criminology* 24 (1934): 1015.

148. Pound, "Needed Reforms in Criminal Procedure," *Tennessee Law Review* 13, no. 2 (February 1935): 114–116.

149. Pound, "Toward a Better Criminal Law," *ABA Journal* 21, no. 8 (August 1935): 499–500.

150. Pound, "Unification of Law," *ABA Journal* 20, no. 11 (November 1934): 696.

151. Pound, "Practical Advantages of Rules of Court for Criminal Procedure," *ABA Journal* 25, no. 10 (October 1939): 825.

152. Cummings to Vanderbilt, 8 July 1939, PHSC, box 114.

153. Holtzoff to Cummings, 5 May 1939, PHSC, box 114.

154. Cummings to Holtzoff, 20 June 1939, PHSC, box 114.

155. Cummings to Harley, 2 July 1940, PHSC, box 114; H.R. 4587, Public No. 675, 54 Stat. 688.

156. "Reform in Criminal Procedure," *Yale Law Journal* 50 (1940): 108.

157. In the late 1930s and onward some hoped for a more aggressive adoption of federal rights protections in such state proceedings as indictments. See Dunn, "Our Dangerous Criminal Procedure," 899. Others continued calling for constitutional amendments to empower the prosecutorial state. See John Henderson, "Necessary Reforms in Criminal Procedure," *Tennessee Law Review* 16, no. 5 (December 1940): 503–511.

158. Cummings, "Modernizing Federal Procedure."

159. On the 1990s, see Michelle Alexander, *The New Jim Crow: Mass Incarceration in the Age of Colorblindness* (New York: New Press, 2010). On the 1960s, see Elizabeth Hinton, *From the War on Poverty to the War on Crime: The Making of Mass Incarceration in America* (Cambridge, MA: Harvard University Press, 2016). On the 1940s, see Naomi Murakawa, *The First Civil Right: How Liberals Built Prison America* (Oxford: Oxford University Press, 2014).

160. Public No. 156, 50 Stat. 304; Public No. 571, 52 Stat. 596; Public No. 587, 52 Stat. 640; Public No. 676, 52 Stat. 779.

161. Public No. 437, 52 Stat. 82; Public No. 465, 52 Stat. 197.

162. Jerome Hall, "Committee on Survey of Crime, Criminal Law and Criminal Procedure," *American Institute of Criminal Law and Criminology* 29 (1938): 562.

6. WORSE THAN MURDER

1. Laying of the Corner Stone, 29 July 1933, OF431, folder: Narcotics, 1933–1943; Assistant Surgeon General to Mulhall, 27 July 1933, HAP, box 3, file 7.

2. H.R. 6906, Public No. 238, 2 August 1937, 50 Stat. 551.

3. "Roosevelt's New Deal war on crime grew out of the prohibition wars," writes Lisa McGirr, *The War on Alcohol: Prohibition and the Rise of the American State* (New York: W. W. Norton, 2015), 218.

4. With origins in 1930s international, regulatory, and tax laws, 1940 was the beginning of "a militant drug war," writes Kathleen J. Frydl, *The Drug Wars in America, 1940–1973* (Cambridge: Cambridge University Press, 2013), 12.

5. According to Alexandra Chasin, "Anslinger's war on drugs" turned America into "Anslinger's nation," thanks to "considerable, if conservative" support and the passive complicity of Roosevelt. Chasin, *Assassin of Youth: A Kaleidoscopic History of Harry J. Anslinger's War on Drugs* (Chicago: University of Chicago Press, 2016), 4–5, 175.

6. Anslinger's "precarious" job was saved by conservatives and the "powerful pharmaceutical lobby," aided by his opportunistic treaty emphasis, according to John C. McWilliams, *The Protectors: Harry J. Anslinger and the Federal Bureau of Narcotics, 1930–1962* (Newark: University of Delaware Press, 1990), 30, 86.

7. David F. Musto, "The Marihuana Tax Act of 1937," *Archives of General Psychiatry* 26, no. 2 (1972): 101–108; Susan L. Speaker, "'The Struggle of Mankind against Its Deadliest Foe': Themes of Counter-Subversion in Anti-Narcotic Campaigns, 1920–1940," *Journal of Social History* 34, no. 3 (Spring 2001): 591–610, 58.

8. On the global drug war, especially after World War II, see Matthew R. Pembleton, *Containing Addiction: The Federal Bureau of Narcotics and the Origins of America's Global Drug War* (Amherst: University of Massachusetts Press, 2017), 66, 117–120.

9. As with the 1914 Harrison Narcotics Act, "the most 'liberal' spokesmen were among the most eager" about marijuana control, according to David F. Musto, *The American Disease: Origins of Narcotic Control* (New Haven, CT: Yale University Press, 1973), 228.

10. Actual grassroots anxiety about Hispanic users is elusive, according to John F. Galliher and Allynn Walker, "The Puzzle of the Social Origins of the Marihuana Tax Act of 1937," *Social Problems* 24, no. 3 (1977): 367–376.

11. On populist fears in Mexico, see Isaac Campos, *Home Grown: Marijuana and the Origins of Mexico's War on Drugs* (Chapel Hill: University of North Carolina Press, 2012).

12. "Government Will Ask States to Ban Growing of Marijuana," *New York Times,* 16 September 1931.

13. Wildman to Morgenthau, 30 August 1934, OF21, box 20, folder: Dept. of the Treasury—Alcohol Tax Unit, 1934–1935.

14. "Asks Uniform Laws to Curb Narcotics," *New York Times,* 20 February 1931.

15. Minutes of the Meeting, 11 September 1934, ROLEC, box 1.

16. Musto, *The American Disease,* 211.

17. Murphy to Anslinger, 20 October 1932; Jaurez, Attn: Bureau of Narcotics, 22 November 1932—both HAP, box 3, file 8.

18. Hoover to Anslinger, 2 August 1933, HAP, box 3, file 7.

19. Ewing to Conboy, 21 December 1932, HAP, box 3 file 8.

20. Anslinger to Gaston, 30 January 1935, HAP, box 3, file 5.

21. Anslinger to Gaston, 6 February 1934, HAP, box 3, file 6; Memorandum for Mr. Gaston, 12 December 1933, HAP, box 3, file 7; Herbert Gaston, 7 January 1938, HAP, box 3, file 2.

22. Thienes to Anslinger, 13 December 1935, HAP, box 3, file 5.

23. Memorandum for Assistant Secretary Lowman, 11 February 1933, HAP, box 3, file 7.

24. Memorandum for H. E. Gaston, 4 August 1934; Anslinger to Gaston, 5 February 1934—both HAP, box 3, file 6.

25. Anslinger to Kelly, 5 September 1932, HAP, box 3, file 8.

26. Brownmeyer to Anslinger, 6 October 1932, HAP, box 3, file 8.

27. Russe to President, 4 April 1933, HAP, box 3, file 7.

28. Memorandum for Assistant Secretary Gibbons, 30 July 1938, HAP, box 3, file 2.

29. Crowe to Anslinger, 17 June 1932, HAP, box 3, file 8.

30. Anslinger: Memorandum for Mr. Gaston, 28 June 1934, HAP, box 3, file 6.

31. Williams to Peck, 10 June 1934, HAP, box 3, file 6.

32. Williams to Peck, 6 June 1934, HAP, box 3, file 6.

33. Herbert L. May, "A Few Words about Opium," World-Wide Broadcast, 19 August 1933.

34. Memorandum, 25 September 1931; Williamson to Anslinger, 23 June 1932—both HAP, box 3, file 8.

35. To Harry, 13 September 1933, HAP, box 3, file 7.

36. Anslinger to Walker, 6 July 1933, HAP, box 3, file 7.

37. Anslinger to Miller, 2 December 1935, HAP, box 3, file 5: Correspondence (1935).

38. Williamson to Anslinger, 3 March 1933, HAP, box 3, file 7.

39. Recommendation XII, 29 November 1933; Hobson to Roosevelt, 19 October 1933; To Richmond P. Hobson, 11 November 1933; Attorney General, 15 March 1935—all OF431, folder: Narcotics, 1933–1943.

40. *Pittsburgh Post-Gazette*, 12 July 1933.

41. Hon. A. J. Sbaath, 26 May 1934; McDonald to Farley, 25 April 1933—both OF21, folder: Narcotics Bureau.

42. To Miss Mary Deston, 7 March 1933, OF21, folder: Narcotics Bureau; Oscar Ewing to Martin Conboy, 21 December 1932, HAP, box 3, file 8.

43. Under Secretary of State William to Anslinger, 9 March 1933, HAP, box 3, file 7.

44. Musto, *The American Disease*, 212.

45. Enfield to Howe, 15 May 1934, HAP, box 3, file 6.

46. Louis Ruppel, Memorandum for the President, 28 November 1933, OF21, box 19, folder: Narcotics Bureau.

47. Cummings to Hobson, 5 April 1933; Berger to Mallinckrodt Chemical Works, 21 November 1933; Berger to Russe, 28 November 1933; Russe, Mallinckrodt Chemical Works, 19 December 1933; Russe to Berger, 24 November 1933—all HAP, box 3, file 7.

48. Memo for the Under Secretary of State, 20 April 1933, OF21, box 19, folder: Narcotics Bureau.

49. Wood to Copeland, HAP, box 3, file 8 (1932).

50. *Altoona Mirror*, 18 March 1933, HAP, box 3, file 7; Memorandum for the President, and the Acting Secretary of the Treasury, from Ruppell, 28 November 1933, OF21, box 19, folder: Narcotics Bureau.

51. Musto, *American Disease*, 213.

52. To Russe, 15 February 1933, HAP, box 3, file 7.

53. Williamson to Anslinger, 3 March 1933, HAP, box 3, file 7.

54. Retail druggists to Douglas, 6 April 1933 HAP, box 3, file 7.

55. Hon. Phillips, 12 April 1933; Memo for the Under Secretary of State, 20 April 1933—both OF21, box 19, folder: Narcotics Bureau.

56. Walker to Anslinger, 30 October 1933, HAP, box 3, file 7; Memorandum for Howe, 27 November 1933, OF21, box 19, folder: Narcotics Bureau; Louis Ruppel, Deputy Commissioner of Treasury Dept, OF21, box 19, folder: Narcotics Bureau.

57. McAdoo to President, 27 October 1933; Hallerman to Newton, 16 November 1933; Memorandum for Howe, 27 November 1933; Louis Ruppel, Deputy Commissioner—all OF21, box 19, folder: Narcotics Bureau.

58. McAdoo to President, 31 October 1933, OF21, box 19, folder: Narcotics Bureau; 31 October 1933, OF431, folder: Narcotics, 1933–1943.

59. Memorandum for the President, 29 December 1933; Roosevelt, Memorandum for Director of the Budget, 30 October 1933—both OF21, box 19, folder: Narcotics Bureau.

60. Newton to Howe, 22 November 1933; Howe to McAdoo, 2 January 1934—both OF21, box 19, folder: Narcotics Bureau.

61. Howe, Cable from Geneva, 18 November 1933, OF431, folder: Narcotics, 1933–1943.

62. Assistant Secretary of State to Anslinger, 8 May 1933, HAP, box 3, file 7.

63. Anslinger to Sharman, 28 April 1934, HAP, box 3, file 6; Sharman to Anslinger, 21 October 1936, HAP, box 3, file 4.

64. Anslinger to La Guardia, 20 September 1932, HAP, box 3, file 8; Memorandum for McReynolds, 1 October 1937, HAP, box 3, file 3.

65. "Anslinger Invited to address Temple University," 20 April 1933, HAP, box 3, file 7.

66. Blanco to Sato, 6 March 1937, HAP, box 3, file 3.

67. Anslinger to Young, 25 March 1938, HAP, box 3, file 2.

68. Memorandum for Acting Assistant Secretary, Report for week ended March 25, 1933, HAP, box 3, file 7.

69. Attention: Bureau of Narcotics, 5 June 1935, HAP, box 3, file 5.

70. Memorandum for Mr. Anslinger in re Bookmaking, 25 March 1937 HAP, box 3, file 3.

71. To Sir, 19 December 1932, HAP, box 3, file 8; From Ralph H Oyler, 17 July 1933; W. North and Bertin to Oyler, 22 August 1933; Reily to Anslinger, 1 August 1933; Walle to Anslinger, 27 October 1933; HTN to HJA, 18 October 1933; Meinke to Anslinger, 1(2) November 1933 (Universal Service Inc); Middlebrooks to Anslinger, 20 November 1933—all HAP, box 3, file 7.

72. Anslinger to Gibbons, 5 January 1935, HAP, box 3, file 5.

73. Memorandum Suggesting a National Organization of Horse Racing Associations, undated, HAP, box 3, file 6; Buchanan to Anslinger, 1933, California Horse Racing Board; Fink to Anslinger, 2 January 1934, HAP, box 3, file 6; Stevenson to Yyler, 7 April 1938, HAP, box 3, file 2.

74. Conor to Anslinger, 25 June 1936, HAP, box 3, file 4.

75. Chao to Anslinger, 21 February 1933, HAP, box 3, file 7; Anslinger to Sharman, 22 March 1934, HAP, box 3, file 6; Anslinger to Hearst, 23 November 1933, HAP, box 3, file 7; Anslinger to Hearst, 23 November 1933, HAP, box 3, file 7.

76. Musto, *The American Disease,* 216; Memorandum in Favor of Proposed Uniform Narcotic Drug Act, HAP, box 3, file 6.

77. Hobson to Roosevelt, 8 April 1933, HAP, box 3, file 7.

78. Hornblower to Bureau of Narcotics, 28 March 1933, DEASF, box 95.

79. Field Secretary, Anti-Narcotic Society on 580 Market Street, SF, 5 January 1932, DEASF, box 95.

80. To Mrs. Bradford, President Parent & Teachers Organization, 9 May 1933, HAP, box 3, file 7.

81. Camp to Wood, 3 April 1935, DEASF, box 95.

82. "Why the Legislature Should Enact the Proposed Uniform Narcotic Drug Law," DEASF, box 95.

83. Anslinger to Pinkham, 27 December 1932, DEASF, box 95.

84. Camp to Draper, June 1935, DEASF, box 95.

85. Wood to Camp, 9 February 1935, DEASF, box 95.

86. Davis to Governor, 15 January 1934, HAP, box 3, file 6.

87. To Mrs. Bradford, 9 May 1933, HAP, box 3, file 7; McWilliams, *The Protectors,* 52.

88. Young to Anslinger, 18 February 1935, DEASF, box 95.

89. *Washington Herald,* 6 April 1933, DEASF, box 95.

90. Kim A. Smith to Anslinger, 31 March 1933, DEASF, box 95; To Governor James Rolph, 7 April 1933, DEASF, box 95.

91. Manning to Anslinger, 11 August 1937, DEASF, box 95.

92. Bliss to Wood, 31 May 1935, DEASF, box 95.

93. Camp to Greeson, 29 May 1935, DEASF, box 95; E.L. Camp to Greeson, DEASF, box 95; Camp to Greeson, New Orleans, 8 January 1935, DEASF, box 95; Camp to Greeson, Received 4 January 1935, DEASF, box 95.

94. Wright to Anslinger; Baker to Anslinger, 17 July 1935—both DEASF, box 95.

95. Camp to Greeson, 9 August 1935, DEASF, box 95.

96. Anslinger to Honorable Draper, 26 July 1935, DEASF, box 95; Hobson to Anslinger, 25 July 1935, DEASF, box 95; Camp to Greeson, 17 August 1935, DEASF, box 95. For a critical account distinguishing cannabis from marijuana see Sarah Brady Siff, "Targeted Marijuana Law Enforcement in Los Angeles 1914–1959," *Fordham Urban Law Journal* (2022).

97. Anslinger to Baker, 24 July 1935, DEASF, box 95.

98. Camp to Gresson, 16 September 1935, DEASF, box 95.

99. McWilliams, *The Protectors*, 84.

100. Vann to Howe, 17 December 1934, OF21, box 19, folder: Narcotics.

101. "Roosevelt Asks Narcotic War Aid," *New York Times,* 22 March 1935.

102. Minutes of the Meeting, 20 November 1935, ROLEC, box 1.

103. Stanley Parker, Memorandum for Mr. Graves, 2 July 1935, ROLEC BOX 1.

104. Coast Guard Headquarters, 8 May 1935, ROLEC, box 1.

105. Minutes of the Meeting, 3 July 1935, ROLEC, box 1.

106. Coast Guard Headquarters, 7 October 1936, ROLEC, box 1.

107. Minutes of the Meeting, 7 April 1938, ROLEC, box 2.

108. Minutes of the Meeting, 22 May 1935, ROLEC, box 1.

109. Minutes of the Meeting, 15 June 1938, ROLEC, box 2.

110. To Heads of Treasury Enforcement Agencies, 23 June 1936, ROLEC, box 1.

111. Sec of Treasury to Commissioner of Internal Revenue et al., 21 April 1936, ROLEC, box 1.

112. Coast Guard Headquarters Report, 15 November 1935, ROLEC, box 1.

113. Coast Guard Headquarters, 28 October 1936, ROLEC, box 1.

114. Coast Guard Headquarters, 11 November 1936, ROLEC, box 1.

115. Minutes of Meeting, 8 April 1936, ROLEC, box 1.

116. Irey to Anslinger, 14 March 1939, DEASF, box 168: "Income Tax Violators."

117. *Washington Herald,* 28 April 1933, DEASF, box 168: "Income Tax Violators."

118. Anslinger to Commissioner of Internal Revenue, 20 October 1932, DEASF, box 168: "Income Tax Violators."

119. Baldridge to Commissioner of Narcotics, 17 May 1933; Ruppel to Smith, 14 July 1933; Oyler, Chicago, 14 July 1933; G.W. Cunningham, 14 July 1933; LJ Ulmar; Manning to Commissioner, 17 July 1933; Forrer to Commissioner, 19 July 1933; Greeson to Ruppell, 21 July 1933; Oyler to Ruppel, 18 July 1933; Forrer to Commissioner, 19 July 1933; Middlebrooks to Ruppel, 20 July 1933; Joerling to Ruppell, 11 September 1933; Wall to Commissioner, 19 July 1933; Memorandum for Mr. Irey, 18 September 1936; Oyler to Grunewald, 18 December 1938—all DEASF, box 168: "Income Tax Violators."

120. Anslinger to District Supervisors, Circ. Letter no. 384, 27 March 1936; Memorandum for Assistant Secretary Gibbons, 24 November 1936; Greeson to Berry, 24 March 1939; Greeson to Berry, 20 November 1939; Anslinger to Colf, 4 December 1939; Circ. Letter no. 384, Supplement no. 1, 1 March 1937; Irey to Anslinger, 23 October 1937—all DEASF, box 168: "Income Tax Violators."

121. Anslinger to Irey, 5 March 1938; Memorandum to all District Supervisors, 18 April 1938; Memorandum for all District Supervisors, 16 May 1938; Memo for Commissioner, 1 August 1938; Palmer to Chief Intel Unit, 15 December 1936; Abstract of telephone call from Williams to Anslinger, 15 September 1938; Williams to IR Intelligence Unit, NY, 11 March 1937; Memorandum for all District Supervisors, 12 August 1938; Ulmer to Special Agent in Charge, 17 August 1938; Grunewald to Oyler, in re: Yee Long, 16 November 1938; Wood, Memo for all District Supervisors, 20 August 1938—all DEASF, box 168: "Income Tax Violators."

122. Earle to Ramsey, 28 June 1933, DEASF, box 63.

123. Wood to Edwards, 2 September 1930; Anslinger to Chief, Food, Drug and Insecticide Administration, 8 October 1930; Attention: M. E.L. Earle, July 1933; Marsulli to Internal Revenue Dept., 18 January 1935; Marzulli to Sale, 8 January 1934; Anslinger to Marzulli, January 1934; Anslinger to Jelks, 24 September 1930—all DEASF, box 63.

124. Ruppel to Highball, 11 May 1934; Anslinger to Maywood Chemical Works, 14 September 1934; Anslinger to Maywood Chemical Works, 3 October 1934; To Mr. Alfred Tennyson, 21 August 1934; Head, Narcotic Section: Memorandum for Mr. Opper, 113 September 1934—all DEASF, box 63.

125. DEASF, box 63: Coca-Cola.

126. Ralph Hayes, VP Coca-Cola, 20 April 1937, HAP, box 3, file 3.

127. Day to Tennyson, 12 July 1936; Tennyson to Day, 15 July 1936; Attention: Food and Drug Administration, 1934; Anslinger to Day, 12 August 1936; Igoe to

Commissioner, 7 April 1934; Igoe to Commissioner, 7 April 1934; Gibbons to Secretary of Agriculture, 17 April 1934; DeLoon to Walton, 10 August 1936; Tugwell to Secretary of Treasury, 19 April 1934; Kola Gighball Company to Secretary of Commerce, 28 April 1934; Ruppel to Kola Highball, 11 May 1934; Ruppel to Owens, 15 May 1934; Owens to Day, 27 April 1934; Owens responds, 25 May 1934; Owens to Sir, 28 May 1934; Day to Commissioner, 12 June 1934; Ruppel to Owens, 28 May 1934; Ruppel to Day, 11 June 1934—all DEASF, box 63.

128. Rafecz to Commissioner, 23 September 1933, DEASF, box 40.

129. Roosevelt to Thomson, 29 June 1933, OF431: Narcotics; Morgenthau to President, 28 January 1937, OF21, box 19: Narcotics; Assistant Surgeon General to Fosler, 4 June 1934, DEASF, box 40; Wood to Colle, 29 January 1935, DEASF, box 40.

130. Memorandum for District Judges, et al., 15 January 1935, DEASF, box 40.

131. *Washington Herald*, 28 August 1935, DEASF, box 40.

132. Proposed Draft of Letter from the President, 13 February 1937, OF21, box 19.

133. Regulations Governing the Admission of Persons, Effective April 1 1935; Edmund to Anslinger, 16 February 1935; Edmund to Anslinger, 16 February 1935; Memorandum for United States District Judges . . . , 15 January 1935; Morison to Morgenthau, 9 December 1934; Achilles to Strong, 12 January 1934—all DEASF, box 40, folder: Addiction: Narcotics Farms General.

134. Wilkinson to Greeson, 14 December 1934, DEASF BOX 95: Uniform Narcotics Laws, Alabama.

135. Anslinger to Oyler, 5 September 1934; Igoe to Anslinger, 28 October 1935; Duffy to Bangs, 11 September 1935; Oyler to Commissioner, 17 September 1935; Anslinger to Treadway, 20 September 1935; Bangs to Commissioner, 18 September 1935; Meeds to Martin, 14 December 1935; Anslinger to Treadway, 26 December 1935—all DEASF, box 40, folder: Addiction: Narcotics Farms General.

136. Anslinger to Treadway, 17 January 1934, DEASF, box 40.

137. Martin to Brice, 26 April 1935, DEASF, box 40.

138. Anslinger to Jacobson, 11 October 1933; Anslinger to Johnson, 17 December 1934; Anslinger to Hassell, 7 March 1939—all DEASF, box 40: Addiction: Narcotics Farms General, 1933 through 1940.

139. Wood to Treadway, 13 June 1935. Middlebrooks to JB Greeson, 24 June 1935, DEASF, box 40.

140. Middlebrooks to ALL Narcotic Officers, District No. 5, 26 November 1935, DEASF, box 40.

141. McMike to Smith, 14 May 1935, DEASF, box 40.

142. See Anne L. Foster, *The Long War on Drugs* (Durham, NC: Duke University Press, 2023), chap. 4.

143. Morenthaugh to President, 8 November 1934, OF431: Narcotics.

144. Hobson to Anslinger, 11 December 1936, HAP, box 3, file 4.

145. Memorandum in Respect to H.R. 10586, 1 February 1936, HAP, box 3, file 4; McIntyre to Mr. Johnson, 24 February 1936, OF21, box 20: Dept. of the Treasury—Alcohol Tax Unit, 1934–1935.

146. Ford to Anslinger, 9 February 1936, HAP, box 3, file 4.

147. Hobson to President, 4 March 1936, OF431.

148. Kelly to Anslinger 24, September 1936, HAP, box 3, file 4.

149. Jones to Sir, 27 February 1936, HAP, box 3, file 4.

150. Proposed Amendment to the Doughton Bill, Anslinger Papers, box 3, file 4.

151. Oliphant to McIntire, 7 February 1936. OF431: Narcotics.

152. Resolution of the Board of Directors, HAP, box 3, file 4.

153. Copy of Letter to all Members of the Board of Directors of the World Narcotic Defense Association, Inc., 3 February 1936, HAP, box 3, file 4.

154. Hobson to Doughton, 3 February 1936 HAP, box 3, file 4.

155. Hobson to President, 4 March 1936, OF431.

156. Memorandum in Respect to H.R. 10586, 1 February 1936, HAP, box 3, file 4.

157. Address of Charles H. Tuttle, "The Menace of Narcotic Drugs," Chairman of Exec Committee. New York City, 27 February 1936, HAP, box 3, file 4.

158. The United States valued the conference to "mandate domestic control of marihuana and opium-poppy cultivation," writes Musto, *The American Disease*, 216.

159. Report of Celebration of the Third Anniversary of the Ratification of the Geneva Narcotics Limitation Convention of 1931, April 1936, OF431.

160. Report of Celebration.

161. William to Anslinger, 9 May 1938, HAP, box 3, file 2.

162. Ann Grover, 13 July 1937, HAP, box 3, file 3.

163. Letter to Gaston and Anslinger, 18 August 1936, HAP, box 3, file 4.

164. Golden to Chief of Narcotics, 30 June 1937; Adams Jr. to Sir, 14 April 1938; To Commissioner of Narcotics, 17 November 1936, from A.M. Bangs—all HAP, box 3, file 3.

165. Letter from Jernigan, 12 November 1933; Jernigan to Oregon State Ag. College, 1 March 1936—both HAP, box 3, file 4.

166. McCord to Mrs. Roosevelt, 25 January 1937, HAP, box 3, file 3, Correspondence (1937).

167. Richard J. Bonnie and Charles H. Whitebread, *The Marihuana Conviction: A History of Marijuana Prohibition in the United States* (Charlottesville: University of Virginia Press, 1974), 143, quotation at 157.

168. Biggins to Anslinger, 1 October 1937; DL Yutronich to Martin, 20 October 1937, HAP, box 3, file 3.

169. Bell to Wood, 7 October 1937, HAP, box 3, file 3.

170. Camp to Greeson, received 1 July 1935, DEASF, box 95: folder: Uniform Narcotics Laws, Alabama.

171. Jackson to Biggins, 25 August 1937; Tom to Biggins, 21 September 1937—both HAP, box 3, file 3.

172. Hobson to Anslinger, 11 December 1936, HAP, box 3, file 4.

173. Bonnie and Whitebread, *The Marijuana Conviction*, 118–122.

174. Memorandum for Assistant Secretary Gibbons, 3 February 1936, HAP, box 3, file 4.

175. Bonnie and Whitebread, *The Marijuana Conviction*, 126. See also McWilliams, *The Protectors*, 69.

176. Bonnie and Whitebread, "The Forbidden Fruit and the Tree of Knowledge: An Inquiry into the Legal History of American Marijuana Prohibition," *Virginia Law Review* 56, no. 6 (October 1970): 989; David F. Musto, "The Marijuana Tax Act of 1937," *Archives of General Psychiatry* 26, no. 2 (February 1972).

177. Bonnie and Whitebread, *The Marihuana Conviction*, 163.

178. Dear Senator, 20 March 1936, HAP, box 3, file 4.

179. McWilliams, *The Protectors*, 75.

180. Anslinger memorandum, 14 March 1938, HAP, box 3, file 2.

181. Memorandum for the 1937 Report, 12 October 1937, HAP, box 3, file 3.

182. Anslinger to McReynolds, 7 July 1938, HAP, box 3, file 2; Oyler to Anslinger, 1 October 1937, HAP, box 3, file 3; Ward to Morgenthau, 30 November 1937, HAP, box 3, file 3.

183. Oyler to Commissioner, 9 December 1938, HAP, box 3, file 2.

184. Garland Williams, in re: Marihuana, 16 June 1938, HAP, box 3, file 2.

185. Murphy to Williams, 20 May 1938, HAP, box 3, file 2.

186. Bowers to Dear Sir, 27 October 1937 HAP, box 3, file 3.

187. Anslinger to Ball, 18 October 1937, HAP, box 3, file 3.

188. Minutes, 13 July 1938, ROLEC, box 2.

189. Larry "Ratso" Sloman, *Reefer Madness: The History of Marijuana in America* (New York: St. Martin's Griffin, 1998).

190. Presidential Memorandum for Commissioner H. J. Anslinger, 25 April 1942, OF21, box 19.

191. Memorandum for Jim Rowe, 4 October 1940, OF431: Narcotics, 1933–1943.

192. Lawrence Kolb, "Medical and Social Effects of Drug Addiction," Chicago Academy of Criminology, 10 February 1939, HAP, box 3, file 1.

193. Kolb to Anslinger, 29 June 1939, HAP, box 3, file 1.

194. Office of District Supervisor to FDR, 18 March 1938; Bureau of the Budget to McIntyre, 23 May 1938; Secretary of Treasury to President, 27 June 1940— all OF21, box 20: Dept. of the Treasury, Alcohol Tax Unit, 1934–1935.

195. Haas to Morgenthau, Treasury Criminal Cases–Enforcement, November 1940, 31 December 1940, HMP, box 383, Criminal Statistics–1940.

196. Greeson to Anslinger, 3 January 1942, DEASF, box 95: Uniform Narcotics Laws, Alabama.

7. SOUTHERN STRATEGIES

1.   White to Norris, 24 February 1938, NAACPHV, General Office File: Anti-Lynching Bill Misc., 1936–1939 (001529_030_0618).

2.   David Fellman, "The Liberalism of Senator Norris," *American Political Science Review* 40 (1946): 27–41.

3.   White to Norris, 24 February 1938, NAACPHV, General Office File: Anti-Lynching Bill Misc., 1936–1939 (001529_030_0618).

4.   David Blight, *Race and Reunion: The Civil War in American Memory* (Cambridge, MA: Harvard University Press, 2009); Nina Silber, *The Romance of Reunion: Northerners and the South, 1865–1900* (Chapel Hill: University of North Carolina Press, 1997).

5.   Nancy Joan Weiss, *Farewell to the Party of Lincoln* (Princeton, NJ: Princeton University Press, 1983); Eric Schickler, *Racial Realignment* (Princeton, NJ: Princeton University Press, 2016).

6.   Christopher Waldrep, "National Policing, Lynching, and Constitutional Change," *Journal of Southern History* 84, no. 3 (2008): 589–626; Daniel Kato,

Liberalizing Lynching: Building a New Racialized State (New York: Oxford University Press, 2015); Michael James Pfeifer, *Rough Justice: Lynching and American Society, 1874–1947* (Urbana: University of Illinois Press, 2004).

7. Risa L. Goluboff, *The Lost Promise of Civil Rights* (Cambridge, MA: Harvard University Press, 2007), 112, 117.

8. Waldrep, "National Policing," 618.

9. On tensions between civil rights in political realignment and the war on crime, see Matthew G. T. Denney, "'To Wage a War': Crime, Race, and State Making in the Age of FDR," *Studies in American Political Development* 35, no. 1 (2021): 19–27.

10. Marshall to Allen, 21 December 1943, NAACPHV, Legal File: Crime— Allen, John 1943 (1532_001_0251).

11. Christopher Waldrep, *African Americans Confront Lynching: Strategies of Resistance from the Civil War to the Civil Rights Era* (Plymouth, UK: Rowman and Littlefield, 2009); Brandon T. Jett, *Race, Crime, and Policing in the Jim Crow South: African Americans and Law Enforcement in Birmingham, Memphis, and New Orleans, 1920–1945* (Baton Rouge: Louisiana State Press, 2021); Megan Ming Francis, *Civil Rights and the Making of the American State* (New York: Cambridge University Press, 2014).

12. Moss to White, 23 September 1933, NAACPHV, SF: Crime, 1933 (001530_014_0467).

13. Further Statement of George Crawford, 2 February 1933, NAACPHV, LFCS: George Crawford (001530_006_0271).

14. Memorandum on the George Crawford Case; NAACP to "my dear sir," 15 June 1933—both NAACPHV, LFCS: George Crawford (001530_006_0743).

15. Wilson to White, 18 February 1933, NAACPHV, LFCS: George Crawford (001530_006_0271).

16. At least once, federal–local arrangements overcame state-level protection. New York governor Lehman refused to extradite a Black man who fled Georgia fearing he would be lynched, but federal–local cooperation overruled his prerogative. Daniel C. Richman and Sarah Seo, "How Federalism Built the FBI, Sustained Local Police, and Left Out the States," *Stanford Journal of Civil Rights and Civil Liberties* 17 (2022): 462.

17. James H. Chadbourn, *Lynching and the Law* (Chapel Hill: University of North Carolina Press, 1933), 5.

18. H. L. Mencken, "A New Deal Constitution," *American Mercury,* June 1937, 129–136; Mencken, "The Eastern Shore Kultur," *Evening Sun* (1931).

19. White to FDR, 29 November 1933; White to FDR, 6 December 1933; Country Is Called to Fight against Lynching, 1 December 1933, 002-0196—both NAACPHV, SF: Anti-Lynching (001529_002_0196).

20. Resolution for Federal Anti-Lynching Legislation, NAACPHV, SF: Nat'l Crime Conf 1934–35 (001529_004_0521).

21. Holmes to White, 19 December 1934; Secretary to Charlie, 21 December 1934—both NAACPHV, SF: Memorials Anti-Lynching (001529_028_0560).

22. Memo to cooperating organizations, 4 May 1934, NAACPHV, SF: Cos-Wag Bill (001529_005_1350).

23. Franklyn Waltman, "Anti-Lynching Bill Fight Marks Emergence of Negro Race as Political Force," *Washington Post*, 27 January 1938, NAACPHV, General Office File: Anti-Lynching Bill Misc., 1936–1939 (001529_030_0618).

24. For Immediate Release, 25 September [1933], NAACPHV, SF: Anti-Lynching Measures 1932–1934 (001529_002_0196).

25. Honorable Arthur W. Mitchell of Illinois, Radio, 6 Tuesday 1937, NAACPHV, General Office File: Anti-Lynching Bill Misc., 1936–1939 (001529_030_0618).

26. Homer Cummings and Carl McFarland, *Federal Justice: Chapters in the History of Justice and the Federal Executive* (New York: Macmillan, 1937), 248.

27. Daniel Kato argues that judicial affirmation of federal nonintervention was a case of "constitutional anarchy." See Kato, *Liberalizing Lynching*.

28. "Secret Romance Led to Last Florida Lynching," *Afro-American*, 24 November 1934.

29. "Renewed Support for Anti-Lynching Bill," *New Journal and Guide*, 8 December 1934.

30. "Lynching Put Off for Fear of Disorder," *Baltimore Sun*, 27 October 1934.

31. Note from Marianna, Florida, 7 November 1934, NAACPHV, SF: Lynching—Nov. 1934 (001527-004-0628).

32. Civil Rights Division, Notice to Close File, file no. 144-17-792, 1 October 2013, NAACPHV, SF: Lynching—Claude Neal.

33. "Group Kills Negro; Disappoints Crowd," *New York Times*, 28 October 1934.

34. Civil Rights Division, Notice to Close File, file no. 144-17-792, 1 October 2013, NAACPHV, SF: Lynching—Claude Neal.

35. "Fla. Mob Attacked Everyone after the Lynching of Neal," *Afro-American*, 24 November 1934.

36. "Mother, Aunt of Mob Victim Thrown in Jail," *New Journal and Guide,* 8 December 1934.

37. Note from Marianna, Florida, 7 November 1934, NAACPHV, Administrative File: Lynching Nov. 1934 (001527_004_0628).

38. "Claude Neal, Mob Victim, Was Innocent," *New Journal and Guide,* 15 June 1935.

39. "Secret Interracial Romance Blamed for Florida Lynching," *Cleveland Call and Post,* 24 November 1934.

40. "The Lynching of Claude Neal," 26 October 1934, NAACPHV, SF: Lynching of Claude Neal (001527_009_0927).

41. "Sends Report to Roosevelt," *New York Amsterdam News,* 1 December 1934.

42. Release for Sunday November 4 Papers; "Pickens Says US Should Apologize to Dillinger and Floyd Relatives," New York, 9 November; "Lindbergh Law Can Be Used against Florida Mob, President Is Told," 2 November 1934—all NAACPHV, SF: Lynching—Nov. 1934 (001527_004_0628).

43. White to Cummings, 27 October 1934; White to Cummings, 30 November 1934—both NAACPHV, SF: Lynching of Claude Neal (001527_009_0927).

44. Keenan to White, 9 October 1934; Wilkins to White, 21 November 1934; Suggested Slogans for Picket Placards . . . 28 November 1934—all NAACPHV, SF: Nat'l Crime Conf 1934–35 (001529_004_0521).

45. Police Arrest NAACP Pickets at National Crime Conference, 14 December 1934, NAACPHV, LFCS: Kater Stevens, October–December 1934 (001530_011_0425).

46. Douglas to White, 20 December 1934; Lovett to White, 20 December 1934—both NAACPHV, SF: Memorials (1529_028_0560).

47. Harvey Dawes Memorandum, 22–31 December 1934, NAACPHV, SF: Cos-Wag Bill (001529_006_1052).

48. Lehman, Memorial to President Franklin D. Roosevelt; List of Signers to Date, 21 December 1934; List of Liberal-Minded Southerners—all NAACPHV, SF: Memorials (001529_028_0560).

49. Wilson to White, 24 December 1934, NAACPHV, SF: Cos-Wag Bill (001529_006_1052).

50. Frederick Reese, 14 December 1934, NAACPHV, SF: Memorials (001529_028_0560).

51. Beard to White, 12 February 1936, NAACPHV, SF: Cos-Wag Bill (001529_009_0684).

52. "Certain Objections Which Have Been Raised," NAACPHV, General Office File: Anti-Lynching Bill Misc., 1936–1939 (001529_030_0618).

53. MFTAG, 28 February 1935, OF10, box 3.

54. To Attorney General, February 1935, OF10, box 3.

55. Attorney General, 13 March 1935, OF10, box 3.

56. White to Cummings, 18 January 1935, NAACPHV: SF: Lynching of Claude Neal (001527_009_0927).

57. Attorney General to President, 3 February 1936, OF10, box 3.

58. Secretary to Baldwin, 19 February 1936, NAACPHV, SF: Cos-Wag Bill (001529_009_0684).

59. White to Cummings, 16 December 1936; White to Cummings, 24 December 1936—both PHSC, box 135: NAACP.

60. Louis Howe, Respectfully Referred to the Attorney General, 20 August 1933, OF10, box 1.

61. Harriet Shadd Butcher, 14 May 1934, OF10, box 2.

62. Memorandum for Mr. Stanley Reed, 31 August 1935, OF10, box 2; Rep. Arthur W.–Illinois, 4 September 1935, OF10, box 3.

63. Memorandum on Interview of the Secretary of NAACP with President, on July 2, 1936; To the Democratic National Convention, Philadelphia, PA, 23 June 1936—both NAACPHV, General Office File: Anti-Lynching Bill Misc., 1936–1939 (001529_030_0618).

64. J. E. Taylor to Charles H. Houston, 16 November 1937, NAACPHV, SF: Police Brutality 1937 (001530_014_0643).

65. Secretary to C. A. Scott, 4 January 1935, NAACPHV, LFCR: W. A. Scott (001530_013_0646); Assistant Special Counsel to Gordon, 2 December 1937, NAACPHV, Legal File: Gordon, John (001530_016_0049).

66. Marshall to Brashear, 18 August 1938, NAACPHV, LFCR: Richard Hammond (001530_013_0056).

67. McLaughlin, The State v. Arthur Perry, Motion for New Trial, August Term 1937, NAACPHV, LFCS: Oscar Perry (001530_010_0467).

68. Houston to Browne, 22 March 1938, NAACPHV, LFCS: Lonnie Mitchell (001530_010_0067).

69. Assistant Sec. to Marshall, 5 June 1935, NAACPHV, LFCR: P–S 1935 (001530_012_0443).

70. Houston to Campbell, 6 March 1936, NAACPHV, LFCR: C–D 1936 (001530_012_0456).

71. Assistant Sec. to Jackson, esq, 29 April 1935, NAACPHV, LFCR: T–Y 1935 (001530_012_0452).

72. Assistant Sec. to Wolinsky, 25 August 1933, NAACPHV, LFCR: Edward Gray (001530_012_0929).

73. Assistant Secretary to Harris, 13 August 1935, NAACPHV, LFCR: Freeman & Stark (001530_012_0841).

74. Assistant Special Counsel to McCall, Esq, 30 November 1936, NAACPHV, LFCR, K–L 1936 (001530_012_0483).

75. Counsel to Capshaw, 4 October 1935, NAACPHV, LFCR: Ernest Womack (001530_013_1023).

76. Todd to Marshall, 30 May 1938, NAACPHV, LFCR: Cox & Ford (001530_012_0692).

77. Munro to Marshall, 23 November 1937, NAACPHV, LFCS: Kater Stevens (001530_011_0425).

78. Houston to McDougald, 11 February 1936, NAACPHV, LFCR: Booker T. McDonald (001530_013_0431).

79. Houston to Patrick, Sr., 22 May 1936, NAACPHV, Legal File: Extradition–Fleetwood (001530_001_0663).

80. Marshall to Allen, 21 December 1943, NAACPHV, Legal File: Crime–Allen, John 1 (001532_001_0251).

81. Houston to McDougald, 2 April 1936, NAACPHV, LFCR: Booker T. McDonald (001530_013_0431).

82. Houston to Owens, 28 October 1937, NAACPHV, SF: Police Brutality: 1937, NJ, NY (001530_014_0643).

83. J. H. Pope, Re: William Gibson Jr. and Robert Wilson, NAACPHV, Legal File: Crime–Gibson (001530_016_0028).

84. Marshall to Woulfe Esq, 26 January 1939, NAACPHV, Legal File: Crime–Pierre (001530_016_0321).

85. Browne to NAACP, 14 November 1938, NAACPHV, LFCS: Lonnie Mitchell (001530_010_0067).

86. Re: State vs. James Poindexter, 7 June 1935, NAACPHV, LFCR: P–S 1935 (001530_012_0443).

87. Jones to White, 21 August 1935; Newell to White, 6 September 1935—both NAACPHV, LFCR: Givens (001530_012_0857).

88. Assistant Secretary to McCall, 8 December 1936, NAACPHV, LFCR: K–L 1936 (001530_012_0483).

89. McGill to Houston, 11 September 1935, NAACPHV, LFCR: Givens (001530_012_0857).

90. Shores to Marshall, 2 August 1939; In the Matter of Will Hall vs. George Williams, 27 July 1939—both NAACPHV, SF: Police Brutality: 1939 Alabama, Florida (001530_014_0806).

91. Houston to Frasier, 4 March 1936, NAACPHV, LFCR: Frazier (001530_012_0825).

92. Scott to Darrow, 27 September 1934, NAACPHV, LFCR: W.A. Scott (001530_013_0646).

93. Memorandum to Mr. Wilkins from Mr. White, 3 April 1933, NAACPHV, SF: Crime, 1933 (001530_014_0467).

94. Gates to White, 8 September 1933, NAACPHV, LFCS: Kelly-Bullock (001530_009_0629).

95. Secretary to Police Commissioners, 12 October 1939, NAACPHV, SF: Police Brutality: 1939 Alabama, Florida (001530_014_0806).

96. Memorandum from Mr. White to Mr. Turner, 3 October 1938, NAACPHV, LFCS: Angelo Herndon (001530_008_0775).

97. "Snow Hill to Send Vagrants out of Town," 20 September [1938]; *New York Post,* 28 September 1938—both NAACPHV, SF: Police Brutality: 1938 Maryland (001530_014_0775).

98. Press Service of the NAACP Florida Governor Asked to Probe Killing of Boy, 3 September [1937]; Davis to Civil Liberties Union, 29 August 1937; ACLU (Ward and Baldwin and Hays) to Honorable Fred P. Cone, 31 August 1937; News Release: ACLU, 31 August 1937; Report Rendered to ACLU and NAACP on the Killing of Stafford G. Dames, Jr, on July 27, 1937; Wirin to S. G. Dames, 31 August 1937; Preliminary report submitted on Demes murder case . . . , 1 September 1937—all NAACPHV, SF: Police Brutality, Stafford Dames, July–September 1937 (001530_014_1017).

99. Carson to Dames, 16 November 1937; Miami Tribune Clipping, "Red Activity Here Charged by Quigg"—both NAACPHV, SF: Police Brutality, Stafford Dames, October 1937–February 1938 (001530_014_1124).

100. See Robin D. G. Kelley, *Hammer and Hoe: Alabama Communists during the Great Depression* (Chapel Hill: University of North Carolina Press, 2015).

101. "James Person: Please Send This to the NAACP," Pittsburg Branch; Memo to Wilkins from White, 10 November 1937—both NAACPHV, SF: Police Brutality: 1937 (001530_014_0643).

102. Marshall to Curlin, 1 September 1937, NAACPHV, SF: Police Brutality, Stafford Dames July–September 1937 (001530_014_1017).

103. Pickens to Dames, 9 September 1937; McCallister to Wirin, 13 September 1937—both NAACPHV, SF: Police Brutality, Stafford Dames July–September 1937 (001530_014_1017).

104. Mary L. Dudziak, *Cold War Civil Rights: Race and the Image of American Democracy* (Princeton, NJ: Princeton University Press, 2011).

105. Gordon Dean, MFTAG, 1 October 1936, PHSC, box 75.

106. Memorandum for Attorney General, 17 November 1936, PHSC, box 75.

107. Brian McMahon, MFTAG, 24 November 1936, PHSC, box 75.

108. Sara Anita Downer, "Guilty Arkansas Peonage Planter Seeks New Trial: Probation Is Offered," *Chicago Defender*, 5 December 1936.

109. "Slavery Verdict Won by 'G' Men," *New York Times*, 29 November 1936.

110. Downer, "Guilty Arkansas Peonage Planter."

111. "Mr. Cummings Wakes Up," *Afro-American*, 12 December 1936.

112. *New York Times*, 27 November 1936.

113. Goluboff, *Lost Promise of Civil Rights*, 118.

114. International Labor Defense, Summary of Herndon Case, NAACPHV, LFCS: Angelo Herndon (001530_008_0775).

115. In the Supreme Court of the United States, October Term, 1934, no. 665, Herndon v. Georgia, Brief of Amici Curiae in Support of Motion for Rehearing; Herndon to National Executive Committee, NAACP, 24 May 1935—both NAACPHV, LFCS: Angelo Herndon (0530-008-0617).

116. International Labor Defense, Summary of Herndon Case, NAACPHV, LFCS: Angelo Herndon (001530_008_0775).

117. Herndon to White, 12 June 1935, NAACPHV, LFCS: Angelo Herndon (0530-008-0617).

118. Special Counsel to Miss Mary Fox, League for Industrial Democracy, 19 September 1935, NAACPHV, LFCS: Angelo Herndon (001530_008_0668).

119. Supreme Court, Angelo Herndon v. Georgia, Brief of Amici Curiae; Herndon to NAACP Exec. Committee, 24 May 1935—both NAACPHV, LFCS: Angelo Herndon (0530-008-0617).

120. Herndon Freed: Georgia Insurrection Law Unconstitutional, International Labor Defense Statement on Herndon Decision, 26 April 1937; Angelo Herndon Issues Statement, April 26 1937—both NAACPHV, LFCS: Angelo Herndon (001530_008_0775).

121. Jon S. Blackman, *Oklahoma's Indian New Deal* (Norman: University of Oklahoma Press, 2013), 23, 29, 47.

122. Richmond L. Clow, "The Indian Reorganization Act and the Loss of Tribal Sovereignty," *Great Plains Quarterly* 7, no. 2 (1987): 125–134.

123. Graham D. Taylor, *The New Deal and American Indian Tribalism: The Administration of the Indian Reorganization Act, 1934–1945* (Lincoln: University of Nebraska Press, 1980), 91.

124. Lawrence C. Kelly, "The Indian Reorganization Act: The Dream and the Reality," *Pacific Historical Review* 44, no. 3 (1975): 291–312.

125. Melissa Walker calls the TVA the first federal "development of an entire region." Walker, "African Americans and TVA Reservoir Property Removal: Race in a New Deal Program," *Agricultural History* 72, no. 2 (Spring 1998).

126. Graves to Miller, 8 June 1939, TVAPC, box 10, folder: NAACP, 1933–1934.

127. Miller to Graves, 21 June 1939, TVAPC, box 10, folder: NAACP, 1933–1934.

128. Report of Hearing Held by the Director of Personnel of the Tennessee Valley Authority regarding Complaints Filed by the NAACP . . . , 17 October 1938, Gordon Clapp. Hearing conducted 7 and 8 September, 1938, TVAPC, box 10, folder: NAACP, 1933–1934.

129. Anthony Gregory, "Policing Jim Crow America: Law Enforcers' Agency and Structural Transformations," *Law and History Review* 40, no. 1 (2022).

130. Silvan Niedermeier explores police torture's modernizing effect in *The Color of the Third Degree: Racism, Police Torture, and Civil Rights in the American South, 1930–1955*, trans. Paul Cohen (Chapel Hill: University of North Carolina Press, 2019). On the history of the evolution from mob violence to state executions, see Seth Kotch, "The Making of the Modern Death Penalty in Jim Crow North Carolina," and Vivien Miller, "Hanging, the Electric Chair, and Death Penalty Reform in the Early Twentieth-Century South," both in *Crime and Punishment in the Jim Crow South*, ed. Amy Louise Wood and Natalie J. Ring (Urbana: University of Illinois Press, 2011); 297 U.S. 278 (1936).

131. Secretary to Senator Capper, 25 March 1939, NAACPHV, General Office File: Anti-Lynching Bill Misc., 1936–1939 (001529_030_0618).

132. David T. Beito, "New Deal Mass Surveillance: The 'Black Inquisition Committee,' 1935–1936, *Journal of Policy History* 30, no. 2 (2018).

133. "Anti-Lynch Act Shelved by Filibuster," *Pittsburgh Post-Gazette*, 2 May 1935.

134. Secretary to Mr. Chappell, 10 June 1937, NAACPHV, SF: Wagner (001529_021_0786).

135. "Opposed to Black," *New York Amsterdam News*, 21 August 1937.

136. "Sen Black is 'Black Eye' to Hope in Race," *Chicago Defender*, 21 August 1937.

137. "United War Veterans Protest against Black," *Chicago Defender,* 9 October 1937.

138. "Black Voted to Supreme Court Despite Klan Charge," *Washington Post,* 18 August 1937.

139. For Immediate Release, Department of Justice, 13 September 1937, OF10, box 4.

140. To White, 4 June 1937, NAACPHV, SF: Wagner (001529_021_0786).

141. Memorandum to MR Houston from Mr. White, 7 October 1937, NAACPHV, SF: Police Brutality: 1937, Alabama, Arkansas, D.C. (001530_014_0569).

142. Franklyn Waltran to White, 21 December 1937, NAACPHV, SF: Wagner (001529_022_0442).

143. NAACP Sends Protest on Sumners for High Court, 7 January [1938], NAACPHV, SF: Conferences: Presidential Anti-Lynching (001529_004_0658).

144. Robert L. Fleegler, "Theodore G. Bilbo and the Decline of Public Racism, 1938–1947," *Journal of Mississippi History* 68, no. 1 (2006): 1–27, 9.

145. Secretary to Senator Capper, 25 March 1939, NAACPHV, General Office File: Anti-Lynching Bill Misc., 1936–1939 (001529_030_0618).

146. Secretary to Philip Randolph, 26 March 1938; Secretary to Bob, 11 April 1938—both NAACPHV, SF: Presidential Anti-Lynching (001529_004_0658).

147. NAACP Investigator Says Secret Interracial Romance Was Basis of Florida Lynching, NAACPHV, SF: Lynching (001527_004_0628).

148. NAACP: AFL Backs Federal Anti-Lynching Bill and Vetoes Discrimination, 13 October 1939; Resolution Adopted by Unknown Soldier Post American Legion, 28 February 1938—both NAACPHV, General Office File: Anti-Lynching Bill (001529_029_0839).

149. Memo to Mr. Marshall from Mr. White, 15 April 1940, NAACPHV, Legal File: Police Brutality: Gildersleeve (001532_019_0598).

150. Wilkins to White, 1 February 1940, NAACPHV, General Office File: Anti-Lynching Hearing (001529_032_0172).

151. Ransom to White, 27 September 1939, NAACPHV, General Office File: Anti-Lynching Special Session (001529_035_0001).

152. O'Reilly, "The Roosevelt Administration and Black America," *Phylon* 48, no. 1 (1987): 12–25.

8. BUILDING CARCERAL LIBERALISM

1. Cummings, "Why Alcatraz Is a Success," *Colliers,* 29 July 1939.

2. Cummings, "Why Alcatraz Is a Success."

3. Observing that Harry Elmer Barnes and Negley K. Teeters saw the new penology's "paradoxes" in Alcatraz, Ward and Kassebaum observe that this novel "prison explicitly designed to hold and punish the nation's criminal elite" complicates the "progressive evolution of American penology" toward "corrections." David Ward with Gene Kassebaum, *Alcatraz: The Gangster Years* (Berkeley: University of California Press, 2009), 2.

4. David M. Kennedy, *Freedom from Fear: The American People in Depression and War, 1929–1945* (New York: Oxford University Press, 1999), has no index entries for "Alcatraz," "jails," or "prisons," although it has a robust entry on "prisoners of war"; see 879, 903, 919.

5. US Department of Justice Bureau of Justice Statistics, *Historical Corrections Statistics in the United States, 1850–1984,* 29, 35. Qualitative changes accompanied quantitative rise, as definite sentencing peaked in 1940— 61 percent of sentences were definite sentences, up from 51 percent a decade earlier (41).

6. One exception is Matthew G. T. Denney, "'To Wage a War': Crime, Race, and State Making in the Age of FDR," *Studies in American Political Development* 35, no. 1 (2021): 17.

7. On the WPA and cultural consciousness, see Christine Bold, *The WPA Guides: Mapping America* (Jackson: University Press of Mississippi, 1999), xiii. On the WPA's transformative political role, including a discussion of Japanese internment camps, see Jason Scott Smith, *Building New Deal Liberalism: The Political Economy of Public Works, 1933–1956* (New York: Cambridge University Press, 2006).

8. Tracing the story to the nineteenth century, Marie Gottschalk suggests that there was a predicament for national authority in the 1920s, quoting Virgil W. Peterson: "Uncontrolled crime had become one of the most serious threats to democracy." Gottschalk, *The Prison and the Gallows: The Politics of Mass Incarceration in America* (Cambridge: Cambridge University Press, 2006), 59. Ruth Wilson Gilmore identifies the "balance of power relations" and "state illegitimacy" in modern carceral origins, considers the welfare contradictions peaking with World War II, and relates the building of the carceral state to southern Democratic loyalties. Gilmore, *Golden Gulag: Prisons, Surplus, Crisis, and Opposition in Globalizing California* (Berkeley: University of California Press, 2007), 80, 79, 9, 136.

9.   For Michel Foucault's theory of discipline as "essentially *corrective*" and socially functionalist, see Foucault, *Discipline and Punish: The Birth of the Prison,* trans. Alan Sheridan (New York: Vintage Books, 1995 [1977]), 179, inter alia. David J. Rothman found Foucault's "mode of analysis" excessively deterministic; Rothman argues that prisons arose from "decisions" regarding a "*theory* of punishment" rather than wholesale "from some capitalist spirit." Rothman, *Conscience and Convenience: The Asylum and Its Alternatives in Progressive America* (Boston: Little, Brown, 1980), 11. While Rothman channeled Foucault's focus on normalization, shed of his materialism, McLennan has shared Rothman's stress on contingency while re-centering political economy. Rebecca M. McLennan, *The Crisis of Imprisonment: Protest, Politics, and the Making of the American Penal State, 1776–1941* (New York: Cambridge University Press, 2008), 278n113, 417–467.

10.   On the core tensions, see Matthew Pehl, "Between the Market and the State: The Problem of Prison Labor in the New Deal," *Labor: Studies in Working-Class History* 16, no. 2 (2019): 77–97. On how the "New Deal labor compromise had operationalized reformist politics by renovating structures of the racial state," see Gilmore, *Golden Gulag,* 136. For PIRA's limits, see Maria Ponomarenko, "The Department of Justice and the Limits of the New Deal State, 1933–1945" (diss., Stanford University, 2010).

11.   Emphasizing his focus on one "prison in its historical epoch" and not "the prison experience as a whole," Bright examines the "parallel constitution of political order" and maximum-security incarceration. Charles Bright, *The Powers That Punish: Prison and Politics in the Era of the "Big House," 1920–1955* (Ann Arbor: University of Michigan Press, 1996), 4, 29.

12.   On mass incarceration as a distinctively late-twentieth-century story, see Jordan T. Camp, *Incarcerating the Crisis: Freedom Struggles and the Rise of the Neoliberal State* (Berkeley: University of California Press, 2016), 3. Also see Jonathan Simon, *Governing through Crime: How the War on Crime Transformed American Democracy and Created a Culture of Fear* (Oxford: Oxford University Press, 2009), 22–31. In *From the War on Poverty to the War on Crime: The Making of Mass Incarceration in America* (Cambridge, MA: Harvard University Press, 2016), Elizabeth Hinton suggests that mass incarceration is both constitutive of and a deviation from postwar welfare statism. On New Deal liberalism and postwar carcerality, also see Margot Canaday, *The Straight State: Sexuality and Citizenship in Twentieth-Century America* (Princeton, NJ: Princeton University Press, 2011).

13.   "By 1935, the managerial system of imprisonment . . . anticipated and distilled the basic dynamics of the post-industrial prison order." McLennan, *The Crisis of Imprisonment,* 466.

14. Foucault attributes unforgiving criminal categories and punitiveness to nineteenth-century bourgeois liberalism, after the French Revolution and "landed property became absolute property." Foucault, *Discipline and Punish*, 85.

15. To explain the US and British "penal-welfare state," David Garland describes the social-contractual war on crime as emerging from classical liberalism and cresting in the 1970s. The early modern "*Hobbesian* problem of order" had given way to "a *Marxist* problem of order—the social and political instability caused by class antagonism and unregulated economic exploitation" before being addressed in the New Deal era. Garland, *The Culture of Control: Crime and Social Order in Contemporary Society* (Chicago: University of Chicago Press, 2001). Also see Garland, *Punishment and Welfare: A History of Penal Strategies* (Aldershot: Gower, 1985).

16. Sanford Bates, *Prisons and Beyond* (New York: MacMillan, 1937), 306.

17. Bates, *Prisons and Beyond*, 3, 14.

18. Memorandum for Mr. Caldwell, 30 December 1933, BOPAF, box 2, entry 9.

19. Bates, *Prisons and Beyond*, 17, 27.

20. Bates, *Prisons and Beyond*, 5, 8, 19, 20.

21. The new penologists exposed indignities and emphasized justice and inmate participation. Lawes developed the "original new penological project into a new, managerialist penal order." McLennan, *The Crisis of Imprisonment*, 448.

22. David Rankin Barbee, "Five Prison Revolts Make Nation Wonder," *Washington Post*, 15 December 1929.

23. "Behind the Walls of New York's Prisons," *New York Times*, 22 December 1929.

24. W. A. Warn, "Legislature Passes Roosevelt's Bill for Prison Relief," *New York Times*, 7 January 1930; McLennan, *The Crisis of Imprisonment*, 458.

25. Homer Cummings and Carl McFarland, *Federal Justice: Chapters in the History of Justice and the Federal Executive* (New York: Macmillan, 1937), 352-365.

26. *SRP*, 5:308, 311.

27. *SRP*, 1:1-2, 7, 17.

28. *SRP*, 5:310, 40, 27.

29. Bright, *The Powers That Punish*, 10-14, critiques the self-referential whiggish outlook.

30. Hudspeth to Ingersol, 27 February 1933; Hudspeth to APC Hansen, 12 April 1933; Hudspeth to Donelan, 19 April 1933; Hudspeth to Stucker, 19 July 1933; Hudspeth to Lucas, 29 March 1933; Hudspeth to Rehorn, 24 May 1933; To General Inspection Service, 4 December 1933; Director to Paulett, 30 December 1933—all BOPAF, box 235, DOJ Mails and Files, folder 4-2-4-0.

31. Bates to Attorney General, 17 March 1932, BOPAF, box 2, entry 9, DOJ Mail and Files, folder 4-01-9.

32. "Pennsylvania Convicts Fire Prison, Quelled," *New York Times,* 22 November 1933.

33. *SRP,* 5:43.

34. Caldwell to Bates, 21 December 1933, BOPAF, box 2, entry 9, DOJ Mail and Files, folder 4-01-10.

35. Zerbst to Director, 2 October 1934; Memo for Director of Bureau of Prisons, J. E. Hoover, 17 September 1934; H. S. Cumming to Bureau of Prisons Director, 17 March 1934—all BOPAF, box 235, DOJ Mails and Files, folder 4-2-4-0.

36. Bates, *Prisons and Beyond,* 10.

37. Hudspeth to Director, 14 February 1934; Director to Warden, 7 February 1934; Zerbst to Director, 26 September 1933; Singer to Hudspeth, 18 August 1933, Hudspeth to Director, 2 August 1933; Memo of Disturbance, 22 August 1933—all BOPAF, box 235, DOJ Mails and Files, folder 4-2-4-0.

38. Office memorandum to Keenan, 1 August 1933, *SPHC,* 29; Memorandum from Bates, 8 August 1933, *SPHC,* 30.

39. Cummings, "Why Alcatraz Is a Success," *Colliers,* 29 July 1939; Bates, *Prisons and Beyond,* 143.

40. "The root causes of these problems were lax management and a system that tolerated—even encouraged—influence peddling, the buying of favors, and other improper relations among prisoners and guards." Ward with Kassebaum, *Alcatraz,* 42–43.

41. Cummings, "Alcatraz by the Men Who Made It," PHSC, box 70: Alcatraz Misc.

42. Bates to Vollmer, 20 November 1933, AVP, box 31: U.S. Bureau of Prisons 1929–1952.

43. Zerbst to Director, 2 October 1934, BOPAF, box 234: DOJ Mails and Files Division, file 4-2-4-0.

44. Ward with Kassebaum, *Alcatraz,* 81; Angelo Paris, no. 20, AWN.

45. Ward with Kassebaum, *Alcatraz*, 81.

46. William J. Simmons, no. 57, AWN.

47. Harry E. Dean, no. 41, AWN.

48. Ward with Kassebaum, *Alcatraz*, 81.

49. Ward with Kassebaum, *Alcatraz*, 111–113, identifies the tension: "The practical concerns of running the prison were not always well served by rules rooted in the need to project a harsh image."

50. Ward with Kassebaum, *Alcatraz*, 124.

51. Bennett to Rumple, 1 November 1932, BOPAF, box 1, folder: Prisoners and National Parks. See Matthew Pehl, "Between the Market and the State: The Problem of Prison Labor in the New Deal," *Labor: Studies in Working-Class History* 16, no. 2 (2019): 77–97.

52. Director to Chief of the Forest Service, 9 April 1935; Memorandum for the Files, 24 August, 1936—both BOFAF, box 1, folder: Prisoners and National Parks.

53. Frank T. Flynn, "The Federal Government and the Prison-Labor Problem in the States," *Social Service Review* 24, no. 2 (June 1950): 216–228.

54. PIRA Progress Report, 15 May 1937; Executive Order: Establishment of the Prison Industries Reorganization Administration, no. 7194, 26 September 1935, APPUCSB.

55. Flynn, "Prison-Labor Problem"; PIRA Progress Report, 15 May 1937, 6.

56. Gustav Peck, "The Prison Labor Situation," *Proceedings of the Annual Congress of the American Prison Association* (1937): 237.

57. PIRA Progress Report, 15 May 1937.

58. "Laws Affecting the Labor of Prisoners and the Sale and Distribution of Prison-Made Products in the United States," 1, 8, in PIRA, Bulletin no. 1, AGAC SF, box 16.

59. *America Builds: The Record of PWA* (Washington, DC: Division of Information, US Government Printing Office, 1939), 100, 106, 199–200.

60. *America Builds*, 199–200, 73, 197, 100.

61. "Alcatraz Prison Improvements and Guard Housing," LND.

62. *Final Report on the WPA Program, 1935–1943* (Washington, DC: US Government Printing Office, 1947), 52. One study found 3,469 American jails in 1923. Without including prisons, the figure gives a sense of the WPA's impact. Another study estimated 2,317 jails; yet another reported 4,037. See *Historical Corrections Statistics*, 92.

63. "National Training School for Boys (former)—Washington DC," LND; *Final Report on the WPA Program,* 34, 118; "Los Prietos CCC Camp (former)—Santa Barbara CA," LND.

64. "Reformatory Improvements—Framingham MA"; "Whittier State School/ Fred C. Nelles School for Boys—Whittier CA"—all LND.

65. "Old Somervell County Jail—Glen Rose TX"; "Rikers Island Penitentiary Improvements—East Elmhurst NY"; "Civil Prison (demolished) Improvements—Brooklyn NY"; "Baja County Courthouse Annex— Springfield CO"; "Contra Costa County Jail Improvements—Martinez CA"; "Camden County Detention Home (Former) Renovation—Pennsauken NJ"; Kingfisher County Jail—Kingfisher OK"; "Santa Cruz City Jail (former)— Santa Cruz CA"; "Jailhouse—Carbon Hill AL"; "Lincoln County Jail and Sheriff's Residence—Canton SD"; "Trinity County Jail—Groveton TX"; "Peoria Jail Museum—Peoria AZ"; "Eddy County Courthouse and Jail— Carlsbad NM"; "Jefferson County Jail (former) Improvements—Monticello FL"; "Maries County Courthouse—Vienna MO"; "Ellicott City Jail (former) Reparis—Ellicott City MD"; "Rowan County Jail and Superintendent's Office—Morehead KY"; "City Hall—Pineville KY"; "Jasper County Jail (former)—Jasper TX"; "Montrose County Jail (former)—Jasper TX"; "Montrose County Jail—Montrose CO"; "San Francisco Hall of Justice and County Jail (demolished)—San Francisco CA"; "Hale Pa'ahao Prison Improvements—Lahaina HI"—all LND.

66. The final report said the survey came "in response to an increasing volume of protest against the use of parole." *SRP,* 1:vii.

67. From the *Journal of Criminal Law and Criminology,* March 1936 Federal Survey, 7 January 1935, AGAC SF, box 1, folder: Executive Committee.

68. *SRP,* 5:9.

69. *SRP,* 5:2–5, 29, 30.

70. On federal attempts to make the nation legible through miscegenation law, see Peggy Pascoe, *What Comes Naturally: Miscegenation Law and the Making of Race in America* (Oxford: Oxford University Press, 2009). Also see James C. Scott, *Seeing Like a State: How Certain Schemes to Improve the Human Condition Have Failed* (New Haven, CT: Yale University Press, 1998).

71. *SRP,* 1:v.

72. Miller to Metz, 31 January 1936; Sanders to Burgess—both AGSRP GC, box 5, folder: WPA.

73. To Whom It May Concern, 16 May 1936, AGSRP GC, box 1, folder: Advisory Committee.

74. Miller, MFTAG, 10 October 1936, AGSRP GC, box 1, folder: Advisory Committee.

75. He reasoned that even the juvenile courts that qualified as criminal courts effectively suspended the sentences of boys put on probation—and because these convicted juveniles were not technically "serving sentence," they "should not be excluded." Miller, Memorandum for Assistant Solicitor Bell, 29 January 1936, Report from Hiller, "Probationers in CCC Camps," AGSRP GC, box 1, folder: Memorandum.

76. Miller, MFTAG, 10 October 1936, AGSRP GC, box 1, folder: Advisory Committee.

77. *SRP,* 1:xi, viii, xi.

78. Miller to Parsons, 9 October 1936, AGSRP GC, box 1, folder: Advisory Committee.

79. Miller Memorandum for Mr. Bates, 22 May 1936; Gill to Miller, 2 April 1936; Sanders, Memorandum for Mr. Justin Miller, 7 April 1936—all AGSRP GC, box 1, folder: Executive Committee.

80. Hutcheson to Cummings, 7 January 1936, AGSRP GC, box 1, folder: Advisory Committee.

81. Miller, Memorandum for Bates, 9 January 1936; Bates, Memorandum for Miller, 3 January 1936, AGSRP GC, box 1, folder: Memorandum.

82. From the *Journal of Criminal Law and Criminology,* March 1936, Federal Survey, 7 January 1935, AGSRP GC, box 1, folder: Executive Committee.

83. Advisory Committee: Attorney General's, *SRP,* 1 December 1936, AGSRP GC, box 1, folder: Advisory Committee.

84. Memorandum for Miller, 5 December 1936, AGSRP GC, box 1, folder: Memorandum.

85. Sanders, Memorandum for Miller, 28 January 1936; Miller, Memorandum for Bates, 2 June 1936; Miller, Memorandum for McMahon, 12 December 1935—all AGSRP GC, box 1, folder: Memorandum.

86. Joseph N. U. to Miller, 16 November 1936, AGSRP GC, box 1, folder: Conference.

87. Miller, Memorandum for Mr. McMahon, 20 February 1936, AGSRP GC, box 1, folder: Memorandum.

88. To Miller, 14 November 1936, AGSRP GC, box 1, folder: Conference, Attorney General's Survey, November 19th and 20th.

89. Halpern to Miller, 6 November 1936, AGSRP GC, box 5, folder: WPA.

90. Technical Director, Memo for Miller, 7 January 1936, AGSRP GC, box 1, folder: Memorandum.

91. Gill to Miller, 4 March 1936, AGSRP GC, box 1, folder: Advisory Committee.

92. George T. Scully, 16 December 1935, AGSRP GC, box 1, folder: Executive Committee.

93. Gill to Miller, 19 March 1936, AGSRP GC, box 5, folder: WPA.

94. MFTAG, 15 February 1936, AGSRP GC, 1925–1938, box 1, folder: Advisory Committee.

95. Morse, Memorandum for Mr. Ray Huff, 10 February 1937; Lovell Bixby to Miller, 12 March 1936—both in AGSRP GC, box 1, folder: Memorandum.

96. Stout to Sanders, 13 November 1936, AGSRP GC, box 5, folder: WPA.

97. Halpers to Miller, 6 November 1936; Sterle to Ames, 5 October 1936—both AGSRP GC, box 1, folder: Advisory Committee.

98. MFTAG, 6 January 1936, AGSRP GC, box 1, folder: Advisory Committee.

99. Glueck to Miller, 6 January 1936; Miller, MFTAG, 10 January 1936; MFTAG, 14 February 1936—all AGSRP GC, box 1, folder: Advisory Committee.

100. Miller, Memorandum for Assistant Solicitor General Bell, 29 January 1936; Report from Francis H. Hiller, Field Director of National Probation Association, "Probationers in CCC Camps"; Edmund A. Clune, Memorandum for Mr. Miller, 14 January 1936—all AGSRP GC, box 1, folder: Memorandum.

101. Miller, Memorandum for the Assistant to the Attorney General, 5 March 1936, AGSRP GC, box 1, folder: Memorandum; Miller to Johler, 9 October 1936, AGSRP GC, box 1, folder: Advisory Committee.

102. Miller to Cummings, 21 September 1936, AGSRP GC, box 1, folder: Advisory Committee.

103. Attorney General to Huff, 2 December 1936, and Miller to Cox, 30 January 1936—both AGSRP GC, box 1, folder: Advisory Committee; Attorney General to Whom It May Concern, February 1936, and Bartelt to Miller, 22 January 1936—both AGSRP GC, box 1, folder: Memorandum.

104. Miller, Memorandum for Mr. McMahon, 25 January 1936, AGSRP GC, box 1, folder: Memorandum.

105. WPA Operating Procedure no. W-9, 11 March 1937, AGSRP GC, box 5, folder: WPA.

106. Miller to Gill, 20 February 1936, AGSRP GC, box 5, folder: WPA; Miller, MFTAG, 18 November 1936, AGSRP GC, box 1, folder: Advisory Committee.

107. Miller, Memorandum for Brien McMahon, 19 December 1935, AGSRP GC, box 1, folder: Memorandum.

108. Gill to Miller, 18 February 1936, AGSRP GC, box 5, folder: WPA.

109. Sanders, Memorandum for Mr. Justin Miller, 19 December 1935, AGSRP GC, box 1, folder: Executive Committee.

110. Memorandum for Joseph B. Keenan, 6 February 1936, AGSRP GC, box 1, folder: Advisory Committee.

111. Miller, Memorandum for Mr. Gordon Dean, 6 February 1936, AGSRP GC, box 1, folder: Memorandum.

112. Memorandum for the Records, 18 June 1936, AGSRP GC, box 1, folder: Executive Committee.

113. Report on the Executive Committee Meeting, 3 June 1936, AGSRP GC, box 1, folder: Executive Committee.

114. Attorney General to Gill, 21 July 1936, AGSRP GC, box 5, folder: WPA.

115. My Dear Mr. Hopkins, 15 December 1936, AGSRP GC, box 5, folder: WPA.

116. Miller to Rice, 17 November 1936, AGSRP GC, box 1, folder: Advisory Committee.

117. Meeting of the Exec. Committee, 14 May 1936, AGSRP GC, box 1, folder: Executive Committee.

118. Rice to Miller, 9 November 1936; Miller to Rice, 17 November 1936—both AGSRP GC, box 1, folder: Advisory Committee.

119. Miller to Bates, 11 November 1936; To Miller, 14 November 1936; Miller to Boach, 11 November; Miller to Bechkham, 11 November 1936; Miller to Best, 11 November 1936; Miller to Coy, 11 November 1936; Miller to Hannan, 16 November 1936; Miller to Laune, 11 November 1936; Kavanaugh to Miller, 6 January 1937; Miller to Gillin, 2 December 1936; Miller to Best, 16 November 1936; Miller to Schroeder, 22 December 1936; Miller to Hannan, 21 December 1936—all AGSRP GC, box 1, folder: Conference, Attorney General's Survey, November 19th and 20th.

120. Petition to the Federal WPA, AGSRP GC, box 5, folder: WPA.

121. Emerson Ross to Miller, 21 April 1936, AGSRP GC, box 5, folder: WPA.

122. Clune, Memorandum for Mr. Miller, 7 January 1936, box 1, folder: Memorandum.

123. Miller, MFTAG, 10 December 1936; Morse to Cooke, National Secretary, 10 March 1937; The Arbitration Board, 28 April 1937; McIntosh to Morris, 2 June 1937; Minutes, 18 April 1936, Workers Alliance Local 3, Chairman David Dixon Presiding; Ray Huff and David Dixon to Benedict Wolfe, 25 April 1937; The Arbitration Board, 28 April 1937; Morse to David Dixon, 17 April 1937; Morse to Dixon, 17 April 1937—all AGSRP GC, box 5, folder: WPA.

124. Dear Mr. Hopkins, 3 February 1937, AGSRP GC, box 5, folder: WPA.

125. Morse to Bennett 4 February 1937, AGSRP GC, box 1, folder: Executive Committee; Wayne Morse, MFTAG, 1 February 1937, AGSRP GC, box 1, folder: Attorney General.

126. Report of the Executive Committee: Suggested Plans for the Preparation and Publication of the Reports; Weihofen and Raymond, Memorandum for the Executive Committee and the Attorney General, 26 March 1937; Meeting of the Executive Committee, 15 June 1937—all AGSRP GC, box 7, folder: Executive Committee.

127. Memorandum for Mr. Justin Miller, 7 November 1936, AGSRP GC, box 1, folder: Executive Committee.

128. Attorney General to Poindexter, 7 December 1936, AGSRP GC, box 1, folder: Advisory Committee.

129. Morse to Rice, 20 March 1937, AGSRP GC, box 5, folder: WPA.

130. The Executive Committee (Miller, McMahon, Bennett, Bixby): Memorandum to Dr. Rice, 7 April 1937, AGSRP GC, box 5, folder: WPA.

131. Meeting of the Exec Committee and the Coordinating Committee Held Thursday, 1 April 1937, AGSRP GC, box 1, folder: Executive Committee.

132. Attorney General to Dr. Stuart Rice, 10 April 1937, AGSRP GC, box 5, folder: WPA.

133. Agenda for the Meeting of the Executive Committee; Memorandum for Members of the Executive Committee, 9 July 1937; Morse, Memorandum to the Members of the Executive Committee, 26 February 1938; Morse to Bennett, 23 March 1938; Gill to Morse, 5 February 1938; Morse to Bennett, 23 March 1938; Gill to Morse, 5 February 1938; Morse, Memorandum for Director James Bennett, 15 April 1938—all AGSRP GC, box 7, folder: Executive Committee.

134. See Christopher Mueller, "Northward Migration and the Rise of Racial Disparity in American Incarceration, 1880–1950," *American Journal of Sociology* 118, no. 2 (September 2012): 287.

135. *SRP,* 1:233.

136. *SRP,* 1:321.

137. *SRP,* 1:743.

138. *SRP,* 2:365.

139. *SRP,* 1:1009.

140. *SRP,* 3:67–68.

141. *SRP,* 2:341, 364, 366, 367, 319.

142. *SRP,* 4:319.

143. *SRP,* 4:421.

144. *SRP,* 4:541.

145. *SRP,* 4:323.

146. *SRP,* 4:558.

147. Bates, *Prisons and Beyond,* 303, 278, 118.

148. Bates, *Prisons and Beyond,* 215, 293, 94.

149. Bates, *Prisons and Beyond,* 92–93, 125, 177, 249, 260.

150. Bates, *Prisons and Beyond,* 145.

151. Cummings to Stydan,14 June 1939, PHSC, box 70: Alcatraz Misc.

152. Bates to Cummings, 16 June 1939, PHSC, box 70: Alcatraz Misc.

153. Cummings, "Why Alcatraz Is a Success," *Colliers,* 29 July 1939.

154. To Johnston, 26 June 1939, PHSC, box 70: Alcatraz Misc.

155. Bensinger to Cummings, 20 July 1939, PHSC, box 70: Alcatraz Misc.

156. Bates to Cummings, 24 July 1939, PHSC, box 70: Alcatraz Misc.

157. Cummings to Early, 24 July 1939; Roosevelt to Cummings, 27 July 1939— both PHSC, box 70: Alcatraz Misc.

158. *SRP,* 5:311, 86, 87, 298.

159. *SRP,* 5:41, 76.

160. *SRP,* 5:109, 71, 117, 113, 72.

161. *SRP,* 5:35.

162. *SRP,* 5:35, 362.

163. *SRP,* 5:68.

164. Bixby to Miller, 12 March 1936, AGSRP GC, box 1, folder: Memorandum.

165. Christopher Muller argues for a longer-term and chronologically earlier focus. Muller, "Northward Migration and the Rise of Racial Disparity in

American Incarceration, 1880–1950," *American Journal of Sociology* 118, no. 2 (September 2012): 281–542.

166. *Final Report on the WPA Program, 1935–1943* (Washington, DC: US Government Printing Office, 1947), 61.

167. Mueller, "Northward Migration and the Rise of Racial Disparity," 282, 287, 289.

168. Demographics hardly shifted on gender—95 percent of federal prisoners were men throughout the decade. The racial change was hardly subtle. *Historical Corrections Statistics,* table 3.32, 66.

169. *Historical Corrections Statistics,* table 3.8, 61.

9. PREVENTION, REPRESSION, AND NEW DEAL CRIMINOLOGY

1.   AGAC GC, box 1, folder: Agenda.

2.   Roosevelt, Address to the Conference on Crime, 10 December 1934, APPUCSB.

3.   Intellectual histories often highlight Edwin Sutherland's sociological approach as triumphing over the Gluecks' multidisciplinarity. John H. Laub and Robert J. Sampson, "The Sutherland-Glueck Debate: On the Sociology of Criminological Knowledge," *American Journal of Sociology* 96, no. 6 (May 1991): 1402–1440. John Galliher traces roots from Bentham and Lombroso through modern social science, yielding a theoretical "positivism [with] liberal reformist political implications" and "perhaps reflecting widespread sentiment supportive of New Deal politics." John F. Galliher, "The Life and Death of Liberal Criminology," *Contemporary Crises* 2 (1978): 246.

4.   Claire Bond Potter, *War on Crime: Bandits, G-Men, and the Politics of Mass Culture* (New Brunswick, NJ: Rutgers University Press, 1998), 184. Also see Janis Appier, "'We're Blocking Youth's Path to Crime': The Los Angeles Coordinating Councils during the Great Depression," *Journal of Urban History* 31, no. 2 (2005): 207.

5.   Kathleen J. Frydl, "Kidnapping and State Development in the United States," *Studies in American Political Development* 20 (Spring 2006): 40.

6.   Priorities of "social security, development, and economic justice" lost the budget and influence contest to priorities of "national security," writes Richard J. Barnet in "The Ideology of the National Security State," *Massachusetts Review* 26, no. 4 (Winter 1985): 486. In contrast, David Garland, *The Culture of Control: Crime and Social Order in Contemporary Society* (Chicago: University of Chicago Press, 2001), situates the New Deal era in the Atlantic arc of penal-welfarism.

7. Accounts often criticize Vollmer-style progressive professionalization and postwar developments more than New Deal criminology. Compare Tony Platt, "Prospects for a Radical Criminology in the United States," *Crime and Social Justice,* no. 1 (Spring–Summer 1974): 2–10, to Platt, "Criminology in the 1980s: Progressive Alternatives to 'Law and Order,'" *Crime and Social Justice,* no. 21/22 (1984): 191–199.

8. On juvenile justice, see Máximo Langer and David Tanenhaus, *The Arc of American Juvenile Justice: From Flexible Due Process to Adversarial Power, 1870–2020* (Oxford: Oxford University Press, forthcoming).

9. Khalil Gibran Muhammad, *The Condemnation of Blackness: Race, Crime, and the Making of Modern Urban America* (Cambridge, MA: Harvard University Press, 2010), 146–191. Also see Anthony M. Platt, *The Child Savers: The Invention of Delinquency* (New Brunswick, NJ: Rutgers, 2009 [1969]), and Geoff K. Ward, *The Black Child-Savers: Racial Democracy and Juvenile Justice* (Chicago: University of Chicago Press, 2012). By the early 1930s, most "crime prevention" material concerned juvenile delinquency. See, for example, Harry M. Shulman, "Crime Prevention and the Public Schools," *Journal of Educational Sociology* 4, no. 2 (October 1930): 69–81; 545–555; Frederic M. Thrasher, "Juvenile Delinquency and Crime Prevention," *Journal of Educational Sociology* 6, no. 8 (April 1933): 500–509; Max W. Nohl, "Crime Prevention from the Cradle Up," *Journal of Criminal Law and Criminology* 28, no. 2 (Summer 1937): 220–231; Benedict S. Alper, "Progress in Prevention of Juvenile Delinquency," *Annals of the American Academy of Political and Social Science* 212, "Children in a Depression Decade" (November 1940): 202–208.

10. Marcus to Cummings, 13 December 1934, AGAC GC, box 2, folder: Crime Prevention.

11. See William G. Hale, "Crime: Modern Methods of Prevention, Redemption and Protection," *Journal of Criminal Law and Criminology* 9 (August 1918); Robert H. Gault, "Psychiatric Clinics for the Prevention of Delinquency," *Journal of Criminal Law and Criminology* 9 (1919): 477–479.

12. See F. W. Jenkins, *Crime Prevention and Crime Repression,* Russell Sage Foundation no. 81, February 1927; Thomas Orbison, "The Prevention of Crimes in Mental Delinquency," *Journal of Delinquency* 11 (1927).

13. Geiger to Waters, 11 July 1932, MVWP, box 15, folder 71.

14. Harry M. Shulman, "Social Agencies and Crime Prevention," *Journal of Criminal Law and Criminology* 22, no. 4 (Fall 1931): 545–555; Augustus Frederick Kuhlman, "Crime Prevention," in *A Guide to Material on Crime and Criminal Justice* (New York: H. W. Wilson, 1929); Neva R. Deardorff, "Some Aspects of Juvenile Delinquency," *Annals of the American Academy of Political*

and Social Science 125 (1926): 68–78; Outline of Crime Prevention, Memo to EH Randolph, AGAC SF, box 5, folder: Crime Prevention. On the Committee on Social Hygiene, see Edith Rockwood and Augusta J. Street, "Social Protective Work of Public Agencies, with Special Emphasis on the Policewoman" (Washington, DC: National League of Women Voters, Committee on Social Hygiene, April 1932).

15. "Educational Programs for Crime Prevention," AGAC SF, box 5, folder: Economic Factors in Crime.

16. Dorothy E. Bradbury, *Four Decades of Action for Children: A History of the Children's Bureau* (Washington, DC: Children's Bureau, 1956), 19.

17. National Commission on Law Observance and Enforcement, no. 14, Report on Police, Washington DC, 26 June 1931, 111.

18. Vollmer to Bowler, 21 May 1934, AVP, box 43; To Alida C. Bowler, 15 August 1933, AVP, box 42.

19. Vollmer to Wilson, 1 September 1933, AVP, box 43.

20. "Reformatories That Do Not Reform," *Literary Digest*, 1 March 1930, PETSG, box 24, folder 7.

21. Sheldon and Eleanor Glueck, Memorandum on Characteristics of Delinquent Boys as Found in 1,000 Juvenile Delinquents, 1933, AGAC SF, box 3, folder: Causes of Crime (2).

22. AGAC SF, box 1, folder: Agenda.

23. Franklin Roosevelt, Address to the Conference on Crime, 10 December 1934, APPUCSB.

24. MFTAG, 10 October 1936, AGAC GC, box 1.

25. Summary of Crime Prevention Conference, Buffalo, New York, 1937, AGAC SF, box 5, folder: Crime Prevention Conference.

26. Federal Judicial Center, "Miller, Justin," Biographical Directory of Federal Judges, https://www.fjc.gov/history/judges/miller-justin.

27. MFTAG, 24 December 1934, signed by Justin Miller, AGAC GC, box 1, folder: Agenda.

28. MFTAG, Subject: Attorney General's Crime Conference—Public Opinion and Crime, 4 January 1935, AGAC GC, box 1 (emphasis in original).

29. MFTAG, 3 January 1935; "Introduction"—both AGAC GC, box 1.

30. Report on the Attorney General's Advisory Committee on Crime, 1 May 1935, AGAC GC, box 1.

31. MFTAG, 2 May 1935, AGAC GC, box 1.

32. "To Every Member of the Advisory Committee on Crime," AGAC GC, box 1, folder: Advisory Committee.

33. MFTAG, 3 January 1935, AGAC GC, box 1, folder: Agenda.

34. Scope of Activities, AGAC GC, box 1, folder: Advisory Committee.

35. MFTAG, 20 August 1935, AGAC GC, box 1.

36. MFTAG, 21 February 1936, AGAC GC, box 1.

37. MFTAG, 7 April 1936, AGAC GC, box 1.

38. MFTAG, 4 November 1935, AGAC GC, box 1.

39. MFTAG, 6 January 1936, AGAC GC, box 1.

40. MFTAG, 28 May 1935, AGAC GC, box 1.

41. Glueck to Sheldon, 11 September 1935, AGAC GC, box 1.

42. MFTAG, 24 July 1936, AGAC GC, box 1.

43. MFTAG, 14 February 1935; Betters to Cummings, 8 February 1935; Cummings to Hoan, 14 February 1935—all AGAC GC, box 1.

44. Attorney General to Hoan, 14 February 1935, AGAC GC, box 1.

45. Memorandum for Mr. Suydam, 13 January 1936, AGAC GC, box 1.

46. MFTAG, 24 October 1935, AGAC GC, box 1.

47. MFTAG, 14 July 1936, AGAC GC, box 1.

48. Miller to Ragsdale, 19 November 1935; MFTAG, 29 May 1936—both AGAC GC, box 1.

49. MFTAG, 6 December 1936, AGAC GC, box 1.

50. MFTAG, 3 January 1935, Re: Departmental Organization, AGAC GC, box 1.

51. Bureau of Publicity, Democratic National Committee, Women's Division, National Press Building, Washington, D.C, for Release after Thursday, October 31st, 1935, MWDP, box 9.

52. MFTAG, 4 March 1936; MFTAG, 1 October 1936; MFTAG, 3 June 1936; MFTAG, 14 July 1936; Miller to Ragsdale, 19 November 1935; MFTAG Cummings, 29 May 1936—all AGAC GC, box 1.

53. MFTAG, 16 February 1935, AGAC GC, box 1.

54. MFTAG, 6 June 1935, AGAC GC, box 1.

55. Director to Lee, 2 July 1935, AGAC GC, box 2.

56. MFTAG, 30 June 1936, AGAC GC, box 1.

57. MFTAG, 9 July 1936, AGAC GC, box 1.

58. Cummings to Mass, 25 January 1937, PHSC, box 114; Lee to Bates, 1 July 1935, AGAC GC, box 2, folder: Crime Prevention.

59. MFTAG, 2 May 1935, AGAC GC, box 1.

60. MacLean Memorandum, 23 May 1935, AGAC GC, box 2, folder: Crime Prevention.

61. MFTAG, 24 May 1935; Memorandum for Mr. MacLean, 24 May 1935; Department of Justice Appropriation Act 1936, Title II Pub. no. 22 74th Congress—all AGAC GC, box 2, folder: Crime Prevention.

62. MFTAG, 25 June 1935, AGAC GC, box 1.

63. Memorandum for Mr. Justin Miller, 21 December 1935, AGAC GC, box 2, folder: Crime Prevention.

64. Attorney General's Advisory Committee on Crime Report, AGAC SF, box 1, folder: AGAC Report. Roosevelt only acknowledged the CCC's crime prevention function in 1939, but insiders saw it in these terms. John A. Pandiani, "The Crime Control Corps: An Invisible New Deal Program," *British Journal of Sociology* 33, no. 3 (1982): 352.

65. MFTAG, 9 April 1936; MFTAG, 7 April 1936—both AGAC GC, box 1.

66. "A Plan for the Crime Prevention Conferences," AGAC SF, box 5, folder: Crime Prevention.

67. Miller to Atkinson, 14 June 1935, AGAC SF, box 3, folder: Child Welfare; Miller to Big Brother & Big Sister Federation in NYC, 1 July 1935, AGAC SF, box 3, folder: Child Welfare.

68. MFTAG, 7 April 1936, AGAC GC, box 1.

69. AGAC Report, AGAC SF, box 1, folder: AGAC Report; AGAC SF, box 2: folder: Bibliographies.

70. Report on Sub-Committee on Plan and Scope of Attorney General's Advisory Committee on Crime, 29 April 1935, AGAC GC, box 1, folder: Advisory Committee.

71. "Apathy of Public Cited by Milligan as Ally of Crime," *Kansas City Mo. Journal-Post,* 10 October 1936, AGAC SF, box 3, folder: Causes of Crime; "Greed and Cruelty of Individuals" and "Moral Weakness," *Portland Oregonian,* 20 June 1936, AGAC SF, box 3, folder: Causes of Crime; Editorial, "Society Must Assume Blame," *Pueblo Colorado Chieftain,* 31 March 1936; "A Job for Schools," *Jackson Mississippi News,* 13 June 1936.

72. Atkinson to Miller, 27 June 1935, AGAC SF, box 3, folder: Child Welfare.

73. Johnstone to Miller, September 27, 1935, AGAC SF, box 3, folder: Child Welfare.

74. *Paterson NJ News,* 23 March 1936.

75. Undated Speech, ERP, box 1403: Speech and Article file, 1935.

76. MFTAG, 19 November 1935; MFTAG, 5 January 1937—both AGAC GC, box 1.

77. Keuhme to Cummings, 27 December 1934; Lukamski to Cummings, 15 December 1934; Castle to Cummings, 15 December 1934—all AGAC SF, box 2, folder: Crime Prevention.

78. Paul H. Douglas, Child Welfare Pamphlets no. 38, "The Impact of Recent Social and Economic Changes upon the Family," 1934, AGAC SF, box 5, folder: Economic Factors in Crime.

79. *Scranton PA Times,* 5 May 1936.

80. Herbert D. Williams, "Causes of Social Maladjustment in Children," *Psychological Monographs* 43, no. 1 (1932): 293; "Portrait of a Criminal" *Philadelphia Ledger,* 2 October 1936.

81. "Crime Prevention Objectives," *Journal of Criminal Law and Criminology* 27, no. 2 (July–August 1936): 289–290; Herbert D. Williams, "A Survey of Pre-Delinquent Children in the Mid Western Cities," Big Brother and Sister Federation, 1933.

82. Justin Miller, "Does Prolific Breeding Cause Crime?," *Birth Control Review,* April 1930, 105, in AGAC SF, box 3, folder: Birth Control.

83. "Sterilization laws," AGAC SF, box 22, folder: Sterilization.

84. Miller to Gosney, 6 December 1935; Gosney to Miller, 16 November 1935—both AGAC SF, box 6, folder: Eugenics.

85. Norton to Miller, 10 April 1936, AGAC SF, box 3, folder: Causes of Crime (2).

86. Glueck to Sheldon, 11 September 1935, AGAC GC, box 1.

87. Sheldon Glueck, "Crime Prevention," Address at Annual Meeting of Big Brother and Sister Federation, Inc., 15 April 1935, AGAC SF, box 7, folder: Glueck.

88. MFTAG, 30 March 1936, AGAC GC, box 1.

89. Baldwin to Miller, 17 March 1936; Miller to Baldwin, 25 March 1936—both AGAC SF, box 4, folder: Civil Liberties.

90. Scott to Miller, 30 July 1935; Schain, National Director of Girl Scouts; Miller to Kirland, 11 April 1936—all AGAC SF, box 3, folder: Child Welfare.

91. Franklin D. Roosevelt, "Announcement of the Appointment of Interdepartmental Committee for Coordination of Federal Health Activities," 15 August 1935, APP UCSB.

92. Robyn Muncy discusses Roche and the Interdepartmental Committee in *Relentless Reformer: Josephine Roche and Progressivism in Twentieth-Century America* (Princeton, NJ: Princeton University Press, 2014).

93. Membership, Financial Committee; Membership of Working Subcommittee; Membership of the Full Committee—all PICCHWA, box 43: Vol. 3; MFTAG, 23 October 1936, AGAC GC, box 1.

94. MFTAG, 28 October 1936, AGAC GC, box 1.

95. Conference of Technical Committee, 15 April 1937, PICCHWA, box 43: Vol. 3.

96. MFTAG, 7 April 1936, AGAC GC, box 1.

97. Memorandum for Mr. Miller (from Fuller), 20 May 1936, AGAC GC, box 1.

98. Fuller to Gillin, 16 June 1937, AGAC SF, box 5, folder: Economic Factors in Crime.

99. AGAC SF, box 3, folder: Bills; Fuller to Heimlich, 12 August 1938; Heimlich to Fuller, 8 August 1938; Heimlich to Fuller, 20 June 1938; Fuller to Heimlich, June 15, 1937; Heimlich to Fuller, 14 June 1938; Fuller to Heimlich, 8 July 1938—all AGAC SF, box 3, folder: Building America.

100. Minutes of Conference of Working Committee, 15 July 1937, PICCHWA, box 43: Vol. 3.

101. Summary of Conference of Working Committee, 7 October 1937, PICCHWA, box 43: Vol. 3.

102. Report for Technical Committee, undated draft, PICCHWA, box 39, folder: Parole and Crime, Prevention, Miscellaneous, 1936–1938.

103. "Bureau of Prisons," PICCHWA, box 6: Correspondence with Government Agencies 1935 to 1938: DOJ.

104. John Ryan, *Crime Prevention: Correction Department Officers Should Be Assigned to Work with Police Squad, Combined Force Would Prevent Many Crimes* (1932), indexed in *Bibliography of Crime and Criminal Justice, 1932–1937,* compiled by Dorothy Campbell Culver, Bureau of Public Administration, University of California (New York: H. W. Wilson Co., 1939), 333.

105. Max Schlepp, "A Plan for the Reduction of Criminality," *National Municipal Review* 15 (September 1924).

106. Herman Adler, "The Prevention of Crime," *Journal of Criminal Law and Criminology* 23, no. 1 (May–June 1932): 81–84.

107. See Sanford Bates, "The Next One Hundred Years in Probation: Progress Is Being Made," 31 May 1941, in *Vital Speeches of the Day* 7, no. 20 (1941): 625–627.

108. Miller to Bates, 11 November 1936, AGSRP GC, entry 422, box 1, folder: Conference—Attorney General's Survey, November 19th and 20th.

109. Interview with Dr. Sanders, 10 March 1937, PICCHWA, box 6.

110. Minutes of Conference of Working Committee, 18 January 1938, PICCHWA, box 39, folder: Records of the Technical Committee, 1937–1940. Others working the final report included Donald Beattie (Administration of Criminal Statistics), Wayne Morse (Survey of Release Procedures), Richard Chappell (Federal Parole System), and Benjamin Frank (Educational Director, Bureau of Prisons), but Fuller was essentially the lead. Membership, Financial Committee; Membership of Working Subcommittee; Membership of the Full Committee—all PICCHWA, box 43: Vol. 3.

111. Peck to Leukhardt, 17 February 1938; Peck to Lowrie, 21 March 1938; Leukhardt to Lowrie, 22 March 1938; Lowrie, Draft of letter to Gustav Peck, 11 April 1938—all PICCHWA, box 39, folder: Records of the Technical Committee, 1937–1940.

112. Memorandum: Technical Committee, PICCHWA, box 43: Vol. 3.

113. See generally PICCHWA, box 43: Vol. 3.

114. Memorandum: Technical Committee, PICCHWA, box 43: Vol. 3.

115. Cummings to Roche, 5 October 1938, PICCHWA, box 43: Vol. 3.

116. Cummings to Roche, 10 October 1938; Memo: "Should the Federal Prison System Be Transferred to a Department of Welfare?"—both PICCHWA, box 43: vol. 3.

117. Memorandum for Chapman, from Commissioner of Education, 31 May 1938, PICCHWA, box 39.

118. Memorandum from Leukhardt to Altmeyer, 25 October 1938; Parole and Crime Prevention Report 1938—both PICCHWA, box 39, folder: Parole Crime Prevention Report 1938.

119. Blaisdell to Watson, 5 April 1940, PICCHWA, box 39, folder: Records of the Technical Committee, 1937–1940.

PART V. THE LIBERAL SECURITY STATE, 1935–1945

1. Roosevelt, Radio Address on the Election of Liberals, 4 November 1938, UCSB.

2.   See Andrew Preston, *The Invention of National Security* (Cambridge, MA: Harvard University Press, 2024); Risa L. Goluboff, *The Lost Promise of Civil Rights* (Cambridge, MA: Harvard University Press, 2007), 150.

3.   Jonathan Simon argues that there is a trade-off in governance among three values—"liberty, security, and community." The "Crime Deal" has undercut the "New Deal's version of the liberty-security-community paradigm." Simon, "From the New Deal to the Crime Deal," in *After the War on Crime: Race, Democracy, and a New Reconstruction*, ed. Mary Louise Frampton, Ian Haney López, and Jonathan Simon (New York: New York University Press, 2008), 50.

4.   In assessing World War II's impact, historians often distinguish the welfare state from the security state. See James T. Sparrow, *Warfare State: World War II Americans and the Age of Big Government* (New York: Oxford University Press, 2013); Carl Boggs, *Origins of the Warfare State: World War II and the Transformation of American Politics* (New York: Routledge, 2017).

5.   Historical sociologist Jason Scott Smith tracks liberalism through policy experimentation, even considering WPA's construction of internment camps, in *Building New Deal Liberalism: The Political Economy of Public Works, 1933–1956* (New York: Cambridge University Press, 2006). Alan Brinkley ponders the shift from New Deal fiscal philosophy to wartime quasi-Keynesianism in *The End of Reform: New Deal Liberalism in Recession and War* (New York: Vintage Books, 1996 [1995]), 14. Lizabeth Cohen concurs on the shifting ethos of political economy in *A Consumers' Republic: The Politics of Mass Consumption in Postwar America* (New York: Vintage Books, 2003), chaps. 1 and 2. Also see Robert Higgs, *Crisis and Leviathan: Critical Episodes in the Growth of American Government* (New York: Oxford University Press, 1997); Arthur A. Ekirch, *The Decline of American Liberalism* (New York: Longmans, Green, 1955).

6.   The idea that the New Deal war on crime ended in the mid-1930s has long resonated with scholars. See John A. Conley, "The New Deal's Response to Crime: The Politics of Law and Order" (master's thesis, Michigan State University, 1971), https://www.ojp.gov/pdffiles1/Digitization/68672NCJRS.pdf.

10. THE NEW POLITICAL ECONOMY OF LAW AND ORDER

1.   Roosevelt, Radio Address on the Election of Liberals, 4 November 1938, APPUCSB.

2.   Barry Latzer, *The Rise and Fall of Violent Crime in America* (New York: Encounter Books, 2016).

3.   G. William Domhoff and Michael J. Webber, *Class and Power in the New Deal* (Stanford, CA: Stanford University Press, 2020); Marlene Park, "City and Country in the 1930s: A Study of New Deal Murals in New York," *Art Journal* 39,

no. 1 (1979): 37–47; Jefferson Cowie, *The Great Exception: The New Deal and the Limits of American Politics* (Princeton, NJ: Princeton University Press, 2016).

4. An early sarcastic usage is in Edward A. Steiner, *Sanctus Spiritus and Company* (New York: George H. Doran Company, 1919), 284. On its application to Prohibition, see Oliver Herford and Karl Schmidt, *What'll You Have?* (New York: Henry Holt, 1925), 25.

5. These class paradoxes had an analog in interwar racist criminology: The receding of eugenic obsessions regarding European immigrants, along with what Khalid Muhammad calls the "Condemnation of Blackness," crescendoed, and by the 1930s the "long" civil rights era began grappling toward outward colorblindness. Khalil Gibran Muhammad, *The Condemnation of Blackness: Race, Crime, and the Making of Modern Urban America* (Cambridge, MA: Harvard University Press, 2010). By 1928, literature was retreating from the most deterministic racist criminology, even as racist law enforcement continued in practice. See Thorsten Sellin, "The Negro Criminal: A Statistical Note," *Annals of the American Academy of Political and Social Science* 140, no. 1 (1928): 52–64.

6. "28 More for Digits Are Indicted," *Atlanta Daily World*, 10 April 1932, 1.

7. "73 Are Indicted in Laundry Racket," *New York Times*, 26 April 1934, 19.

8. "Exterminate the 'Lawyer Criminal'" *ABA Journal* 19, no. 11 (November 1933).

9. Roosevelt, Statement on Signing Crime Bill, 18 May 1934, APPUCSB.

10. Roosevelt, Acceptance Speech for the Renomination for the Presidency, 27 June 1936, APPUCSB.

11. White-collar crime "typically encompasses the following offences committed mainly by corporations, their owners, executives or employees as well as by government or municipal officials and members of the professions: fraud, corruption, embezzlement, misappropriation and malfeasance, tax fraud, intellectual property theft, insider trading, money laundering, Ponzi schemes, misrepresentation of financial statements, price-fixing, illegal cartels, and collusion as well as the breach of environmental, health and safety regulations." Hartmut Berghoff and Uwe Spiekermann, "Shady Business: On the History of White-Collar Crime," *Business History* 60, no. 3 (2018): 289–290.

12. Dusey to Moley, 11 August 1933, RMP, box 211.

13. Edwin H. Sutherland, "White Collar Criminality," *American Sociological Review* 5, no. 1 (1940): 2.

14. Berghoff and Spiekermann, "Shady Business," 291, 289–290.

15. Sutherland, "White Collar Criminality," 2, 9, 6, 4.

16. Sutherland, "White Collar Criminality," 3, 4, 5, 6.

17. John H. Laub and Robert J. Sampson, "The Sutherland-Glueck Debate: On the Sociology of Criminological Knowledge," *American Journal of Sociology* 96, no. 6 (May 1991): 1402–1440.

18. Sutherland, "White Collar Criminality," 10, 11.

19. William J. Hausman, "Howard Hopson's Billion Dollar Fraud: The Rise and Fall of Associated Gas & Electric Company, 1921–1940," *Business History* 60, no. 3 (2018): 381–382.

20. Hausman, "Howard Hopson's Billion Dollar Fraud," 388–390.

21. Richard Schneirov, "Urban Regimes and the Policing of Strikes in Two Gilded Age Cities: New York and Chicago," *Studies in American Political Development* 33, no. 2 (2019): 258–274.

22. Williams to Merriam and Rossi, 17 September 1934; Williams to Merriam, 12 October 1934—both NCB, Subseries 1.2, carton 5, folder 98: General Correspondence, 1934.

23. Ernest Besig, "To All Churches, Trade Unions, Fraternal Organizations, etc.," 26 August 1935, ACLUNC, Subseries 2.24, carton 35, folder 742: Police Accountability, 1934, 1952.

24. Williams to Addis, 21 November 1934, NCB, carton 5, folder 98: General Correspondence, 1934.

25. Minutes, 7 October 1935, ACLUNC, Subseries 1.1, carton 1, folder 8.

26. Minutes, 22 August 1938, ACLUNC, Subseries 1.1, carton 1, folder 9.

27. Besig to McGinty, 15 February 1936; McMahon to Besig, 26 February1936—both ACLUNC, Subseries 2.24, carton 35, folder 748.

28. Packard to Besig, 21 March 1936, ACLUNC, Subseries 2.24, carton 35, folder 100.

29. Minutes, 4 April 1938; Minutes, 27 June 1938—both ACLUNC, Subseries 1.1, carton 1, folder 9.

30. Minutes, 24 May 1937, ACLUNC, Subseries 1.1, carton 1, folder 8.

31. Minutes, 16 May 1938, ACLUNC, Subseries 1.1, carton 1, folder 9.

32. See Jerold S. Auerbach, "The La Follette Committee and the CIO," *Wisconsin Magazine of History* 48, no. 1 (1964): 3–20.

33. See Simon Balto and Max Felker-Kantor, "Police and Crime in the American City, 1800–2020," *Oxford Research Encyclopedia of American History* (Oxford: Oxford University Press, 2022).

34. George B. Vold, "Crime in City and Country Areas," *Annals of the American Academy of Political and Social Science* 217 (September 1941): 40.

35. Stone, "Substitution of the Summons and Notice for Expansive Arrest Procedure," RMP, box 197.

36. Daniel C. Richman and Sarah Seo, "How Federalism Built the FBI, Sustained Local Police, and Left Out the States," *Stanford Journal of Civil Rights and Civil Liberties* 17 (2022).

37. Kathleen Battles, *Calling All Cars: Radio Dragnets and the Technology of Policing* (Minneapolis: University of Minnesota Press, 2010), 80, 86.

38. "Burma White Case," *Calling All Cars,* 6 December 1933, https://www
.oldtimeradiodownloads.com/crime/calling-all-cars/burma-white-case-1933
-12-06.

39. CaptO#33, 19 February 1936, SFPD9, box 3, folder 3.

40. CaptO#100, 28 April 1934, SFPD9, box 3, folder 9.

41. CaptO#107, 5 May 1934, SFPD9, box 3, folder 8.

42. CaptO#60, 23 February 1935, SFPD9, box 3, folder 6.

43. CaptO#122, 21 May 1936, SFPD9, box 3, folder 2.

44. CaptO#111, 9 May 1934, SFPD9, box 3, folder 8.

45. CaptO#123, 21 May 1934, SFPD9, box 3, folder 8.

46. CaptO#124, 28 May 1934, SFPD9, box 3, folder 9.

47. Quinn to Bonner, 10 August 1934, ACLUNC, Subseries 1.2, carton 5, folder 99.

48. CaptO#132, 9 June 1934, SFPD9, box 3, folder 9.

49. CaptO#3, 2 January 1936, SFPD9, box 3, folder 3.

50. CaptO#228, 29 October 1934, SFPD9, box 3, folder 7.

51. Captain's Order, 25 April 1934, SFPD9, box 3, folder 6.

52. CaptO#184, 21 August 1934, SFPD9, box 3, folder 2.

53. CaptO#240, 28 September 1935, SFPD9, box 3, folder 4.

54. CaptO#50, 27 February 1934; CaptO#28, 13 February 1934; CaptO#40, 21 February 1934; CaptO#41, 23 February 1934—all SFPD9, box 3, folder 9.

55. CaptO#242, 31 October 1934, SFPD9, box 3, folder 7; CaptO#275, 29 October 1935, SFPD9, box 3, folder 4; CaptO#251, 27 October 1936, SFPD9, box 3, folder 1.

56. CaptO#179, 29 July 1936, SFPD9, box 3, folder 2.

57. CaptO#272, 24 October 1935, SFPD9, box 3, folder 4.

58. CaptO#167, 17 July 1936, SFPD9, box 3, folder 2.

59. CaptO#225, 27 September 1936, SFPD9, box 3, folder 1.

60. CaptO#30, 15 February 1934, SFPD9, box 3, folder 9.

61. CaptO#148, 1 July 1934, SFPD9, box 3, folder 8.

62. CaptO#257, 9 December 1934, SFPD9, box 3, folder 7.

63. CaptO#78, 19 March 1935, SFPD9, box 3, folder 6.

64. CaptO#108, 5 May 1934, SFPD9, box 3, folder 8.

65. CaptO#169, 20 July 1936, SFPD9, box 3, folder 2.

66. CaptO#72, 19 March 1934, SFPD9, box 3, folder 9.

67. CaptO#272, 27 December 1934, SFPD9, box 3, folder 7.

68. CaptO#219, 27 August 1935, SFPD9, box 3, folder 5.

69. CaptO#157, 11 July 1934, SFPD9, box 3, folder 8; CaptO#15, 8 January 1935, SFPD9, box 3, folder 6; CaptO#181, 9 July 1935, SFPD9, box 3, folder 5.

70. CaptO#81, 21 March, 1935, SFPD9, box 3, folder 6; CaptO#182, 9 July 1935, SFPD9, box 3, folder 5.

71. CaptO#120, 29 April 1935, SFPD9, box 3, folder 6.

72. CaptO#98, 29 April 1936, SFPD9, box 3, folder 3.

73. CaptO#72, 19 March 1934, SFPD9, box 3, folder 9.

74. Anne Gray Fischer, *The Streets Belong to Us: Sex, Race, and Police Power from Segregation to Gentrification* (Chapel Hill: University of North Carolina Press, 2022). On rising administrative expertise alongside everyman rationales for sexual policing amid new positivist understandings, see Anna Lvovsky, *Vice Patrol: Cops, Courts, and the Struggle over Urban Gay Life before Stonewall* (Chicago: University of Chicago Press, 2021).

75. On how morals policing shaped the very structure of the New York Police Department, see Emily M. Brooks, *Gotham's War within a War: Policing and the Birth of Law-and-Order Liberalism in World War II–Era New York City* (Chapel Hill: University of North Carolina Press, 2023), 38–43.

76. Minutes of Meeting of Executive Committee, 16 January 1935, RSPC, box 14: Excomm Minutes, 31–36.

77. Citizens Committee on the Control of Crime in New York, 21 October 1936, ILP, MC085, box 56, folder 8.

78. Lindbergh to Harry, 22 May 1936, ILP, MC085, box 56, folder 8.

79. Released for Publication, Wednesday, 9 June, 15 June 1937, ILP, MC085, box 56, folder 8.

80. "Lehman Loads Gun for War on Crime," *Baltimore Sun*, 29 June 1935, 3.

81. Lehman to Guggenheim, 15 June 1937, ILP, MC085, box 56 folder 8.

82. Cass to Dewey, 21 April 1945, RSPC, box 1: Dewey.

83. "Dewey Warns City Legal Overlapping Balks Crime War," *New York Times*, 12 May 1937.

84. "Dewey Warns City."

85. Lehman to Roosevelt, 21 April 1930, FDRGP, box 48: Series 1, Lehman.

86. Egbert to Lehman, 3 May 1935, RSPC, box 1.

87. Lehman to Wald, 19 December 1934, LDWP, box 31, microfilm, reel 22; Lehman to Wald, 13 November 1935, LDWP, box 32, microfilm, reel 22.

88. Russell Owen, "Dewey Seeks Allies for a War on Crime," *New York Times*, 7 July 1935, E10.

89. See Jewel Bellush, "Roosevelt's Good Right Arm: Lieutenant Governor Herbert H. Lehman," *New York History* 41, no. 4 (October 1960): 436, 438.

90. James M. Kieran, "Lehman Maps Out State Crime War," *New York Times*, October 6, 1935, 68.

91. Moley, "Crime and Society," Address before the Governor's Conference on Crime, "The Criminal and Society," Albany, NY, 30 September 1935, RMP, box 120.

92. Moley, "Crime and Society."

93. In his 1939 anti–New Deal broadside, Moley remains proud of the war on crime and of keeping Hoover at the FBI. Moley, *After Seven Years* (New York: Harper, 1939), 274–275.

94. Moley to Cummings, 18 May 1936, RMP, box 11, folder 56.

95. Moley to Cummings, 2 June 1936, RMP, box 11, folder 56.

96. Moley, *After Seven Years*, 274–275.

97. W. A. Warn, "Lehman Opens Way for War on Crime," *New York Times*, 12 January 1936, E12.

98. Lewis to Lehman, 6 August 1936; Cunningham to Mahoney, 19 February 1936—both HLP, box 253, folder 2.

99. Message of Governor Herbert H. Lehman to the Legislature, 6 January 1937, HLP 1405, folder: Annual Messages to NYS legislature, 1933–1938.

100. Troy to Lehman, 27 September 1939, HLP, box 211, folder 10.

101. Lehman to Ellis, 18 September 1937; Lehman to McCormick, 10 October 1939—both HLP, box 211, folder 19.

102. Abel to Lehman, 17 January 1938, HLP, box 253, folder 1.

103. Woolley, White, et al. to Lehman, 6 February 1939, HLP, box 211, folder 3.

104. Allen to Lehman, 24 June 1938, HLP, box 253, folder 5.

105. Lehman to Cummings, 6 January 1936, AGSRP Correspondence with State Officials, Entry 424, box 1, folder: New York.

106. Moore to Lehman, 26 July 1937, HLP, box 237, folder 29.

107. Lehman to Hartshorne, 20 September 1937, HLP, box 237, folder 29.

108. DeFrantz to Lehman, 26 January 1938, HLP, box 253, folder 7.

109. French to Lehman, 24 January 1938, HLP, box 253, folder 7.

110. Shea to Lehman, 29 January 1938, HLP, box 253, folder 7.

111. Publisher of *Post-Standard* to Lehman, 25 January 1938, HLP, box 253, folder 7.

112. "Dewey Plans to Continue War on Crime," *Baltimore Sun,* 30 September 1938, 1.

113. Radio Address on the Election of Liberals, 4 November 1938, APPUCSB.

114. "Lehman Plurality Officially 64,004," *New York Times,* 8 December 1938. See also Mary M. Stolberg, *Fighting Organized Crime: Politics, Justice, and the Legacy of Thomas E. Dewey* (Boston: Northeastern University Press, 1995).

115. In early 1939 Samuel Marcus resigned as director, accusing the Society of partisan investigations of Albany machine politics. Statement of the Society for the Prevention of Crime in Answer to the Charges Made by Samuel Marcus, MHB, box 596: Society for the Prevention of Crime, 1937–1941.

116. "'Dewey Bills' Back Evidence Seizure without Warrant," *New York Times,* 3 February 1939.

117. Newman Award Won by Dewey: New York Prosecutor to Receive 1938 Medal . . . , *Los Angeles Times,* 26 April 1939; ProQuest Historical Newspapers: *Los Angeles Times,* 9.

118. To R. W. Morris, 12 August 1940, HLP, box 253, folder 2.

11. ANALOGUES OF WAR

1.   J. Edgar Hoover, "Soldiers in Peacetime," 19 September 1938, OF10b, box 10: 1937–1938.

2.   Hoover, "Soldiers in Peacetime."

3. On the World War I origins of the New Deal state, see William E. Leuchtenburg, "The New Deal and the Analogue of War," in *Change and Continuity in Twentieth-Century America,* ed. John Braeman, Robert H. Bremner, and David Brody (Columbus: Ohio State University Press, 1968), 81–143.

4. "Free Speech for Nazis?," 9 November 1933, RBP, MC 005, box 22, folder 10: Debs.

5. On left-wing splits over the "Brown Scare," see Leo P. Ribuffo, *The Old Christian Right: The Protestant Far Right from the Great Depression to the Cold War* (Philadelphia: Temple University Press, 1983), 178–224, 183.

6. Baldwin to Winston, 6 November 1934, RBP, MC 005, box 10, folder 9: New Deal.

7. "What Liberty under the New Deal?," RBP, MC 005, box 23, folder 7.

8. Laura M. Weinrib argues that the New Deal fractured the interwar civil liberties coalition, pitting anti-state legalists and conservatives against reformers and organized labor. Baldwin managed a "flexibility," balancing "credibility in radical circles while studying the limits of liberal tolerance." Weinrib, "The Liberal Compromise: Civil Liberties, Labor, and the Limits of State Power, 1917–1940," (diss., Princeton University, 2011).

9. "Challenge to American Liberties?," 1935, Baldwin Papers, Race Relations.

10. Extracts from Diaries of Osmond K. Fraenkel, OFD, box 1, folder 1.

11. Roger Baldwin to Miller, 17 March 1936, AGAC SF, box 4, folder: Civil Liberties. Also see Robert Cottrell, *Roger Nash Baldwin and the American Civil Liberties Union* (New York: Columbia University Press, 2001.

12. "The Constitution in the 20th Century: Personal Liberty; Differing Views, John W. McCormack vs. Baldwin," American Academy of Political and Social Science (reprint), 2 June 1936, NBC, "You and Your Government," Series 13, Lecture 18, RBP, box 22: Race Relations.

13. "How Shall We Fight War and Fascism?," February 1935, RBP, MC 005, box 23, folder 1: Radicalism.

14. "The Strike Breaking Militia," RBP, MC 005, box 23, folder 1: Radicalism

15. MFTAG, 25 June 1935, OF10b, box 10: 1933–1940.

16. Postmaster General, 5 February 1935, Dingell, Rep John D., 8 February 1935, OF10b, box 10: 1933–1940.

17. Attorney General, 7 February 1936, OF10b, box 10: 1933–1940.

18. Hoover to Howe, 17 October 1935, OF10b, box 10: 1935–1936.

19. Hopping to Lagadon, 25 May 1936, OF10b, box 10: 1935–1936.

20. Curt Gentry, *J. Edgar Hoover: The Man and the Secrets* (New York: W. W. Norton, 1991), 204–205, 207.

21. Beverly Gage, *G-Man: J. Edgar Hoover and the Making of the American Century* (New York: Penguin Random House, 2022), 206.

22. Ira Katznelson, *Fear Itself: The New Deal and the Origins of Our Time* (New York: W. W. Norton, 2013), 326.

23. Hoover, 23 December 1938, OF10b, box 10: 1933–1940.

24. For an emphasis on Hoover's agency over FDR's, arguing for a minimalist reading of the 1936 and 1939 presidential directives, see Athan Theoharis, *Spying on Americans: Political Surveillance from Hoover to the Huston Plan* (Philadelphia: Temple University Press, 1978), 67. Others stress Hoover's postwar influence, but Melissa Graves argues that it declined after the 1930s; see Graves, "FBI Historiography: From Leader to Organisation," in *Intelligence Studies in Britain and the US,* ed. Christopher R. Moran and Christopher J. Murphy (Edinburgh: Edinburgh University Press, 2013), 139. Christopher Andrew stresses the "enduring element of vagueness" in the word "subversion" in Roosevelt's 1939 directive. Andrew, *For the President's Eyes Only: Secret Intelligence and the American Presidency from Washington to Bush* (New York: Harper Collins, 1995), 91. In any event, Kenneth O'Reilly argues that Roosevelt willingly exploited "the FBI's resources for political as well as national- security purposes"; see O'Reilly, "A New Deal for the FBI: The Roosevelt Administration, Crime Control, and National Security," *Journal of American History* 69, no. 3 (December 1982): 647.

25. David T. Beito, "New Deal Mass Surveillance: The 'Black Inquisition Committee,' 1935–1936," *Journal of Policy History* 30, no. 2 (2018).

26. Carusis, Hon. Ugo, Exec. Assistant to the Attorney General, 23 October 1936, OF10b, box 10: 1933–1940.

27. Attorney General, 30 June 1937, OF10b, box 10: 1933–1940.

28. Hopkins, Hon. Harry L., 8 July 1937; Attorney General, 13 August 1937; Hoover, John Edgar, 12 January 1938; Hopkins, Hon. Harry L., 15 June 1938—all OF10b, box 10: 1933–1940.

29. Meigs to La Follette, 20 July 1938; Fechner to Besig, 24 March 1938; To John J. O'Connor, 21 March 1938—all ACLU Subseries 2.24: Police 1935–1972, carton 35, folder 103.

30. 19 April 1937, folder 8, Natl Minutes–Board of Directors, 1934–1937.

31. Besig to Britchey, 11 December 1939, Poverty & Civil Liberties, Dust Bowl, 1936–1940, Subseries 2.24: Police 1935–1972, carton 35, folder 748.

32. MFTAG, 17 April 1935, OF10b, box 10: 1935–1936.

33. Address by Pennington, 2 May 1940, LPP, box 16, folder 1.

34. Memorandum for the President, 19 January 1935, OF10b, box 10: 1935–1936.

35. Charles Stevenson, "Roosevelt's Budget Slaps at Cummings," OF10b, box 10: 1935–1936.

36. To Dear Mr. Bell, 15 June 1935, OF10b, box 10: 1935–1936.

37. MFTAG, 23 May 1935, OF10b, box 10: 1935–1936.

38. Arthur Vandenberg to President, 6 May 1936, OF10b, box 10: 1935–1936.

39. Miller, Fred, 29 September 1937, OF10b, box 10: FBI 1933–1940.

40. Daniel C. Richman and Sarah Seo, "How Federalism Built the FBI, Sustained Local Police, and Left Out the States," *Stanford Journal of Civil Rights and Civil Liberties* 17 (2022): 455.

41. Morris to President, 26 August 1938, OF10b, 1937–1938.

42. MFTAG,15 March 1935—from J. Edgar Hoover, OF10b, box 10: 1935–1936.

43. Roosevelt to Attorney General, 23 November 1937, OF10b, box 10: 1937–1938.

44. Cummings to Roosevelt, 16 March 1935, OF10, box 3.

45. Fechner, Hon. Robert, 29 February 1936, OF10b, box 10: 1933–1940.

46. Attorney General, 2 March 1936, OF10b, box 10: 1933–1940.

47. Attorney General, 26 December 1935, 27 February 1936—both OF10b, box 10: 1933–1940.

48. MFTAG, 26 July 1935, OF10b, box 10: 1933–1940.

49. J. Edgar Hoover, "Your Task as a Citizen," 21 June 1939, OF10b, box 10: 1939.

50. Thanks to Anders Stephanson for the turn of phrase.

51. Andrew Preston, "Monsters Everywhere: A Genealogy of National Security," *Diplomatic History* 38, no. 3 (2014): 491–492.

52. Address Delivered by J. Edgar Hoover, Penn Athletic Club, Philadelphia, 14 April 1937, OF10b, box 10: 1937–1938.

53. Remarks of John Edgar Hoover, "Law Enforcement and the Publisher," 22 April 1937, OF10b, box 10: 1937–1938.

54. "Lawlessness—A National Menace," 14 November 1939, OF10b, box 10: 1937–1938.

55. Address by Lee R. Pennington, 13 January 1938, LPP, box 16.

56. Pennington, "The FBI and Its War on Crime," 21 April 1938, LPP, box 16.

57. See Leuchtenburg, "The New Deal and the Analogue of War."

58. Minutes, 28 July 1937, ROLEC, box 1.

59. Minutes, 7 April 1938; Minutes, 22 September 1937; Minutes, 5 January 1939; Memo for Coordination File, on 7 September 1939; Minutes, 20 September 1939—all ROLEC, box 2.

60. Hoover to Roosevelt, 29 July 1937, OF10b, box 10: 1937–1938.

61. Roosevelt worked in "a short period, and in complete secrecy," to build a "formidable U.S. security structure," writes Raymond J. Batvinis, *The Origins of FBI Counterintelligence* (Lawrence: University Press of Kansas, 2007), 1, 258.

62. Some see the post-1937 developments as a "new New Deal" or "Third New Deal." John W. Jeffries, "The 'New' New Deal: FDR and American Liberalism, 1937–1945," *Political Science Quarterly* 105, no. 3 (Autumn 1990): 397.

63. Laura Weinrib, *The Taming of Free Speech: America's Civil Liberties Compromise* (Cambridge, MA: Harvard University Press, 2016), 258.

64. Hoover, "Your Task as a Citizen."

65. Attorney General to President, 17 June 1939; Memorandum for . . . 26 June 1939—both OF10b, box 10: 1939.

66. Presidential Memorandum for the Secretary of State et al., 26 June 1939, OF10b, 1933–1940.

67. Secretary of Treasury, 29 June 1939; Postmaster General to President, 30 June 1939—both OF10b, box 10: 1939.

68. Memorandum for Secretary of State, 26 June 1939, OF10b, box 10: 1939.

69. Memorandum for the President, 7 December 1939, OF10b, box 10: 1933–1940.

70. Attorney General to President, 6 September 1939, OF10b, box 10: 1939.

71. The President Issued a Following Statement on 6 September 1939, OF10b, box 10: 1939.

72. Hoover, "Your Task as a Citizen."

73. Presidential Memorandum, 15 December 1939, OF10b, box 10: 1933–1940.

74. Wisconsin Chiefs of Police Association, 26 October 1939, OF10b, box 10: 1939.

75. The Attorney General, 23 October 1939, OF10b, box 10: 1933–1940.

76. John M. Walker, 6 June 1940, OF10b, box 10: 1940.

77. Lazare, Ben, 2 January 1936, OF10b, box 10: 1933–1940.

78. Attorney General to President, 5 January 1939, OF10b, box 10: 1939.

79. Hon. J. Edgar Hoover, 12 June 1940, OF10b, box 10: 1933–1940.

80. Hoover, 20 March 1939, OF10b, box 10: 1933–1940.

81. Hoover, 13 December 1938, OF10b, box 10: 1933–1940.

82. Curran, Joseph, 19 October 1940, OF10b, box 10: 1933–1940.

83. Attorney General to President, 5 January 1939, OF10b, box 10: 1939.

84. Hon. J. Edgar Hoover, 14 November 1938; Dies, Hon. Martin, 9 October 1940—both OF10b, box 10: 1933–1940.

85. American Civil Liberties Union, June 1939, HLP, box 211, folder 3.

86. ACLU Board of Directors, Minutes, 9 October 1939, ACLUNC, carton 1, folder 9.

87. J. Edgar Hoover, before NU Herald-Tribune Forum, 24 October 1939, "Law Enforcement in a Crisis," OF10b, 1939.

88. "What Shall We Do," 25 January 1939, RBP, MC 005, box 10, folder 10: New School.

89. The left's solidarity against the far right helped set up the postwar atmosphere when other extremists became "suspect themselves." Ribuffo, *The Old Christian Right,* 178, 181. Also see Wendy L. Wall, *Inventing the "American Way": The Politics of Consensus from the New Deal to the Civil Rights Movement* (Oxford: Oxford University Press, 2008).

90. Baldwin to Frank, 30 December 1938, JFP, box 21, folder 24.

91. American Civil Liberties Union, June 1939, HLP, box 211, folder 3.

92. See Risa Lauren Goluboff, *The Lost Promise of Civil Rights* (Cambridge, MA: Harvard University Press, 2007), 111–140; Paul L. Murphy, *The Constitution in Crisis Times, 1918–1969* (New York: Harper and Row, 1972), 170–171.

93. "Should the Dies Investigation Be Continued?," *Town Meeting: Bulletin of America's Town Meeting of the Air,* Wolcott D. Street, 8 January 1940, vol. 5, no. 13, RBP, MC 005, box 22, folder 1: Race Relations

94. Theoharis, *Spying on Americans,* 41.

95. Roosevelt to Attorney General, 13 September 1939, OF10b, box 10: 1939.

96. Pennington, "The FBI's National Defense Program," 21 April 1941, LPP, box 16, folder 1.

97. Attorney General to President, 18 December 1939, OF10b, box 10: 1939.

98. Pennington, "Americanism and the Citizen," undated, LPP, box 16, folder 1.

99. Lehman to Appleton, 14 December 1939, HLP, box 211, folder 9.

100. Batvinis, *Origins of FBI Counterintelligence,* 92–93.

101. Batvinis, *Origins of FBI Counterintelligence,* 94–95.

102. Public No. 443, 54 Stat. 55; Gage, *G-Man,* 239.

103. Dale to McIntyre, 1 March 1940, OF10b, box 10: 1940.

104. Robert Justin Goldstein, *Political Repression in Modern America from 1870 to 1976* (Urbana: University of Illinois Press, 2001), 252–254.

105. Stephen Early to J. Edgar Hoover, 18 May 1940, OF10b, box 10: 1940.

106. Memo to J. Edgar Hoover from Rudolph Forster, 23 May 1940, OF10b, box 10: 1940.

107. Early to Hoover, 29 May 1940, OF10b, box 10: 1940.

108. Watson to DOJ, 4 June 1940, OF10b, box 10: 1940.

109. Paul W. Arndt, Jr, 18 June 1940; Peter Brown, 18 June 1940; Paul Bruno, 18 June 1940; Louis Fagin, 18 June 1940—all OF10b, box 10: 1940.

110. Graf, Charles, 18 June 1940, OF10b 1940; Memo to J. Edgar Hoover, 27 May 1940, OF10b, box 10: 1939; Roosevelt to Hoover, 14 June 1940, OF10b, box 10: 1940.

111. Gentry, *J. Edgar Hoover,* 235.

112. Dies, Hon. Martin, 1 June 1940, OF10b, box 10: 1933–1940

113. Batvinis, *Origins of FBI Counterintelligence,* 130–131.

114. Excerpts from Speech by Roger Baldwin at University of Chicago Law School, 6 June 1940, "National Defense and Civil Liberty," RBP, MC 005, box 22, folder 1: Race Relations.

115. Gage, *G-Man,* 239.

116. Jackson, Hon. Robert, 29 November 1940, OF10b, box 10: 1933–1940.

117. Watson to Jordan, 8 March 1940, OF10b, box 10: 1940.

118. Pennington, "Citizenship Today," before American Legion of Ohio, 13 July 1940, LPP, box 16, folder 1.

119. Francis Biddle, 31 July 1940, OF10b, box 10: 1933–1940.

120. Dies, Hon. Martin, 25 November 1940, OF10b, box 10: 1933–1940.

121. Attorney General Jackson to Roosevelt, 9 July 1940; House Resolution 571, Permitting Wiretapping in Certain Cases, 76th Congress 3rd Session House of Rep. Report no. 2374—both OF10b, box 10: 1940.

122. Pennington, "Citizenship Today."

123. Edgar Dale to Marvin McIntyre, 1 March 1940, OF10b, box 10: 1940.

124. Watson to Walker, 26 June 1940, OF10b, box 10: 1940.

125. Letter to a Conference of Law Enforcement Officials on National Defense, 31 July 1940, APPUCSB.

126. Secretary to President, 22 January 1938; Secretary to President, 18 February 1938—both NAACPHV, SF: Presidential Anti-Lynching Conference 1938 (001529_004_0658).

127. Christopher Waldrep, "National Policing, Lynching, and Constitutional Change," *Journal of Southern History* 84, no. 3 (2008): 614.

128. NAACP Statement on Anti-Lynching Legislation, NAACPHV, General Office File: Anti-Lynching (001529_035_0001).

129. Mr. Ames Speaks for Self Alone, 17 May 1940, Thursday May 9 1940: South Ends First Lynchless Year.

130. Statement by Walter White to the Sub-Committee of the Senate Judiciary Committee, 6 February 1940 (032-0172, 031-0362).

131. "Abstract of Speech on National Defense and the Fifth Column," 6 October 1940, RBP, MC 005, box 22, folder 1: Race Relations.

132. "Abstract of Speech on National Defense and the Fifth Column."

133. Weinrib, *Taming of Free Speech*, 3. "And as they changed the law," writes Weinrib, "the law changed them" (12).

134. Indeed, "the New Deal order created new obstacles to statist ambitions," write Disnet M. Milkis and Jerome M. Mileur, editors, *The New Deal and the Triumph of Liberalism* (Amherst: University of Massachusetts Press, 2002), 10. "The ACLU retained its hostility toward state overreaching, even as the New Deal demonstrated that industrial interests were separable from state power," writes Weinrib, *Taming of Free Speech*, 302.

135. "The Enemies within the Gate," RMP, box 217, folder 20.

136. "Draft for Dewey," 7 October 1940, RMP, box 217, folder 20.

137. Remarks of Governor Lehman over the Radio, 6 November 1940, HLP, box 263, folder 5.

138. Landon to Moley, 3 December 1940, RMP, box 217, folder 145. On the discourse around relief and federalism, see Karen M. Tani, *States of Dependency: Welfare, Rights, and American Governance, 1935–1972* (Cambridge: Cambridge University Press, 2016).

139. Landon to Moley, 8 April 1941, RMP, box 217, folder 15.

140. Blackett to Moley, 11 January 1941, RMP, box 217, folder 14.

141. Carr to Roosevelt, 19 April 1941, OF10b, box 11: 1941–1942.

142. Stimpson and Knox to President, 29 May 1941, OF10b, box 11: 1941–1942.

143. Memorandum for the Secretary of War and the Secretary of the Navy, 4 June 1941, OF10b, box 11: 1941–1942.

144. Carlisle to Early, 11 June 1941, OF10b, box 11: 1941–1942.

145. Memorandum for Henry Morgenthau, Jr., OF10b, box 11: 1941–1942.

146. FDR to Attorney General, 3 February 1941, OF10b, box 11: 1941–1942.

147. Goldstein, *Political Repression,* 252.

148. Pennington, Address before Banquet . . . , 18 February 1941, LPP, 16, folder 1.

149. Ryan to Roosevelt, 24 November 1941, OF10b, box 11: 1941–1942.

150. McIntyre to Ryan, 24 November 1941, OF10b, box 11: 1941–1942.

151. Pennington, "The FBI's National Defense Program," 21 April 1941, Open Meeting . . . , LPP, box 16, folder 1.

152. Speech delivered by Lee H. Pennington, 7 October 1941, LPP, box 16.

153. *Edwards v. California,* 314 U.S. 160 (1941).

154. Baldwin, *150 Years of the Bill of Rights,* ACLUNC Subseries 1.1: National Office 1918–1974, carton 1.

155. "Liberalism and the United Front," 1941, RBP, MC 005, box 22, folder 2.

156. "The Threats to Liberty," 17 July 1941, RBP, MC 005, box 22, folder 2.

157. Pennington, "Citizenship Today."

158. "To the War Resisters League," 27 January 1942, RBP, MC 005, box 10, folder 24 (emphasis in original).

12. TRIAL BY FIRE

1. Shultz to Conway, Administrative Code on Fingerprinting Program, 13 May 1942, TVAPC, box 100, folder: Crimes, Offenses, Criminals.

2. Allen to Clapp, 4 December 1942; Supplementary Statement Required of Public Safety Officer-Trainee Applicants, 15 September 1942; Announcement of Examinations—all TVAGM, box 533, folder:421–17 Uniforms and Costumes.

3. Public Safety Service Receives "E" Guides from US Army, 13 April 1944; Campbell to Clapp, Office Memorandum, 6 November 1944—both TVAGM, box 419, folder: 211.2 (1770), Guards, Guides, Policemen, Detectives.

4. See Hugh Rockoff, "World War II and the Growth of the U.S. Federal Government," *Japan and the World Economy* 11, no. 2 (April 1999): 245–262.

5. In World War II, successes and failures of economic mobilization inspired and tempered activist liberalism, while the totalitarian foil abroad stood as a

parable against planning. See Alan Brinkley, "The Two World Wars and American Liberalism," in *Liberalism and Its Discontents* (Cambridge, MA: Harvard University Press, 1998), 79–94. Alonzo L. Hamby notes World War I's negative impact on "the nascent 'Wilson Coalition' of 1916." Hamby, "High Tide: Roosevelt, Truman, and the Democratic Party, 1932–1952," in *The Achievement of American Liberalism: The New Deal and Its Legacies,* ed. William H. Chafe (New York: Columbia University Press, 2003), 43.

6. For works emphasizing the contrast between welfare and the security state, see James T. Sparrow, *Warfare State: World War II Americans and the Age of Big Government* (New York: Oxford University Press, 2013), 110; Carl Boggs, *Origins of the Warfare State: World War II and the Transformation of American Politics* (New York: Routledge, 2017), 3, 7, 11; and Hamby, "High Tide," 46–47.

7. Ryan Madden, "The Forgotten People: The Relocation and Internment of Aleuts during World War II," *American Indian Culture and Research Journal* 16, no. 4 (1992): 55–76.

8. It took a generation for historians to confront 1930s FBI mobilization. See Athan Theoharis, "The FBI and the American Legion Contact Program, 1940—1966," *Political Science Quarterly* 100, no. 2 (Summer 1985): 271–286.

9. I.C. #61-7632, 13 November 1941, Friedrich Ernst Auragen, LPP, box 3, folder 3.

10. Memorandum for the President re: Intelligence Work in Western Hemisphere, 22 December 1941, OF10b, box 11: 1941–1942.

11. Proposed Directive, 23 December 1941; Biddle to McIntyre, 23 December 1941; McIntyre to Attorney General, 23 December 1941; MFTAG, Undersecretary of State et al., 30 December 1941; MFTAG, 13 February 1942—all OF10b, box 11: 1941–1942.

12. I.C. #45-1923, 14 December 1943, LPP, box 3, folder 2.

13. "War Duty Suggestions for Police Executives," Federal Bureau of Investigation, United States Department of Justice, J. E. Hoover, January 1942, OF10b, box 11: 1941–1942. See also *FBI Law Enforcement Bulletin* 11, no. 3 (1942), 23.

14. See Emily M. Brooks, *Gotham's War within a War: Policing and the Birth of Law-and-Order Liberalism in World War II–Era New York City* (Chapel Hill: University of North Carolina Press, 2023), 152.

15. NPAI #27, NPA Graduate Catches Arsonist in Michigan, 7 October 1944, LPP, box 3, folder 3.

16. I.I.L. #154, Expert Testimony Helps Convict Hit-and-Run Driver, 25 May 1943, LPP, box 3, folder 3.

17.   I.I. #L-162, Fibers Convict a Hit-and Run Driver, 31 July 1943, LPP, box 3, folder 3.

18.   I.I.L. #143, Murderer Confesses When Confronted, 12 April 1943, LPP, box 3, folder 3.

19.   I.I.L. #155, Firearms Identification Assists in Obtaining Admission of Guilt Just before Trial, 8 June 1943, LPP, box 3, folder 3.

20.   I.I.L. #145, FBI Laboratory Assists Memphis Police, 24 March 1943, LPP, box 3, folder 3.

21.   I.I. #491, Drunken Driver Identified as Escaped Murderer, 23 July 1943, LPP, box 3, folder 3.

22.   I.I. #500, Fingerprints Identify Aircraft Victims, 9 November 1934, LPP, box 3, folder 3.

23.   I.I. #497, Applicant's Extensive Record Revealed by Prints, 19 October 1943, LPP, box 3, folder 3.

24.   I.I.L. #180, Fingerprint on Trigger Convicts Georgia Murderer, 11 December 1943, LPP, box 3, folder 3.

25.   I.I. #499, English Given Record on American Criminal, 9 November 1943, LPP, box 3, folder 3.

26.   Pennington, "Citizenship Today," 13 July 1940, Pennington, box 16, folder 1.

27.   I.I. #489, Deceased Soldier Identified by Fingerprints, 7 April 1943, LPP, box 3, folder 3.

28.   I.I.L. #151, Federal Bureau of Investigation Assists in Solving 'Perfect Crime,' 13 May 1943, LPP, box 3, folder 3.

29.   I.I. #L.-160 Microscopic Analyses Convict Murderer, 10 June 1943, Pennington, box 3, folder 3.

30.   I.I.L. #148, Life Imprisonment Given to Young Murderer as Result of Ballistics Examination, 28 May 1943, LPP, box 3, folder 3.

31.   I.I.L. #156, Murderer Sentenced to Electric Chair, Accomplice to Life Imprisonment as Result of FBI Identification of Firearms, 3 July 1943, LPP, box 3, folder 3.

32.   Address of L. R. Pennington, "The Challenge to Law Enforcement," 23 February 1944, LPP, box 16, folder 1.

33.   I.C. #31-67289, Ellen Lucille Moore, 14 December 1943, LPP, box 3, folder 2.

34.   I.C. #71-1630, 71-1677, 71-1594, 71-1593, Lucky Strike Lottery Company, 15 January 1944, LPP, box 3, folder 3.

35. I.C. #9-9370, Samuel Rubin, 12 November 1942, LPP, box 3, folder 3.

36. I.C. #49-9956, Mrs. Benson Kramer, 30 November 1943; I.C. #47-30025, Frances Johnson, 9 November 1943—both LPP, box 3, folder 2.

37. I.C. #25-96330, Arturo Bernardo Vela, 20 January 1944; Lotis Florine Ross, 30 September 1944; I.C. #25-248512, Walter Alvin Johnson, 7 September 1944—all LPP, box 3, folder 3.

38. I.L. 498, Embezzlement, Forgery Record Revealed by Fingerprints, 19 October 1943, LPP, box 3, folder 3.

39. I.I.L. #167, Application for Government Position, 23 September 1943, LPP, box 3, folder 3.

40. I.I. #540, Body in River Identified as Escaped War Prisoner, 30 October 1944, LPP, box 3, folder 3.

41. I.C. #98-4819, Michael William Etzel, Glenn L Martin Company Sabotage, 1 December 1941, LPP, box 3, folder 3.

42. I.C. #65-39300, Dr. Theodore Aurelius Schmidt, 19 February 1944, LPP, box 3, folder 3.

43. I.C. #100-30234, Waldemar Othmer, 12 October 1944, LPP, box 3, folder 3.

44. I.C. #65-40673, Herman Tracy Green, 3 June 1942, LPP, box 3, folder 3.

45. #65-43379, John Da Silva Purvis, 22 December 1943, LPP, box 3, folder 3.

46. I.C. #98-17301, Starting Forest Fires Is Sabotage, 29 May 1943, LPP, box 3, folder 3.

47. I.C. #98-7719, James Howard, 2 June 1942, LPP, box 3, folder 3.

48. I.C. #98-6354, Stokes McCreay, 2 June 1942, LPP, box 3, folder 3.

49. I.C. 100-124410, Peace Movement of Ethiopia, 23 October 1943, LPP, box 3, folder 3.

50. I.C. #65-40879, Pacific Movement of the Eastern World, 8 September 1943, LPP, box 3, folder 3.

51. I.C. #39-1150, Max Stephan, Theodore Donay, 31 December 1943, LPP, box 3, folder 3.

52. I.C. #39-1150, Max Stephan, Theodore Donay, 31 December 1943, LPP, box 3, folder 3.

53. "American Liberties in War-Time," 11 October 1943, RBP, MC 005, box 22, folder 1: Race Relations.

54. "For the Pacific Citizen," 7 December 1943, RBP, MC 005, box 22, folder 1: Race Relations.

55. "The Evacuation of Citizens and the Law," Baldwin, July 1942, RBP, MC 005, box 22, folder 1: Race Relations.

56. By the 1980s, researchers of declassified archives questioned the wartime regime's liberal reputation. Theoharis, "FBI and the American Legion," 272.

57. See Geoffrey Stone, *Perilous Times: Free Speech in Wartime from the Sedition Act of 1798 to the War on Terrorism* (New York: W. W. Norton, 2004), 285-286; "State Apologizes for Mistreatment of Italian Residents during WWII," *Los Angeles Times,* 23 August 2010.

58. Compare Harold M. Hyman, *To Try Men's Souls: Loyalty Tests in American History* (Berkeley: University of California Press, 1959), to Robert Justin Goldstein, *Political Repression in Modern America from 1870 to 1976* (Urbana: University of Illinois Press, 2001), 194-195. See also David T. Beito, *The New Deal's War on the Bill of Rights: The Untold Story of FDR's Concentration Camps, Censorship, and Mass Surveillance* (Oakland, CA: The Independent Institute, 2023), chap. 9.

59. On labor, see Rosa L. Swafford, *Wartime Record of Strikes and Lockouts, 1940—1945* (Washington, DC: US Government Printing Office, 1946). On conscription, see John O'Sullivan, *From Voluntarism to Conscription: Congress and Selective Service, 1940-1945* (New York: Garland, 1982).

60. Marshall B. Clinard, *The Black Market: A Study of White Collar Crime* (New York: Rinehart, 1952), 3.

61. Hugh Rockoff, *Drastic Measures: A History of Wage and Price Controls in the United States* (Cambridge: Cambridge University Press, 1984), 139-140.

62. Rockoff, *Drastic Measures,* 141-142.

63. Clinard, *The Black Market,* 23, 37.

64. Rockoff, *Drastic Measures,* 141-143.

65. Clinard, *The Black Market,* 227-228.

66. State of the Union, 6 January 1945, APPUCSB.

67. Black gains in the 1930s were "only by contrast with . . . before," writes William H. Chafe, "Race in America: The Ultimate Test of Liberalism," in *The Achievement of American Liberalism,* 162.

68. Hamby, "High Tide," 40.

69. Christopher Waldrep, "National Policing, Lynching, and Constitutional Change," *Journal of Southern History* 84, no. 3 (2008): 618; Risa L. Goluboff, *The Lost Promise of Civil Rights* (Cambridge, MA: Harvard University Press, 2007),112, 128-129, 133, 137, 133.

70. Chafe, "Race in America," 163.

71. Dominic J. Capeci Jr. and Martha Wilkerson, *Layered Violence: The Detroit Rioters of 1943* (Jackson: University Press of Mississippi, 1991), 34 and inter alia.

72. See Stuart Cosgrove, "The Zoot Suit and Style Warfare," in *Zoot Suits and Second-Hand Dresses: Youth Questions,* ed. A. McRobbie (London: Palgrave Macmillan, 1984), 3–22.

73. See Los Angeles Committee for American Unity, "Investigations of the Los Angeles Committee for American Unity," 11 June 1943, reprinted in Kevin Hillstrom, *The Zoot Suit Riots* (Detroit: Omnigraphics, 2012), 172–174.

74. Robert Bruns, *Zoot Suit Riots* (Santa Barbara: Greenwood Press, 2014).

75. "First Lady Traces Zoot Riots to Discrimination," Associated Press, 17 June 1943.

76. "Mrs. Roosevelt Blindly Stirs Race Discord," *Los Angeles Times,* 18 June 1943.

77. Unnamed document, 2 June 1942, OF10b, box 11: 1941–1942.

78. MFTAG from FDR, 4 August 1942, OF10b, box 11: 1941–1942.

79. Patrick S. Washburn, "J. Edgar Hoover and the Black Press in World War II," *Journalism History* 13, no. 1 (1986): 26–33.

80. J. Edgar Hoover, "Legionnaires Aid the FBI," LPP, box 16, folder 3.

81. Address of J. Edgar Hoover, "Our Future," 10 May 1942, OF10b, box 11: 1941–1942.

82. Hoover, "Legionnaires Aid the FBI."

83. Goldstein, *Political Repression,* 283.

84. Arnold to Norris, 29 February 1940, OF10b, box 10: 1940.

85. Civil Rights and the F.B.I., 12 March 1942, RBP, MC 005, box 22, folder 1: Race Relations.

86. Memo by Roger Baldwin, July 1943, RBP, MC 005, box 22, folder 1: Race Relations.

87. Sparrow's formulation, associating state repression with the FBI and domestic welfarism with New Deal liberalism, invites questions about the mutual constitution of these different parts of the government. Sparrow, *Warfare State,* 89.

88. Louis Fisher, *Nazi Saboteurs on Trial: A Military Tribunal and American Law* (Lawrence: University Press of Kansas, 2003), 43–53.

89. William D. Hassett, *Off the Record with F.D.R., 1942–1945* (New Brunswick, NJ: Rutgers, 1958), 74–75.

90. Johnston to Bennett, 4 May 1942, AAF, box 7.

91. Harry N. Scheiber and Jane L. Scheiber, *Bayonets in Paradise: Martial Law in Hawai'i during World War II* (Honolulu: University of Hawai'i Press, 2016), 14.

92. Quoted in Scheiber and Scheiber, *Bayonets in Paradise,* 17.

93. Scheiber and Scheiber, *Bayonets in Paradise,* 23, 2, 16.

94. Scheiber and Scheiber, *Bayonets in Paradise,* 214, 9, 3, 46, 44.

95. "Nearly every civil liberty guaranteed in the Bill of Rights of the Constitution and its subsequent amendments was set aside for some or all of the civilian population of Hawai'i," write Schieber and Scheiber, "including the First Amendment rights of freedom of religion, of speech, of press, and of assembly; the Fourth Amendment guarantee of freedom from unreasonable search and seizure; the Fifth Amendment's guarantee of due process; the Sixth and Seventh Amendments' rights to trial by jury, confrontation of witnesses, and right to counsel; and the Fourteenth Amendment's right to equal protection of the laws." Scheiber and Scheiber, *Bayonets in Paradise,* 4.

96. Scheiber and Scheiber, *Bayonets in Paradise,* 55, 74.

97. Gabrielson to Vollmer, 20 April 1942 and 25 April 1942, AVP, box 11: Gabrielson, William A., 1940–1953.

98. Greg Robinson, *By Order of the President: FDR and the Internment of Japanese Americans* (Cambridge, MA: Harvard University Press, 2001), 4.

99. Jason Scott Smith, "New Deal Public Works at War: The WPA and Japanese American Internment," *Pacific Historical Review* 72, no. 1 (February 2003): 64.

100. 56 Stat. 173, 18 U.S.C.A. 97a.

101. Brooks, *Gotham's War within a War,* 147.

102. Police Record of Complaints, 3 June 1932, JAERR, box 35, microfilm, reel 14.

103. War Relocation Authority Internal Security Case Report #260, WESP, box 1, folder 9.

104. Memorandum of Agreement, 1 December 1943, WESP, box 1, folder 6.

105. Black to Schmidt, 2 June 1944, WESP, box 1, folder 2.

106. Standard Position Description, 13 May 1943, WESP, box 1, folder 6.

107. Standard Position Description: Patrolman, May 1943, WESP, box 1, folder 6.

108. Standard Position Description: Internal Security Officer, 14 May 1943, WESP, box 1, folder 6.

109. Standard Position Description: Chief of Internal Security, 1 December 1943, WESP, box 1, folder 6.

110. Schmidt to Best, 28 February 1944, WESP, box 1, folder 2.

111. Meyer to Best, 20 May 1944, WESP, box 1, folder 2.

112. Graves, The New Officer, Gile River Project Internal Security Rivers, Arizona, WESP, box 1, folder 2.

113. Schmidt to Provinse, War Relocation Authority, 13 January 1945, WESP, box 1.

114. Memorandum, To: Advisory Council, From: Co-ordinating Committee: Subject: Employment of Priests and Social Workers and Educational Lecturers, 16 March 1944, WESP, box 1, folder 1.

115. Standard Position Description: Internal Security Officer, 14 May 1943, WESP, box 1, folder 6.

116. Tommy Tomlinson, 19 May 1944, WESP, box 1, folder 9.

117. Report of the Informal Meeting of the Stockade Internees and the Co-Ordinating Committee of the Tule Lake Center, 5 February 1944, WESP, box 1, folder 5.

118. Tulare Lake Center to Co-Ordinating Committee, February 1944; Black to Best, 8 February 1944—both WESP, box 1, folder 1.

119. Memorandum: Co-Ordinating Committee to Mr. W. Schmidt, 9 March 1944, WESP, box 1, folder 5.

120. Historians have increasingly focused on Roosevelt's responsibility. See Robinson, *By Order of the President,* 6, and Beito, *The New Deal's War on the Bill of Rights,* chap. 7.

121. Robinson, *By Order of the President,* 60, 57, 60, 71, 62.

122. Mae M. Ngai, *Impossible Subjects: Illegal Aliens and the Making of Modern America* (Princeton, NJ: Princeton University Press, 2014), 176.

123. Quoted in David M. Kennedy, *Freedom from Fear: The American People in Depression and War, 1929–1945* (New York: Oxford University Press, 1999), 749.

124. Kennedy, *Freedom from Fear,* 751, 752.

125. Robinson, *By Order of the President,* 85; Kennedy, *Freedom from Fear,* 757.

126. Francis Biddle, *In Brief Authority* (Westport, CT: Greenwood Press), 224.

127. Americans' Views of Japanese Internment, Gallup, December 1942, https://news.gallup.com/vault/195257/gallup-vault-wwii-era-support-japanese -internment.aspx.

128. "What Future for Japanese Americans?," RBP, MC 005, box 22, folder 1: Race Relations; see also Sparrow, *Warfare State,* 100–108.

129. World War II is often seen as accelerating the collision of New Deal racial contradictions. On the other hand, John W. Dower's study of the Pacific Theater as a race war suggests an obsessive precision in differentiating "good" Asians from the "bad." Dower, *War without Mercy: Race and Power in the Pacific War* (New York: Pantheon Books, 1996), 79.

130. Scholars still split on whether to credit Myer and the administration for eschewing "concentration camp" terminology. Compare Bill Hosokaw, *Nisei: The Quiet Americans* (Boulder: University Press of Colorado, 2002), to Richard Drinnon, *Keeper of Concentration Camps: Dillon S. Myer and American Racism* (Berkeley: University of California Press. 1987). Also see Greg Robinson, "Updating Historiography of Japanese Americans," *Journal of American Ethnic History* 22, no. 4 (Summer 2003): 67–71.

131. Dillon S. Myer, address, 16 November 1943, LPP, box 16, folder 2.

132. Mae Ngai notes the "greater irony" that "WRA's assimilationism led to the most disastrous and incendiary aspects of the internment experience—the loyalty questionnaire, segregation, and renunciation of citizenship." See Ngai, *Impossible Subjects,* 179.

133. 21 November 1944, quoted in Robinson, *By Order of the President,* 2.

134. Robinson, *By Order of the President,* 103–104.

135. See Elaine Elinson and Stan Yogi, "During Japanese American Incarceration, the ACLU Lost—and Then Found—Its Way," 2 December 2019, ACLU, https://www.aclu.org/issues/civil-liberties/during-japanese-american -incarceration-aclu-lost-and-then-found-its-way.

136. Cheryl Greenberg, "Black and Jewish Responses to Japanese Internment," *Journal of American Ethnic History* 14, no. 2 (Winter 1995): 15.

137. R. C. Hoiles, "The Evacuation of the Japanese in Retrospect," *Santa Ana Register,* 14 October 1942.

138. See Larry Ceplair and Steven Englund, *The Inquisition in Hollywood: Politics in the Film Community, 1930–1960* (Urbana: University of Illinois Press, 2003 [1973]), 197–198; Beverly Gage, *G-Man: J. Edgar Hoover and the Making of the American Century* (New York: Penguin Random House, 2022), 258–261.

139. Vollmer to Fisher 12 October 1942, AVP, box 46.

140. *Hirabayashi v. United States,* 320 U.S. 81 (1943).

141. *Korematsu v. United States,* 323 U.S. 214 (1944).

142. *Ex parte Endo,* 323 U.S. 283 (1944).

143. Malick W. Ghachem and Daniel Gordon, "From Emergency Law to Legal Process: Herbert Wechsler and the Second World War," *Suffolk University Law Review* 40 (2006): 333. They write, "The spirit of the New Deal glided easily toward the policy of Japanese internment because the New Deal had already decisively diminished enthusiasm for strict judicial scrutiny of government programs" (348).

144. Ira Katznelson, *Fear Itself: The New Deal and the Origins of Our Time* (New York: W. W. Norton, 2013), chap. 7.

145. "Civil Liberties—1944," 27 February 1945, RBP, MC 005, box 22, folder 2.

146. Wendell Willkie, "How the Republican Party Can Win in 1944," *Look,* October 4, 1943, RMP, box, 217 folder 3.

147. Roosevelt, "Address to the Democratic National Convention in Chicago," 20 July 1944, APPUCSB.

148. Robinson, *By Order of the President,* 126–127.

149. Keynote Address of Governor Warren, 26 June 1944, RMP, box 57, folder 62.

EPILOGUE

1.   Naomi Murakawa, *The First Civil Right: How Liberals Built Prison America* (Oxford: Oxford University Press, 2014).

2.   Truman, "Address before the Attorney General's Conference on Law Enforcement Problems," 15 February 1950, APPUCSB.

3.   Elaine Carey and Alfred J. Andrea, eds., *Protests in the Streets: 1968 across the Globe* (Indianapolis, IN: Hackett, 2016); Kyle Longley, *LBJ's 1968: Power, Politics, and the Presidency in America's Year of Upheaval* (Cambridge: Cambridge University Press, 2018); Jeremi Suri, *The Global Revolutions of 1968* (New York: W. W. Norton, 2007); Mark Kurlansky, *1968: The Year That Rocked The World* (New York: Random House, 2005).

4.   See Elizabeth Hinton, *America on Fire: The Untold Story of Police Violence and Black Rebellion since the 1960s* (New York: Liveright, 2021).

5.   "The Warren Court itself backed off quickly from any real attempt to limit the criminalizing or punishing capacity of state governments," writes Jonathan Simon. "It remains unclear how committed Chief Justice Warren, former district attorney of Alameda County, former attorney general of

California, and son of a murder victim, was to making significant limitations on crime control)." Jonathan Simon, *Governing through Crime: How the War on Crime Transformed American Democracy and Created a Culture of Fear* (Oxford: Oxford University Press, 2009), 51.

6.   Christopher Andrew, *For the President's Eyes Only: Secret Intelligence and the American Presidency from Washington to Bush* (New York: Harper Collins, 1995), 310.

7.   See Daniel C. Richman, "The Past, Present, and Future of Violent Crime Federalism," *Crime and Justice* 34, no. 1 (2006): 377–439; Jessica Bulman-Pozen and Heather Z. Gerken, "Uncooperative Federalism," *Yale Law Journal* 118, no. 7 (2009): 1256–1310.

8.   See Stuart Schrader, "A Carceral Empire: Placing the Political History of U.S. Prisons and Policing in the World," in *Shaped by the State: Toward a New Political History of the Twentieth Century,* ed. Brent Cebul, Lily Geismer, and Mason B. Williams (Chicago: University of Chicago Press), 296.

ARCHIVAL AND PRIMARY SOURCES

MANUSCRIPT COLLECTIONS

Albert and Shirley Small Special Collections Library, University of Virginia, Charlottesville

Papers of Homer S. Cummings

Bancroft Library, University of California, Berkeley

August Vollmer Papers

Berkeley, California, Police Department Records

Frank F. Merriam Papers

Japanese American Evacuation and Resettlement Records, 1930–1974

Orlando Winfield Wilson Papers

San Francisco Police Department Records, Police District No. 9

California Historical Society, San Francisco

American Civil Liberties Union of Northern California Records, 1900–2000

Columbia University Rare Book & Manuscript Library Special Collections, New York City

Herbert Lehman Papers

Records of the Society for the Prevention of Crime

Eberly Family Special Collections Library at Penn State, State College, Pennsylvania

Harry Anslinger Papers

Franklin Roosevelt Presidential Library, Hyde Park, New York

Department of Commerce Bureau of Census

Eleanor Roosevelt Papers

Franklin D. Roosevelt Governorship Papers

Henry Morgenthau Papers

Mary W. Dewson Papers

Official Files 10, Department of Justice

Official Files 10b, Department of Justice, FBI Records

Official Files 21, Department of Treasury

Official Files 117, Crime

Official Files 431, Narcotics

President's Interdepartmental Committee to Coordinate Health and Welfare Activities

Harvard Law School Historical & Special Collections, Cambridge, Massachusetts

Papers of Eleanor T. and Sheldon Glueck, 1911–1972

Hoover Institution, Stanford, California

Herbert Hoover Subject Files

Lee Pennington Papers

Raymond Moley Papers

Library of Congress History Vault (Online)

NAACP Papers: The NAACP's Major Campaigns—Scottsboro, Anti-Lynching, Criminal Justice, Peonage, Labor, and Segregation and Discrimination Complaints and Responses

National Archives at Atlanta, Georgia

Record Group 142, Tennessee Valley Authority

Records of the General Manager's Office

Division of Personnel Correspondence File

National Archives at College Park, Maryland

Record Group 56, General Records of the Department of the Treasury

Records of the Office of the Assistant Secretary for the Enforcement and Operations, Records of the Office of Law Enforcement Coordination, Minutes of Meetings of the Committee on Coordination of Law Enforcement, 1934–1939

Record Group 60, General Records of the Department of Justice

Attorney General's Survey of Release Procedures

Subject File, 1934–1938, Attorney General Advisory on Crime, Records Relating to Special Investigations and Survey

General Correspondence, 1934–1938, Attorney General Advisory on Crime, Records Relating to Special Investigations and Survey

Records of the Attorney General's Survey of Release Procedures

Record Group 129, Records of the Bureau of Prisons

Administrative Files, 1930–1937

Record Group 170, Drug Enforcement Administration

Subject Files, 1916–1970, Department of Justice Bureau of Narcotics (Declassified Authority NND948040)

National Archives at San Francisco, San Bruno, California

Record Group 129, Records of the Bureau of Prisons

Administrative Files, 1934–1963, Textual Records of the U.S. Penitentiary, Alcatraz Island, CA, 1938–63

Wardens' Notebook Pages, 1934–1963, Microfilm, Records of the Attorney General's Survey of Release Procedures

New York Public Library, New York City

Lillian D. Wald Papers

Princeton University Rare Books & Special Collections, Princeton, New Jersey

Ivy Lee Papers

Osmond Fraenkel Diaries

Roger Baldwin Papers

San Francisco Public Library, San Francisco

San Francisco Police Department Records

San Jose State University Special Collections and Archives, San Jose, California

Willard E. Schmidt Papers

Yale University Manuscripts and Archives, New Haven, Connecticut

Jerome Frank Papers

PUBLISHED PRIMARY SOURCES INITIALIZED OR ABBREVIATED IN NOTES

Attorney General's Survey of Release Procedures. Department of Justice, Washington, DC, 1939.

Carl Brent Swisher, ed., *Selected Papers of Homer Cummings, Attorney General of the United States, 1933–1939*. New York: Charles Scribner's Sons, 1939.

Congressional Record, Proceedings and Debates of the Second Sessions of the 73rd Congress of the United States, vol. 78 (1934).

Roosevelt, Elliott, ed. *F.D.R.: His Personal Letters, 1928–1945*. New York: Duell, Sloan and Pearce, 1950.

Proceedings of the Attorney General's Conference on Crime. Washington, DC, 1934.

ONLINE PRIMARY SOURCES

The American Presidency Project, University of California, Santa Barbara, by Gerhard Peters and John T. Woolley, www.presidency.ucsb.edu/ws/?pid =14917.

Biographical Directory of Federal Judges, Federal Judicial Center, www.fjc.gov /history/judges/.

Gallup Polls, Gallup.com.

Living New Deal, University of California, Berkeley, Department of Geography, livingnewdeal.org.

NAACP Papers, Library of Congress, History Vault, The NAAC's Major Campaigns—Scottsboro, Anti-Lynching, Criminal Justice, Peonage, Labor, and Segregation and Discrimination Complaints and Responses, https:// proquest.libguides.com/historyvault/NAACP.

Speeches of Attorney General Homer Stille Cummings, Justice Department website, www.justice.gov/ag/speeches-5.

ACKNOWLEDGMENTS

This book owes its existence to many people's guidance and support. I was privileged to begin this project in UC Berkeley's History Department. I thank Rebecca McLennan, the greatest mentor a historian could ask for. Her intellectual engagement in ways big and small drove me to make this book what it is. I also thank Daniel Sargent and, from Berkeley Law, Jonathan Simon, both of whom have continued to provide indispensable intellectual and moral support. These three faculty moreover introduced me to fruitful discussions in Berkeley's Legal History Workshop, its Global History community, and its Carceral Studies Working Group.

Other History faculty whose feedback especially helped with this book include Mark Brilliant, Brian DeLay, Robin Einhorn, David Henkin, Caitlin Rosenthal, Ronit Stahl, and James Vernon. My thinking and writing also benefited enormously thanks to input and advice from Mary Elizabeth Berry, David Hollinger, Kerwin Klein, Tom Laqueur, Dylan Penningroth, and Mark Peterson. I learned a lot from conversations with faculty outside the History Department, including Gabriel Lenz, David Presti, Karen Tani, and Christopher Tomlins. Especially helpful graduate student interlocutors included Cameron Black, Christopher Casey, Gil Rothschild Elyassi, Sophie Fitzmaurice, Grace Goudiss, Gregoria Grigsby-Olson, John Handel, Kyle Jackson, J. T. Jamieson, Craig Johnson, Danny Kelly, Elliott Kramer, Kimberly Killion, Johann Koehler, Christopher Lawson, Joseph Ledford, Brendan Mackie, Anthony Morreale, Amy O'Hearn, Maria Reis, Lois Rosson, Brendan Shanahan, and Varsha Venkatasubramanian.

I must acknowledge archives and archivists for their indispensable accommodations: The Albert and Shirley Small Special Collections Library at the University of Virginia, Crystal Miles and the Bancroft Library at Berkeley, the California Historical Society in San Francisco, Tara Craig and the Columbia University Rare Book & Manuscript Library Special Collections, Rachael Dreyer and the Eberly Family Special Collections Library at Pennsylvania State, Virginia Lewick and the Roosevelt Presidential Library in Hyde Park, Harvard Law's Historical and Special Collections, Haley Maynard and the National Archives at College Park, Meredith Mann and the New York Public Library's Brooke Russell Astor Reading Room, Maureen Hill and the National Archives at Atlanta, Douglas Williford and the National Archives at San Bruno, Princeton's Rare Books & Special Collections, the San Francisco Public Library, San Jose State's Special Collections and Archives, and Yale's Manuscripts and Archives. The Hoover Institution was particularly welcoming with fellowship support.

Over the years this project has benefited from sharp and constructive critique at workshops and conferences. Thanks to Kyle Volk at the 2016 Society for U.S. Intellectual History Conference; the 2017 Summer Graduate Research Fellowship conference hosted by the Institute for Humane Studies, which also provided fellowship support; and the late Lauren Edelman for her invitation to and Liora Israel for great comments at the 2017 Graduate Student Working Conference in Law and Society in Paris. Thanks also to Gary Mucciaroni at the 2018 Policy History Conference, David Kieran at the 2018 conference for the Society for Historians of American Foreign Relations, and Kimber Quinney at the 2018 American Historical Association Pacific-Coast Branch conference. I have also presented research from this project at the 2020 Australian and New Zealand Historical Criminology Symposium, the 2020 Intellectual History Conference, the 2021 Law and Society Conference, and the 2022 Policy History Conference, at which Julie Novkov gave incisive comments.

From July 2020 through June 2022, I was a postdoctoral research associate at Brown University's Political Theory Project (PTP), where I profited from discussions with John Tomasi, David Skarbek, Emily Skarbek, Daniel D'Amico, Alytheia Laughlin, and Ryan Doody. I received excellent chapter comments from colleagues Julia Netter, Lowry Presley, Arthur Ghins, Antong Liu, Sam Director, Emilie Sartre, and Ugur Altundal.

Beverly Gage, Elizabeth Hinton, Anne Kornhauser, and Andrew Preston provided some of this project's most rigorous and generous feedback at a May 2022 manuscript workshop hosted by the PTP. Laura Weinrib also gave many rich and invaluable suggestions. For their helpful readings and comments on excerpts or the whole manuscript late in the process I also thank David Beito, Richard John, Elizabeth Katz, John Moser, and Michael Vorenberg. As I finished this book, I was fortunate to have an institutional home at the Rhode Island School of Design, which also provided some funding through its Humanities Fund and Professional Development Fund.

I cannot adequately thank the editorial team. My editor at Harvard University Press, Andrew Kinney, gave three years of support and outstanding substantive advice. Emily Marie Silk took the helm and was an excellent collaborator in the book's crucial last stages. I also must thank Stephanie Vyce and Kathleen Drummy at the press for their wonderful help, and the outstanding production editor Brian Ostrander and copyeditor Wendy Nelson. The anonymous peer reviewers provided fantastic guidance and encouragement. Thanks also to Lauren Post, the Estate of Rollin Kirby Post, for permission to reprint Figure 10.1.

Finally, this book would be impossible without the support of my family and friends, particularly my wife, Nicole, my son, Alfred, and my father, who has always encouraged me in this and all my proudest endeavors.

Of course, this book's every fault is my sole responsibility.

INDEX

Figures and tables are denoted by *f* or *t* following the page number.